Contesting the Past, Reconstructing the Nation

Contesting the Past, Reconstructing the Nation

American Literature and Culture in the Gilded Age, 1876–1893

Ben Railton

THE UNIVERSITY OF ALABAMA PRESS

Tuscaloosa

Copyright © 2007
The University of Alabama Press
Tuscaloosa, Alabama 35487-0380
All rights reserved
Manufactured in the United States of America

Typeface: Minion

∞

The paper on which this book is printed
meets the minimum requirements of
American National Standard
for Information Sciences-Permanence of Paper
for Printed Library Materials,
ANSI Z39.48-1984.

Library of Congress Cataloging-in-Publication Data

Railton, Ben, 1977–
Contesting the past, reconstructing the nation : American literature and culture in
the Gilded Age, 1876–1893 / Ben Railton.
p.   cm. — (Studies in American literary realism and naturalism)
Includes bibliographical references and index.
ISBN-13: 978-0-8173-1580-1 (cloth : alk. paper)
ISBN-10: 0-8173-1580-2 (alk. paper)
1. American literature—19th century—History and criticism. 2. National characteristics,
American, in literature. 3. Literature and society—United States—History—19th century.
4. Sex role in literature. 5. Race in literature. I. Title.
PS214.R35 2007
820.9′358—dc22

2007005022

Contents

Preface

In May 1876 the advertisements for one of America's longest-running stage productions, the Howards' touring Tom Show, underwent a significant shift. George C. Howard's company had been performing Tom Shows since 1852, and their postbellum performances thus functioned as a reminder of the sectional division and Civil War that *Uncle Tom* had mirrored, presaged, and, as President Lincoln's famous remark to Harriet Beecher Stowe made explicit, furthered. Moreover, while the Tom Shows were always first and foremost about entertainment, spectacle, and profit, the advertisements from their earliest 1850s iterations had characterized the play as an "American moral drama," linking the stage versions to the reform ethos at the heart of Stowe's text. Such characterizations continued throughout the Reconstruction years, so that when the Howards' show advertised itself in February 1876 as "the most complete and realistic picture of Southern life ever presented," the claim to verisimilitude would seem to offer explicit opposition to the many and ongoing Southern attempts to refute the accuracy and consequently impugn the morality of Stowe's depiction of slavery and antebellum life.[1]

Yet just a few months later, a May 21 advertisement for a "new version (adapted to the sentiment of the times)" of the Howards' show, one "careful[ly] prepar[ed] ... in commemoration of the Centennial," promised instead "Old-Time Plantation Melodies of pleasant memory." Tom Shows had been including African American song and dance numbers more and more often over the previous few years, but the depiction of the show itself took on a striking new tone in these May advertisements. Gone was any reference to the show's or the text's morality; the advertisements now characterized the production as "the greatest and most successful of all American plays" or, even more tellingly, as "the amended and popularly approved version of" the novel. At this Centennial moment, the new advertisements suggest, the popular sentiment required a shift in constructions of the Southern past from critical to celebratory, an emphasis on pleasant memories of the old-time plantation rather than moral depictions of life among the lowly (Stowe's subtitle often appeared on early advertisements but was likewise excised from these May 1876 and subsequent characterizations). Such revisions of *Uncle Tom*'s historical function served as precursors to the plantation tradition that would come to dominate Southern and in many ways national literature over the next two decades. And the revision process culminated, five years later, in Joel Chandler Harris's only slightly ironic description (in the Introduction to *Uncle Remus, His Songs and His Sayings* [1881]) of "Mrs. Stowe's wonderful defense of slavery as it existed in the South" (39).[2]

As complete and striking as the revision process may have been for the Howards and the Harrises, however, the moral and realistic historical functions of *Uncle Tom's Cabin* and its stage manifestations remained vital for at least one American coming of age in this postbellum moment: Nat Love, the former-slave-turned-frontier-cowboy-turned-Pullman-porter who narrated his extraordinary Gilded Age life in *The Life and Adventures of Nat Love* (1907). Love promises in his subtitle "A True History of Slavery Days" (among many other things), and the opening chapter focuses on the period between his 1854 birth into slavery in Tennessee and the outbreak of the Civil War. But while Love describes this "greatest curse of all . . . the curses of this fair land" in outraged and graphic detail, he concludes the chapter by admitting that another artistic work has captured that curse's realities much more fully than he. "Go and see the play of 'Uncle Tom's Cabin,'" he implores his audience, for there "you will see the black man's life as I saw it when a child" (13).[3]

The overall shift in *Uncle Tom*'s historical function and Love's resistance to that shift exemplify, respectively, a dominant trend in Gilded Age constructions of the past and the existence of alternative, literary

visions of American history. In the final quarter of the nineteenth century, in response both to the divisive horrors of sectionalism, Civil War,
and Reconstruction and to the progress of industrialization and all its
corollary effects, American culture returned to and reified a monologic
national historical narrative, a unifying, triumphalist vision of the past
and its progressive relationship to the nation's present prosperity and future glory. That narrative was embodied in the 1876 Philadelphia Centennial Exposition and the year's concurrent celebrations; its cultural
dominance was exemplified by a number of key events a decade later;
and it reached its apotheosis at the 1893 Columbian Exposition and in
the imperialist ventures foreshadowed there. Yet the Centennial year
and post-Centennial decade also witnessed the continuing presence of
critical social questions—such as the questions of race, Indians, women,
and the South—that provided focal points for dialogic complications
of the national narrative, opportunities for the introduction of other
American voices and visions of history. And the decade's most complex constructions of those dialogic histories, its most significant contestations of the past and reconstructions of the nation, can be found in
works of historical literature.

The precise contours of my argument about American culture between 1876 and 1893, as well as my study's relationship to the ongoing
dialogues of historical and literary scholarship, are the focus of the Introduction and Conclusion; the specifics of each social question, and
especially of my readings of historical literary texts, constitute the five
chapters in between. At a more theoretical level, this study represents the
first step in a larger critical project: the construction of a poetics of historical literature, a framework for approaching and analyzing literary
texts that are centrally concerned with constructing, conveying, conversing with, or complicating visions of the past. The underlying methodology and driving force behind the close readings that comprise most
of the chapters is my belief that a formalist approach to such texts, one
that does not ignore cultural, political, or evaluative questions but that
allows one's perspective on them to arise out of extended attention to
each work's complexities, is by far the most productive way to analyze
literary visions of history.[4]

In developing that formalist approach, I focus not only on each text's
construction of history, but also on the related element of voice. By voice

I mean each distinct perspective expressed in a text. There are two key terms in that phrase: "expressed," to indicate that these are ideas given explicit expression (often in spoken dialogue or free indirect speech, but also in the narrator's voice, an author's voice in forewords or peripheral materials, the voice of an included document, and so on) in the text; and "perspective," to indicate that what these voices express is a standpoint on a particular issue, a vision of something—specifically, here, a vision of history. That vision may not be, indeed usually is not, simple, static, one dimensional, or perfectly consistent, but it is unique to each voice in question, and can thus be traced and analyzed through attention to a voice's various expressions. And at the contextual level, my overall argument—about the rise and reification of a monologic national historical narrative over these years and the dialogic alternative narratives offered in the decade's historical literature—is centrally concerned with the visions of history expressed by a nation's cultural and literary voices.[5]

Acknowledgments

This project has benefited enormously from conversations with many colleagues and friends, especially Michael Kaufmann, Allen Davis, Jeff Renye, Sari Edelstein, Mark Rennella, Ian Williams, Heidi Kim, Maria Gapotchenko, and Dan O'Hara. Thanks also to Paula Bernat Bennett, Carolyn Sorisio, Michael Hoberman, Patrice Gray, Lorene Lamothe, Coleman Hutchison, Frank Portella, Michael Parker, Chile Hidalgo, Gina Masucci Mackenzie, John Stauffer, Dan Ellis, Kelley Wagers, Veronica Hendrick, and Tara Powell. Very little of the research for this book would have been imaginable without the resources and staff of Harvard's Widener Library; chapter 5 is due largely to the holdings and help of the Special Collections staff at Houghton Library. And my chairs, administrators, and colleagues in the Temple English department, the Boston University Writing Program, the University of Massachusetts Boston English department, and especially the Fitchburg State College English department have been uniformly supportive and collegial.

My experiences with The University of Alabama Press deserve special mention here. And to the two anonymous readers I owe thanks not only for their painstakingly thorough and impressive comments, but also for helping me produce a book of which I'm very proud.

This book itself is the best way I can acknowledge my debts and gratitude to Miles Orvell and Carolyn Karcher—well, that and doing everything I can do to live up to their models as scholars, teachers, friends, and people. Thanks for everything!

Of the many ways in which I'm lucky, none can compare with the degree of love and support that I've received from my family. Thanks so much to Annie Railton, Arthur Railton, Mike and Anna Tsao, Jack Tsao, and Joan Han. Both of my grandmothers, Rae Fine and Margery Railton, passed away while I was working on this project, but it, like everything else in my life, connects back to their spirit and love. They also raised some amazing kids—Mom and Dad, my earliest and best readers, the source of all that is best in me, and my best models for the other project that I'm just beginning. And to Connie, Aidan, Kyle, and Linus, this book will be one small part of the house and life that we're building and filling together. Without you, it wouldn't mean a thing.

Contesting the Past, Reconstructing the Nation

Introduction

An Ahistorical Exposition and a Historicist Argument

The 1876 Centennial Exposition at Philadelphia was, above all, a celebration of America's material progress and prowess. Of the Centennial's ten categories of exhibits, nine were direct manifestations of material culture ("I. Raw Materials," "V. Tools, Implements, Machines, and Processes"); only the tenth, "Objects illustrating efforts for the improvement of the Physical, Intellectual, and Moral Condition of Man," pointed toward other aspects of culture, and there the reference to improvement was a telling one (McCabe 221–23). The nominal subject of any Centennial—the events of a hundred years ago—was here so buried beneath the accumulated stuff that there was an "almost complete absence . . . of any reminder of the event it was designed to commemorate" (Goodheart 55). The Exposition's official accompanying text, J. S. Ingram's *The Centennial Exposition Described and Illustrated,* reiterated this emphasis, consisting of a catalogue of especially impressive items, "a popular presentation of only those things possessing . . . superior attractions" (5), with virtually no discussion of the historical or cultural issues to which those items or their exhibits might relate.[1] And such elision of the past in favor of America's present and future glories occurred not only implicitly in the Exposition's materially focused exhibits but also explicitly in one of its central texts: John Greenleaf Whittier's Centennial Hymn, performed at the May 10 opening ceremonies, expressed the fervent hope that "the new cycle shame the old!" (Cawelti 325–26).[2]

This material and progressive focus exemplified the overall tenor of the year's celebrations and reflections.[3] The most prominent such reflection was a text published late in the year entitled *The First Century of the Republic: A Review of American Progress.* As the Publisher's Advertisement notes, the book focuses not on official affairs of state, but rather on "the part taken by the American people in the remarkable material progress of the last hundred years"; its goal is to "connect the present with the past, showing the beginnings of great enterprises, tracing through consecutive stages their development, and associating with them the individual thought and labor by which they have been brought to perfection" (7-9). The move toward perfection is indeed the book's central image: of its seventeen chapters on subjects as wide ranging as agriculture, jurisprudence, and humanitarianism, nine include the word "progress" in their title and four others the word "development." The point is obvious: the first century has all been prelude to the present pinnacle, and things can only get better from here.

Such an attitude would seem to preclude any sense of the past, any vision of history as a distinct and meaningful entity. Indeed, Michael Kammen, the foremost historian of American cultural memory, argues that the 1876 events "tended to celebrate the present at the expense of the past," and that in such cases "we must be careful not to confuse commemoration with genuine remembrance" (135-37). Yet it is more accurate to argue that a central belief in progress requires a particular construction of history, one which sees the past as part of a reverse linear trajectory and which moves backward from the present's accomplishments to their foundations. This triumphalist take on history's meaning is nicely delineated by Kammen's distinction between commemoration—an act of celebration significantly shaped by present cultural value systems—and the more ostensibly value-neutral concept of remembrance. The commemorative historical construction does not discount the value of nor entirely elide the past—*First Century*'s chapters are full of historical facts, figures, and events—so much as exclude those details which do not fit into the linear progression and portray the rest as almost typological precursors of the present perfection.

My reference to the commemorative model's use of typology is deliberately suggestive of religious historical perspectives; the progressive historical visions which dominated the 1876 celebrations can be seen as a postbellum reincarnation of a Protestant millennialism that had been essential to virtually every important act of American national self-fashioning, from Winthrop's Arabella sermon to the Prospect Poems to the Gettysburg Address. Apropos of the latter occasion, Ernest Tuveson, whose *Redeemer Nation: The Idea of America's Millennial Role* (1968) remains this view's definitive history, argues that the Civil War represented the millenial historical narrative's apotheosis, but adds that, "despite post–Civil War disillusionment, the myth of the Redeemer Nation kept a hold on the deepest feelings of the country, and in critical moments asserted itself" (209). Certainly the first centennial of American nationhood would count as such a critical moment, and the millennial, progressive historical visions expressed at that moment would seem very much a part of an ongoing American religious and philosophical tradition.[4]

Contemporaneous with the millennial vision since the Puritan era, of course, has been a second predominant American historical narrative: the declension model, as exemplified by the jeremiad. That construction of the past, in which historical figures occupy a pinnacle from which the present has fallen and to which the nation is implored to return, would seem directly antagonistic to a progressive perspective; yet as Sacvan Bercovitch and others have demonstrated, the jeremiad has often gone hand in hand with the millennial philosophy in constituting America's national identity. The jeremiad, in Bercovitch's summation, "helped sustain a national dream" (*Jeremiad* xi).[5] As historical narratives, both models are equally linear, and equally unwilling to include past details that complicate that linear vision. Moreover, the jeremiad's conservative nostalgia for those who have come before—like the progressive narrative's commemoration of the past—is often closely tied to particular attitudes and emphases in the present. Despite their superficial opposition, then, the declension and progress models are actually quite similar, and the 1876 celebrations often made them compatible: nostalgically gesturing toward the greatness of prominent historical ancestors and events while continuing to believe in the progressive perfection of America's material existence in the present and in the future. Americans in 1876 "wanted to keep the best of their new industrial and urban surroundings yet return to the simplicities of the past" (Dee Brown 344), and in the celebrations' combination of nostalgia and material progressivism they found a way to do just that.

Moreover, while scholars such as Bercovitch and Werner Sollors have certainly established the presence of similar unifications of seemingly disparate historical perspectives—whether described as cultural "rituals of consensus" (Bercovitch, *Rites* 29–67) or individual acts of "consent" (Sollors, *Beyond* 6–7)—throughout American history,[6] I believe that such unifications' 1876 recurrence possessed a character distinct from and more forceful than any prior such appearance. There are a number of reasons for that distinctiveness, all related in one way or another to the previous quarter century's polarizing historical events. Most obvious, the scars of antebellum sectional conflict and the Civil War's much fresher wounds were unavoidable reminders of the damage done by division; the presence of those injuries, as Lisa Long documents, led many postbellum Americans to seek cultural "rehabilitation" (*Bodies* 1–7), and one particularly effective treatment was found in historical consensus (such as that constructed by veterans' groups) about those painful memories and the war that had produced them.[7] Also providing impetus for consensus in 1876 were the more recent memories of Reconstruction, and the new visions of nation and history that the period's very name implied; as Kirk Savage argues, "Reconstruction demanded nothing less than that the nation and its people reimagine themselves," and the reimaginings that took place in the public war memorials Savage analyzes provided an ideal vehicle through which to "yield resolution and consensus" about the past (4).[8] And on a broader level, those traumatic and divisive historical experiences produced a generation with a new worldview, "a philosophical foundation for the concept of union" (Dawes 24) that centered on two crucial components: what Anne Rose calls the late Victorians' "resilient humanism built on the sense of personal triumph" from having survived history's traumas (255); and a corresponding shift from a cyclical to a progressive notion of time, in which such traumas could be seen as obstacles to be transcended in the movement toward an evermore glorious future.[9]

For all those reasons, the kinds of consensus about the past, the unifications of nostalgia and progressivism, that the Centennial's commemorations constructed were distinct in both degree and nature from any that had come before. Those celebrations reached their peak, naturally enough, on July 4; speakers at the Philadelphia Exposition and around the country both honored the past's untouchable grandeur (in the form of the Founding Fathers) and stood entranced at the future's immeasurable heights of material success. "What our fathers were we know. Their life was splendid; their history was registered," intoned Henry Ward Beecher, and yet "there never began to be in the early day such promise for physical vigor and enriched life as there is to-day upon this continent" (Trachtenberg, ed. 69–70). Yet promise was not the only thing evident on that commemorative day: at the Exposition women's suffrage activists staged a protest in the midst of the celebrations; news of General Custer's defeat at Little Big Horn was reaching the East for the first time; and in Hamburg, South Carolina, parading black militiamen refused to cede the street to a white militia and were fired upon, leaving five dead.

Those coincidental July 4 events highlighted some of the less celebratory aspects of American life in 1876, elements of its history that fit much less neatly into the progressive narrative and represented areas on which there was clearly not national consensus; and they were far from isolated occurrences. Throughout the year there were signs of unrest over gender, the frontier, race, and region: in January the New York Women's Suffrage Society went before Congress to protest the Centennial fund, arguing that it "imposed upon a disfranchised and unrepresented sex the enormous burden of half a million dollars" (Nugent 56), and in May the National Women's Suffrage Association met in Philadelphia on the day the Exposition opened; in February the Department of the Interior gave the army full jurisdiction for all Native American lands in the Black Hills, site of an ongoing gold rush, prompting the Sioux reprisals that led to Little Big Horn and the nation's final major Indian war; and November's contested presidential election paved the way for the end of Reconstruction and the spread of segregation and race violence in the South, while Congress continued to debate the question of amnesty for former Confederate leaders and soldiers.

All four of these issues, which I call for simplicity (echoing the period's language) the woman question, the Indian question, the race question, and the South question, were present in some form on the Centennial Exposition's grounds; together they constituted a much more dialogic vision of American history than those comprised by the Exposition's materialist exhibits or voiced in its ceremonial texts. Women had a chance to address the woman question on their own terms at the Women's Pavilion, which was entirely funded and planned by the all-female Women's Centennial Exposition Committee. That committee explicitly sought to represent American women as a whole, bringing before Congress letters from average women to prove female enthusiasm for the Centennial and secure a spot for the Pavilion. Yet the Pavilion's exhibits offered a particular vision of women's past contributions to and present role in America, one focused on material advancements related to domestic work and crafts. That vision not only complemented the Exposition's overall emphasis on material progress, but also failed to include in any significant way such historical counter-narratives as women's advancements and obstacles in the workplace, the public arts, and politics. And the latter exclusion was one cause of the suffragists' July 4 protest: reading their "Declaration of Women's Rights" from a separate stage near the official one, they articulated an alternative vision of women's histories and futures, highlighting the dialogic nature of and stakes inherent in the question of which histories would be presented and which elided.[10]

Native Americans were likewise given exhibits (if not a pavilion) of their own at the Exposition, but their level of participation drastically differed from the women's. These exhibits were planned and executed by the Smithsonian Institution and the Department of the Interior, with the help of federal Indian agents who "collected" (often through underhanded means) artifacts from a variety of Native American tribes. The Indian question, then, was addressed at the Centennial by the same federal government that was in the process of giving Indian land to the army, and the representations of Native Americans reflected this "great ambiguity" (Trennert 129).[11] While the exhibits apparently contained objects of genuine beauty and power, they also depicted Indians as part of America's history, rather than its present; that image was reinforced by the Smithsonian's textual introduction to the exhibits, which read (in part): "the monuments of the past and the savage tribes of man are rapidly disappearing from our continent" (Rydell, All 23).[12] The exhibits thus fit Native Americans into the progressive historical narrative, portraying their seemingly inevitable extinction as a necessary part of that progress; the alternative vision of separate cultures facing ongoing conquest and brutality, which after decades of neglect was just beginning to be re-voiced at this time by Native Americans and their reformer advocates, was nowhere to be found at the Exposition.[13]

The Centennial's presentation of the race question fell somewhere between these two positions of limited self-expression (the Women's Pavilion) and stereotypical classification (the Indian exhibits). For over a year African Americans fought for the chance to take part in the Exposition on their own (if still progressive) terms, to "claim," as one editor put it, "that [their] labor of the past had added something to the glory of the country" (Kachun 309).[14] That battle yielded two significant but somewhat ambiguous triumphs. First, Frederick Douglass was seated on the main platform at the opening ceremony, although he was almost turned away by overzealous policemen and was not allowed to give a speech. Second, the African Methodist Church led a movement to erect on the Exposition grounds a statue of Bishop Richard Allen, the church's founder and an important abolitionist; the statue was greatly delayed (due to an artistic misunderstanding and a railway accident) but was raised just before the Centennial's closing and became "the earliest successful effort by black Americans to honor one of their own with a commemorative statue" (Kachun 300). The Exposition's inclusion of Douglass and Allen was significant not only because it acknowledged that important Americans could be black but also because it hinted, if only obliquely and (in Douglass's case) silently, at the history of slavery and abolitionism that constituted another alternative to the consensus, progressive vision that dominated the Exposition.[15]

The self-expressed vision of African American history exemplified by the Allen statue, however, had its own alternative within the Centennial grounds. At the statue's dedication, one speaker identified "the South question" as "a central issue for the destiny of the entire nation" (Kachun 317), and the Exposition's most explicit attempt to address that question was a troubling one. Among the many culinary exhibits was a concession called "The South," or "The Southern Restaurant," which attempted to recreate the feel of an antebellum plantation, down to the "band of old-time plantation 'darkies'" which performed at all times (Rydell, *All* 28). This nostalgic vision of Southern and racial history, obviously antithetical to the slavery narrative represented by Douglass and

Allen, was also literally dangerous in its refusal to acknowledge either the historical grounding for or the current realities of the postbellum South. And yet neither did the Southern Restaurant fit smoothly into the consensus historical narrative of the Civil War; to view a plantation as a preferable place to dine would be to differ implicitly from the view that the war was a traumatic but necessary stage in the nation's ongoing upward development. Thus the visions of history constituted by the exhibits concerning these four questions, like the year's current events, undermined the Exposition's unified, progressive historical narrative at the same time that they were often closely linked to it, indicating some of the deep-seated complexities in the nation's past and present in the Centennial year.

Those complexities would only deepen over the next decade, yet the progressive, consensus national historical narrative grew concurrently more unified and more dominant in American cultural life. Part of that developing dominance involved the specific responses to the social questions that frame my next four chapters: the amalgamation of the national and Southern historical perspectives—or, more exactly, conversion of the former to the latter perspective—that I discuss in chapter 4, and the concurrent cooption of African American dialect voices to articulate a nostalgic vision of slavery that frames chapter 1; the rise of a new nationalist narrative of Western American history, one predicated, I argue in chapter 2, on the explicit forgetting and silencing of Native American histories and voices; and, in a quite different but ultimately connected vein, prominent public women's construction of a narrative from their own perspective that began as explicitly alternative to the existing national narrative but that, in its unified presentation of female voice, ended up excluding the variety of women's voices and experiences that I trace in chapter 3. Yet these direct responses to the social questions' dialogic historical narratives were part of a larger process taking place over this period: the development of a powerful new national monologue on America's history and identity, its past and future.

Benedict Anderson, whose *Imagined Communities: Reflections on the Origin and Spread of Nationalism* (1983) remains one of the definitive accounts of nationalism's processes, argues that different kinds of communities (national and otherwise) "are to be distinguished ... by the

style in which they are imagined" (15). More specifically, Anderson links
the rise of nationalist narratives to a new historical imagination, a progressive concept of time, noting that "The idea of a sociological or-
ganism moving calendrically through ... time is a precise analogue of
the idea of the nation, which also is conceived as a solid community
moving steadily down (or up) time" (31). The progressive historical vision both expressed at and embodied by the Centennial can thus be
seen as an early formation of a nascent postbellum nationalism, and
the subsequent decade's consolidations of that vision as the blooming
of that nationalist narrative. In the words of Priscilla Wald, such historical consensus is "the task of the official story of the nation": "to enable a smooth transition," to mold a nostalgic narrative of the past with
a progressive vision of the future "in order simultaneously to transform
and preserve 'us.'" And Wald's definition of such "official stories" as the
narratives "through which a nation—'a people'—spoke itself into existence" nicely identifies the centrality of voice to the production of such
consensus (1–2). Indeed, what arose over these years can be described as
a national historical monologue, one that required for its successful development the concurrent elision or assimilation of the kinds of dialogic
histories that undermined any unified sense of the American "us" and
that were represented by the social questions.[16]

   That monologue's successful development is illustrated by many of
the period's cultural trends. Philosophically, two predominant ideas were
a rejuvenated patriotism and the newly articulated Social Darwinism;
the necessity for a national historical monologue is more obvious for the
former, but Social Darwinism too depends on consensus about a progressive movement from past to future, and more exactly about explanations for individual failures that enable the overall belief in progress to
remain intact.[17] Significant political policies such as the embrace of corporations and the rise of imperialism (and its concomitant economic,
cultural, and religious expansionisms) can be similarly linked to the
consensus over a progressive historical narrative; both of those policies
depended on an understanding of past economic and expansionist developments as signs of progress in order to justify the further pursuit of
such developments, while imperialism also required a view of America
as more advanced than the nations it would be civilizing.[18] As for the
period's historiographic trends, I have already noted how Civil War me-

morials brought the country together, helping the war become a "central component of the new nationalist mythology" (Grant 206); and a similar consolidation occurred with the founding of the American Historical Association, one of many professions to experience a "consensus of the competent" during these years (Lasch 228–29).[19] While, as I argue throughout this study, much of the period's literary production constituted dialogic complications of the national monologue, there were certainly links between some particularly popular genres and that monologic narrative: dime westerns, for example, tended to feature a heroic lead who vanquished alternative Americans (often Native Americans) to ensure a glorious future; while local color writing allowed for an embrace of regional differences within an implicitly (and sometimes explicitly) unified nation.[20] And even turn-of-the-century movements that might seem diametrically opposed to the monologue can be seen as attempts to build on its essential elements (if with certainly distinct goals): Progressivism, for example, with its emphasis—made overt in the movement's name—on a glorious possible future (often directly linked to a lost past, as in the jeremiad) and on change as an ever-present and generally positive force in American life; or literary naturalism, with its central tenets of determinism (certainly a unifying vision of history and one related to Social Darwinism) and decline (which locates the future in a linear relationship to the past).[21]

As connected to and reflected by those diverse trends, then, the monologic historical narrative was reified in post-Centennial American culture. As I argue in the Conclusion, the 1893 World's Columbian Exposition in Chicago both represented that narrative's apotheosis and pointed toward the imperial ventures that would in the following years become the narrative's next and most sweeping incarnation. Yet I believe that four quite distinct but equally significant 1886 events illustrate how by a decade after the Centennial the monologue had truly taken hold. One such event was the official opening ceremony for the Statue of Liberty, the first pieces of which had been displayed at the Philadelphia Exposition ten years before. The Statue's original idea was provided by French liberal Édouard René de Laboulaye, and was linked not only to the joint American and French traditions of liberty, but also to the specific historical realities of American slavery and emancipation; Laboulaye opposed French alliance with the Confederacy during the Civil War, arguing that "to intervene in this struggle on the side of slavery would be to deny our past," and he first voiced the Statue idea at a dinner party in 1865, shortly after the war's end (Moreno 57–58, 133–37).[22] Yet when, six years later, he instructed his friend, the sculptor Auguste Bertholdi, to "go to see that country" in order to gain ideas for the sculpture (Leslie Allen 21), Bertholdi responded by focusing entirely on the present and future of what he called, upon arrival in New York, "indeed the New World" (Gilder 12); in no account of his travels is there any indication that Bertholdi investigated issues of African American slavery and freedom.[23] President Grover Cleveland's speech at the 1886 opening cemented the statue's assimilation into the progressive narrative of both past ("We will not forget that Liberty has made here her home") and future ("a stream of light shall pierce the darkness of ignorance and man's oppression when Liberty enlightens the world") [Bell and Abrams 55]. And subsequent popular and scholarly responses to the Statue have fully endorsed this progressive interpretation.[24]

If the Statue of Liberty's incorporation into the progressive national narrative required a revision—or at least an elision of key elements—of Laboulaye's original idea, the man and ideas at the center of the second 1886 event were much more fully in concert with that narrative. That event was the publication of Josiah Strong's best-selling *Our Country: Its Possible Future and Its Present Crisis,* a combination of jeremiad and progressive prophecy that linked Protestant millennialism to both a budding imperialism—particularly in chapter 14, "The Anglo-Saxon and the World's Future," in which Strong argues that he "know[s] of nothing except climatic conditions to prevent this race from populating Africa as it has peopled North America" (215)—and the Gilded Age's corporate realities (in the concluding chapter 15, "Money and the Kingdom"). As William Berge argues, the previous fifteen years of Strong's life had been a "period of unrest" in which he "always seemed to be groping for some elusive goal or idea" (167–210); but in 1885 he came to just such an idea, a vision of his era as one of those "great focal points in history toward which the lines of past progress have converged, and from which have radiated the molding influences of the future" (Strong 13).[25] And within the next year Strong expressed that vision in at least three significant ways: not only writing and publishing *Our Country,* but also starting an even more explicitly expansionist sequel, *Our World* (published in 1914) and beginning his work as "an ecclesiastical politician involved with the actualities of foreign policy decision-making" (James Reed 232).[26] The late 1890s' connection between and expansion from the national to the imperial progressive narrative were thus already in development in 1886.

The final two noteworthy 1886 events are likely the best known, reflecting as they do the two issues—the rise of corporations and labor conflicts—that have been at the heart of many scholarly assessments of the Gilded Age. Both, however, are also worth revisiting as representations of the progressive historical narrative's dominance. One would be the Supreme Court's May 10 ruling on *Santa Clara County v. Southern Pacific Railroad Company;* or, more exactly, Justice Morrison Waite's preamble to the ruling, subsequently included as the published decision's first line, in which he stated that "the court does not wish to hear argument on the question whether the provision in the Fourteenth Amendment to the Constitution, which forbids a State to deny to any person within its jurisdiction the equal protection of the laws, applies to these corporations. We are all of the opinion that it does" (Korten 185–86).[27] This striking revision of the Fourteenth Amendment represented more than just a victory for big business; it was another illustration of how dialogic histories connected to the social questions (in this case, the race question) had by 1886 been assimilated into the national monologue. It would be easy to see the second event, the Haymarket bombing (May 4, the same week as the Supreme Court ruling), as precisely such a dialogic complication; after all, the strikes and protests with which that bombing was connected—like the first national strikes of 1877, or the Pullman conflicts of 1894—were in direct contrast to the Court's position that corporations and people were in a sort of unified consensus.[28] Yet I would argue that those persistent Gilded Age labor conflicts, which unquestionably represented dissent over America's present condition and ideal future, were by the same token part of the developing national consensus on the past. That is, the participants in the debates over labor and corporations tended—with the exceptions of extremists such as the Chicago anarchists, who were usually portrayed by both sides as distinctly outside of America and its narrative—to take for granted interrelated concepts such as the nostalgia for an ideal agrarian past and the potential for a glorious, world-leading future, both core elements of the

progressive historical narrative. Disagreements over the best way to establish continuity with that past and achieve that future, of which there
were many, do not necessarily represent distinct historical visions.[29] The
past was thus often an assumed starting point from which the respective
social or political positions diverged; and as I argue below, many subsequent scholars have unintentionally replicated that assumption with
their focus on the period's relationship to its twentieth-century future.

However, if the years between the Centennial Exposition and Haymarket comprised the progressive historical narrative's ascendance, that
consensus about the past did not go uncontested. The social questions
remained as prominent throughout the decade as they had been in 1876,
and the two central and intertwined issues from each question's representation at the Centennial—what histories would be articulated and
in whose voices—remained the principal elements of the dialogic historical spaces constituted by the questions. And historical literature in
all its forms—the texts centrally concerned with constructing, conveying, conversing with, or complicating visions of the past—provided the
best vehicle through which those dialogic possibilities could be voiced
and engaged with. Thus over the next five chapters, each of the first four
structured around one of the social questions and the fifth focused on a
text that includes them all, I analyze works of historical literature from
the post-Centennial decade; they construct dialogic historical visions
that contest—in multiple forms, to distinct degrees, and with varying
effectiveness, but all with complexity that demands close attention—the
progressive, monologic national narrative.

In that central argument about the consensus narrative's consolidation on one cultural level and literary texts' contestations on another, my
study can and should be seen as part of a long tradition of assessments
of the Gilded Age. Those assessments begin with that very name for the
period, coined by Mark Twain and Charles Dudley Warner two years
before the Centennial; the term "Gilded" provides perfect shorthand for
arguments about the period's dual and divided nature, its polished and
attractive surface under which hid the at best tarnished and workman-
like and at worst false and ugly realities. Both the term and its implied
analysis have carried over into twentieth-century scholarship; a compi-
lation of primary documents is titled *The Land of Contrasts* (Harris ed.),

and many of the most prominent scholarly engagements with the Gilded Age have focused on variations of one central contrast: between the numerous conscious attempts to construct a unified and coherent vision of American society, usually related to industry and material progress, and the disunified and chaotic realities of an increasingly diverse nation in which many were left out of and behind by that progress. That contrast is found in foundational concepts such as C. Vann Woodward's "reunion and reaction," Robert Wiebe's "search for order" in "a society without a core" (12), and Alan Trachtenberg's "incorporation of America" that "proceeded by contradiction and conflict" (*Incorporation* 7); in more recent analyses including T. Jackson Lears's "complex blend of accommodation and protest" in antimodernism (xv), Lawrence Levine's opposition of "Culture" to "growing fragmentation" in "the emergence of cultural hierarchy" (175–77), Gail Bederman's "discourse of civilization" and its gendered and racial alternatives (5), and Michael Elliott's "culture concept" with its narratives of similarity and difference; and in literary critical arguments like Susan Donaldson's "competing voices" and Kate McCullough's "enabling national fiction . . . masking the amalgamation of other categories that constituted it" (1–4).

I would certainly categorize my study as another such literary critical argument, one grounded in precisely the kinds of historicist perspectives about the era this impressive body of scholarship has constructed over the last half century. Yet I believe that my project differs in two important ways from the majority of those earlier studies, differences that are partly matters of emphasis but that also reflect essential elements of my project that have been underrepresented in Gilded Age scholarship. For one thing, that scholarship has tended to focus on Gilded Age society's links to its future (i.e., twentieth-century America) rather than its past. The title of a recent anthology, *The Gilded Age: Essays on the Origins of Modern America* (Calhoun ed.), is a telling piece of evidence for that forward-looking mindset, but more important are the date ranges covered by most individual studies: 1877–1920; 1880–1940; and so forth. Literary critics, perhaps guided by survey courses' penchant to divide at 1865, have likewise tended to connect the era to its future, as exemplified by Jay Martin's seminal *Harvests of Change: American Literature, 1865–1914,* and the aforementioned Donaldson (1865–1914) and McCullough (1885–1914) projects. Even historians who focus on Reconstruction and its immediate aftermath, a subject that would seem deeply grounded in the period's particularities and past—race historians such as Eric Foner and Joel Williamson, Southern historians such as C. Vann Woodward—have also tended to link Gilded Age developments with the twentieth century (as exemplified by Woodward's *Origins of the New South, 1877–1913*).

Moreover, two of the essays in a recent *American Literary History* forum on the continuing importance of Trachtenberg's *Incorporation* contend that it is precisely this forward-looking emphasis that both distinguishes the Gilded Age from other periods and characterizes Gilded Age scholarship in Trachtenberg's vein. David Shumway articulates both parts of that position, arguing first that "American culture and society change[d] fundamentally during the late decades of the nineteenth century and the first decade of the twentieth, defining the century that would follow," and then that Trachtenberg's book provided a "starting point . . . for a systematic rereading of American culture that focused on the late nineteenth and early twentieth centuries rather than on the mid nineteenth century" (754). And Trachtenberg's own reassessment of his book concludes that a significant element of its continuing value is its ability to explain the manifold ways in which the Gilded Age was "a turning point in US history" ("Incorporation" 759).[30] Despite their many critiques and revisions of the consensus narrative, then, these scholars have in a certain way reified its elision of history and constructed a twentieth-century extension to its focus on the future. And even their revisionist stance has contributed to that construction: when scholars with this forward-looking orientation analyze the role of the past in the Gilded Age, they often focus on the progressive narrative, and thus view the era's visions of history as entirely concurrent with developments of national consolidation and consensus, as part of the problem rather than (at least potentially) part of the solution.[31]

One historian who has written extensively about the era's relationship to the past is Michael Kammen. Part 2 of his *Mystic Chords of Memory: The Transformation of Tradition in American Culture* covers "Circa 1870 to 1915"; while that date range indicates that even Kammen links the Gilded Age with its immediate aftermath, he is more fully concerned than other scholars with how the era related to and looked back on its history. Moreover, he argues that "between 1861 and 1907,

American memory began to take form as a self-conscious phenomenon," and describes the period as "an age of memory and ancestor worship by design and by desire" (100, 12). Much of Kammen's emphasis here, as his reference to "ancestor worship by design" indicates, is on the nostalgic and self-serving commemorations of the past which fit neatly into a progressive vision of history. But Kammen also mentions memory as an important aspect of the era's vision of history, and his analysis of that concept reveals the dialogic nature of its relationship to the past: "memory is more activated by contestation, and amnesia is more likely to be induced by the desire for reconciliation" (13). Kammen's inclusion of memory in his description of Gilded Age historical visions, then, indicates that the period's sense of the past comprised more than the consensus narrative visible in the nostalgia and progressivism of the official celebrations (as well as in the many other cultural arenas that I have discussed); it is my focus on those multiple historical constructions that differentiates my study from most scholarship on the era. As Trachtenberg (among many others) has noted, many of the Gilded Age's conflicts transcended particular issues to become "controversies over the meaning of America" (*Incorporation* 8); and while most scholars have focused on those controversies' ramifications in the Gilded Age present and for the twentieth-century future, I argue that the controversies themselves, the contested definitions of America's identity and future, were just as closely tied to visions of the past.

Such contestations over the meaning of America and visions of its history were played out in numerous cultural arenas during the post-Centennial decade, but nowhere with more complexity and power than in historical literature. And the second significant differentiation between my critical position and that of much Gilded Age scholarship is precisely in that literary emphasis, in the analytical use to which I put literary texts. In Brook Thomas's introduction to the *American Literary History* (*ALH*) panel, he argues that a salient feature of *Incorporation* was the way in which it "brought literature and material social life together" and demonstrated that in both cases "their role is ideological." For Trachtenberg, Thomas rightly notes, those ideologies are in contrast, with texts and the market "generat[ing] competing senses of reality"; but as Thomas acknowledges, subsequent scholars have taken the ideological premise in a different direction, arguing that literature and materialism reified the consensus narrative in quite similar ways. Perhaps the pioneer of this reading was Walter Benn Michaels, who explicitly references and diverges from Trachtenberg in his argument that many if not most of the period's literary texts served as "endorsement[s] of consumer capitalism" (17); and this approach, which constructs an either-or framework in which texts either abet or counter dominant cultural or political trends (often with little room for middle grounds), has been extended in a variety of ways since.[32]

Certainly there are literary texts that seem clearly and unequivocally to endorse a particular cultural viewpoint; I reference one such text in chapter 1: Thomas Nelson Page's short story "Marse Chan" (1884), which uses an ex-slave's dialect voice to describe slavery as "good ole times . . . de bes' [he] ever see" (10).[33] Yet identifying individual examples does not provide sufficient rationale for a methodology; and my methodology is instead grounded in analyzing each text's complex engagement with the past on its own terms, rather than deciding into which preestablished category the text might fit. Many scholars of Gilded Age literature take a similar position, but interestingly many argue for that literature's value by constructing a literary historical contrast that mirrors the surface and reality arguments: a conflict between a genteel literature, which in this view tended to ally with the progressive historical vision, and the new realism, which often stressed the realities beneath that vision. George Santayana, who coined the term "genteel tradition," described it as "a survival of the beliefs and standards of the fathers," "the back-water" of the era's literary and intellectual work; a recent chronicler of the tradition connects that description more fully to the period's contrasting historical forces, arguing that genteel literature "embodied conservatism in a threatening age" (Tomsich 1, 195).[34] On the other side, realist fiction was described by the early twentieth-century critic Fred Pattee as "teeming . . . with the freshness, the vitality, and the vigor of a new soil and a newly awakened nation" (*History* 18); while there has been famous disagreement on many of the defining characteristics, figures, and attitudes of realism, most post-formalist critics would still agree with Amy Kaplan's claim that "realism's relation to social change" is in "the foreground of [realist novels'] narrative structure" (9).[35] As further evidence of the established critical contrast between these two literary modes and that contrast's connections to Gilded Age historical forces, one need look no further than the ongoing debates over whether William Dean Howells was a conservative (and thus genteel) or a Progressive (and thus realist).[36]

Such broadly historicist literary criticism is undoubtedly important and necessary, particularly as a response to formalist readings of realism which entirely ignored its relation to its complex social context. And my own readings of the period's historical literature are interconnected with my historicist arguments, both the study's overall analysis of the monologic national narrative and its dialogic complications and the chapters' specific variations on that unifying idea. Yet I could not agree more strongly with Philip Barrish's argument that "in the impulse to make literary works line up with what we already know (or think we know) about broader historical developments ... we risk moving too quickly past some of the wrinkles and folds that distinguish literature itself" (11). The historians and cultural studies scholars I have referenced throughout this introduction, along with many others, have traced and will continue to trace those broader historical developments in all their complexity; while we literary critics should not pretend that such studies have no relevance for our own projects, neither should we simply seek to duplicate (and inevitably simplify) their work by extending it wholesale to literature. Too often, as Barrish hints, that leads us to treat literary works as mere reflections or extensions of a period's history, rather than as separate and complex entities which demand close and extended attention before their thematic depth and social relevance can be understood. That limiting tendency has been especially pronounced in critical accounts of historical fiction. And my own readings of historical literature, while connected to the cultural issues that I have discussed here (and in my research of which I have attempted to be as thorough and responsible as possible), thus seek, through both their breadth and their reliance on extended formal attention to each text and its many distinct voices, to approach and understand literary constructions of history on their own complex terms.

In discussing the social questions' Centennial presence, I highlighted the interconnections of history and voice. Here I would add the literary historical corollary that such a connection may be particularly apt for Gilded Age texts; many accounts of the period's literary production have focused on its unique developments in the concept of voice. Two of the earliest critics to consider the vernacular style in American literature, Leo Marx and Richard Bridgman, locate that style's primary development in the late nineteenth century: Marx writes of "a new language" spoken by narrators in the era's texts (112), and Bridgman elaborates the distinction into a full analysis of "the stylistic revolution . . . at the end of the century" (46). The critical question addressed by this new form of literature was "how the ordinary American spoke," and the answer "required the establishment of a characteristic diction (the vernacular) and of a characteristic way of using it (colloquial)" (Bridgman 62). If both Marx and Bridgman focus largely on defining this new literary style, rather than on connecting their readings to themes or historical contexts, Marx's final point that "the vernacular was more than a literary technique—it was a view of experience" (122) points toward such connections.

More recent scholars have followed that lead and connected Gilded Age texts' use of voice to broader questions, while maintaining Marx's and Bridgman's assessments of the late nineteenth century as a period of radical literary change. The narratologist critic Janet McKay, for example, argues in *Narration and Discourse in American Realistic Fiction* (1982) that novelists such as Henry James, William Dean Howells, and Mark Twain "redefin[ed] the role of the narrator, . . . foreground[ed] the voices of characters, and . . . combin[ed] these two changes to present a variety of perspectives" in their works (4). "Never before in our fiction," she posits, "had discourse been so crucial to the telling of the tale," and she connects this new emphasis to another argument about realism's relationship to social change: the variety of perspectives illustrates the "egalitarian faith" of the novelists in question (191–92).

Other critics complicate McKay's utopian picture of these literary developments, however. Barbara Hochman does so in reader-response terms, portraying the realists' shift in the use of perspective as an attempt to supplant an earlier model of "friendly reading" with a more removed authorial position; a change based not only on new formal ideas and goals but also on nascent anxieties about the constitution and desires of the reading public (29–47). More overtly political analyses of these developments are found in two works by Elsa Nettels: *Language, Race, and Social Class in Howells's America* (1988) and *Language*

and Gender in American Fiction: Howells, James, Wharton, and Cather
(1997). Nettels's arguments, while comprised of impressive close readings that are sensitive to nuance, in their overarching analyses often
echo Michaels's either-or approach: in the former work she claims that
Howells had largely democratic impulses but that his use of dialect
"emphasize[s] the forces that sever rather than unite humanity" (194);
and in the latter she investigates whether the writers "helped perpetuate or subvert their culture's ideology of language and gender" (2). Yet
rather than giving in entirely to that binary evaluation, Nettels comes to
the conclusion that the writers' use of "conflicting voices [is] suggestive
of conflicting sympathies" (*Fiction* 184), an argument that parallels my
analysis of historical literature's multivocality and dialogic relationship
to the social questions and national narrative.

Perhaps late nineteenth-century literature's most striking stylistic development was the use of dialect, a subject which Gavin Jones thoroughly and impressively explores in his *Strange Talk: The Politics of Dialect Literature in Gilded Age America* (1999). As Jones notes, "this new
movement, dubbed 'the cult of the vernacular,' was judged to be the
most significant literary event of its generation" (1); his work reiterates that judgment, arguing that "the distinctiveness of late-nineteenth-
century American literature lay largely in the generative role of dialect
within it" (3). He acknowledges dialect's potential for nostalgia and racism but also traces its ability to "record the subversive voices in which
alternative versions of reality were engendered," a Bakhtinian point that
connects his individual texts and readings to the larger, "crucial cultural
debate in which ideological attempts to forge an ideal America . . . were
constantly undermined by new and strange ways of talking" (11–12). And
while Jones certainly takes a political side in that debate, "stress[ing] dialect's counterhegemonic, disruptive potential" in preferred writers such
as Cable and Dunbar (211–13), he does so in much the same way that I
hope to: through a balance of nuanced cultural commentary on the one
hand and close and extended attention to particular literary texts' uses
of dialect on the other.[37]

Jones's work, then, like many of the texts I have referenced, has much
to offer my project, both in its specific argument and individual readings and as a model of the kind of analysis I hope to perform. I would

like to close by reiterating a few of the most salient points. First, my readings of particular texts are not primarily historicist, since I am most interested in each text's voices and historical visions, rather than its contexts; but neither are they entirely formalist, for I link their constructions of history and voice to thematic conclusions about the texts' connections to the four social questions, their dialogic complications of the monologic national narrative, and that narrative itself. Second, my study is not an exhaustive treatment of the decade; my focus on constructions of history has led me away from some presentist or futurist topics—economics and labor, immigration, Howells and the rise of realism—which would be central to such a treatment (and which have been central to cited projects such as Trachtenberg's).[38] Third and finally, what it is: a close reading of how texts written between 1876 and 1886 use a variety of voices to construct visions of history, and a connection of those dialogic historical constructions to the era's social questions and national narrative.

Each of the next four chapters centers on historical literary texts that deal in some central way with one of the four questions: race, Indian, woman, and the South. The particular valences of voice and history vary—dialect and slavery in chapter 1; silence and forgetting in 2; public debates and private experiences in 3; the lure of the Southern voice and history in 4—but in each they connect to this chapter's historical and literary contexts. In chapter 5 I focus on an exemplary case study for my argument: George Washington Cable's *The Grandissimes* (1880), a novel that I argue is one of the decade's most complex and important literary treatments of voice and history. In a coincidental but fascinating development, its manuscripts contain an additional level of dialogue, in the form of comments by its editor and the two publisher's readers and responses by Cable himself; all four figures use those conversations to articulate, defend, and adjust their own readings of the novel's constructions of voice and history. I believe that an analysis of Cable's novel, first on its own complex terms and then in the context of that historical dialogue, perfectly illustrates and effectively concludes my analyses of history and dialogue in American literature. And if the monologic national historical narrative had gained dominance by 1886 and, as I argue in the Conclusion, reached its apotheosis at the 1893 Columbian Exposition and in the imperialist ventures foreshadowed there, Cable's novel and all of the decade's dialogic literary contestations of that narrative serve as models on which future historical literature could build and remain powerful and profoundly relevant reconstructions of American histories and voices.

1

"He Wouldn't Ever Dared to Talk Such Talk in His Life Before"

Dialect, Slavery, and the Race Question

On May 30, 1885, Alexander Crummell delivered the commencement address to the graduating class of Storer College, a freedmen's college located in Harper's Ferry. Despite that West Virginia town's singular importance in the histories of slavery and African Americans, "thrilling memories" that Crummell could not entirely ignore, he nonetheless argued that the era's blacks too often "settle[d] down in the dismal swamps of dark and distressful memory." In response to that tendency, he used the occasion to advocate a "shifting of general thought from past servitude, to duty and service, in the present." That argument's presentist and progressive focus exemplified Crummell's overall role, as Wilson Moses describes it, "as the philosopher of uplift in post-Reconstruction America"; and that emphasis and role overlapped with the progressive historical narrative's increasing national dominance by a decade after Reconstruction's end. In fact, as Moses notes, the years between 1873 and 1898—the same period in which the millennial national narrative was consolidated and then extended onto the world stage—were for Crummell "characterized by attempts to adapt his Christian nationalism to an American environment." But Crummell's 1885 attempt, like the national narrative, did not go unchallenged; present in the audience at Storer was Frederick Douglass, who lodged what Crummell called an "emphatic and earnest protest" to the presentist position and instead "urge[d] his hearers to a constant recollection of the slavery of their race."[1]

Crummell and Douglass's 1885 debate was on one level simply another salvo in a long series of exchanges between these two philosophical and political African American leaders. But the debate and the divergence in thinking it revealed also illustrate a complex historical question at the heart of the period's explorations of African American issues and identity: what emphasis should be placed upon the African American past in general, and on slavery in particular? Both Crummell and Douglass were in many ways progressives, practical-minded men who believed that African Americans must focus on gaining rights in the present and equality in the future.[2] Yet the Storer College debate highlighted the deeply distinct roles that the past could play in such otherwise similar philosophies: depicted as an earlier, lesser stage of life to be moved past and triumphed over, in Crummell's articulation; or as a critical element in the formation of African American identity to be remembered and even stressed in the current debates, in Douglass's reply. Many of the literary texts that explored the race question between 1876 and 1886 engaged with precisely this historical issue, analyzing and attempting to answer two connected questions: what vision of the African American past in general, and slavery in particular, texts should construct; and what was at stake in that decision.

Not so effectively represented by Crummell's and Douglass's highly educated and articulate voices, but inextricably intertwined with the period's historical debates, was the issue of African American speech, and particularly their use of or progression past nonstandard, dialect English. To give two examples of such interconnections: unreconstructed white Southerners often made African Americans' continued use of dialect central to their paternalistic arguments about slavery's benefits and the need for related postbellum forms of racial hierarchy, as George Frederickson argues; while Wilson Moses and David Howard-Pitney analyze how African American messianic thinkers used the Anglo-American jeremiad's linguistic and rhetorical sophistication for their own racialist, progressive purposes.[3] And the decade's literary texts likewise explored issues of voice: how texts should represent the way in which many African Americans talked, their unique dialect (if indeed they had one); what importance texts should place on both that style of speech and its literary representations; and how the African American voice related to other (particularly white) American voices. As was the case with Crummell and Douglass at Storer College, for many authors, including four of the five analyzed in this chapter, engaging either the historical or vocal question in a complex way that challenged existing definitions and national narratives seems to have required flattening the other question: on the one hand, Joel Chandler Harris's *Uncle Remus* and *Nights with Uncle Remus* and Mark Twain's *Huckleberry Finn* both construct visions of African American voice's potential subversive power but reinforce more nostalgic narratives of slavery; the autobiographical narratives of Douglass and Sojourner Truth, on the other hand, construct importantly revisionist histories at the expense of multifaceted portrayals of dialect. But Charles W. Chesnutt, perhaps the most conflicted of all five authors in his thoughts on the race question, overtly analyzes in his early journals and short fictions this seeming conflict between voice and history and produces, in "The Goophered Grapevine," a story that engages both dialect and slavery with revisionist complexity.

For many years, historians and critics argued that slavery was a largely forgotten subject in the postbellum era. In this they were often following the lead of Stanley Elkins, who claims in his influential *Slavery: A Problem in American Institutional and Intellectual Life* (1959) that "throughout a good part of the postwar generation ... a moratorium on that subject was observed everywhere with surprising unanimity" (5).[4] Certainly it seems likely that the reconciliationist attitudes toward the South that took hold during Reconstruction and dominated its final years would have required a public code of silence about the peculiar institution that had so prominently caused the sectional tensions and Civil War.[5] Yet over the last thirty years, a number of scholars have demonstrated that postbellum constructions of race were closely linked to slavery on at least two distinct levels: racial attitudes associated with slavery continued into the postbellum era; and the period's early historical works on slavery were almost always intimately intertwined with contemporary debates over race and Reconstruction.[6]

It stands to reason that the white supremacists of the postwar years took their cues from the social structures and racial attitudes inherent in the slave system.[7] But as many historians have argued, even the period's more liberal white visions of race often connected to particular narratives of slavery; more exactly, many of those liberals viewed African

American history with a combination of progressive emphasis and nostalgic underpinnings quite similar to the core of the national narrative.
For these whites, the abolition of slavery was an unquestionable sign
that race relations were making progress, yet the ideal social relationship
between the races was one based (often implicitly, sometimes explicitly) on the imagined understanding and harmony that had existed between master and slave.[8] The racial visions of both conservative and liberal postbellum whites, then, were interconnected with constructions of
slavery; and the same can be said of those African Americans who publicly articulated racial visions in the period, whether like Crummell they
made an "utterly conscious effort to forget the past" (Charles Johnson
297) or like Douglass "despised the politics of forgetting that the culture
of reconciliation demanded" (Blight, *Reunion* 316–17). And those white
and black authors who attempted in the post-Reconstruction decade to
explore the race question—"the problem of determining the place that
Negroes should occupy in American life" (Rayford Logan 3)—in literary
works would likewise connect those explorations with constructions of
the African American past.

Moreover, literary memories of slavery were often explicitly connected to depictions of the African American dialect voice. In some contexts those connections could further racist constructions of African
Americans and their history; it is in that vein that Charles Johnson locates in "the generation in whom lingered memories of the powerful
degradation of slavery" an instinctive antipathy toward dialect and its
literary depictions (297). But in other ways, as Gayl Jones argues, depictions of dialect and the oral tradition with which it was intertwined
could provide African Americans with a discursive space of their own,
distinct and possibly liberated from white versions of them and their
history (1–14). As they did with the balance between forgetting and remembering the history of slavery, individual texts had to negotiate this
tension between racist and liberating visions of dialect, and scholarly
analyses of the literary presence and role of African American dialect
have likewise engaged with that tension.

As Kenneth Lynn and others have convincingly demonstrated, dialect literature's roots can be found in the early nineteenth-century traditions of American (and particularly Southwestern) humor.[9] But dialect was particularly prominent in late-nineteenth century literature; the

"cult of the vernacular" dominated literary representations of the nation from New York City to rural Indiana, the West's mining communities to the Maine woods, immigrant tenements to former slaves' cabins. Much of the movement's literary criticism has focused on the last category: the era's representations of African American dialect. And after the initial linguistic work of pioneers such as Sumner Ives and J. L. Dillard, scholars of dialect literature, replicating the tension discussed above, have tended to fall into one of two dominant strains of interpretation. For the first group, the period's representations of black dialect were inherently racist, part of what Jeffrey Hadler labels "Remus orthography." Such representations, Michael North argues, were "almost exclusively a matter of white mimicry and role-playing" (22); even when African American writers like Chesnutt began to use dialect in their own works, such writers still usually operated, in these critics' opinion, under the umbrella of "traditional literary dialect" (Gayl Jones 9).[10]

For critics who read dialect literature this way, the period's founding text is often taken to be Irwin Russell's poem "Christmas-Night in the Quarters" (1878). While Thomas Dunn English and the Lanier brothers (Clifford and Sidney) had published dialect poems earlier in the decade, Russell's was the first to achieve nationwide popularity, and it also established a number of the central components critics have identified in racist dialect literature: it sets its nostalgic depiction of slave life in the present tense, illustrating that environment's status as a postbellum ideal; it argues that antebellum blacks were better off for being "unlearned and untaught," since their ignorance gave them the freedom to "say and do/[things] That never would occur to you" (such as promising "Mahsr" that they will work harder than ever because he has given them the Christmas holiday) [8]; and it concludes with an extended "legend of the olden time," narrated by the slave Booker, which tells of Ham, who remains "de happiest ob niggers" even as Noah prepares for the flood (17–23), thus constructing African Americans' carefree and dependent nature as grounded in both historical precedent and their own storytelling.[11] Those critics attempting to connect Russell's poem's nostalgic, racist precedent to the works of a later dialect writer such as Joel Chandler Harris are aided by Harris's introduction to an 1888 edition of Russell's poetry, in which he argues that in "Christmas-Night" "the old life before the war is reproduced with a fidelity that is marvelous."

Yet Harris also points out (in what is otherwise a positive account) that his "dialect . . . is often carelessly written," indicating that Russell's construction of African American voice did not necessarily provide a model for later dialect writers (Russell x–xi).[12]

With that possibility of other approaches to dialect in mind, the second group of critics, while acknowledging dialect's racist potential, emphasizes instead its subversive qualities. Perhaps the first, and certainly the most significant, such critic was Henry Louis Gates Jr., who calls dialect, at its "most effective," a "speech-segment of natural language" that can function as "a verbal mask" ("Dis" 118, 105, 90). More recent critics in this group, like Gavin Jones, have reiterated the "double function of black English," its ability to reify and subvert, often at one and the same time, categories such as "standard English" (10–11); these critics further argue that dialect's reifying and racist capabilities have been rather thoroughly documented and that it is now time to "reread ethnic dialect" for its "subversive potential" (Kersten 95–98).[13] Lisa Cohen Minnick, for example, attempts to answer the question "Does dialect literature limit or liberate?" by adding "the important theories and methods of empirical and computational linguistics" to literary criticism's "qualitative literary methods" (xiii–xvi); while Minnick concludes that "the decision to incorporate African American dialectical speech was one that clearly involved controversy and contradiction as well as both limitation and liberation" (152), her methodology indicates the seriousness with which this second group of critics take their reevaluation of dialect literature.[14]

That seriousness is warranted, as there is a great deal at stake in any analysis of the era's representations of dialect. The connections to voice are obvious and crucial in an era when African Americans were struggling to define and articulate their place and role in the postbellum nation. Just as central, however, was the question of history, of how and by whom the African American past would be remembered and portrayed. And such historical questions, to reiterate, were also intimately connected to the period's uses of black dialect. Dialect, Gates argues (quoting Hugh Kenner), is "a broken mirror of memory" ("Dis" 105), and many of the decade's literary engagements with the race question attempted to reconstruct that mirror in one form or another. An analysis of those texts can thus illuminate the complex connections between dialect and slavery, voice and history. In this chapter, I read closely the works of five figures who exemplify those connections—or, more accurately for the first four, disconnections. Harris and Twain develop complex fictional visions of voice but are ultimately unable to do the same for their historical subjects; while Douglass and Truth's autobiographical narratives construct deeply revisionist histories but do so at the expense of multifaceted portrayals of voice. Recognizing in both his own philosophies and his culture the presence and potential dangers of such disconnections between African American voice and history, Chesnutt produces in his early journals and short fictions the group's most nuanced and significant visions of dialect, slavery, and the race question.

In the Introduction to *Nights with Uncle Remus* (1883), the second volume in the series inaugurated by *Uncle Remus* (1881), Joel Chandler Harris tells a peculiar and complex autobiographical story. One night in 1882, while waiting for a train at a small Georgia station, Harris found himself among a group of African American workers who "seemed to be in great good-humor." After "listening and laughing awhile" to "one of the liveliest talkers in the party," Harris himself told "the 'Tar Baby' story by way of a feeler"; although he claims that "the story was told in a low tone, as if to avoid attracting attention," his auditor's loud responses drew the remainder of the crowd, and by the end of Harris's second tale, "two or three could hardly wait for the conclusion, so anxious were they to tell stories of their own." And so the storytelling, and Harris's work as compiler of such stories, commenced in earnest:

> It was night, and impossible to take notes; but that fact was not to be regretted. The darkness gave greater scope and freedom to the narratives of the negroes, and but for this friendly curtain it is doubtful the conditions would have been favorable to story-telling. But however favorable the conditions might have been, the appearance of a note-book and pencil would have dissipated them as utterly as if they had never existed.
>
> Moreover, it was comparatively an easy matter for the writer to take the stories away in his memory. (xv–xvii)

With that, Harris concludes his story and returns to the learned discussion of African American folktales' origins with which much of his
Introduction is concerned.

The temptation to move outward from the text at this point, to connect this story with other details of Harris's biography and thus to analyze him and his relationship to writing, folktales, and African Americans, is almost overwhelming. It becomes even more so when coupled
with one of the most famous American literary letters, an 1898 mis-
sive from Harris to his daughter Julia in which he describes his writing
process for the Uncle Remus tales in these terms: "When night comes, I
take up my pen, surrender unconditionally to my 'other fellow,' and out
comes the story" (MacKethan, *Dream* 62). Numerous critics, particularly those trying to complicate the portrayals of Harris as inveterate
racist, have made just such biographical and psychoanalytic leaps, arguing that Harris's Uncle Remus texts represent his own divided personality, his intentions and worries as a writer, his region's conflicted relationship with both African Americans and its own history, and any
number of other external themes (including, in at least one case, Harris's speech impediment).[15]

While Harris invites such biographical readings through his inclusion of the personal story in *Nights*' Introduction, to give in to that
temptation is to move away from the text and, more important, to subsume it permanently into a reading of Harris himself. That is, once Harris becomes the central critical subject, he is likely to remain in that position of priority, and his texts to remain evidence in an analysis of his
(and his region's) psyche. Moreover, the railway station story is, like all
of *Nights* (and, to a somewhat lesser extent, *Uncle Remus*), an extremely
complex text in its own right. The themes it raises are central to Harris's works: the relationship between African American voice and white
memory and writing; the setting and environment of storytelling, as
well as its potentially dangerous or masked qualities; the responses of
African Americans to the stories that comprise much of their oral history. Just as significant is the issue that the story carefully elides: the use
of dialect. Did Harris tell his stories using the African American dialect
in which he has Uncle Remus narrate them? It seems likely that he did;
if so, how would that fact relate to his use of a "low tone" and his desire
not to "attract attention"? In all these ways, the story provides an exem-

plary introduction to the complex dynamics of voice, race, and history in Harris's first two Uncle Remus collections.

The Introduction to *Uncle Remus* establishes Harris's narratorial voice and lays out that narrator's positions on African American voice and history. The first word of the Introduction is "I," and the section's purpose, as Harris defines it in the first sentence, is to allow that "I" to speak directly to the reader about his book—to "give [Harris] an opportunity to say" some noteworthy things about the text. More specifically, he wants to delineate his goals: "to preserve the legends themselves in their original simplicity, and to wed them permanently to the quaint dialect—if, indeed, it can be called a dialect—through the medium of which they have become a part of the domestic history of every Southern family; and I have endeavored to give to the whole a genuine flavor of the old plantation" (39). *Uncle Remus,* then, is centrally concerned with voice and history, and the two are seemingly inseparable: the history which the Brer Rabbit legends encapsulate can only be narrated through this "quaint" voice, which is inextricably linked to the region's history. Moreover, both voice and history are, as Harris portrays them in the Introduction, almost literally past, and in danger of being forgotten: Uncle Remus is "venerable enough to have lived during the period which he describes"; "the dialect of the legends has nearly disappeared." And that historic dialect voice contains a particular vision of the past: Remus "has nothing but pleasant memories of the discipline of slavery" (46-47).

That final quote illustrates the source of much of the critical opposition to Harris: the nostalgic component of his narrative voice which participates in (even, many argue, helps to inaugurate) the myth-making surrounding the antebellum South which became so prevalent in the region's (and nation's) literature during this era. Certainly that component is part of Harris's voice here in the Introduction, and in the book which follows. Yet it is not uniformly present throughout that book. The full title of this first volume in the series is *Uncle Remus, His Songs and His Sayings,* and what the tendency to shorten the title elides is the fact that the book comprises two distinct sections: Remus's recounting of the Brer Rabbit stories, entitled "Legends of the Old Plantation"; and sections of songs and contemporary sketches, under the "His Songs" and "His Sayings" headings. Those distinct sections, moreover, emphasize different aspects of the book's central themes: the Legends privilege the complex issue of voice, while the Songs and especially the Sayings focus on Harris's more simplistic, distinctly nostalgic vision of Southern and African American history.

The opening paragraph of the first Legend, "Uncle Remus Initiates the Little Boy," exemplifies the importance and use of voice in this section of the book. "One evening recently," the narrator begins, "the lady whom Uncle Remus calls 'Miss Sally' missed her little seven-year-old. Making search for him through the house and through the yard, she heard the sound of voices in the old man's cabin, and, looking through the window, saw the child sitting by Uncle Remus. . . . This is what 'Miss Sally' heard" (55). The narrative frame, which opens every chapter of this section and closes many of them, is, as many critics have noted, clearly composed in correct standard English; one need only compare the above sentences (with their use of "whom," for example) with the beginning of Remus's story that follows ("Bimeby, one day, arter Brer Fox bin doin' all dat he could fer ter ketch Brer Rabbit") to prove that point. In terms of language conventions, the narrator's voice thus seems authoritative. Yet within that narrative voice, Uncle Remus's dialect voice occupies a privileged position. It is privileged linguistically, as the woman on whom the sentences focus is identified (twice) through Remus's designation for her; and it is privileged structurally, as Sally listens to what Remus says and, quite literally, disappears behind his voice for the remainder of the book.[16] This privileging of a seemingly weaker voice is reiterated in the legends themselves: the first full story that Remus narrates, and the only one that stretches over multiple chapters, is the famous "Wonderful Tar-Baby Story," in which the imprisoned Brer Rabbit escapes from the powerful Brer Fox's clutches using only his "mighty 'umble" voice (63).[17]

This initial portrayal of voice's power extends throughout the remainder of the Legends section, with a couple of interesting twists. First, there are moments in which Remus's vocal power transcends Harris's capabilities as transcriber of it. For the most part, Harris works extremely hard to reproduce that voice; in the definitive account of Harris's use of dialect, Sumner Ives notes that "interpretation reveals a consistent phonology, and . . . this phonology is clearly based on accurate observation of a genuine folk speech" ("Phonology" 3). Yet there are moments when the narrator must admit that he cannot accurately represent an element of Remus's voice, that "no typographical combination or description could do justice to ... [his] peculiar intonation," or that "no explanation could convey an adequate idea of the intonation and pronunciation which Uncle Remus brought to bear upon this wonderful word" (88, 92). Here again aspects of authoritative, written, standard English—typographical combinations, rational explanations—fall short of the wonderful tones of the storyteller's oral, dialect voice; while it would be possible to read these moments as condescending toward that voice, it is important to note that the boy who serves as its ideal audience takes no such position: "He [is] in thorough sympathy with all the whims and humors of the old man, and his capacity for enjoying them [is] large enough to include even those he [can] not understand" (134).

It is precisely the boy's relationship to Uncle Remus's voice and stories that comprises the section's other interesting twist. For much of this book (as opposed to *Nights,* as we will see), the boy is portrayed only as "occupying the anxious position of auditor" (80), and his voice exists simply to provide Remus with appropriate responses which allow the storytelling to continue: "But what became of the Rabbit, Uncle Remus?" (76). Yet there is at least one scene that complicates that structure and reveals that the boy's voice is not without its own power in this relationship. Uncle Remus begins to tell a story about Brer Wolf, and the boy "breaks in" to point out, correctly, that Remus had "said the Rabbit scalded the Wolf to death a long time ago." Remus is "fairly caught and he [knows] it," but his response is to "frown ... upon the child" with "both scorn and indignation," and to remark to an "imaginary person" that there was a time when no child of his Mistress would "dast ... ter come 'sputin' longer me." Up to this point the vocal power still seems mostly located with Remus, but at the same time the boy's voice has prompted this assertion of authority, and Remus aims his rebuttal not directly at the boy but rather at a presumably less sensitive proxy. Moreover, it is the boy who ends the confrontation; when his "eyes [fill] with tears and his lips [begin] to quiver, but he [says] nothing," Remus "immediately [melts]" and they return to their normal state. The narrator concludes the account by noting that "Uncle Remus had conquered him and he had conquered Uncle Remus in pretty much the same way before" (110–11). The precise meanings of these codependent conquests are debatable, but I would argue that Remus has maintained his story-teller's authority without directly challenging his auditor, that the boy has indicated to Remus his responses' importance without overstepping the bounds of his listener's role, and that both have finally admitted (without ever saying as much) that they are dependent upon each other for the continuance of this mutually beneficial relationship.

If voice is thus a paramount and complex aspect of the Legends section, history is almost nowhere to be found in this part. As numerous critics have argued, the Brer Rabbit stories themselves can be read as an ironic commentary on slavery, one in which the less powerful, constantly threatened, wily Rabbit consistently outwits figures of authority such as Fox and (much less frequently, but more significantly for this argument) Man. It is in this context, for example, that Eric Sundquist defines Harris as a "double-voiced trickster" (*Wake* 345). Yet this reading, while faithful to the content and spirit of many of the stories, seems to me to give too much credit to Harris for those aspects. He simply repeats those particular legends, as he does the ones in which Brer Rabbit acts maliciously or stupidly (legends from which critics such as Sundquist do not try to extrapolate allegories for slavery). However, and despite his Introduction's nostalgic description of Remus's historical attitudes, neither does Harris use the Legends section as a platform to expand on that nostalgia. Even the relationship between Remus and the boy, reminiscent as it might occasionally be of certain ideal slave-master dynamics, is, as I have argued, ultimately a good deal more complex than that.

Instead, it is in the book's latter sections that Harris's nostalgic vision of history comes to the forefront, almost entirely displacing the first section's voice-related themes in the process. The change begins in the stand-alone "Story of the War," originally published in 1878, slightly (if meaningfully) revised for the book, and placed by Harris just before the final section, "His Sayings." As with the Legends, this story begins with an external narrator's voice setting the scene—in this case the visit of a Northern woman to her brother's newly adopted Southern home—and moves into an Uncle Remus story. But while Remus's dialect here is essentially the same as in the Legends, his voice is defined by a new attribute: "Uncle Remus spoke from the standpoint of a Southerner, and with the air of one who expected his hearers to thoroughly sympathize with him" (180). And this new regional vocalization is far from coincidental, as the story deals not with a mischievous rabbit but instead with Remus's Civil War–era loyalty to his absent master; that loyalty includes efficiently running the plantation as overseer and, most important, staying behind after emancipation and wounding a Northern soldier who is about to kill his master. In the revised version Harris (a supporter of the New South, if with reservations[18]) does include a hopeful image of national Reconstruction—the wounded Yankee, who had been killed in the newspaper story, ends up marrying the master's sister and fathering the boy who becomes the Legends' auditor—but that in no way detracts from the nostalgic vision of slavery that dominates the story. Moreover, putting that vision in Remus's voice, having him say, at the story's climax, that he "disremembered all 'bout freedom en lammed aloose" at the Yankee (185), couples his storytelling orality to Harris's historical project for the first time in the book.[19]

In the final section, "His Sayings," really a series of brief sketches about Remus's life in the post-Reconstruction South, that coupling comes to dominate Remus's voice and identity. Here Remus, reporting his views of various situations to a group of white journalists, becomes a mouthpiece for Harris's positions on Reconstruction and its legacy, and it is his fellow African Americans who bear the brunt of his derision. Far from telling stories in his own distinct voice, Remus now simply takes issues like "Race Improvement" and Arkansas "Emigrants" as his "texts" (194) and supplies glib glosses that provide his white auditors with a great deal of amusement. Without a doubt the most troubling of these sketches, in light of the first section's emphasis on both voice and Remus's relationship with the boy, is entitled "As To Education." In it Remus encounters a "little colored boy carrying a slate and a number of books"; the two exchange "unpleasant" words, the "exact purport [of which] will probably never be known," and Remus remarks to a "sympathizing" white policeman that "I 'aint larnt nuthin' in books. . . . Put a spellin'-book in a nigger's han's, en right den en dar' you loozes a plow-hand" (215–16). Certainly the power of Remus's voice in the Legends section did not derive from books or instruction in the elements of standard English (like spelling), but neither did it have much to do with plowing; moreover, that power would be far less likely to find a sympathetic ear among post-

Reconstruction white law enforcement than Remus's new nostalgia. If voice dominates the first section of *Uncle Remus,* history becomes the the final section's focus, and the change is not for the better.[20]

Two years later, in response to the first collection's overwhelming popularity, Harris published a sequel: *Nights with Uncle Remus: Myths and Legends of the Old Plantation.* While the majority of *Nights'* chapters are structured identically to those in *Uncle Remus's* Legends section—a narrator's voice frames a story which Uncle Remus tells to the boy—the book's constructions of history and voice significantly differ. In terms of history, Harris defies the laws of narrative continuity and moves his characters decades backward in time, setting the stories "before the war" so as "to give in their recital a glimpse of plantation life in the South" in that era (xlii). In other words, the historical and social commentary that Harris locates in the first book's Sayings section has now been folded into the tales' frames, which Harris thus expands to include a good deal more description of both Remus and his interactions with other members of the plantation community.

Moreover, as *Uncle Remus's* slavery past becomes *Nights'* present setting, the nostalgic picture of that world is not altered in the slightest. Uncle Remus and his fellow slaves are presented as doing virtually no work of any kind (aside from occasional craftsmanship that seems to be more of a hobby), as having the ability to come and go freely from the plantation, as courting and marrying one another at will and with no apparent potential for separation, and generally as enjoying full, rich, and easy lives that would certainly explain Remus's later contempt for the results of Emancipation and Reconstruction. Of course, within the chronology of Harris's publications those emotions are not later but earlier, a subtle point but one that helps make his portrait of slave conditions seem inevitable and, I would argue, easier to accept. That is, having already witnessed Remus's historical judgments on and preference for slavery from without, it logically follows that his experiences of the institution from within will be pleasant. This is historical propaganda at its most potent and dangerous.[21]

Despite that historical component, however, *Nights* constructs, overall, a more complex and rich picture of African American life than *Uncle Remus,* and it achieves that effect through its multifaceted and shifting use of voice.[22] The first area in which voice plays a new and more intricate role is the relationship between Remus and the boy: the nuances visible at times in *Uncle Remus* (as in the confrontation scene) take center stage in *Nights,* beginning with the book's first few stories. The first two, though seemingly no different from any number of previous tales, produce only silence, rather than the boy's normal excited responses; the first such pause has "a depressing influence upon Uncle Remus" (8), and the second, "prolonged silence" causes the boy to grow "restless enough to cast several curious glances" around the cabin (13). Remus is nothing if not conscious of the effects of his voice and story-telling, and so he immediately seeks to remedy these lapses in power. And the story and tone with which he does so are both significant.

The story that Remus chooses to tell, which Harris titles "Brother Rabbit and the Little Girl," is one of the few that does not pit animal against animal. Instead, Brer Rabbit encounters and befriends the human Little Gal, daughter of the dangerous Mr. Man (the Mr., significantly, has been added since *Uncle Remus*'s references to this figure). On a subsequent visit to Little Gal, Brer Rabbit is caught by Mr. Man, but he escapes by using his powers as a performer: first he sings for Little Gal, which makes her laugh, and then he convinces her that his dancing will be even better and she unties him, allowing him to make his escape. It is Brer Rabbit's performative nature, then, that undermines Mr. Man's authority, seduces his child, and allows Brer Rabbit to maintain control of his own destiny. Remus clearly recognizes the import of his story: he says "with unusual emphasis" that "en dem days Brer Rabbit wuz a singer," and performs the song "with a curious air of attempting to remember something," indicating that the story has meaning in his own past as well. Moreover, he this time receives the desired responses from his auditor: at the story's two key moments, the boy asks "What did he sing, Uncle Remus?" and "Did the rabbit dance, Uncle Remus?" The boy has been seduced once again by Remus's vocal power, and at the end of the tale it is now Remus, his storyteller's authority fully restored, who pauses and sighs, "as though he had relieved his mind of a great burden" (12–17).

As these first few stories indicate, the relationship between Remus and the boy, and particularly voice's role on both sides, becomes newly prominent in *Nights.* More exactly, the boy is developing a voice of his own, if one that consistently relates to and is guided by Remus's voice and stories. He begins to express his opinions about and preferences on the stories, and thus to add his voice to the narrative frames' exchanges (rather than the formulaic responses which he had always provided within the stories). Remus notices this change, exclaiming that he "'clar' ter goodness ef dat ar chile aint gittin' so dat he's eve'y whit ez up-en-spoken ez w'at ole Miss ever bin" (274). Soon the boy is even taking part in the storytelling, interjecting into one of Remus's purposeful pauses "the climax of a story that Uncle Remus had told a long time before" (285). As that reference indicates, the boy's developing voice takes its cues from Remus's, and in the next chapter it is still the boy who asks "Uncle Remus, what did [Brer Rabbit] say?" and still Remus who "proceed[s] to tell the story in his own way" (287). But the boy's voice has unquestionably become a significant part of the stories' oral environment.

The boy's is not *Nights*' only new voice, however, nor its most important. That designation must go to the three additional African American voices that populate many of the book's chapters and eventually contribute their own stories to the mix: Tildy, Aunt Tempy, and Daddy Jack. At first, these new visitors serve mostly as supplementary respondents to Remus's tales, providing reactions like Tildy's "Dar, now!" (64) and "Truth, too!" (65) or Aunt Tempy's "Oh-ho, Mr. Rabbit! How you feel now?" (151). But the arrival of Daddy Jack, a "genuine African" (132) who speaks an entirely new dialect but is quite capable of fitting into the existing storytelling dynamic ("the little boy [understands his] rapidly-spoken lingo perfectly well" [135]), signals that Remus is no longer the only qualified vocal performer in the cabin. It is not long before Tildy and Tempy are likewise chiming in with their own stories and voices, to the delight of Remus (who tells Tempy after her first attempt that she "better jine in wid us some mo'" [248]). And this multivocality produces the ultimate heteroglossic moment: Remus, Jack, Tempy, and then Remus again all tell versions of the same tale, with each successive story building on the previous ones while contributing its own unique voice and perspective at the same time. Moreover, the tale at this heteroglossia's center is the famous "Cutta Cord-La," which, as a number of critics have noted, itself focuses on voice: Brer Wolf attempts to pass his own voice off as Brer Rabbit's but fails because he is unable to pronounce a key word correctly (230–54).[23]

This scene of successive storytelling is heteroglossic not only because it provides three distinct and four total perspectives on the same tale of multivocal struggle, but also because of each teller's reaction to the previous version. Daddy Jack responds to Remus's initial attempt by first lapsing into his unique voice so thoroughly that he is temporarily unable to communicate with the others—"mumbl[ing] to himself in a lingo which might have been understood on the Guinea coast, but which sound[s] out of place in Uncle Remus's Middle Georgia cabin"—but ultimately moves past his belief that Remus has not told the tale "stret" to share what the story "soun' lak" to him (236–37). Aunt Tempy, in turn, is "very much interested in Daddy Jack's story," and reveals that her interest has been piqued because the story reminds her of a voice from her past, a "tale w'at [she] year long time ago" in "Ferginny"; with her unique history and perspective so engaged for the first time, Tempy is willing to tell her version of the "tale 'long side er Brer Remus un Daddy Jack" (241–42). And having heard and approved of both alternate versions, Remus cannot help but give it his own spin one final time, noting that "dat ar hollerin' 'bout shucky-cordy" has "put [him] in min' er one" additional story (250). In its content, its overlapping but distinct acts of storytelling, and its engagement with each storyteller's particular voice, perspective, and history, this extended scene truly exemplifies Remus's cabin's heteroglossic potential.

I use "heteroglossic" purposefully, for an explicit turn to Bakhtin's terminology drives home both the complications of voice found in *Nights*' latter sections and those complications' thematic stakes. The storytelling segments of *Uncle Remus* are essentially monologic, with Remus's voice dominant and the boy's voice serving as an occasional respondent. Such monologia is significant in its acknowledgment of the African American voice's power, yet it is also easily co-opted by an equally monologic but much more regressive vision such as the Sayings' nostalgia. From the outset of *Nights*, Harris depicts the storytelling situation as much more dialogic: the boy's voice takes on a power of its own, one that crucially does not undermine Remus's voice or power (that, in fact, owes its growth to them) but does challenge and enrich both the narrative frames and the tales themselves. And with the introduction of the other African American voices, the environment in the cabin becomes truly heteroglossic, with distinct voices and dialects not only coexisting but also contributing to a final voice that is still centrally Remus's yet comprises something more creative and powerful than it or any particular one of them.

It is only with that heteroglossic ideal in mind that one can read the book's final chapters as something more than the simple nostalgia and racial hierarchy evident in *Uncle Remus's* Sayings. Certainly those elements are present in *Nights'* concluding scenes, a vision of the slaves' Christmas celebrations (somewhat reminiscent of Russell's poem) where they gather to perform, to "the fine company of men and women at the big house," a "powerful and thrilling" song entitled "My Honey, My Love"; afterward Remus carries the boy to the big house and puts him to bed, singing the book's closing line of "Good night" (402–4). Yet Harris's description of the performance unmistakably echoes the cabin setting, with Remus's voice—"strong, and powerful, and sweet, . . . its range as astonishing as its volume"—dominant yet fully supported by the "hundred voices almost as sweet and as powerful as his own" (401–2). It is thus no surprise that the boy's "ready delight" in the African American celebrations "has been trained and sharpened, if the expression may be used, in the small world over which Uncle Remus presided" (396), nor that the boy's final sensation, as he drifts to sleep, is of "floating in the air, while somewhere near all the negroes were singing, Uncle Remus's voice above all the rest" (404).

The strength of Harris's construction of African American voice, ultimately, lies precisely in that combination: the power of Remus's voice, the contributions of distinct yet related fellow voices, and the potential effects of those voices upon their chief auditor, the boy. Certainly Harris's visions of history and slavery, whether developed in *Uncle Remus's* contemporary Sayings or *Nights'* narrative frames, are nostalgic and reductive in the extreme. Yet his construction of voice is neither of those things, and at its best, as in *Nights'* heteroglossic moments, it is a powerful alternative vocalization in its own right. Just before the Christmas song, Remus and the boy sit and gaze into his fireplace, and the narrator initially describes them as entirely distinct: "old age and youth, one living in the Past and the other looking forward only to the Future." Yet their "shadows," reflected on "the wall behind them," are "clinging together," and even when the two of them are roused by the supper horn, the change has "no perceptible effect upon the Shadows" (382). If history in the Uncle Remus tales depicts African Americans as entirely distinct from both their actual past experiences and white Americans, voice is the shadow in which those elements cling together, inseparably bound in the dialect stories of Uncle Remus and his compatriots and in the responsive voice of his young auditor.

Voice and the relationship between a black slave and a young white boy are likewise at the heart of Mark Twain's *Adventures of Huckleberry Finn* (1884) and have provided focal points for much of the critical commentary and controversy that have surrounded the novel since its publication. In fact, two of the most recent and famous critical works on the novel have concerned themselves with precisely the combination of voice and race, albeit from diametrically opposed positions: Shelley Fisher Fishkin's *Was Huck Black?: Mark Twain and African-American Voices* (1993), which attempts to trace "the ways in which African-American voices shaped Twain's creative imagination at its core" and thus to argue that "the voice we have come to accept as the vernacular voice in American literature . . . is in large measure a voice that is black" (4); and Jonathan Arac's *Huckleberry Finn as Idol and Target: The Functions of Criticism in Our Time* (1997), which argues that "Huckleberry Finn has less 'dialogue' than we might imagine," and thus that its portrait of race is much less progressive than we critics would like to admit (38).

My goal in this section is not to side with one or the other of these arguments, nor with any of the manifold established scholarly takes on this controversial text. In fact, I hope to avoid altogether the issue of sides; one limitation of much recent *Huck* criticism, I would argue, is that it reads like a lengthy opinion essay, with a clear, qualitative thesis supported by extensive supporting evidence and thorough rebuttals of the opposing positions. Fishkin's and Arac's books are exemplary models of this type of criticism, for better and for worse. *Huckleberry Finn* has indeed become an idol or a target, but in neither position is it likely to receive a reading that pays close attention to its particulars and allows an analysis of issues such as voice, history, and race to emerge in all their (perhaps irresolvable) complexity. Certainly there are critics who are performing just such analyses of *Huck,* if without yet the same attention as that received by Fishkin and Arac—Laurel Bollinger, Joseph

Coulombe, Stacey Margolis, Lisa Cohen Minnick, and Peter Schmidt
have done so within the last few years alone—and it is in their company
that I would locate the following analysis of voice, history, and race in
the novel.

Huck's prefatory materials contain two interesting indications that
the novel will focus on voice and history. The first is the oft-discussed
"Explanatory" note, which identifies the novel's seven "dialects," claims
that their "shadings" have been done "painstakingly, and with the trust-
worthy guidance and support of personal familiarity with these several forms of speech," and concludes with the statement that the signed
"Author" "make[s] this explanation for the reason that without it many
readers would suppose that all these characters were trying to talk alike
and not succeeding." Critics have tended to take one of two positions on
this note: taking it seriously, and attempting to identify and judge the
authenticity of the novel's dialects; or treating it as another in Twain's
long history of satirical commentaries on his fellow writers (in this case,
on dialect writers such as Harris who worked hard to prove their own
authenticity).[24] The latter case is certainly helped by both the comic self-
seriousness of the author's tone and the note's proximity to the even
more infamous and clearly humorous "Notice" from the "Chief of Ord-
nance" about what "persons" are not to do. Yet even if the Explanatory
functions principally as humor, it nonetheless clearly brings up issues of
voice and dialect, of close attention to how and where people speak in
particular ways, from the novel's outset.[25]

Less clear, and certainly less famous, is the novel's prefatory reference to history. Yet there on the first edition's title page, just under the
title and rarely repeated subtitle (*Tom Sawyer's Comrade*), are dramatic cues identifying the book's "Scene: The Mississippi Valley" and
its "Time: Forty to Fifty Years Ago." The latter identification is strangely
vague, particularly in contrast with the Explanatory's linguistic specificity (humorous or not). Yet such chronological ambiguity has literary
precedent: the first historical novel (as it is often described), Sir Walter
Scott's *Waverly,* was subtitled *'Tis Sixty Years Since,* with its events' "precise date," Scott later admitted, "withheld from the original edition, lest
it should anticipate the nature of the tale by announcing so remarkable
an era" (37). Twain's literary criticisms of Scott and his American heir
Cooper are well known, as are the ways in which those criticisms inform

various sections and themes of *Huck;* yet this titular echo places Twain's work within the tradition of the historical novel. Moreover, his vagueness on that history's specifics anticipates his tale's critique of the antebellum era and its preference for the raft's ahistorical, timeless world.

As many critics note, the novel's opening paragraph clearly and efficiently both establishes its unique narrative voice and distinguishes it from the author's voice. In both senses, the paragraph locates its narrator as an outsider in significant ways: outside of the world of "Mr. Mark Twain," and able to look objectively at his "book by the name of *The Adventures of Tom Sawyer*" and judge that it "is mostly a true book; with some stretchers"; and outside of the conventions of standard English, as exemplified by the famous and ungrammatical first sentence: "You don't know about me, without you have read [*Tom*], but that ain't no matter" (1).[26] Moreover, much of the remainder of the novel's opening (generally described as ending with Huck's chapter 7 escape to the island) consists of identifying other linguistic systems on the outside of which Huck finds himself: the widow's biblical language; Tom's Romantic literary language; even Pap's vulgar, anti-educational language. Each of these languages, which could be broadly defined as "dialects," holds a potential appeal for Huck—particularly Pap's language, which closely resembles Huck's and temporarily seduces him back into its world—but ultimately none can satisfy his combination of pragmatism ("I couldn't see no advantage in going where she was going" [3]), realism ("I reckoned he believed in the A-rabs and the elephants, but as for me I think different" [16]), and rebelliousness ("I didn't want to go to school much, before, but I reckoned I'd go now to spite pap" [26]). While he does not often voice his objections to these languages—"I never said so, because it would only make trouble, and wouldn't do no good" (3) could be the section's epigraph—he makes his disagreements clear through actions, beginning with his sneaking out of the widow's house and culminating in his elaborate escape from Pap's cabin. Yet if these opening pages make abundantly clear what Huck and his voice are not—Mark Twain, grammatical, religious, literary, or his father—it remains to be seen what they are.[27]

The novel's first section also introduces, if only in broad strokes, the character and voice of its other central character: "Miss Watson's big nigger, named Jim" (5). By his status as slave—a status implicit in that possessive identification of him and, as the subsequent derogatory term indicates, a status that is as much linguistic as economic or social—Jim is located entirely within the period's most controversial system and thus (by 1884) within history. And the opening chapters' depiction of Jim contains many attributes of a particular historical conception of slaves to which Twain's critics have objected most vigorously: his superstitions, his use as an object of humor (by Tom, but also, to some extent, by Twain), his ignorant misinterpretations of the world. Yet within those characteristics are also hints of a more unique and stronger voice: Jim's creative storytelling in response to Tom's practical joke results in his becoming a powerful vocal force in the community, so much so that other blacks "will come miles to hear [him] tell about it" (6); and Huck asks Jim if his magic hairball will "talk" about Pap and takes Jim's resulting monologue entirely seriously (19). Perhaps it is most apt to say that Jim's first spoken words in the novel, "Who dah?" (5), can be applied reflexively as well: Jim's identity and voice are not fully comprised by his historical identification as comic, ignorant slave and are instead, at this point in the text, open to further definition.[28]

Despite their many differences, then (not just of race, but also their distinct relationships to the era's language systems), Huck and Jim share an undefined quality in the novel's opening section. And by that section's end they also share a physical location: the island from which they will set off on their shared journey down the Mississippi. The voyage and raft world have been dissected from virtually every critical angle; for my purposes I would emphasize the novel's depiction of voice on the raft and its relation to the historical world through which their journey takes them. At the outset, it seems that the raft will be just another linguistic system which requires its participants' silence: Huck promises Jim that he will not say a word about Jim's escape, despite the fact that "people would call [him] a low down Ablitionist [sic] and despise [him] for keeping mum" (48); and when they have their first adventure and find the floating house with the corpse, Jim does not want to discuss the dead man and so there is no further conversation about him (58). If either were to break these silences, the raft's world would collapse: Jim would be tracked down and returned to a state of slavery; Huck (once he learned that the corpse was Pap, a fact that Jim knows but keeps to himself) would have no reason to continue his faked death and flight.

These initial silences, in which one person's future and fate are dependent (for good or for ill) on the other's refusing to give voice to the truth, seem to highlight the separation between the two figures; each may resemble the other in the power granted by his unshared knowledge, but such a similarity is hardly one which tends to build a spirit of community. Yet as the journey continues, the raft's silences do become more evenly shared between the two, and thus more communal. When Huck returns from his disastrous masquerade as Sarah Williams/George Peters and alerts Jim to their pursuers, "Jim never ask[s] no questions, he never [says] a word," and as the raft slips away from the island toward safety, it is both of them whom Huck describes as "never saying a word" (69). This shared need for silence in the face of danger, in turn, yields a more positive type of silence, which Huck identifies at the next chapter's outset, in the first of his pastoral descriptions of life on the raft: "we didn't ever feel like talking loud, and it warn't often that we laughed, only a little kind of low chuckle" (71). The raft's communal identity is most obvious at such a moment: the use of "we" in these phrases becomes the dominant identification in this and all the pastoral descriptions, including the most famous, chapter 19's opening paragraph.

That description is best known as the agreed-upon exemplification of the novel's revolutionary use of the vernacular voice, an aspect illustrated by the chapter's first sentence: "Two or three days and nights went by; I reckon I might say they swum by, they slid along so quiet and smooth and lovely" (129). Certainly Huck's narrative voice in this description, as in all the pastoral moments, takes on a poetic beauty while maintaining its vernacular grammar, structures, and tone; it is, I would argue, not a coincidence that his voice is at its most individual and strong in his descriptions of life on the raft with Jim.[29] Yet the aspect of the chapter 19 pastoral description that I would emphasize is historical, or more exactly ahistorical; chronological time becomes almost entirely meaningless at these moments in the novel. The first sentence, with the vagueness of "two or three days"—a vagueness that does not resonate with the novel's usual specificity on the question of time, although it echoes the title page's "forty to fifty years ago"—exemplifies this timelessness, as do the remaining description's shifts between past and present tenses and its sense of habitual action ("Here is the way we put in the time" each day [129]). During these ideal pastoral moments on the raft, Huck and Jim are outside of history, and that ahistoricity directly connects to the communal voice that surfaces most strongly at these moments.[30]

Both that escape from history and their shared voice, however, are threatened in two key ways throughout their journey. The first, and for my argument less significant, group of threats comes from outside the raft: the intrusions of various historical aspects of Southern society. Such famous episodes as the feud, the aborted lynch mob, and the adventures with the King and Duke all fall into this category and can be read as satirical commentaries on aspects of the antebellum South: its chivalric code's superficial civility and underlying violence, the power of mob passions, the obsession with nobility. These degraded aspects of Southern society are directly related to false language systems— Emmeline Grangerford's terrible Romantic "tributes" to the dead (114); the King's and the Duke's constant lying and double-talk, along with their mangling of Shakespeare—and produce in Huck the same silence which was his only response to the opening section's languages. After the climactic battle between the Grangerfords and the Shepherdsons, for example, Huck admits that he "ain't agoing to tell all that happened— it would make me sick again" (127); later he sees through the King's and the Duke's lies but "never [says] nothing, never let[s] on" (138). These historical intrusions, then, push Huck further toward his outsider status and back to the raft's ideal world and communal voice: after the aforementioned battle, Huck hears "Jim's voice," and notes that "nothing ever sounded so good before" (128).

Even when they are alone on the raft, however, Jim's voice does not always sound so good to Huck, and it is those moments that reveal the second type of threats to the raft's world. Those threats come from inside Huck's consciousness and represent the recurrence of the language systems with which he was faced at the novel's outset.[31] Many of Huck's less communal moments on the raft can be attributed precisely to the influence of one or another of those systems: his sour assertion that "you can't learn a nigger to argue" (88) sounds like Pap's vulgar and overtly racist voice; while both the cruel trick he plays on Jim after their separation in the fog and his willingness to use Jim as a prop in the King and Duke's schemes echo Tom's literary voice and insensitivity to Jim's humanity or dignity.

Yet the system which causes the most pressure on and division in Huck's voice (and conscience) is the widow's religious language and worldview, closely coupled with the slave system's. It is that combination which prompts, first implicitly and then explicitly, the two famous moments in which Huck almost returns Jim to slavery. The first such moment arises because of Jim's voice: the raft's ideal world has begun to feel so comfortable to Jim that he is willing to give unfettered voice to his desire for freedom. It makes Huck "all over trembly and feverish . . . to hear him," and suddenly the raft's communal voice dissolves into two monologues: "Jim talked out loud all the time while I was talking to myself." The more Huck talks it through, the more he realizes that the raft world is responsible for this new voice of Jim's, that "he wouldn't ever dared to talk such talk in his life before." Moreover, he admits that he has helped create this new world, and thus that "this is what comes of [his] not thinking." While Huck does not explicitly mention religion as the cause of this newly conscientious voice, he does connect that voice to Miss Watson and her rights as a slaveowner, and it is on those counts that his "conscience [gets] to stirring [him] up hotter than ever" (97–98).

Just as this moment of newfound conscience is created by Jim's voice, it is likewise diffused by it. As Huck paddles away to "tell" on Jim, Jim notes that he will soon have full use of his voice and that he owes this capability to Huck: "Pooty soon I'll be a-shout'n for joy, en I'll say, it's all on accounts o'Huck." This "seem[s] to kind of take the tuck all out of" Huck, and when Jim follows it up by commending Huck's voice— "Dah you goes, de ole true Huck; de on'y white genlman dat ever kep' his promise to ole Jim"—he makes it impossible for Huck to give in to his conscience's voice and turn Jim in (98–99).[32] This externally dialogic battle of voices—a battle, that is, between two different monologic versions of what has happened on the raft and what is about to happen off of it—has been won by Jim, and the religious language system does not resurface in Huck's voice (at least not in relation to Jim or slavery) for over a hundred and thirty pages.[33]

When the religious system does reappear in Huck's voice, however, Jim is no longer around to oppose it with his own voice. Huck finds out that Jim has been captured and taken back into slavery at the Phelps plantation; the ensuing debate about what Huck should do with this information takes place entirely within his head and can thus be described as internally dialogic. The debate's first salvo is fired by the religious voice, now explicitly identified as "the plain hand of Providence slapping [Huck] in the face" and later described as "something inside of [him that keeps] saying, 'There was the Sunday school, you could a gone to it; and if you'd a done it they'd a learnt you, there, that people that acts as [you'd] been acting about that nigger goes to everlasting fire.'" Huck attempts to listen to this voice and follow its mandate, but when he tries to pray, "the words wouldn't come"—he has not truly aligned his own voice with the religious one, and realizes that "you can't pray a lie." Next he tries to make the religious voice more authoritative by putting its mandate in writing, which he hopes will prompt his own voice: "I'll go and write the letter [to Miss Watson]—and then see if I can pray." Yet immediately afterward his mind returns to memories of the raft's pastoral ideal, of the communal language shared there ("we a floating along, talking, and singing, and laughing"), and of Jim's voice (which has now become an internal part of Huck's own) commending him for his loyalty. Huck realizes that such memories cannot coexist with this religious voice, and thus that he has "to decide, forever, betwixt two things." And decide he does, in the novel's most important single vocalization: "I studied a minute, sort of holding my breath, and then says to myself: 'All right, then, I'll go to hell'—and tore it up" (233–35).

Much scholarly attention has been paid to this moment, and some critics have decided that it is not, after all, quite so revolutionary as it might seem. Arac, for example, notes that Huck's binary opposition between Providence and hell does not take into account moral anti-slavery forces such as abolitionism and asks why, "if other voices can sound through [Huck's], [is there] so limited a repertory?" (54). Besides expecting a bit more of Huck than might be reasonable given his upbringing, age, and region, however, such critics miss three key points about this moment. First, the limited "repertory" of voices within Huck's is not a creative limitation of Twain's but rather an apt comment upon the language systems available to Huck; moreover, that repertory has significantly expanded since the first confrontation scene to include Jim's voice. Second, his decision to break definitively with the religious system and side "for good" with hell, "which [is] in [his] line" (235), is one of his only affirmative statements of identity; while its effect is lessened because it is made only to himself, it is nonetheless something quite different from his normal silences, escapes, or other evasions in the face of attempts to circumscribe his identity. And third, his decision is prompted by memories of the raft's pastoral, ahistorical linguistic community, demonstrating both the very real effects of and the narrative voice's preference for that community.

Unfortunately, it is at this moment that the raft ceases to serve as the novel's defining world, or even as a potential such world for Huck and Jim. Instead, the novel's infamous closing section takes place on the Phelps plantation, a world in which the entirely historical system of slavery and Tom's equally destructive literary system take center stage once more. How critics read *Huck*'s ending has long reflected their overall judgments on its aesthetic and moral accomplishments or failures, and thus very few fail to discuss this section; I do not have a great deal to add to the mix.[34] Certainly the return to slavery seems to be historically inevitable and thematically necessary, given the novel's antebellum setting (and, to a degree, the post-Reconstruction world of its composition).[35] Just as certainly, the return of Tom's literary system, with its constant and entirely unnecessary humiliations and struggles for Jim—made even more unnecessary when Tom reveals his own silenced secret, that Jim has been freed—is a failure on both aesthetic and moral levels. The collision of both aspects—the inevitable return to slavery and the regrettable focus on Tom—comes when Jim and Huck have the chance to escape once more on the raft with a badly wounded Tom. Here Jim's voice fits perfectly into the dominant language systems: "Say it, Jim," Huck instructs, and when Jim says that he would never escape if that would endanger Tom, Huck notes that "I knowed he was white inside, and I reckoned he'd say what he did say" (301). Once again their voices are in communal harmony on the raft, but this time, ironically, their shared goal is to subsume their voices to the needs of Tom and the "white" society of which he is so clearly a part.[36]

Perhaps that is the final section's most egregious failure: the way in which Huck's and Jim's voices, individually and, more importantly, communally, become so thoroughly dominated by the systems around them, both Tom's and slavery's. Yet that is not necessarily, or not only, a failure of Twain's (although we must lay the blame more squarely on him for the humorous use to which he puts much of that domination).

After all, the world of the raft, one separate from history and in which a white boy and a black slave can share a communal voice, did not stand much chance of survival in the antebellum South, and likely seemed scarcely more imaginable in the mid-1880s.[37] Yet Twain did imagine such a world, if only for a short time, and the voice which that world's inhabitants share provides a revisionist rejoinder to the dominant language systems of Huck's and Twain's times.

Harris and Twain, then, took meaningful steps toward imagining alternative African American voices, although both were ultimately unable to sustain those voices or to make the same progress in their visions of history. One possible reason for their shortcomings, of course, is that, while both men had grown up around the system of slavery, neither of them (nor any white author) could rely on personal experiences or knowledge of that system's realities and effects for African Americans. There were, however, former slaves who could narrate just such experiences and knowledge, and the decade saw the final new autobiographical publications from two of the most famous and respected such figures: Frederick Douglass's third autobiography, *Life and Times of Frederick Douglass: Written by Himself* (1881); and the reissued and greatly updated *Narrative of Sojourner Truth: A Bondswoman of Olden Time* (1878), cowritten by the white former abolitionists Olive Gilbert and Frances Titus.[38] Both Douglass and Truth, moreover, were explicitly interested in revising the dominant visions of African American history, and both, due to their roles as orators, relied heavily on their strength of voice to do so. Yet aspects of both narratives led their authors away from the representation of dialect and toward positions that silenced some important aspects of the African American voice.

Before getting to those specific texts, however, a few words are in order about the generic shift from fiction to autobiography, and particularly to the subgenre known as the slave narrative. This shift certainly does not require any substantive change in thematic focus: if history and voice are central to the fictional works I examine in this chapter, they are equally central, in fact defining, elements of the genre of autobiography. That is, the purpose of any autobiography is for its author to narrate, in his/her own voice, his/her life history and, usually, the larger human history with which that life history has come into contact. That purpose becomes even clearer and more focused in the slave narratives, which existed so that their authors could give voice to personal evidence about their life and experiences in the larger human system of slavery. Carver Waters defines the slave narrative as "the recollecting voice of a slave" (35), and both his conjunction of recollection and voice and his linkage of them with the status of slave are precisely correct about the genre's purposes.[39]

If the slave narratives are thus hyperexamples of history and voice's importance to the genre of autobiography, however, there are aspects of those two themes which are distinct to (and often more complex within) the narratives. On the issue of history, the slave narratives contain at least three such distinctive aspects. First, the author's memories, obviously the source of any autobiographical narrative, are in these cases often limited and always painful; as W. J. T. Mitchell argues, the usual role of memory in autobiography, to serve as a "transparent window into past experience," is here complicated by "strange gaps and blind spots" (202). Second, the identification of the narrative's author as identical to its protagonist, another defining characteristic of an autobiography, is weakened by the many gaps (in social status, literacy, and name, among others) between those two figures; the author here is "only . . . an ex-slave, already removed from the experience" (Mitchell 204), and thus the slave narrative "by its very existence underscores the gap between 'I' as writer and 'I' as protagonist" (Niemtzow 97). Third, the narratives' central subject is no longer the author's life, but rather that life's relation to the system of slavery, and this focus dictates not only what is included in the narrative, but also what is left out; as James Olney argues, "the ex-slave is debarred from use of a memory that would make anything of his narrative beyond or other than the purely, merely episodic" (150).

The slave narratives are similarly distinct in at least three ways from other autobiographies on the theme of voice. First, the narratives' overtly political purpose requires the authors to make use of a certain tone and structure of address, both of which can be described as oratorical; as Stephen Butterfield notes, the "tone . . . is that of the impassioned orator, speaking directly to an audience" (77). Second, both that political purpose and the slaves' previous illiterate status (a status that was vital to the abolitionist critique of slavery) require the authors to prove that they are in fact writing their own narrative, and thus (ironically, given their oratorical styles) to distance themselves from the oral traditions so central to slave life.[40] Third, the narratives generally contain voices other than the author's, for at least two reasons: the need for authentication requires the presence of white voices in support of the author (or, in Truth's pseudo-autobiographical narrative, as coauthors), a presence which can "create something close to a dialogue" (Stepto 178); and the gaps and stages in the author's memories and life produce a variety of narrative positions, so that, as Carver Waters puts it, "multiple identities generate multiple voices" (29–30).

All these complications of history and voice in the slave narratives are relevant to a close reading of Douglass's and Truth's texts. It is also important at the outset to note a difference between the two books which necessarily informs my readings of them. As the title changes from Douglass's 1845 *The Narrative of Frederick Douglass, An American Slave, Written By Himself* to the 1881 *Life and Times of Frederick Douglass, Written by Himself* indicate, this final narrative moves a good deal closer to the genre of autobiography; certainly there are still aspects of the slave narrative in *Life*, as the continued use of *Written by Himself* suggests, but those aspects now constitute only a portion of Douglass's goals and subjects, and are balanced by much more contemporary (if still historically significant) subjects such as Douglass's relationship with Lincoln and his postbellum political activities.[41] The title of the 1878 *Narrative of Sojourner Truth; A Bondswoman of Olden Time*, however, reiterates its continued emphasis on her story as slave; the book's new concluding sections, identified as "A History of Her Labors and Correspondence, Drawn from Her 'Book of Life,'" expand but do not significantly alter (and certainly do not draw attention away from) that central story.[42]

Despite that difference, however, Douglass's and Truth's works share a central and revisionist historical goal. Both authors are interested in giving voice to realities of the slave experience that have been (to their minds) greatly underrepresented, thus correcting the dominant story of slavery as it has been narrated. Douglass gives clearest articulation to this historical purpose, as well as the continued (and evermore urgent) need for it, in *Life*'s "Conclusion," when he notes that "The time is at hand when the last American slave and the last American slaveholder will disappear behind the curtain which separates the living from the dead and when neither master nor slave will be left to tell the story of their respective relations or what happened to either in those relations. My part has been to tell the story of the slave. The story of the master never wanted for narrators" (478–79). Douglass's portrait of the disappearing slave resonates with Harris's description of the "venerable" Uncle Remus, whose dialect has "nearly disappeared." And in fact, both Harris and Twain can be seen in some sense as telling "the story of the slave." Yet despite their efforts in regard to voice, both men remained in significant ways narrators of the master's story: not only racially but also in nostalgia for the slave system (in Harris's case) or a view of that system's unassailable power over the languages and lives within it (in Twain's). It thus remained essential and imperative for slaves to tell their own stories; no one else could do so in the same way, because, as is noted of Truth near the end of her narrative, "Her parallel exists not in history. . . . Her memory is a vast storehouse of knowledge," and the chief purpose of her book (as of Douglass's) is to give voice to that knowledge (253–54).

The history which Douglass and Truth relate in their works is not free of the aforementioned limitations common to slave narratives. Both figures address candidly the existence of gaps in their historical narratives: Douglass in discussing his escape from slavery, which he had withheld from his first two autobiographies and of which he admits to having "sometimes thought it well enough to baffle curiosity by saying that while slavery existed there were good reasons for not telling the manner of my escape, and since slavery had ceased to exist there was no reason for telling it" (197); and Truth in a lengthy passage on "some hard things that crossed [her] life while in slavery, that she has no desire to publish," whether because "they are not all for the public ear," because "'they'd call me a liar! . . . and I do not wish to say anything to destroy my own character for veracity," or, most simply, because of "forgetfulness" (81–82). Both likewise admit to a significant distance between their past lives as slaves (and protagonists of their narratives) and their present states of freedom (and as authors of those narratives): Douglass precedes a lengthy quotation of his famous 1845 passage on his grandmother's death—one of many sections from the earlier narratives that he includes and comments upon, thus remembering and revising his literary as well as personal and cultural history—by noting that at that writing, "the distance between the past then described and the present was not so great as it is now" (99)[43]; Truth admits that "she now looks back upon her thoughts and feelings [as a slave] . . . as one does on the dark imagery of a fitful dream" (37–38).

These inevitable limitations on their historical narratives, however, do not undermine Douglass and Truth's revisionist historical purpose. In fact, both figures make significant use of one of the genre's potential weaknesses—its demand for personal, episodic evidence of slavery, at the expense of all other subjects or themes—and convert the limitation into a strength of their revisionist rhetoric. Douglass, for example, relates a specific episode in which a slave unknowingly complains to his master about his treatment and is harshly punished; the narrative then moves directly and effortlessly to a larger, revisionist point about slaves' testimony on their conditions: "It was partly in consequence of such facts," Douglass argues, "that slaves, when inquired of as to their condition and the character of their masters, would almost invariably say that they were contented and their masters kind" (63–64). His pointed contrast of the "facts" that he has just narrated with the history as it has previously been reported intimates both history's fictional quality and its unreliability in the face of authentic testimony such as his. Truth is similarly adept at moving from personal details to broad abolitionist rhetoric, as when she describes the whippings she suffered at a young age and then seamlessly shifts to a present analysis: "And now . . . when I hear 'em tell of whipping women on the bare flesh, it makes my flesh crawl, and my very hair rise on my head! Oh! my God! . . . what a way is this of treating human beings?" (27). Again, her individual experiences become a necessary foundation for her current abolitionist sentiments, a move that is perfectly illustrated by the connection between her body's memories of pain and her heart and mind's disgust with slavery.[44]

History in Douglass's and Truth's narratives, then, constitutes a strong, unequivocal response to *Uncle Remus*'s nostalgia and *Huck*'s concluding surrender. However, both texts' constructions of voice, and specifically of African American and dialect voices, are more problematic. William Andrews argues, in fact, that "narrating voice" is "the most problematic aspect of either the writing or the reading of [slave] narrative as authoritative" ("Novelization" 23), and these narratives bear out that claim. Moreover, both do so in part because they acknowledge and respond to the slave narratives' perceived lack of vocal authority. That is, both authors were well aware that their protagonists' status as former slaves could serve as an obstacle in their path toward vocal authority—an authority without which, to reiterate, autobiography cannot successfully communicate its historical narrative—and both texts seek, in distinct ways, to surmount that obstacle. And the strategies which they employ relate closely to their protagonists' connections to dialect and positions as orators.

For Douglass, a principal lesson of his history as abolitionist orator was the necessity of speaking in his own voice, even if (perhaps precisely because) that voice defied his auditors and supporters' expectations. The problem with Douglass's voice was that it sounded too educated, too rhetorical, to belong to an ex-slave, and thus that it prompted doubt of its historical authenticity.[45] "They said I did not talk like a slave," Douglas notes of many early responses to his orations, "and that they believed I had never been south of Mason and Dixon's line." The connection between voice and history in such responses is clear, and was certainly apparent to Douglass's abolitionist friends, who counseled him, paradoxically, to "Be yourself, and tell your story. . . . Better to have a little of the plantation speech than not." Yet since for Douglass the "plantation speech" was not part of himself, his story could not be told in that voice, and so he concludes that "still I must speak just the word that seem[s] to *me* the word to be spoken *by* me" (218).

This emphasis on his own voice, one entirely divorced from the dialect which was historically (and accurately) associated with so many ex-slaves, translates fully into *Life*'s narration.[46] A central goal of the book's first few chapters, in which Douglass describes his upbringing and formative years, is to document the genesis and development of that distinctive (even unique) voice. One of the few details he provides about his mother, for example, is to note that "she was the only one of all the colored people of Tuckahoe who could read," and to "attribute" his own "love of letters" to her "native genius" (36). And shortly after, Douglass describes his "association with Daniel Lloyd," his master's youngest son, in order to explain "the mystery" of "how [he] happened to have so little of the slave accent in [his] speech" (44). The slave accent is absent not only from Douglass's own voice and narration, however, but also from his transcription of other slaves' speech. This elision is most noticeable in Douglass's encounter and conversation with Sandy (he of the famous magical root); Sandy is, like Harris's Daddy Jack, "a genuine African," but Douglass (unlike Harris) does not attempt to represent his speech, narrating their conversation in free indirect discourse ("He told me that he could help me") so that, as he parenthetically notes, he can "put his words in my own language" (137).[47]

There is certainly nothing wrong with Douglass's choice to use his own voice, free from dialect as it was; he had worked hard to develop that voice, to prove that he could master standard English as well as any white orator or scholar, and his speeches and narratives provide ample proof of his success.[48] Yet there is an important difference between oration, which of necessity constitutes a univocal performance, and narration, which (as the conversation with Sandy indicates) at least occasionally requires the inclusion and representation of other voices. As Douglass's unwillingness to include dialect in *Life* illustrates, he pursues in the narratives the same degree of univocality that he achieved in his orations; perhaps it is for that reason that he notes, near the book's end, that "writing for the public eye never came quite as easily to [him] as speaking to the public ear" (511). His voice in the text is just as strong and focused as in his speeches, but here that strength and focus are limiting as well as liberating; and what they limit most fully is the inclusion of the dialect that constituted a central element of slave and African American voices throughout Douglass's life and times.[49]

In this respect, as in many others, Sojourner Truth could be seen as providing an interesting contrast to Douglass.[50] After all, Truth's most famous oration, usually entitled "Ain't I a Woman?" (a misquotation or modernization of the speech's actual refrain, "and ar'n't I a woman?"), was delivered entirely in dialect, as her *Narrative*'s transcription of its first sentence indicates: "Well, chilern, whar dar is so much racket dar must be something out o' kilter."[51] And at every stage *Narrative* stresses not only that her speech as freed woman remains the same as when she was a slave, but also that she derives much of her oratorical power from that naturalness of voice. The text's first direct quotation from Truth, in which she asks the Lord to "send de good angels to feed me while I live on dy footstool," is identified as "language from the depths of her soul" (ix), and the book represents Truth's dialect whenever she is quoted. Moreover, passages compiled in the "Book of Life" section stress that dialect's power: Harriet Beecher Stowe describes a song of Truth's in which she "mispronounc[es] the English, but seem[s] to derive as much elevation and comfort from bad English as from good" (159); and a newspaper transcript of a speech indicates that "the piquancy of [Truth's] remarks [was] greatly heightened by the inimitable patois, if it may be so called, of her expression" (212–13). Truth's rhetorical authority, her ability to be passionate and convincing on a subject such as slavery, is thus explicitly tied in *Narrative* to her dialect voice, a position that would seem directly opposed to Douglass's purposeful distancing of himself from that voice.

As the final two quotes' references to "bad English" and "inimitable patois" indicate, however, *Narrative*'s presentation of Truth's dialect voice is not without its own difficulties. More exactly, the text's positive position on Truth's voice does not diminish the facts that the book's narrative voices are white (Gilbert in the first section, from the 1850 edition; Titus in the second, new in 1878), that they narrate in their eras' correct "good" English, and that they too tend to represent Truth's speech as, in some fundamental way, "inimitable," impossible to duplicate on the page. Much has been said about the interplay of Truth's, Gilbert's, and (less often) Titus's voices in *Narrative*'s composition, but central to that interplay is the fact that "as an accurate representation of Truth's linguistic skills, it fails" (Samra 158).[52] While no Truth scholar can discount Nell Irvin Painter's arguments that the transcribed "Ain't I a Woman" speech was largely created by Frances Gage and that Truth spoke in a less pronounced dialect voice than that speech or her amanuenses indicate, the fact remains that *Narrative* consistently creates a distance between its depictions of Truth's voice and that voice's presence and effects; that distance resonates with Painter's own description of the ways in which *Narrative*'s postbellum editions "sought to efface the shortcomings of the figure of Truth from the first edition" (*Life* 260–61).[53] Time and again, often at moments of heightened import, the text resorts to phrases like "with emphasis that cannot be written" (39) to describe Truth's voice; such references are clearly meant to highlight the importance of what Truth is about to say, but they paradoxically diminish the text's depiction of her orality. This becomes particularly apparent in *Narrative*'s descriptions of her two signature vocal acts, her public orations and her private "talks with God": of the former, the narrator notes that "The impressions made by [Truth] on her auditors, when moved by lofty or deep feeling, can never be transmitted to paper" (45); and the latter are described as "perfectly original and unique, and ... well worth preserving, were it possible to give the tones and manner with the words; but no adequate idea of them can be written while the tones and manner remain inexpressible" (60).[54]

As with Douglass's refusal to add elements of dialect to his speech, these failures to represent the power of Truth's dialect voice are perfectly understandable; but just as the univocality of Douglass's oratorical mode does not translate to written narrative without a sense of limitation, so too is Truth's *Narrative* limited by its inability to capture her voice's strength and importance. Both texts succeed significantly in their attempts to revise the standard narrative of slavery, and both give voice to a vision of African American history that is grounded in the details of individual experience and knowledge but that transcends those details to construct an entirely new perspective on race in the American past. Yet ironically, the voice in which both texts convey that vision is limited—by its univocality in Douglass and its unrepresentability in Truth—and ultimately unable to capture dialect's complexities and importance in, and to, the history of slavery.

In the same years that saw the publication of Truth's and Douglass's final autobiographies, Charles W. Chesnutt was in the midst of recording, in a series of private journals (1874–1883), his ambitions and dreams, doubts and fears, and, most importantly, attempts to develop his skills as a writer. Chesnutt is perhaps most famous for the divisions in his psyche—between his black and white heritages, identification with and hatred of the South, longing for and dissatisfaction with popular success—and critics have thus most often turned to the journals for evidence of those divisions, and of Chesnutt's early discovery of the potential for a writer of fiction to transcend (or at least vocalize and communicate to a mass audience) such psychological, racial, regional, and commercial concerns. Certainly the journals contain a great deal of such evidence, as exemplified by the famous (and oft-quoted) sections on Albion Tourgée's *A Fool's Errand* ("why could not a colored man ... write a far better book about the South?" [125]) and on Chesnutt's racial ambitions for his fiction ("If I can exalt my race" [93]; "The object of my writings would be ... the elevation of the whites" [39]). Yet such critics do not always give enough credit to Chesnutt's own statement of the journal's purpose, as identified in the first entry of its 1877 incarnation: "My principal object is to improve myself in the art of composition" (85).[55]

To read the journals with a focus on "composition" is, ironically, to uncover another division, if one that develops out of close reading rather than authorial psychoanalysis. For Chesnutt's early ideas about writing contain two distinct, and in many ways opposed, perspectives on an author's use of words: one in which the author is in full control over his creation and deployment of language, and one in which he makes use of the language of others for his own artistic purposes. The first position is most clearly illustrated in Chesnutt's interest in the compositional theories of Hugh Blair, whose *Lectures on Rhetoric and Belles Lettres* (1783) Chesnutt discusses and quotes at length in his October–November 1878 journal entries (93–99). Blair focuses, in the lectures with which Chesnutt is concerned, on the necessities of stylistic exactness; Blair identifies this aspect as "perspicacity" and notes that, "with respect to words and phrases," it requires "three qualities in them, *purity, propriety,* and *precision.*" Precision is defined as the art of being "correct and exact in the choice of every word"; propriety as "the selection of such words and phrases . . . as the best and most established usage" indicates, with a corresponding "avoidance of vulgarisms or low expressions"; and purity as "the use of such words . . . as belong to the idiom of the language which we speak" (93). Given the sophisticated, indeed perspicacious style in which Chesnutt writes this section, along with virtually all of his journal entries, it is clear that "the idiom of the language" he speaks is synonymous with that of learned rhetoricians like Blair, and thus that (under these carefully transcribed rules) he must likewise compose his artistic productions in that idiom.

A year and a half later, however, Chesnutt records an artistic interest in a very different kind of idiom. In his entry of March 11, 1880, Chesnutt makes note of "the great revival which is going on" and, more significantly, of his potential plan to compile "a collection of the ballads or hymns which the colored people sing with such fervor." Chesnutt readily admits that "the songs are not of much merit as literary compositions," but argues that "they have certain elements of originality which make them interesting to a student of literature, who can trace, in a crude and unpolished performance, more of the natural ability or character of the writer than in the more correct production of a cultivated mind." Such a "cultivated" production resembles (whether deliberately or not) precisely the kind of artistic endeavor on which Blair would insist—"crude and unpolished" have no place in a perspicacious style—yet Chesnutt here recognizes that raw originality has a particular communicative and thematic value as well. "The [songs'] verse is generally the merest doggerel," he concedes, "but the ideas are often good." And Chesnutt's job as compiler of such productions would entail more than simply collecting them: "Elder Davis has kindly furnished me with the words for several," he notes, "and the music I myself must write" (121–22). The author's role in this kind of artistic production, then, is to take others' unpolished words and compose a form into which they can fit (and in which, presumably, they can best communicate their ideas).

It is just after Chesnutt recognizes the value of this other type of authorial interaction with words that he articulates for the first time a specific literary goal, in response to Tourgée's success. The section's most famous quote, noted above, is "why could not a colored man" write such a novel; but just as significant is the path that Chesnutt decides to follow in order to write his own Southern fiction. "There are many things about the Colored people which are peculiar, to some extent, to them," he notes, and his plan is to "record" such details "with a view to future use in literary work" (125–26). Once again, that is, the writer's task is not to create the perfect words and themes, but instead to gather them from those around him—to whom they are unique—and shape them into a coherent literary production.

There is, of course, another crucial consideration for any young writer desiring publication: the issue of audience. Shortly after Chesnutt has articulated his compositional plans, he considers that issue in regard to Elder Davis, a popular local preacher. Davis expounds his understanding of a congregation's multiple audiences—the "educated," the "moderately intelligent, but with very little learning," and the "largest class," the "ignorant, unlettered, naturally stupid ones who can't be reached by anything but excitement and extravagance"—and the simple performative fact that, in order to "please 'em all, . . . you must preach to suit them all." He then relates the story of two preachers, Frederick Jones and Brudder Sam: Sam preaches in dialect and is by far the more successful, and "the elegant Fred Jones," in order to win over the congregation, is forced to "imitate old Brudder Sam as closely as possible" (129–32). While these experiences would certainly impress upon Chesnutt the necessity of using dialect in order to reach a key part of his African American audience, they do so in a rather condescending and unsatisfactory way; the implied attitude toward both that audience and the use of the vernacular suggests that for Elder Davis (and, by extension, for Chesnutt himself) the battle between Blair's sophisticated idiom and a "crude and unpolished" one has not been entirely decided.

Yet if Chesnutt has at this point not settled upon his preferred artistic weaponry, the overall campaign is now clear to him. Despite the fact that he has "so little experience in composition," he admits that he "think[s] [he] must write a book" (139). The subject of this undertaking is equally clear: "I expect the *Cleveland Herald* would pay me for Southern Correspondence," he notes, since he has "a vast fund of raw material on hand for stories and sketches, and [he] ought to be able to work some of it up" (149). And a good number of the remaining journal entries comprise attempts to produce just such sketches, many of them, including an exchange between two "colored parties" at a circus (153) and the series of short anecdotes which conclude the 1882 journals (180–81), composed in African American dialect. It seems that, in order to convey artistically the regional and racial histories about which he believes he has a good deal of expertise, Chesnutt is willing to use an idiom—a voice—that is not his own but is undeniably related to those histories.[56]

As two of his earliest published fictions indicate, however, texts which share the use of dialect could still construct distinct visions of African American history and voice. Chesnutt's first published story, "Uncle Peter's House" (1885), and his next story to deal with specifically racial themes, "The Fall of Adam" (1886), nicely illuminate the different stylistic and thematic possibilities inherent in his use of dialect.[57] "Uncle Peter's House" is a deeply historical story, one that is concerned with both the recent (Reconstruction) and the antebellum past; the first phrases, in fact, set the story's events in the gray area between those historical moments: "Ever since the broad column of Sherman's army swept through central North Carolina, leaving the whites subjugated and impoverished and the blacks free and destitute" (*Short Fiction* 168). Moreover, the ex-slave protagonist, Peter, is defined by his historical "dearest wish": a desire to own a "great white house" like the plantation whose picture, "around which cluster the most vivid impressions of childhood, remain[s] fresh in his memory" (168–69). If Peter's experiences and memory drive the story's plot, however, virtually all of the narrative is told in the third-person narrative voice's standard English, which identifies Peter as "Uncle" and sets off the story's rare dialect moments (such as the use of "chist" for chest [169]) in quotation marks. Those facts would seem to identify the narrative voice as separate from and nostalgic toward a dialect voice such as Peter's, which is heard for the first time pleading in stereotypical phrases with the Ku Klux Klan mob: "No, Marse, I 'clare to de Lo'd it's jes' my own house" (173). Yet Peter lives to see the Klan become "a thing of the past" (174), and the story's climactic moment, his death-bed vision of the "hebbenly big white mansion" which awaits him (an image which foreshadows the actual house which his son, Primus, will complete in "several years"), is narrated in the dialect of Peter's "strong, clear voice" (175). "Uncle Peter's House" thus modulates between the primacy of its narrative voice and the struggles and ascendancy of Peter's dialect voice, much as its historical themes straddle two historical epochs and, in the completed house, point (however preliminarily) toward a third.[58]

"The Fall of Adam" is likewise set in the Reconstruction South, where its protagonist, the black preacher Brother Gabriel Gainey, presides over the newly founded Hallelujah Chapel. The story's events are, once again, introduced through direct reference to their historical moment: Gabriel, who as "Br'er Gabe was the slave preacher on a large plantation" before the war, sees "his chance [to found a church of his own] in the breaking up of society which follow[s] the abolition of slavery." But whereas Peter was primarily identified by his experiences and memory, Gabriel is defined by his voice and language: the first description of him notes that "his pulpit powers were developed under circumstances somewhat unfavorable to . . . any acquaintance with the rules of grammar" but that he has "strong lungs," and as the story opens he has "just decided upon a satisfactory pronunciation for a word of four syllables with which he [has] been wrestling" (177). Much of what follows is a straightforward example of a comic dialect tale, comprising Gabriel's unique and ridiculous responses to a parishioner's difficult questions about "Adam's Fall" and the "Origins of Races" (179). Yet within the comedy, Chesnutt still locates interesting conflicts between voices: Gabriel's explanations are met with a "murmur" that is not "one of unqualified approval," and one parishioner's probing follow-ups lead Gabriel to assert in the concluding lines that he "wants dis tawkin' in de chu'ch stopped" (182). If "Adam" thus falls more clearly into the preestablished tradition of dialect humor (one with which "Uncle" cannot be aligned), it still indicates that voice is as complex a subject as history in Chesnutt's early stories.[59]

Those early texts' promise would be fulfilled, over the next decade, with the publication of Chesnutt's most famous short fictions, the conjure stories. The first such story, "The Goophered Grapevine," appeared in the *Atlantic Monthly* in 1887 and contained the core elements which would recur throughout the conjure tales: John, the pragmatic Yankee narrator who moves to the postbellum South seeking a "change of climate" for his ailing wife, Annie, and whose standard English narration begins and ends the story (782); and Uncle Julius, the ex-slave who tells Annie and John, in dialect, the slavery-era conjure tales that form each text's heart.[60] As that brief synopsis suggests, the conjure tales bear a striking formal resemblance to texts in the plantation tradition, as exemplified by Harris's Uncle Remus stories. The publishers of *The Conjure Woman,* the 1899 collection of Chesnutt's conjure tales, certainly did not downplay the similarities: that book's cover featured a drawing of Uncle Julius flanked by two grinning rabbits (despite the absence of any such creatures from the book's stories). And critics have paid a great deal of attention to Chesnutt's relationship with Harris and the plantation tradition; so much so, in fact, that Tynes Cowan argues that "Chesnutt's identity as a writer is largely determined by how critics interpret Chesnutt's response to Harris's influence" (232).[61]

The echoes of Harris, Thomas Nelson Page, and the plantation tradition are certainly present and significant—if decidedly ambiguous—in Chesnutt's conjure tales, and would have been even more so to contemporary audiences; those echoes are only amplified by Chesnutt's admission that he read the Uncle Remus stories to his children and by his famous 1890 comment to George Washington Cable that Harris is one of those writers who "give us the sentimental and devoted negro who prefers kicks to half-pence" (Sundquist, *Wake* 357).[62] As that quote indicates, however, Chesnutt saw his conjure stories as representing a departure from, not a continuation of, the work of writers such as Harris. And most of Chesnutt's divergences are already apparent in "Grapevine": the white auditors are two adults who have distinct and shifting reactions to the conjure tales; the narrator is one of those auditors, and thus part of and directly affected by the tales; Julius's conjure tales are explicitly set in the slave south, are (at least nominally) based on events that he witnessed first-hand, and mix realistic human interactions under slavery with elements of the supernatural. For all those reasons, and more important for the sake of evaluating Chesnutt's vision of African American history and voice as he constructs it in this earliest conjure tale, there is value in reading "Grapevine" on its own terms.

The story's opening paragraphs set the scene, and, as in "Uncle" and "Fall," that setting is a South on the borderline between two historical eras. Literally the story takes place in "central North Carolina," where the narrator has decided to move his "grape-culture" business and ailing wife, at the end of Reconstruction (the 1887 story's first words are "About ten years ago"). But figuratively, the shadows of the antebellum South and the war that destroyed it are immediately present: the narrator describes his proposed purchase as "at one time a thriving plantation" with a vineyard that has "not been attended to since the war, and [has] fallen into utter neglect," and as he and his wife drive "between the decayed gate-posts—the gate itself had long since disappeared"—he remarks that "the house had fallen a victim to the fortunes of war, and nothing remain[s] of it except the brick pillars on which the sills had rested" (782). Unlike the perfect but unattainable white house of Uncle Peter's memories, this remnant of slavery is more degraded and yet more omnipresent; it is entirely unable to sustain either its commercial or symbolic functions, but, as the narrator's focus on it illustrates, it still dominates the literal and figurative landscape on which it sits.[63]

It is in the heart of that landscape, on the grounds near the vineyard which the narrator hopes to rejuvenate, that John and Annie encounter Uncle Julius for the first time. His relation to the place's history is immediately apparent, as John describes him as "venerable-looking" (an interesting echo of Harris's initial description of Uncle Remus[64]) and then inquires if he knows "anything about the time when this vineyard was cultivated," to which Julius replies: "I knows all about it. Dey ain' na'er a man in dis settlement w'at won' tell yer ole Julius McAdoo 'uz bawn an' raise' on dis yer same plantation." Just as crucial as Julius's historical knowledge is his orality: he is described as "smacking his lips with great gusto" over some grapes, in a "performance" which John intuits is "no new thing." Julius is thus identified from the first as intimately connected to both the history of slavery and a history of oral performance, and the two aspects are further connected by his role as explanatory mediator. That is, just as John cannot gain access to the plantation's history without Julius's narrative, he cannot understand that narrative's dialect terms without additional aid: Julius notes that "dis yer old vimya'd is goophered," and John, "not grasping the meaning of this unfamiliar word," must ask for clarification (782–83).

To provide that clarification, to "'splain to yer how it all happen," Julius begins to tell the conjure tale which forms the story's center. And as he does so, he undergoes a transformation which—along with John's description of it—exemplifies the story's explorations of history and voice: "We assured him that we would be glad to hear how it all happened, and he began to tell us. At first the current of his memory—or imagination—seemed somewhat sluggish; but as his embarrassment wore off, his language flowed more freely, and the story acquired perspective and coherence. As he became more and more absorbed in the narrative, his eyes assumed a dreamy expression, and he seemed to lose sight of his auditors, and to be living over again in monologue his life on the old plantation" (783). After the introductory first sentence, each subsequent clause and image in the paragraph operates on two significant levels: as a purposeful depiction of the workings of Julius's voice and memories; and as an unconscious portrait of John's attitudes toward those aspects of Julius's character.

In terms of Julius, it is first worth noting that, in the decade and more since the Civil War's end, he has apparently not revisited his memories of the plantation and slavery. This provides an immediate contrast with Uncle Peter, whose goals for the future are entirely dictated by his memories of that past; Uncle Julius seems instead to have been able to exist quite happily without recourse to those memories. However, the act of giving voice to such memories certainly does change Julius, and, it would seem, for the better: his voice becomes stronger and more assured and, perhaps more important for a storyteller, his narrative's form becomes clearer and more effective. Yet at the same time that he is regaining those vocal capabilities, he is losing perspective on the present conditions of

and auditors for his tale, and instead moving back into the history itself; that shift is accompanied by the replacement of the dialogic potential with which his story began (John's query about "goophered," for example) with its final form as an uninterrupted "monologue."

All those vocal and historical qualities, of course, are described by
John, and thus are contingent upon his observations and understanding
of Julius. Critics have long disputed those two central voices' respective
authority in the conjure tales, usually linked to their analysis of Chesnutt's own position and views: most have argued that Chesnutt would
identify with Julius, so that John is constantly subverted through irony
and distance; some that John is the more likely identification, making
his voice and vision generally authoritative; while a few have brought
Annie's voice and viewpoints into the mix, arguing that she represents
more of an ideal for Chesnutt than either of the men.[65] Leaving aside
the ultimately unanswerable question of Chesnutt's intentions, I would
argue that John and Julius simply represent two distinct voices, each
with its own vision of the other and the world, neither entirely static
nor entirely privileged. That does not mean that one cannot identify
strengths or weaknesses in each voice, of each view, at any individual
textual moment; simply that I would agree with Dean McWilliams's description of the conjure tales as "Julius and John stories," by which he
means "to call attention to the presence of two narrators, two languages,
and two views of the world" (76).[66]

The first significant element of John's voice in the above paragraph
is its unwillingness to make absolute pronouncements, as illustrated by
his repeated use of "seemed." In the story's first few paragraphs, John's
analysis of the setting has no such hesitancy—he is, after all, an authority on the use of land, and his descriptions of "shiftless cultiva-
tion" and "utter neglect," as well as his more hopeful belief that "the site
was admirably adapted to grape-raising," are uttered without reservation (782). When it comes to Julius, however, he cannot be so certain
about what he sees, and he is willing to admit the possibility of alternative readings. Nowhere is that more paramount than in his wavering between Julius's "memory" and "imagination"—the story's status as authentic history or fictional artistry is, as the ending will reveal, crucial to
its meaning, and yet John cannot identify with certainty from which of
those facilities the story emanates. Or at least he initially believes that he

cannot; in his descriptions at the end of the paragraph, which are made some time after the first lines, he portrays Julius as having dreamily vanished into his memories of "the old plantation," and, concurrently, as unable to keep John and Annie within his line of vision. This final interpretation, also relevant to the revelations that accompany the story's conclusion, is much more definitive (although John continues to hedge somewhat with his use of "seemed"), and indicates that John believes he is gaining an understanding of, and thus a heightened ability to read, Julius as the story progresses.

The tale that Julius narrates, of the goophered vineyard and the slave (Henry) whose fate becomes tied to it, is well known, but a few elements are worth reiterating. First, the story contains a number of subtle historical references to life under slavery which paint a far bleaker and less nostalgic picture of that system than other contemporary accounts: such references include Julius's point that "befo' de wah, in slab'ry times, er nigger didn't mine goin' fi' er ten mile in a night, w'en dey wuz sump'n good ter eat at de yuther een" (783); his claim that "ef you'd a knowed ole Mars Dugal' McAdoo, you'd a knowed dat it ha' ter be a mighty rainy day when he could n' fine sump'n fer his niggers ter do" (786); and, most important, his seeming aside about a runaway slave, how the whites "had gone out wid dere guns en dere dogs fer ter he'p 'em hunt fer de nigger," and how "de han's on our own plantation wuz all so flusterated" by the events (785). A second and related element is the nuanced picture of black-white relations, one in which slaves will steal the master's crops (in this case, grapes) at every available moment but in which the free black conjure woman will work for the master and cast a goopher on the vineyard to prevent just such thefts.[67] The tale's portrait of white-white relations under slavery is also far from rosy: the master uses Henry's seasonal transformations to cheat his fellow slave owners, only to be cheated by a Yankee swindler who "bewitche[s]" the master with lies about increasing productivity (787).

What all those elements share, besides their revisionist perspective on the historical details about slavery, is an emphasis on the power of knowledge, and particularly on giving voice to or silencing such knowledge. Julius seems to know more about the horrors of slavery than he is willing to relate to John and Annie; the slaves "all 'nied" their role in the thefts "ter de las'" (784); the conjure woman is willing to share her goopher—an entirely vocal power—with the master in exchange for a basket of gifts and ten dollars; it is the other slaves' silence about the goopher that allows Henry to eat a grape and release the curse; the master lies to his brethren about Henry's condition, just as the Yankee in turn lies to the master; and so on. At each stage of the story, and in each level of the historical society portrayed, it is how one uses one's voice, what one reveals or keeps hidden, that dictates the lives of all those with whom one interacts and, in a very real way, determines how history will unfold for both place (the plantation) and people (both slaves and masters).

Moreover, that vocal power does not merely exist in the past described in Julius's tale, but rather is exemplified by his act of storytelling and its effects in the present. Annie's reaction, which immediately follows the tale, is to ask, "doubtfully, but seriously, . . . 'Is that story true?' "; Julius replies that "it's des ez true ez I'm a-settin' here, miss," and advises John that he "wouldn' 'vise yer to buy dis yer ole vimya'd." John's take on the story's veracity, however, is just as doubting but less serious than Annie's; he buys the vineyard and returns it to "thriving condition," finding out in the process that "Uncle Julius had . . . derived a respectable revenue from the neglected grapevines," which "doubtless, accounted for his advice to [John] not to buy the vineyard, though whether it inspired the goopher story [John is] unable to state" (788–89). Once again, the story here constructs voice on multiple levels. Julius has used his storytelling powers in an attempt to influence his present situation and the people around him, and has, in at least one important respect, succeeded: John refers in the final sentence to "the wages I pay him," indicating that Julius remains employed ten years later (789). Yet that present, pragmatic aspect of his voice does not discount other, historical and supernatural, elements: John has no doubt that the practical concerns accounted for Julius's advice, but he is unable to analyze the goopher story's origins, an uncertainty that echoes Annie's doubtful but serious query about the tale's veracity as well as John's own initial inability to distinguish between memory and imagination. The plot twist at the story's end, then, reveals all while settling nothing; John may understand (and quite possibly empathize with) Julius's selfish and financial motives, but he is, admittedly, no closer to penetrating the more profound mysteries—about the interconnections of past, knowledge, and voice—which lie behind Julius's conjure tale.

History and voice, then, are at once central to and entirely contested within "The Goophered Grapevine." The story's unwillingness to provide definitive statements about those themes resonates with the conflicts over African American dialect and experience which were apparent in Chesnutt's journals and early stories, conflicts that would continue to occupy Chesnutt's imagination throughout the conjure tales and, indeed, the remainder of his career. As Eric Sundquist argues, "the silent, indirect language of African American life . . . ran beneath the language of Chesnutt the published author, who spoke predominantly in the refined voice of the majority literary culture" (*Wake* 392). But it is too definitive to say that Chesnutt "spoke predominantly" in any one voice: the genius of "Grapevine" and the subsequent conjure tales lies in their modulation between voices, their use of both dialect and standard English to construct their complex visions of African American history and language. And it is his ability to portray both dialect and slavery, voice and history, in all their complexity that distinguishes Chesnutt as the decade's most significant literary commentator on the race question.

By the end of the 1880s Chesnutt had seemingly tired of the conjure tales' African American voice, claiming, in a famous letter to Tourgée, "I think I have about used up the old Negro who serves as mouthpiece, and I shall drop him in future stories, as well as much of the dialect" (Andrews, *Literary* 21). Likely wary of being linked to the nostalgic and exploitative use of dialect in popular works such as Thomas Nelson Page's *In Ole Virginia* (1887), Chesnutt would, despite the 1899 publication of the conjure tales in book form, make much less use of the dialect voice in his later works. Yet it would be a mistake to see his shift in narrative voice, like his corresponding turn to more contemporary racial subjects, in works such as *The Wife of His Youth and Other Stories of the Color Line* (1899), *The House Behind the Cedars* (1900), and *The Marrow of Tradition* (1901), as an abandonment of "Grapevine"'s complex historical and vocal revisionism. One need look no further than "The Wife of His Youth" (1898), and particularly the powerful impact of Liza Jane's personal history of slavery and its aftermath, expressed in her carefully rendered dialect voice and then retold by Mr. Ryder in his own (previously repressed) such voice, to see the continued prominence that Chesnutt gave to complex portrayals of dialect and slavery.[68]

Similarly, the apparent victory, in popular and commercial terms, of the thoroughly nostalgic and often racist dialect tradition of Russell and Page—a tradition brought to even greater commercial success by Thomas Dixon, D. W. Griffith, and in her own spectacular way Margaret Mitchell—should not overshadow the import and influence of the more complex writers considered here. Their alternative tradition certainly influenced later African American voices, from Dunbar to DuBois, Hughes to Hurston. And, just as significantly, it provided a contemporary counterpoint to the period's portrayals of African American voice and history. In response to the era's tendencies to forget slavery or remember it nostalgically, to silence the dialect voice or utilize it for conservative purposes, writers such as Harris, Twain, Douglass, Truth, and Chesnutt constructed their own versions of African American history and voice; and if the first four achieved complex revisionism on one theme at the expense of sufficient or consistent depth on the other, Chesnutt demonstrated the possibility and power of creating multifaceted constructions of dialect, slavery, and the race question.

2

"If We Had Known How to Write, We Would Have Put All These Things Down, and They Would Not Have Been Forgotten"

Silenced Voices, Forgotten Histories, and the Indian Question

In the post-Centennial decade, the mythic identity of the American West was undergoing an important shift: the early-nineteenth-century image of the West as an alternative to Eastern progress and development was being replaced by a vision of the West as the best example of American growth and democracy, a progressive vision which found its apotheosis in Frederick Jackson Turner's legendary 1893 address on "The Significance of the Frontier in American History." This new vision argued that the region's voices and histories, often previously unheard and untold, were in fact defining elements of the larger American identity and story. The creation of this mythic, progressive new American West is exemplified by a short story, Mary Hallock Foote's "The Fate of a Voice," that was published in the decade's final months ("Fate" first appeared in *Century Magazine*'s November 1886 issue).

Foote's story begins by describing a West that seems devoid of recognizable history or voices: "There are many loose pages of the earth's history scattered through the unpeopled regions of the Far West," the first sentence asserts, and these "unread pages" are "known but to a few persons, and these unskilled in the reading of Nature's dumb records" (341). The story's heroine, Madeline Hendrie, explicitly connects that description to the West's potential to silence voices: Hendrie is introduced as "a girl with a voice" (342), and she does not intend to abandon her plans for a singing career in order to marry Aldis, a Western engineer. To do so, she tells him, would be to exchange "the real me" for "what you would make of me—the ghost of a voice—and echo of other voices from the world I belonged to once calling in the wild places where you would have me buried alive" (345). And indeed, the West's "wild places" seem to produce precisely the effect that Madeline fears; Aldis falls into a cavern while protecting Madeline from the untamed natural world, and while he lives, "the Voice" is "the victim of this tragedy": Madeline's shock destroys her ability to sing (348).

Yet this narrative of the West is not the story's only option. Aldis himself offers a different interpretation, one in which "this part of the world is not so empty as it looks" (345) and in which Madeline's voice would still have value. Aldis explicitly contrasts this Western notion of value with the more traditional, now corrupted Eastern one: "to a generous woman who believes in the regenerating influence of her art, I should think there would be singular pleasure in giving it away to those who are cut off from such joys. I know there are singers who boast of their thousand-dollar-a-night voices; I would rather boast that mine was the one free voice that could not be bought." If Madeline were to be this "singer of a new people" (346), Aldis implies, her voice would be truer both to itself and to American ideals of freedom and independence. And in the story's climactic section, Madeline regains her voice and triumphantly performs at an Eastern concert hall (the height of traditional history and value), but chooses to return permanently to the West with Aldis.

Following this choice, Foote closes her tale with a brief coda which depicts two different perspectives on Madeline's fate. In the first, an unnamed "they" lament how Madeline's "gifts . . . disappeared," how she "threw away a charming career . . . and went West." But in the second, the narrator notes that, among the solitary routines of Western life, "a voice is sometimes heard, . . . a voice those who have heard say they will never forget." Many critics focus on the first perspective, connecting the story to biographical accounts of Foote's bouts of unhappiness with her Western life and literary prospects; but in light of the story's developments Foote clearly associates the first perspective, located apart from the narrator in the detached voice of the unnamed "they," with the corrupt Eastern past and connects the second, expressed by a specific audience and advocated by the narrator, to the pure, millennial Western (and

American) future.[1] "Lost it may be to the history of famous voices," the narrator admits of Madeline's art, but it "will find its listeners; though it be a voice singing in the wilderness, in the dawn of the day of art and beauty which is coming to a new country and a new people" (358–59).

In "The Fate of a Voice," then, the West represents not simply a disappearance or escape from the East, but rather an alternative and appealing American identity, one which may not have much of a history but certainly has a promising, progressive future (thanks in part to the contributions of voices like Madeline's and Foote's). Yet from the story's first line, there is a problem with that vision: there might not be a great deal of Euro-American history in the West, but to describe the region as "unpeopled" is to ignore—or, more exactly, to silence and forget—the voices and histories of the Native Americans (among other groups, including Mexican landowners and Chinese laborers) who had long called it home.[2] One of the decade's most prominent Native Americans, Ponca chief Standing Bear—whose legal and rhetorical defense of his tribe influenced both Helen Hunt Jackson and William Justin Harsha, whose novels I consider here—articulated his opposition to those processes of silencing and forgetting in an 1881 speech to the Senate. The speech begins with the rhetorical question, "Why should I tell you a different word?" a recognition of the version of Native and Western history that has dominated the American narrative—what Standing Bear describes as what "they say." But he resists that dominant narrative, constructing instead a history of presence—"I have been here two thousand years or more"—that audibly makes present the voices and experiences that have been elided in the mythic national version. And he ends with an implicit call for dialogue between white and Native cultures, noting of the government agents who broke up his tribe that "they came and took me away without saying a word" (1594–1596).[3]

Some of the decade's Western writers took up Standing Bear's challenge and call, struggling to produce dialogic historical texts that work against the period's collective acts of silencing and forgetting. In this chapter I focus on texts by five such authors—Bret Harte, Joaquin Miller, Helen Hunt Jackson, William Justin Harsha, and Sarah Winnemucca—who attempted in their own ways to recover and retell Native American voices and histories. While Harte, Miller, and (in a more complex way) Jackson ultimately portray those voices and histories as tragically lost,

Harsha and Winnemucca construct strong Native voices that will not let their histories be forgotten in the creation of a mythic, progressive American West.

As critics such as Henry Nash Smith, Richard Slotkin, and Annette Kolodny have long documented, the West was from the arrival of its first Euro-American settlers a region particularly prone to mythic construc- tions. Moreover, the image of the West as unpeopled, as "virgin land," was likewise present from the outset, so the silencing and forgetting of Native American voices and histories were similarly foundational. How- ever, the myth of the West underwent a significant shift over the course of the nineteenth century. In the century's early years, the West was often envisioned as an outlet from the East, a less structured, more mo- bile haven to which iconoclastic figures opposed in some way to Eastern notions of progress, frontiersmen like Natty Bumppo and Daniel Boone, could escape. But by the Gilded Age, and due to such diverse factors as the perceived closing of the frontier, dissatisfaction with Eastern cor- ruption, and painful memories of the Civil War, the West had begun to seem to many Americans the best version of America, the purest ex- ample of its ideals of progress, independence, and democracy.[4]

This new, archetypically American version of the Western myth was propagated during this era through two radically distinct media. As the 1885 founding of the American Historical Association exemplified, the period witnessed the rise of the professional, scientific historian, and many of these new historians focused on the West's relation to American history. As Ray Billington argues, "during the last two decades of the nineteenth century . . . an altered intellectual atmosphere created a cli- mate of opinion suited to receive and nurture the frontier theory" (56), and historians such as Theodore Roosevelt and especially Frederick Jack- son Turner were ready to provide that theory.[5] At the same time, the era's two dominant forms of Western popular art, the dime novel and the Wild West show, contributed to the new Western myth in their own way, creating heroes such as Deadwood Dick and Buffalo Bill who, de- spite their violent tendencies, ultimately stood as "glorified and ideal- ized" representations of American values (Curti 179–80).[6]

Besides their efforts to link Western voices and histories to American values and ideals, the historians and popular artists also shared a concurrent position on Native Americans: the need to erase them, and thus their voices and histories, from the Western narrative. For historians such as Turner, this erasure was a natural part of the settling and "civilizing" of the West, and is duplicated in their historical works through the designation of Native Americans as an early stage in, and often an obstacle to, that settlement process.[7] In the dime novels and Wild West shows, the erasure was more aggressive, as illustrated by the touring show entitled "The Red Right Hand; or, Buffalo Bill's First Scalp for Custer" (Stedman 259).[8] Brian Dippie has called the concept of the Indian as "vanishing American . . . a constant in American thinking" (xi), but I would argue that the erasure of Native Americans took on a less complex and more pointed function in this period: earlier mythic frontiersmen such as Bumppo had identified in some way with the Indians and were themselves "vanishing Americans" (Fiedler 121), while the late-nineteenth-century heroes erased the Indians and, like the West itself, remained behind to become more fully Americanized.[9] In the words of Monika Kaup and Debra Rosenthal, "the symptom of the 'Vanishing American' accompanie[d] the process of 'Becoming American'" (xiv–xv).

Unfortunately, the idea of Americanization links even the period's leading advocates for reform with this process of erasure. If the decade's governmental Indian policy combined warfare (egged on by Little Big Horn in 1876 and culminating in Geronimo's late 1886 surrender) with removals to reservations, the reformers—Friends of the Indian, as they called themselves—instead advocated assimilation, with the ultimate goal of full Native American citizenship and participation in American society. While assimilation was by no means the uniformly racist or hegemonic tool some critics have portrayed it to be, it did require for its success a disappearance of Indian languages and traditions—voice and histories—that could gel quite nicely with the larger processes of silencing and forgetting.[10] With even the decade's most avowed reformers taking such a position on Native Americans' unique voices and histories, one can truly appreciate the 1880s lament of a Pawnee chief, in considering his tribe's nearly lost traditions and myths, that "If we had known how to write, we would have put all these things down, and they would not have been forgotten" (Lee Mitchell 160).

In this chapter I examine five texts which attempt to "put all these things down" so that they will not be "forgotten"—texts, that is, which provide narratives of Native Americans' silenced voices and forgotten histories. Four of the five were written by non-Natives, however, and the premise that any white author can construct such Native American narratives would seem directly counter to a number of ongoing scholarly traditions. The depiction of Indian characters and life in white American literature and culture, particularly in the nineteenth century, has been the subject of a great deal of impressive scholarship: Roy Harvey Pearce, Richard Slotkin, Louise Barnett, Robert Berkhofer, Brian Dippie, Lucy Maddox, Joshua Bellin, and many others have identified and traced at length the predominant types, stereotypes, and archetypes with which artists, historians, and mainstream white culture more generally have dismissed, embraced, or otherwise engaged the Indian question.[11] While these critics often develop nuanced analyses of literary and cultural images of Native Americans, they nonetheless explicitly focus on Indians as images, operating from a foundational, if often unspoken, assumption that white Americans and texts (especially pre-twentieth century) were largely unable to envision Native Americans as complex individuals with unique voices and viewpoints. Even the most sympathetic reformers or writers, according to this critical stance, were so limited by dominant images of Native Americans as to be unable to speak for the Indian in any meaningful sense.[12]

Concurrently, much of the recent scholarly attention to Native American texts has been explicitly and centrally concerned with voice, with Indians' struggles to speak as and for themselves. With the historical and theoretical groundwork for Native American literary studies laid by pioneering scholars such as Arnold Krupat, LaVonne Ruoff, and Robert Berner, subsequent critics have been able to concentrate more closely on individual writers and texts, and many such critics—including Dell Hymes, David Murray, Cheryl Walker, Noreen Lape, Siobhan Senier, and Robert Parker—have focused on their subjects' development of and struggles with voice. When such scholars deal at length with white authors—as does Senier in a chapter on Jackson and Lape on Mary Austin, for example—they do so in direct comparison (and, to one degree or another, contrast) with texts produced by Native American authors; the latter writers almost inevitably (and understandably) fare better as constructors of and spokespeople for Indian voices. The Native texts, in reflecting the fact that "plenty of Indians speak perfectly well for themselves" (Parker 16), thus seem to render the white texts deeply problematic and even inauthentic by contrast.[13]

Parker's quote also hints at the connections between this literary critical emphasis on Native voices and authors and the centuries-old and increasingly prominent arguments for Native American sovereignty. Those arguments have always been grounded in historical and legal issues, whether those faced by the Cherokees in their resistance to removal in the early nineteenth century or by the Sioux in their support of a Wounded Knee memorial in the late twentieth.[14] But scholars have increasingly recognized that "the struggle may be over land and sovereignty, but it is often reflected, contested, and decided in narrative" (Jace Weaver 47), and have extended sovereignty arguments to the realms of intellectual, critical, and particularly literary history. In response to what Craig Womack calls "the colonized . . . current state of Native literature" (7), these scholars argue that plenty of Indians have also read and written perfectly well for themselves, and thus attempt to recover "the inconvenient reality that Indian America has always had its own quiet word(s) and language(s)" (Elizabeth Cook-Lynn 64). And such arguments for literary sovereignty have resulted not only in impressive answers to Robert Warrior's call for "a bibliography dominated by the literature and . . . the criticism of American Indian writers" (xvi), but also in concurrent critiques of even the best-intentioned white literary constructions of Indians as "the appropriation of Native issues by non-Natives" (Womack 9).[15]

By reading four white literary works alongside one Native text, I might well be seen as replicating the trend against which these varied scholars work: prioritizing white constructions of Native Americans and their perspectives over the Natives' own articulations (whether written, oral, treaty-based, located in resistance movements, or otherwise) of those perspectives. That critique of my chapter cannot be answered simply by noting the complexities and divisions apparent even within Native perspectives, as illustrated by the tribal controversies over Winnemucca; those divisions do highlight the limitations of any essentialist definitions of Native American identity, what Jace Weaver dismisses as the "seemingly constant, essentializing attempt by some activists and intellectuals to define 'Indianness'" (4), but they do not answer the crucial question, asked (in an entirely friendly tone) by an early reader of this

chapter: "why recover these aesthetically unappealing, politically sus-
pect white guys at all?"[16] Part of my answer would be historicist: these
fictions were essential to the nineteenth century's most elaborated and
organized efforts at Indian reform and must be recovered (in the cases
of Harte, Miller, and Harsha) and read in order to understand those efforts. And part would be literary historical: the genre of the Indian reform novel (a genre which produced, in *Ramona,* one of the century's
most popular and durable texts) has been largely overlooked in scholarship on both reform fiction and postbellum literature.

But the most important reason to read all five of this chapter's works
is that they represent significant attempts by both white and Native authors to perform acts of cultural mediation between distinct but interconnected cultures. The phrase cultural mediation has been used for
decades to describe Native Americans who move between their own
and mainstream American societies, and for recent literary critics it
has captured many Native texts' complex multivocalism, the way they
use "the epistemological frameworks of American Indian and Western
cultural traditions to illuminate and enrich each other" (Ruppert 3).[17]
Jace Weaver criticizes this focus on cultural mediation, admitting that
it may be an "entry point" into Native literature for "Amer-European"
critics but arguing that Native authors "most often privilege the Native reader," for whom there is "something much more intimate going
on" (40–41). While I no more wish to subsume Native readers in my
own (Amer-European) perspective than I want to replace Native writers
with non-Native ones, it seems to me that a central job of all American
literary criticism—and all American literature, for that matter—is to
include multiple writers and multiple readers in its purview, to allow
seemingly disparate groups to illuminate and enrich each other. That
so much criticism and literature has failed to do so, has canonized non-
Native authors who ignored or stereotyped Natives, only highlights the
need for breadth and inclusion as the work of recovery and rereading
moves forward. And in the case of these five books, that work can illuminate texts by a wide variety of authors that attempt to mediate between the cultural traditions, the histories and voices and perspectives,
of white and Native Americans.[18] Despite that shared purpose, the five
texts are far from unified in their forms and themes: Harte's "In the Carquinez Woods" and Miller's *Shadows of Shasta* portray Native American

voices that attempt to narrate their identities and histories, as well as
their connections to white society, but are ultimately silenced and lost;
Jackson's *Ramona* focuses on the complex relationship between one Native American who is struggling to find her voice and history (and who
succeeds, if in temporary or partial ways) and one who seeks only to escape both (and who succeeds much more completely, if tragically); and
Harsha's *Ploughed Under* and Winnemucca's *Life Among the Piutes* are
narrated by strong Native American voices that address a white audience, accept the complexity of their identities, and give full accounts of
their alternative histories.

   While the name Bret Harte is synonymous with the rise of Western
literature after the Civil War, his career trajectory would seem to miti-
gate against including one of his texts in a project that covers 1876 to
1886: Harte's meteoric rise in the late 1860s—with stories such as "The
Luck of Roaring Camp" and "The Outcasts of Poker Flat" (both 1868),
texts so influential that one critic designates Harte the "founding father"
of the local color movement because of them (Morrow, "Popular")[19]—
was followed by a steady decline in popularity throughout the 1870s,
and his departure for Europe in 1878 signals, for most critics, the end
of his American literary career.[20] When critics consider his later works
at all, they tend to argue that in them Harte's sentimental, romantic
side, which struggled with his more satirical and realistic goals in the
earlier works, dominates the texts in ways that drastically reduce their
readability and effectiveness.[21] Certainly the novella "In the Carquinez
Woods" (1882), with its wild beasts, love triangles, unrequited affections,
mysterious family connections, and tragic climax, qualifies as a romantic text; but it also portrays a Native American protagonist whose voice
and history serve as doomed but significant alternatives while inextricably linked to the dominant Western narratives with which he interacts.
   In many ways "Woods" focuses, as its title suggests, on the natural
world, and particularly on the dangers of the untamed nature found especially (by this era) in the West. The story opens with a party of trav-
elers being tracked by a bear, described as "a fragment of one of the
fallen monsters ... become animate" (2); later one of the two heroines,
Teresa, is attacked by a "panting, crowding pack" of "beasts of prey" (16–
17); and the text concludes with an all-consuming forest fire, "a whirl-

wind of smoke and flame" (124–25). The natural world's perils are not simply physical, however; the forest also has the potential to silence and erase voices and histories. The story's first paragraph concludes by equating the woods with "the silence, the solitude of the forgotten past" (1), and these links are repeated throughout, as when Teresa defiantly shouts her name into the forest and finds that her "shrillest tones [are] lost in an echoless space, even as the smoke of her fire had faded into pure ether" (14). Not even echoes, the faintest memories of a voice, can survive in this natural space.

These characterizations of the forest as a realm of silence and forgetting are especially relevant because the story's two most complex and interesting characters are explicitly associated with the natural world. Teresa, a fugitive from both the law and a personal history full of tragedy and heartbreak, is described as speaking "savagely" (7), and she herself identifies her sole remaining purpose in life as "huntin' a hole . . . to die in," much like "a hunted animal" (9). While Teresa is fleeing the civilized world into nature, the story's hero, Low Dorman, has already done so, and in a quite literal way—he has made his home in the trunk of an ancient, giant tree, departing society entirely. Apparently that departure has transformed Low: he is initially described, emerging from the tree, as "a faun who [is] quitting his ancestral home" (6). Despite these similarities between Teresa and Low, there is also a key difference in the two descriptions—for Teresa the move to nature represents a final descent, an escape into death, while for Low it seems to be more of a return to a prior state. And Harte does not wait long in clarifying the latter association's symbolism: Low introduces himself and his racial identity to Teresa through reference to the era's common phrase "Lo, the poor Indian," and Teresa makes the connection between nature, identity, and history explicit when she thinks that Low does "not look like any Indian she [has] ever seen, but rather as a youthful chief might have looked" (11–12).[22] In returning to nature, Low has apparently returned to a past version of Native American identity as well.

While the image of a Native American actually living inside a tree is, as far as I know, an original one, the associations between Indian identity and a primeval, natural state of history seem at this point in the story only too reminiscent of the "Vanishing American" mythology. Moreover, the figure at the center of the text's civilized and moral society, Reverend Wynn—father to Low's love interest, Nellie—goes to great lengths to drive home those associations, informing Nellie that Low is "an Injin . . . an out-and-out Cherokee," that it is "no wonder he prefers to live in the woods," and that she "can't of course have anything to do with him. He must n't come here [to the church] again" (24–25). Yet even at this moment, Harte reveals the distance between Wynn's description of Low's identity and history and the reality of both, and he does so through language: Wynn tells Nellie that "Low Dorman" is "only French for 'Sleeping Water,' his Injin name," and when Nellie replies "You mean 'l'Eau Dormante,'" Wynn's only rejoinder is "That's what I said" (24). But as Harte's spelling highlights, that is not exactly what the Reverend said; Low's name and, implicitly, his ancestry are more complex than Wynn can understand.

Those complications are further developed through three additional characteristics of Low's. First, the text contains a revelation about Low's heritage, one that is not shocking but does complicate Wynn's straightforward social structures and world: Low is of mixed race, and his father turns out to be none other than the town's sheriff, Teresa's former captor, and the other suitor for Nellie's hand, one Mr. Dunn. The figure of "the half-breed," as it was once designated, was a common one in nineteenth-century novels, but the lack of originality does not necessarily lessen the importance of this aspect of Low's identity; in fact, as William Scheick persuasively argues, this mixed figure was often one whom writers "could not treat evasively," who "belonged very much to the present and quite possibly to the future of America" (2).[23] Harte eventually does treat Low all too evasively, but not before he elaborates the potential social subversiveness of Low's connections to both the Native American and white worlds. That subversiveness is exemplified by an exchange between Wynn and Dunn: Wynn, clearly threatened by the existence of half-bloods, argues that "there should be a law, sir, against the mingling of races," and Dunn, officially white law's representative but personally the father of a mixed-race child, rises "with a face livid" to reply "Who dares say that?" (79–80).[24]

A second, and more unique, complication is the element of free will and volition in Low's identification with his Native voice and history. The fear of racial mixing expressed by men like Wynn is contingent on the ability—and assumed desire—of half-bloods to pass for white, thus subverting white society's racial and social systems. Yet as Low himself makes clear, he has chosen to emphasize the Indian side of his identity, and he willingly and confidently shares it with both Teresa and Nellie. In relating his "earlier recollections" of his mixed ancestry to Teresa, Low is described by the narrator as "imperturbable" (55–56), and when Nellie confronts him with his racial identity, he responds by reminding her that he "told [her] all this the day [they] first met" and that it is she who has "forgotten"; she is "obliged to drop her eyes before the unwavering, undeniable truthfulness of his" (38). Moreover, Low's confident adoption of the Native side of his identity is portrayed not as the inevitable triumph of dark blood or racial destiny, but rather as a simple choice, and one which he can make differently: when Nellie expresses dissatisfaction with his name, he replies simply that "if my name annoys you, I can get it changed by the legislature, . . . and I can find out what my father's name was, and take that" (38). For Low, identity and history are mutable and under one's control—not nonexistent or meaningless, but neither left to the cruel hands of inevitable fate.

The third complication of Low's status as stereotypical Native American relates once more to the natural world, and to Low's goals in it. Brace, a particularly racist member of Wynn's cohort, identifies Low as a "Digger," a derogatory term common to the northern California region at the time; Diggers were Indians who did not, in the eyes of whites such as Brace, make proper or authorized use of land (79).[25] Yet not only is Low not literally a Digger (as Wynn himself reluctantly admits), but his relationship to nature is more complex than the term implies. On one level, Low's close affiliation with nature seems entirely consistent with standard images of Native Americans: of his namesake water in particular he notes that "I seem to hear it in my dreams. . . . It is my earliest recollection; I know it will be my last, for I shall die in its embrace" (37). While Low's voice, history, and identity are thus inextricably linked to the natural world, that link is again complicated by Low's will and volition. Specifically, he wants to set a particular element of nature, a hidden spring, apart for himself and Nellie, and to make it their own through language: "I discovered it the first day I saw you, and gave it your name," he tells her, "but you shall christen it yourself. It will be all yours, and yours alone, for it is so hidden and secluded that I defy any feet but my own . . . to find it" (36). This goal of creating a personal, Edenic space within the natural world is perhaps overly idealistic, but it does connect to Low's more practical and deeply significant profession: botanist. What Low does for a living, that is, is to study and attempt to name accurately the natural world, and thus to turn his symbolic link with nature into a rational program for understanding and living with it in precisely the type of relationship he desires for himself and Nellie. In other words, the same honesty and volition which Low demonstrates in regard to his racial identity drive his connection to nature: a desire to vocalize accurate identifications and then construct a meaningful self and life in terms of them.

The complications inherent in Low's identity, then, at once confirm and yet broaden stereotypical elements of the Native American image as it operated in nineteenth-century literature and myth. Low is a half-breed, but that designation does not imply degradedness or tragedy; instead it illustrates subversive social links to white structures of power (such as the sheriff's office). He seeks to name his own racial identity, but not in an attempt to pass for white; his goal is simply to define his own mixed heritage and then to make a life for himself (and, ideally, for Nellie) within that definition. And he is profoundly connected to the natural world, but not in an instinctual or nostalgic way; rather, his profession and goals indicate the volition and rationality within his natural preferences and connections. Using some of the most hackneyed aspects of romantic literature about Native Americans, Harte creates a character that is something more than a simple romantic image, whose voice, history, and identity are unique and interconnected.

It is precisely that successful creation that makes the story's ending so unsatisfying. Believing himself rejected by Nellie, Low undergoes a radical change, becoming a kind of worst version of his own potentially stereotypical traits. Asked by Teresa if he is still seeking Nellie, he replies "Seek her—her? Yes! Seek her to tie her like a witch's daughter of hell to that blazing tree!" Nature has become for Low the realm of savagery and violence with which it has been associated at moments throughout the text, and he recognizes that shift's ramifications when he adds, "in a changed voice," that he is "forgetting [himself]." He is losing control of his own voice, history, and identity, and his change prompts a similar response in Teresa: an "expression of half-savage delight . . . pass[es] across her face" (120–21). As if to mime at the broadest level Low's descent into uncontrolled violence, and the silencing and erasure of his voice and history which are its result, Harte sets this climactic scene amid a raging forest fire, one that serves as a "fiery baptism" for Low and Teresa (120). They momentarily escape to Low's hidden spring, but there the fire catches and kills them; the concluding image of Low is of a permanent and perhaps linguistically inevitable final return to nature: he "seem[s] to be sleeping peacefully in the sleeping water" (125). Far from representing the idyllic future that Low had imagined for himself and Nellie, the spring becomes instead the site of his last, irrevocable return to his primal past.

To drive home the erasure that this final fire accomplishes, its flames also kill Dunn, silencing all connections to Low's heritage and identity. All except Nellie, that is, who, the story's one-paragraph epilogue relates, will soon marry the racist Brace and thus join the society which has sought to name, silence, and forget Low. And indeed, the epilogue, which gives the voice of "contemporaneous history" the final say about Low, describes him as a "wretched tramp," one who "is said to have been a Digger," and of whom it is "not unreasonable to suppose that the fire originated through [his] carelessness" (125). Harte's inclusion of this perspective is of course ironic, but that irony is just another aspect of the ending's weakness: having erased Low and his complications in such a simple and irrevocable fashion, Harte can comment satirically upon his society's views of Native Americans without the need to imagine a way in which Low's voice and history can coexist with that society. Rather than force white society to confront the meaning of the woods as a potential alternative to its structures and stereotypes, he simply destroys them, and his protagonist with them.

If Harte's American popularity had largely faded by the early 1880s, Joaquin Miller, his successor as the exemplar of Western literary production, was at the same moment enjoying the height of his own notoriety; one critic has gone so far as to designate Miller "the most famous writer in America" in this period (White 86). While Harte's fame largely derived from the success of his published works, Miller's resulted more from an overt and lengthy process of self-promotion, his tireless work to "invent himself as a poetic frontiersman" (Lewis 78). And much of that invention relied directly upon Native Americans: Miller took the name Joaquin from Joaquin Murieta, the outlaw hero of the first Native American novel (written by John Rollin Ridge and published in 1854), and his mythic Western identity from his oft-republished autobiographical account of his adoption into an Indian tribe, *Life Amongst the Modocs* (1873).[26] Miller's use of Native American myth and history for his own purposes has led many critics to identify his writings on Indian causes as, in the final summation, simply another example of Euro-American theft and abuse; "in unintentional ways," Miller "represented western conquest" (Lewis 108).[27]

While such arguments certainly resonate for Miller's autobiographical writings, it is more difficult to apply the "self-serving" label to his novel of Indian removal, *Shadows of Shasta* (1881). In fact, *Shadows* is so focused on Native American issues and, at times, so didactic that one biographer calls it "sheer propaganda on behalf of the Indian" (Frost 100).[28] Yet an analysis of the text's three principal voices, and particularly of the relationship between its ever-present first-person narrative voice and its Native American heroine's almost unheard storytelling voice, illustrates how Miller transcends his mythic inclinations and romantic tendencies to produce a novel which manages to capture, if only in momentary glimpses, "the Indian question from an Indian point of view" (Keiser 242).

Miller begins *Shadows* with an extended "Introductory" in which he explicitly addresses the question, "Why this book?" (7). The specific answer is an impassioned account of the recent wrongs committed by the federal government and Western settlers against two Native American tribes, the Poncas and the Cheyennes; Miller documents those wrongs by quoting both government commissioners and Indian chiefs. But the more significant answer can be found in the Introductory's final intimations of a larger narrative of silenced voices and forgotten histories, one in which Miller and his readers are themselves implicated. He warns: "We are making dreadful history, dreadfully fast. How terrible it will all read when the writer and reader of these lines are long since forgotten! Ages may roll by. We may build a city over every dead tribe's bones. We may bury the last Indian deep as the eternal gulf. But these records will remain, and will rise up in testimony against us to the last day of our race" (16). Against the seemingly inevitable destruction of Native American lives, identities, and histories, Miller does posit one defense: the "testimony" of "these records." That is, Miller envisions counter-narratives, alternative histories, the voices of which can speak for the Indian after (Miller implies) he can no longer speak for himself. At its best, Miller's novel serves as such a counter-narrative; at its worst, its romantic conventions and acceptance of Indian voices' inevitable silence and disappearance undermine such alternative histories' effectiveness.

The most prominent example of the latter failings is the novel's nominal hero, the young, attractive, noble, doomed John Logan.[29] Like Low Dorman, Logan is a half-blood; but without the complications that undermine Low's stereotypical aspects, Miller's hero fits more neatly into the "tragic half-breed" cliché. For one thing, while the identity of Low's father is revealed early in "Woods," a revelation that carries with it a good deal of social significance, Logan's mother, a "tawny, silent old woman" (20), never offers her son the details of his heritage or identity. Her silence, moreover, breeds a similar reticence in Logan, so the knowledge is doomed to share her fate: "Who was his father? . . . The boy himself had looked into the deep, pathetic eyes of his mother, and asked the question in his heart for many and many a year; but he never opened his lips to ask her. It was too sad, too sacred a subject, and he would not ask of her what she would not freely give. And now she lay dying there alone on the porch, . . . and her secret hidden in her own heart" (25). The tragic and inevitable aspects of his mother's death are inextricably linked to her silence and his lack of self-knowledge; the Vanishing American takes with her the son's identity and heritage, and he, in failing to resist that process of disappearance, is somehow complicit in it.

Logan is complicit not only in this loss of his heritage, but also, and even more crucially, in the identification with his Native American half that leads directly to his own tragic demise. Miller makes clear from the outset that he views Logan's Indian blood as a blight, describing Logan as having "the awful curse of Cain upon his brow, the mark of Indian blood," and adding in his didactic narrative voice, for those readers who cannot process the allusion, that "You had better be a negro—you had better be ten times a negro, were it possible—than be one-tenth part an Indian in the West" (32). Yet Miller also specifies that Logan is not predestined to the same terrible fate as Cain and Native Americans, that instead he owes his tragedy to his voluntary identification with Indians: "John Logan knew all the wrongs of his people only too well. He sympathized with them. And this meant his own ruin" (78). Given the many wrongs which Miller himself details in his novel, Logan's sympathy is certainly understandable, perhaps even inevitable; but that sense of inevitability only heightens the feeling that his Indian heritage represents not an opportunity, not an alternative to Euro-American society (as it did, however briefly, for Low Dorman), but a tragic curse.

That curse plays out to its foregone conclusion in the novel's final pages. Logan, having aided Indians who are attempting to escape removal to reservations, is himself targeted for such removal; when offered the chance to "go far away," he can only reply that he "was never outside of this." Besides, he knows that "they are waiting for [him] there—everywhere," and that they will always spot "this tinge of Indian blood, that all men abhor and fear, and call treacherous and bloody. Across [his] brow at [his] birth was drawn a brand that marks [him] forever—a brand—a brand as if it were the brand of Cain" (132). Logan has fully accepted his Indian heritage—apparently, has accepted it as utterly defining, something which he has never been "outside"—and with it the inevitable doom; he has listened to what "they call" him, and cannot voice or imagine an alternative to that definition. And so he joins the other Indians on their forced march to the reservation, which he does not survive; somewhere along the harsh path Logan "perishes in darkness, unnamed, unknown" (172).[30]

In his lost history and rapidly vanishing future, Logan strikingly resembles the "little Indian trail" that winds through the novel's mining town setting. The trail must, of course, have come from somewhere, but apparently that knowledge has not been passed down through the years: Miller's question, "Where did it begin?" is purely rhetorical and goes unanswered. Its destination, however, is more precisely known: "Where did the Indian trail lead to? To the West. But leaves were strewn thick along it now. The Indian had gone, to come back no more. Ever to the West points the Indian's path. Ever down to the great gold shore of the vast west sea leads the Indian's path. And there the waves sweep in and obliterate his foot-prints forever" (35). It is a moving image, but one that once again connects the vanishing Indian to a natural world which, according to many Western observers, was similarly disappearing.[31] Yet despite its past tense, its nostalgia and regret for something already lost, it is not Miller's only image of Native Americans: occupying just as central a place in the text is Logan's love interest, the young Indian girl Carrie, whose voice and identity represent real alternatives to his.

Upon her introduction, Carrie seems to be another stereotypical Native character. She and her brother, Johnny, are described by Miller as "babes in the wood," "wild and spirited" children whose parents have been killed by settlers and who now live a more natural life on the mining town's geographic and social borders (25–26). Moreover, these wild children seem, like their figurative half-brother Logan, to have neither discernible past nor meaningful future: some of the miners try "to find out something about [Carrie's] past life," but mostly what they discover is that "the two children [look] as if they had been literally stunted in their growth from starvation and hardship" (50). Wild forest creatures, fated to remain in a childlike state, dependent upon white society but not able to participate in it—Carrie and Johnny at this point embody particular, stereotypical images of Native Americans.

Yet in the first description of Carrie, Miller implies that she does not quite conform to such images: "she [does] not quite look the Indian; men [doubt] if she really [is] an Indian or no, sometimes" (26). And it is through her hesitant, nearly obscured voice, with which she begins to narrate her own and her people's histories, that Carrie truly differentiates herself from what the town's inhabitants would define as "the Indian." The passage in which her voice and storytelling are introduced, the moment where Carrie first speaks of "her life and history," is worth quoting at length: "She did not like to talk; indeed, she talked with difficulty at first, and her few English words fell from her lips in broken bits and in strange confusion. But at length she began to speak more clearly as she proceeded with her story, and became excited in its narration. Then she would stop and seem to forget it all. Then she went on, as if she was telling a dream. Then there would be another long pause, and confusion, and she would stammer on in the most wild and incoherent fashion, till the old miner became quite impatient" (51). The effective performance of Carrie's voice is clearly threatened by obstacles both within (her preference for silence) and without (the language barrier), by her difficult relationships to her own past (the ease with which she can "seem to forget it all") and her white audience (to whom her voice seems "wild and incoherent"). Yet despite those barriers, the use of her narrating voice does have a positive effect: she gains clarity and excitement in producing her narrative. Those effects are certainly partial and impermanent, but they are real, and all the more valuable because of the hostile environment for vocalization out of which they have been produced.

Of course, neither Carrie's newfound clarity nor her excitement can alter a further, and perhaps insurmountable, narrative difficulty: the darkness of her subject matter. As she becomes more comfortable with one particular miner, the old loner Forty-nine—a name itself connected to the history of Anglo-American presence in California—who befriends Logan, Carrie, and Johnny, she begins "to tell strange, wild stories to the old man." But these "wild and terrible dreams of the desert, of blood, of murder and massacre" are so painful that they frighten even the grizzled miner, and the result is a return to silence: "He did not like to hear these dreams, and she soon learned not to repeat them" (55–56). Yet even if Forty-nine no longer wishes to hear Carrie's voice and history, her narrations have introduced them, and all that they represent, into the text, and its own narrative voice cannot remain unchanged in their company. In opposing Carrie's Indian histories to the more sanitized versions produced by Indian agents, the narrator notes that "there [is] a darker story, and told under the breath, and not spoken loud. Let it be told under the breath, and briefly here, also" (53).[32] And for much of the novel, the role of the oft-criticized, admittedly didactic first-person narrative voice is precisely to tell such "darker stories."

From his first words in the Introductory, the narrator introduces themes of silenced voices, lost histories, and alternative narratives into the novel. Moreover, he seems supremely confident about his own ability to produce such an alternative narrative, claiming on the novel's fourth page that "I knew this Indian boy [Logan] and his mother well, and know every foot of the ground I intend to go over, and every fact I propose to narrate. And if you are not prepared to receive this as truth, I prefer you to close this page right here" (21). Despite the final sentence's superior tone and belligerent attitude, this claim actually humanizes the narrator, brings him to the same level as the Native American characters and Western settings about which he will write. Equally significant is the narrator's recognition of his subject's gravity, intimated in the reference to a "darker story" and drawn out when the narrator admits that he "know[s] nothing in history so dark and dreadful as the story of the Indians in this dreaded deadly Reservation" (76). Alliterative and repetitive as this declaration may be, it also compellingly introduces the seriousness with which the narrator will approach his momentous theme. Finally, the narrator also connects his text to its likely audience responses, noting that, in "thinking of only ourselves and our success, we forget others. It is easy, indeed, to forget the misery of others; and we hate to be told of it, too" (81). His subject will be, he knows, an unpopular one, but that unpopularity is precisely what reveals his narrative as an alternative—even, he would argue, a corrective—to the era's ubiquitous success stories.

For much of the text, the romantic tale of Logan and Carrie's courtship, rather than the darker tone of Carrie's dreams, provides the narrative with its momentum. It is in the novel's concluding portrait of the death march to the reservation and the appalling conditions encountered there, however, that the narrator achieves his purpose of giving voice to an alternative Native American history. Once again he derives narrative authority from his own presence in the midst of the history, claiming that he "shall not forget the face of the prisoner [Logan] as we stood beside the trail in the snow" (151); and he likewise brings his readers into, and implicates them in, that same history, demanding that they "keep the picture before" them of the captives "chained together in long lines, marched always on foot in single file, under the stars and stripes" (158). Here, in that final pairing of grim physical reality with mythic national symbol, is social satire chained (quite literally) to specific, present Native American conditions, not cordoned off into a backward-looking coda as in Harte's story.

Yet even while he is presenting this alternative picture, the narrator begins to demonstrate an aversion to his subject's darkness, a desire to return to lighter and more romantic scenes and themes. "Let us hasten on from this subject, and this scene" (157), he requests of his own imagination after a particularly wrenching description, and later, as the Native Americans die and Carrie grows sicker beside them, the request becomes more fervent: "Let us escape from these dreadful scenes as soon as possible. They are like a nightmare to me" (170). Just as Forty-nine could not bear to hear Carrie's dark dreams of past injustices, neither can the narrator bear to witness the nightmarish visions he himself has

created; here his presence amid the history is not an effective authenti-
cating device but a source of genuine pain. And since he cannot escape
the darkness while his characters remain part of it—"the mind turns
back constantly to John Logan lying there" (170)—the narrator must invent a romantic ending for his novel. And so he does: Forty-nine ar-
rives at the reservation to find Carrie dying and honors her last wish
to be taken "back to the mountains" when she dies (178); there she mi-
raculously comes back to life, defying death (which had decided that
"no Indian [will] ever return to his native mountains"), and living out
the remainder of her life with Forty-nine in "the heart of the Sierras"
(182–84).

Even leaving aside the bizarre changes that Carrie undergoes in Miller's sequels to *Shadows*—in which she appears as Forty-nine's wife and
is now apparently (and on at least one occasion explicitly referred to
as) Euro-American—this ending is unsatisfactory on any but the barest
emotional terms. That is, no feeling reader would wish Carrie dead, but
the manner in which she lives—separated from her loved ones, identity,
and history; returned to a nature which seems unreal in its perfection;
made childlike once more in her dependence on Forty-nine (she even
calls him "father" in her deathbed request)—marks a return to the Native American stereotypes which she had seemed for much of the text to
transcend. It is almost impossible to gel this final, beatific reincarnation
of Carrie with the storyteller just gaining her voice and narrating lost,
dark, alternative histories that frighten Forty-nine and even the narrator with their raw pain. Whatever his conclusion's flaws, however, Miller
does allow that earlier version of Carrie to give hesitant voice to those
histories, and he joins his own narrative voice to that project in ways that
are as provocative as they are didactic.

In its creation of that hesitant, developing heroine in service of a didactic, revisionist narrative project, *Shadows of Shasta* foreshadows the
decade's (and century's) most important Indian reform novel, Helen
Hunt Jackson's *Ramona* (1884). While any attention given to Miller's
text has faded with his literary notoriety, the immediate and striking
popularity of Jackson's novel—it sold over fifteen thousand copies in its
first ten months of publication—has endured sufficiently to make plausible John Byers's claim that it is "one of the most popular pieces of lit-

erature ever published in America" (331).[33] Yet the novel's enduring commercial success does not necessarily mean that its message of Indian reform has been heard and internalized by the reading public; in fact, many critics argue that the overwhelming public focus on *Ramona*'s tragic love story and idyllic re-creation of the California past has consistently undermined Jackson's avowed reformist goals. She may have explicitly hoped to write an *Uncle Tom's Cabin* for the Native American, these critics contend, but in the end this little lady started only a big tourism boom in southern California.[34]

Blaming Jackson for the popular reaction to her novel is, it seems to me, a misdirected exercise in reader-response criticism, one which perpetuates the cycle of attention paid to particular aspects of the text at the expense of other, equally present elements. Similarly, those critics who draw a direct line between Jackson's novel and the Dawes Act, the controversial 1887 congressional legislation which allowed for the allotment of reservation land to individual Native Americans, likewise read the novel through a retrospective lens that obscures its complexity.[35] Yet there is no question that Jackson purposefully introduced elements into her novel that drew attention away from its more overtly political themes, with the romance at the top of the list; "I have sugared the pill," she wrote to a friend in comparing *Ramona*'s love story to her more purely polemical *A Century of Dishonor* (1881) [Banning 205], and criticism of the novel on the grounds that such sweetness undermines its bitter revisionist medicine is thus certainly reasonable.[36] But here I argue the opposite: that the romance between the Indian Alessandro and the half-blood Ramona, far from diverting attention away from Jackson's politics, actually constitutes, through its themes of voice, identity, and history, as well as its effects on the novel's principal white character and its continued resonance even in the controversial conclusion, *Ramona*'s most complex and revisionist element.

Ramona begins not with its love story, nor with a revisionist narrative of Native American history, but with what would seem to be another digression: an extended, elegiac portrait of "sheep-shearing" time at Señora Moreno's southern California hacienda (1). Critics have indeed treated this section, and particularly its nostalgic and glowing depiction of the Mission system (with which Jackson apparently became enamored during the time she spent in California researching Indian life and history), as a further detraction from the novel's political effectiveness; more recently, critics with an interest in Mexican-American literature and history have castigated Jackson for her relatively flat portrayals of Señora Moreno, her son Felipe, and the hacienda system as a whole, especially when compared to a contemporary Mexican-American historical novel like Maria Amparo Ruiz de Burton's *The Squatter and the Don* (1885).[37] The text's opening pages deserve all these criticisms, but they also serve another purpose: to introduce the themes of history and voice with which the novel will be centrally concerned. Specifically, Jackson describes the Mexican history of California as apparently lost to narration—"California lost all. Words cannot tell the sting of such a transfer" (16)—but then develops Señora Moreno's voice as a subtle, subversive antidote to such loss. The Señora may seem "quiet" and "reserved," someone who "never . . . said anything about herself," but in the "curious hesitancy" of her voice can be found her power over past and future, her ability both to maintain her late husband's estate and to direct her son Felipe's life (1–2). A historical loss such as that suffered by the Mexican inhabitants of California, Jackson implies from *Ramona's* outset, cannot be countered—or even narrated—directly, but can be opposed by the quiet strength of a minority voice struggling to retain its history and control its destiny.

Having established that theme for her Mexican characters, Jackson then introduces another struggling minority voice: her titular, half-blood heroine, Señora Moreno's adopted daughter. Ramona is initially defined, in direct opposition to the Señora, as possessing a passionate liveliness that grounds her in her own time: "The Señora was of the past; Ramona was of the present" (30). But Jackson quickly complicates this assessment by noting that it is precisely Ramona's own past which, in two distinct ways, defines and limits her in the present. On one level, Ramona's mixed-race status seems to both the Señora and the narrator to be an inescapable and inevitably negative part of her identity: the Señora notes that she "like[s] not these crosses. It is the worst, and not the best of each, that remains" (38); and while the narrator clearly does not agree, she does note of Ramona's heritage that "it [is] a sad legacy, indissolubly linked with memories which [have] in them nothing but bitterness, shame, and sorrow from first to last" (39). And on a second level, Ramona is limited by her lack of knowledge of her own past and identity: "the story of Ramona the Señora never told" (30), and when Ramona inquires about her parents, the Señora replies, "Don't ever speak to me again about this" (41). Not only is Ramona's past inescapable, but it is also, at this early stage in her life and the novel, unnarratable.

Just because a history has not been told, however, does not mean that it has vanished, and Jackson is careful to note that Ramona's past is "not one to be forgotten" (30). In order for it to become a more overt part of Ramona's life in the present, what is required is the presence—and in particular the voice—of another Native American. Thus enters Alessandro, the beautiful, talented son of an Indian chief who has become the leader of a band of roving sheep-shearers. Many critics focus on the ways in which Alessandro is anything but a typical Native American, at least for the era's imagery: he plays the violin, has been taught to read (as part of his father's "trying to make him like white men" [64]), and is generally so deracialized as to make the Señora exclaim: "How the boy makes me forget he is an Indian!" (127).[38] Yet of Alessandro's many attractive aspects, the one which instantly connects him to Ramona, his voice, is both explicitly and implicitly tied to his Indian identity. The inhabitants of the hacienda begin each morning by singing a hymn, and on the first morning that Alessandro adds his "rich new voice" to the chorus, Ramona immediately finds herself drawn to "the Indian who sang"; her explicit association of race with voice continues when she asks Felipe "which one of the Indians it is [who] has that superb voice" (63–64, 68). And what attracts Ramona to Alessandro's voice is not simply its quality, but also its ties to a world she has never known: "Ramona had never heard such a voice. . . . this was from another world, this sound" (63). Implicitly, Alessandro's voice links to the Native American heritage that has never been communicated to Ramona, and her simple statement that she has "never heard anything like it" (68), when connected to the Señora's enforced silence about Ramona's past, exemplifies this new voice's potential to communicate that which has gone unnarrated.

Such communication is precisely what results from Ramona's burgeoning relationship with Alessandro, although not without complications. For one thing, there is a language barrier: Ramona has always spoken Spanish, and while Alessandro is fluent in that language, at times he

speaks "in the Indian tongue," which Ramona does "not at first understand" (72). Moreover, the hacienda is permeated by disdain for and
dismissal of Native American history and identity. The Señora wonders "of what is it that these noble lords of villages are so proud? Their
ancestors—naked savages less than a hundred years ago?" (111), and even
the more tolerant Felipe admits that "the consciousness of Ramona's
unfortunate birth had rankled at times" (132). Growing up around such
opinions, it is no wonder that for Ramona, believing herself Mexican,
"so strong [is] the race feeling" that she can hardly imagine Alessandro
apart from his Indian identity (94–95). Yet Alessandro, "full of venera-
tion for the fathers and their teachings" (84), once again perfectly re-
dresses the gaps in Ramona's knowledge; his pride in his Indian history and identity, like his otherworldly voice, is an ideal vehicle through
which Ramona can come to know and appreciate her own heritage and
voice.

   First, however, she and Alessandro fall in love, and the sequence and
connection of those two processes are crucial. That is, while readers
and critics have often separated the novel's love story from its Native
American themes, the two elements are in fact intertwined. It is after
Alessandro excitedly learns of Ramona's "Indian blood! Indian blood!"
(121), that they first declare their love for one another, and the moment
is founded on a shared, if as yet unspoken, recognition of their similar
identities and histories. Alessandro declares his love while "the whole
story . . . of the girl's birth [is] burning in his thoughts," and he longs to
tell her that "they have made you homeless in your home. . . . The blood
of my race is in your veins." At the same time, Ramona, who has "never
before spoken to Alessandro of her own personal history or burdens,"
admits that "the worst thing is, Alessandro, that she will not tell me who
my mother was" (149). And to cement the link between their developing
bonds and shared Indian heritage, later that night Alessandro symbolically renames Ramona in his own language: he hears two wood-doves'
love songs and thinks that "if [Ramona] is my wife my people will call
her Majel, the Wood-Dove" (155).

   With the couple having formed such a strong connection without a
full narration of Ramona's past, all that remains before they can begin
their life together is for that history to be told and acknowledged by all.

First, the Señora confronts Ramona with her past, bringing out the long-hidden box which contains Ramona's mother's final possessions (literally, her heritage) in an attempt to "explain to you why you will not marry the Indian Alessandro. . . . Your mother was an Indian," she confirms, "a low, common Indian," and it was only a matter of time before "the Indian blood in your veins would show." Yet Ramona, far from rejecting this tragic legacy as the Señora expects, completes the process begun with Alessandro and embraces her identity and history: "Yes, Señora Moreno, . . . the Indian blood in my veins shows to-day. I understand many things I never understood before. . . . Oh, I am glad I am an Indian! I am of his people" (164–65). Now that Ramona knows and accepts her heritage, she can fully share that knowledge with Alessandro, and does so in a climactic courtship scene where her Native American identity is confirmed: "I belong to your people," she tells him; he replies that he has long seen "what it was in your face [that] had always seemed to me like the faces of my own people"; and he shares her new name, the "Indian word," Majel (225–26).

So Ramona and Alessandro are completely united, and even the Señora, hearing the couple sing a duet, cannot deny the rightness of their union: "To hear those two voices! . . . would one suppose they could sing like that? Perhaps it is not so bad as I think" (159). Yet Ramona's is not the only Native American history in the mix; Alessandro likewise brings a past to the relationship, and the revelation of his people's ongoing history is not the cathartic and energizing experience that it was for Ramona. At the same moment that Ramona's past is revealed and the courtship culminated, Alessandro must share the terrible history that has befallen his tribe: "I have no home; my father is dead; my people are driven out of their villages" (218). If Ramona's newfound heritage blesses her with a strength and a voice that she had not previously possessed, Alessandro's blood and past seem both more of a curse and less within his control: "We have no right in Temecula [their ancestral village], not even to our graveyard full of the dead," he exclaims (222). And Alessandro's sufferings even change his voice: as he narrates the horrors, Ramona asks herself, "this voice—this strange, hard, unresonant voice—whose voice was it?" (218). Blessing and curse, gain and loss—Ramona and Alessandro's relationship embodies both the potential and pain of Native American identity and history, and criticism of the novel's romance as a distraction from its politics ignores those elements' interconnections.

In fact, much of the rest of the novel represents a balancing act between the love story and the revisionist Native American history. Ramona and Alessandro leave the hacienda and set out on an epic journey across southern California, one that is at once elopement and escape, continuation of their love and flight from persecution. Their journey contains scenes of romantic beauty that epitomize Ramona's acceptance of her Native American identity: the moment when Ramona admits that she is "Ramona no longer" and will now be "Majella—Alessandro's Majel" (244)[39]; or their brief stay in an Edenic canyon, where Ramona begins to understand the natural world's majesty and thus, for Alessandro, to "speak in the language of our people" (260).[40] Yet it likewise contains reminders of Indian identity's negative aspects in this place and time: their realization that, in taking Ramona's horse Baba away from the hacienda, they have become the popular stereotype of "horse-stealing" Indians (251); or Alessandro's recognition that his cousin Ysidro's land grant for their ancestral village will be useless in the face of American settlers and government agents, who will not "mind the paper" in their quest for Western land (253).

Both sides of their identities and histories can be found in one of the novel's most powerful scenes, Ramona's long vigil in the Temecula graveyard. They have returned to Temecula so Alessandro can bid a painful farewell to cherished aspects of his past: literally because he must sell his father's violin, which, he notes in a "slow, husky voice," is "very old" (273); and figuratively because he must witness the American settlers' encroachment onto his people's land and into their homes. Ramona's time in the graveyard waiting for Alessandro's return could be just as painful an experience, but instead it is the opposite: she relishes her time among the Indian dead, realizing that "they would all help us if they could" (264); and she has for companionship Carmena, a young Temecula widow. Carmena speaks only Luiseno, the Temecula language, but somehow Ramona understands, leading Alessandro to note "delightedly," upon his return, that "she has understood the Luiseno words. . . . She is one of us" (279). For now, then, the positive elements, represented by Ramona's strength and voice, outweigh the historic losses and abuses, and Alessandro does not "dwell long on past wrongs" (276); but as the couple ride away, Carmena speaks a "dire prophecy" for their future, re-peating "One of us! one of us! Sorrow came to me; she rides to meet it!" (279).

Carmena is unfortunately correct, and the negative elements of Na-tive American identity and history increasingly dominate Ramona and Alessandro's lives as the novel moves toward its conclusion. Time and again they witness the losses and pain associated with the settlers' ar-rival, and each incident serves as a "note of the knell of their happi-ness" (318). After one particularly traumatic encounter, which results in the forced sale and evacuation of their home, it is Alessandro who must comfort Ramona as best he can, telling her that she must not "look back. It is gone!" (330). And after the most painful loss, the death of their first daughter due to an Indian agent's inaction and negligence, Ramona's transformation is complete: "Take me where I need never see a white face again," she begs Alessandro, and he feels "a melancholy joy" that she now shares his view (382). Because of the constant presence of loss and pain in this section, even the more positive aspects of Ramona's ongoing growth—their wedding, in which she uses the name Majella and thus takes "the last step . . . in the disappearance of Ramona" (293); her introduction to an elderly Indian woman, where Ramona expresses "reverence" for her "great age" and says that she will "be her daugh-ter if she will let me" (304–5)—are overlaid with a sense of inevitable loss. Ramona's acceptance of her identity and history, while nominally still of her own volition, comes to feel just as inescapable and tragic as it did with Miller's Logan, and the novel's revisionist depictions of her strength and voice suffer because of it.

In fact, in the text's final section Jackson shifts her revisionist agenda onto a new character: Aunt Ri, another strong, vocal woman. Aunt Ri and her family are the novel's only significant white characters, and de-spite their somewhat caricatured dialect,[41] their responses to Ramona and Alessandro's experiences clearly represent an ideal for Jackson (as their last name, Hyers, indicates). Aunt Ri in particular is sensitive to the Native Americans on a variety of key levels: she tells her family not to speak about the couple in English in front of them, since " 't don't seem hardly fair to take advantage o' their not knowin' any language but their own" (355); she contrasts her interactions with Alessandro and Ramona with "her ideas of Indians," which "had been drawn from newspapers, and from ... narratives of massacres," and finds the latter wanting (356); and later she even transcends her Protestant faith and joins a group of Indians in a Catholic prayer, "a moment and a lesson" which she "never forgot" (423). As a result of these responses and an indication of her own stubborn strength and voice, Ri fully converts to the Native American cause: "the last vestige of her prejudice against Indians [has] melted and gone" (431); she predicts that she'll "turn Injun, mebbe, afore [she] git[s] through!" (433); and she devotes most of her time to investigating the wrongs committed by Indian agents (436–38).[42]

The conversion of Aunt Ri is an essential element in the novel, and another indication of the romance's political, revisionist value. Yet this triumph for the Native American cause cannot overshadow that romance's tragic conclusion. Alessandro, consumed by both the horrors of his people's history and the inevitably painful future he foresees, goes mad: "His passionate heart, ever secretly brooding on the wrongs he had borne, the hopeless outlook for his people in the future, and most of all on the probable destitution and suffering in store for Ramona, consumed itself as by hidden fires." Moreover, his voice, through which he first connected to Ramona's Indian identity, entirely abandons him: "Speech, complaint, ... might have saved him; but all these were foreign to his self-contained, reticent, repressed nature" (388). Ramona's singing lover has transformed into the stereotypical stoic Indian; and after his madness causes him accidentally to steal a white settler's horse and the settler responds by murdering him, Ramona is likewise silenced, struck ill with grief and unable to testify on Alessandro's behalf at the subsequent inquest. Just as their voices had once sung together to illustrate their shared identity and history, so at this tragic end to their relationship do Alessandro and Ramona share in a silence that seems the only possible response to the brutality they have witnessed and suffered.[43]

Yet silence is not Ramona's only response to her loss, nor the only way in which her connection to Alessandro will endure into the future. The novel's conclusion, in which Felipe finds Ramona, convinces her to marry him, and moves with her to Mexico, a "new home" where Felipe "might yet live among men of his own race ... , and of congenial beliefs and occupations" (445–47), has often been criticized as just another Vanishing American narrative; not only does Ramona physically leave America, but she also seems to leave behind her Indian identity and history and to adopt once more the Mexican heritage of her child-hood.[44] Yet Ramona's abandonment of her Native American side is less absolute than that. She does tell Felipe, in agreeing to marry him, that "part of [her] is dead . . . can never live again" (448), and while she spe-cifically refers to her love for Alessandro, the connection of that rela-tionship to her Indian identity makes this sentiment racial as well as ro-mantic. But neither Alessandro nor his voice—nor the Native American identity and history to which they are forever linked—have entirely died for Ramona: "It was indeed a new world, a new life. Ramona might well doubt her own identity. But undying memories stood like sentinels in her breast. When the notes of doves, calling to each other, fell on her ear, her eyes sought the sky, and she heard a voice saying, 'Majella!'" (449). And there is a living embodiment of this enduring voice and his-tory, Ramona and Alessandro's surviving daughter Ramona, to whom Ramona has passed along her heritage (the contents of her mother's se-cret box) as well as her name, and with a description of whom the novel closes: Felipe and Ramona's "daughters were all beautiful; but the most beautiful of them all, and, it was said, the most beloved by both father and mother, was the eldest one: . . . Ramona, daughter of Alessandro, the Indian" (449).[45] While Jackson does, along with Harte and Miller, sen-timentalize the tragic loss of Indian voices and histories, she also imag-ines the possibility that a strong Native American voice can bring its his-tory into the future.[46]

Ironically, the novel which featured one of the decade's strongest such Native American voices, William Justin Harsha's *Ploughed Under: The Story of an Indian Chief, Told by Himself* (1881), is now remembered solely for having contributed to *Ramona*'s development. Each Jackson biography tells the story: she was writing a disappointed review of Har-sha's novel for *The Critic*—she admired its politics and purpose, but felt that it "lacked true dramatic ability and power of characterization," and thus "was not a great success" (Banning 159–60)—and the book's editor, her friend J. B. Gilder, suggested that "she was herself the proper person to undertake such a story" (Odell 169). Although Jackson at first de-nied the claim, believing that she did not possess the necessary knowl-edge and experience, the seed was planted, and her California researches were at least partly due to this conversation and her growing desire to write such a novel.[47] Besides Jackson's biographers, the few critics who reference Harsha's text do so only in passing, and more dismissively than Jackson: Francis Prucha makes brief mention of "the unsuccessful Indian novel by William Justin Harsha" (137) while Siobhan Senier goes further, referring to Harsha's "dreadfully dull 1881 'Indian' novel" (44).

It is difficult to disagree with aesthetic criticisms of the novel: Harsha is at best an awkward prose stylist, and his tendency to wax poetic for pages about his story's clichéd and underdeveloped love triangle does not help (this romance contributes nothing to the novel's revisionist or political goals). Yet calling the novel unsuccessful or putting quotes around Indian imply that *Ploughed* also fails thematically and politically, and there I would disagree. Moreover, it is the novel's one formal innovation that allows for its thematic successes: as the subtitle's "Told by Himself" indicates, Harsha creates a fictional Native American first-person narrator (the first in a Euro-American text, as far as I know), and that narrative voice's power and revisionism distinguish Harsha's text from the decade's other Indian fictions.[48]

Ploughed opens with two significant prefatory texts. The first, an "Introduction" by "Inshta Theamba ('Bright Eyes')"—the pseudonym of Susette La Flesche, an Omaha Indian who gained fame through her 1879–1880 lecture tour with the Ponca chief Standing Bear[49]—considers broadly the issue of how "white people have tried to solve the 'Indian Question'" (3) and concludes with an apt metaphor for the novel's principal, revisionist goal. "As the author has so graphically depicted, the huge plough of the 'Indian system' has run for a hundred years, ... turning down into the darkness of the earth every hope and aspiration which we have cherished," La Flesche writes (6), and it is indeed Harsha's purpose to unearth Native Americans' buried histories and identities.[50] In the following brief "Preface," Harsha reiterates that goal, claiming that, "while the narrative has not followed the history of any one tribe, all the scenes depicted have been taken from the great unwritten volume of Indian suffering." And he links his attempt to write one chapter of that volume to voice, arguing that "The dialogue contains the substance of the discussions around the camp-fires and in the lodges and homes of all the Indians of the great North-west. The Indian language is so full of metaphor, that to preserve anything like a true conception of Indian speech, the seemingly excessive richness of its coloring must be preserved" (7). While at times Harsha's prose is unquestionably guilty of "excessive richness" and while its authenticity as "Indian speech" could no doubt be debated—although one current critical website attributes the anonymous authorship to Standing Bear (Welker), while another claims that it was written by Bright Eyes herself (Franks), so its voice has seemed convincingly Indian to at least a few readers[51]—this claim's significance lies in its connection of Native American history to voice. The former, he implies, cannot be adequately narrated without the latter, and his first-person Native American narrator impressively illustrates that principle.

Ironically, the novel opens by separating history and voice: the narrator attempts to describe his "earliest memories," which "are concerned with" his powerful relationship with the natural world, but notes that they are "the suggestion and type of thoughts [he] could never hope in [their] simple [Indian] language to express." But he is quick to add that this expressive failure is not necessarily related to linguistic simplicity or ignorance: "I doubt if they could be defined even in the sweetest and most powerful words that other peoples know so well how to use" (11). Part humble self-deprecation, part pointed response to Euro-American conceptions of their own linguistic skills as greater than Native Americans', this opening paragraph highlights the narrator's willingness to analyze both languages. That is, while ostensibly focused on his own voice's historical limitations, on a broader level he is considering the efficacy of Indian and white words, and recognizing that the latter's expressive efforts can likewise fail.

Indeed, much of the novel's first half constitutes documentation of white language's failure to capture Native Americans' identity and history. The narrator's first words of dialogue, responding to wise man Standing Elk's story of white-Indian interactions, are "Savages! How can they rightly call us savages?" (14), and in fact the opening chapter's title, "The First Puzzle," refers to that "ever-recurring question" over which the narrator "would puzzle" constantly: "Is this to be a savage?" (17). As the narrator's serious consideration of the question indicates, white language has the potential to influence and even alter Native American conceptions of their own identity and history, and lest his readers distance themselves from those processes, the narrator implicates them directly: "think of my people as—ignorant, if you please, but—possessed of a love and sympathy which in any condition avail to make life worth the living" (34). Although "in any condition" seems to grant the possibility that Indians are indeed ignorant, the use of hyphens creates a series of disconnections: between his people, the white image of them, and the reality of their identity.

Moreover, the narrator makes clear that white language affects not only Native Americans' identity, but also their sense of history and their lives in the future. A government agent, summing up both the tribe's past existence and its future under his care, claims that, "In short, you are no longer to be neglected, but will be taken care of and protected by me," to which the tribal chief (the narrator's father) responds that "In short, we are to be thy slaves! . . . Why may we not live as we have always lived and as our fathers have lived before us?" (46). Despite the chief's eloquence, these competing voices are far from equal, as illustrated by a subsequent incident in which the agent strikes a bargain with the chief and his "words [are] taken down, as we suppose, by the interpreter, and under them [his] father and all the head men present [make] their marks" (51). The interpreter, the narrator learns much later, has falsified the treaty to allow for future white profit and abuse; the whites' marks in this linguistic interaction far outweigh, even erase, the Native Americans'. For the Indians "bemoaning much the ruin that had fallen on [their] people in the past, but bemoaning much more the sad prospect that [their] time to bear the white man's unpitying blow might soon come," theirs is, the narrator stresses, "a real fear, . . . a real despair" (119), and that ruined history and sad future are inextricably linked to white language's power to define and erase Native Americans.

Yet that history and future are not the only ones which can be narrated and imagined; nor can white language only be used to stereotype and destroy. Despite the government Indian agent's many abuses, he does, the narrator notes, "establish a school in which more than one hundred of [their] young people [learn] to read and speak the English language," and thus it is "to him" that the narrator "owe[s] the power, which [he] now so poorly use[s], of writing [his] simple history, with the hope of securing sympathy and justice for [his] unhappy people" (52). The self-deprecation of "poorly" and "simple" cannot mask the significance of this "power," of the narrator's ability to tell his history in his own voice to a white audience. At almost exactly the novel's midpoint, a sympathetic white senator asks of a more racist colleague, "Who will write a history of the long years [Native Americans] patiently suffered?" (142), and the answer, unspoken at that moment, is provided at every moment by the text itself. The narrator will write that history; and he will do so for his ideal readers, those who, "if [he] could but write down upon this page the horror and despair and the many intangible emotions of bitterness and dread," would feel "real sympathy" and weep "tears of real sorrow" (128). Such emotions alone cannot change Native Americans' lives or fates, but they are certainly powerful inducements to hear Native voices, learn and remember their histories, and finally act upon their behalf.

That goal has three potential limitations, however: such ideal readers may not be plentiful, nor the ones who most need to hear this alternative voice and history; and, just as crucially, the narrator must have the skill to "write down upon this page" that history's complexity and power. The first two problems, like Jackson's reader responses, fall largely outside of an author's control, but the third does not, and the clichéd love triangle on which the narrator (that is, Harsha) focuses much of his novel's second half reflects badly on his skill in giving voice to Native American history. Moreover, as the novel nears its conclusion the narrator seems to give in to Vanishing American stereotypes of inevitably silenced voices and forgotten histories. In relating his father's final words, the narrator admits that "The Indian chief uses a language far nobler and more picturesque than that employed by ordinary members of his tribe. Hence it is that very few interpreters are able to give the full meaning of a chief's address, while in almost every case the beauty of metaphor and the passion of expression are lost. . . . thus it is difficult to retain the full sweetness and glory in a language less intimately associated with the voices of grove and prairie" (247). Once again the narrator analyzes both Indian and white languages, but here the white language's expressive failure has the unfortunate effect of contributing to the Indian language's loss; so much for the power which English gives the narrator over his own history and identity. His father similarly contributes to the Vanishing American myth, arguing, in his deathbed speech, that "the Indians must always be remembered in this land," because "out of our languages we have given names to many beautiful things which will always speak of us" (249). Such linguistic memories, however abiding, do not speak of, in fact obscure, this land's enduring, actual Native American presence, and it is their identities and histories which need remembering.

Yet if these images and ideas of his father, contained in a chapter entitled "Ploughed Under," seem to accept Native Americans' inevitable burial and disappearance, they are not the narrator's final words on the subject. As the novel's closing chapter, "The Two Voices," makes clear, the narrator himself has not vanished; indeed he has not gone anywhere: "I sit in a little cabin on the shore of the same shining river whose smile is my first remembrance" (266). Memory and narration, past and present become, in this rather astonishing moment, one, and Native Americans become both literally and chronologically present.[52] The narrator once again implicates his readers in the forces which seek to silence and erase his people, noting that he "dare[s] not tell you where [his] cabin stands" out of fear of further white conquest. He also voices a final self-deprecation of his own power to oppose such conquest, exclaiming, "my people—O my people! I long to do something for them in their desolation. Yet what can I do?" (267).

What he can do, of course, is offer his own voice and history in opposition to the dominant white conceptions of both. He illustrates that contrast through the novel's final metaphor of the "two voices" of "the shining river": one which "swells loudly" and "cries, 'The Indian is an evil thing in the path of civilization'"; and "the other" which "comes wailing, 'Are we not human beings?'" As with the novel's first-person narrative voice, the "we" implicitly, effectively responds to the impersonal white definition of "the Indian" as a "thing." And the narrator develops one last, related opposition in the short closing paragraph, concluding that "it is for the Christian public to say which voice in the river shall swallow up the other. Wolf Killer the son of Eagle Wing has spoken" (267-68). Certainly the Christian public's voice will have a significant say in the fate of Native American voices and histories; but as exemplified by the brilliant juxtaposition of that idea with the second sentence's encapsulation of its Native American narrative voice's strength and historical emphasis ("the son of Eagle Wing"), Indians too can have their say.

If that say is provided in fictional form by Harsha's novel, it was embodied in all its complexity by the life and writings of Sarah Winnemucca.

Winnemucca, daughter and granddaughter of chiefs of her Northern Paiute tribe, served throughout her life as a translator, interpreter, and spokeswoman for that tribe in its extended and difficult dealings with the U.S. Government and army.[53] She describes that service and those dealings in *Life Among the Piutes: Their Wrongs and Claims* (1883), generally considered the first autobiographical text published by a Native American woman. Because of that lack of literary precedent, as well as the text's generic complexity and Winnemucca's own controversial history—some tribespeople and some governmental officials attempted to discredit her, while others from both sides praised her and her work—many critics have focused on defining, as precisely as possible, the text's genres and its author's roles.[54] Yet the very hybrid nature of Winnemucca's life and text resists and renders counterproductive such precision, and recent critics such as Andrew McClure, Eric Anderson (112-32), Noreen Lape (19-56), Siobhan Senier (73-120), and Cari Carpenter focus instead on that hybridity. Similarly, I argue that *Life*'s formal hybridity and multivocality both reflect Winnemucca's own complex position as interpreter and spokeswoman and serve as strategies through which she can utilize that situation to further her only and enduring purpose: to voice effectively her and her people's identities and histories.

Life begins, like so many nineteenth-century minority autobiographies, with a "Preface" by its white editor, Mary Mann. In this short piece, Mann identifies a few central issues with which any reading of this "heroic act," as she defines the text, must be concerned. First is voice, and the written text's relation to Winnemucca's history as a lecturer and (implicitly) her preference for oral narration.[55] Mann notes that, "Finding that in extemporaneous speech she could only speak at one time of a few points, [Winnemucca] determined to write out the most important part of what she wished to say. In fighting with her literary deficiencies she loses some of the fervid eloquence which her extraordinary colloquial command of the English language enables her to utter, but [Mann is] confident that no one would desire that her own original words should be altered." Mann thus immediately contrasts Winnemucca's difficulties with written narrative and her voice's power, but at the same time stresses the text's significance ("the most important part") and its close correspondence to Winnemucca's voice ("what she wished to say," "her own original words"). Moreover, she then relates the narrative to

Winnemucca's unique position—her "knowledge of the two races gives her an opportunity of comparing them justly"—and her desire to give voice to her Native American identity and history: "it is of the first importance to hear what only an Indian and an Indian woman can tell. To tell it was her own deep impulse, and the dying charge given her by her father, the truly parental chief of his beloved tribe." Winnemucca may have lost some of her "fervid eloquence" in writing the narrative, but she has retained full possession of her strong voice and clear purpose (2).[56]

That voice and purpose must coexist with the complex realities of Winnemuca's history and tribal status, however, and the opening chapter introduces two paramount such complexities. For one thing, there is the narrative's generic hybridity, and specifically its shifts between personal and tribal histories (and thus between autobiography and ethnohistory). As Winnemucca's opening pages illustrate, that generic hybridity illustrates how any Native American, especially one in a position of authority (Winnemucca is, again, the heir to chiefs) and most especially one who is addressing a white audience, occupies the doubled (and potentially split) position of individual person and representative "Indian." The text's first four sentences exemplify the complex balancing act which such doubling requires: "I was born somewhere near 1844, but am not sure of the precise time. I was a very small child when the first white people came into our country. They came like a lion, . . . and have continued so ever since, and I have never forgotten their first coming. My people were scattered at that time over nearly all the territory now known as Nevada" (5). In some ways these lines echo the openings of innumerable personal narratives: beginning with one's birth[57]; focusing immediately on a defining moment from early life; emphasizing through the power of memory that moment's continuity with the moment of composition. Yet this personal narrative is also a narrative of a people's history, and the defining moment is as much theirs as it is hers—it is "our country" to which the whites come, and so Winnemucca must shift the subject within a few lines from "I" to "my people."

The relationship of the personal to the tribal parallels the second complexity: the text's multivocality. Specifically, Winnemucca introduces the authoritative voice of her grandfather, the chief known as Truckee, but does not allow his narrative of the first white-Indian encounter to go unchallenged. Truckee's version is that of a prophecy ful-

filled, a historical cycle completed: "my long-looked for white brothers
have come at last," he rejoices, telling his people a powerful origin myth
in which four siblings, two light and two dark, are separated at an early
age but will eventually be reunited to "heal all the old trouble" (5–7).
Winnemucca quotes her grandfather at length, establishing his voice's
effectiveness when he convinces his tribe to "promise as he wishe[s]"
that they will welcome the whites when they next arrive (7), but also
makes clear that her own narrative of the encounter, delivered from
the perspective of the nearly forty intervening years, is quite different.
Commenting on her grandfather's later disappointments, she notes that
she "can imagine his feelings, for [she has drunk] deeply from the same
cup. When [she] think[s] of [her] past life, and the bitter trials [she has]
endured, [she] can scarcely believe [she] live[s], and yet [she does]" (6).
Winnemucca at once connects to her grandfather's optimism and dis-
tances herself from it, quotes his voice and undercuts it with her own,
and the moment's personal and vocal hybridity foreshadow her narrative's defining formal and thematic characteristics.[58]

There is, of course, a third set of voices with its own prominent role
in *Life:* the voices of whites. Those voices add not only to the text's
multivocality, but also to its generic hybridity, for in her depictions of
white voices Winnemucca adds an explicit political purpose to the autobiographical and ethnohistorical elements. I refer to plural white voices
because Winnemucca distinguishes at least two: a governmental voice,
as exemplified by her grandfather's "paper" from the president, which
he believes can "talk to him" (18); and her potential white readers' voice,
with which Winnemucca explicitly engages with phrases like "You call
my people bloodseeking" (10). If the former voice has perpetrated the
most overt wrongs against the Piutes, Winnemucca is well aware that
the latter's silent support has enabled that perpetration, and that its opposition could help end it. In a complex moment, Winnemucca refers to
what her people did not say to starving white settlers—"They did not
hold out their hands and say: 'You can't have anything to eat unless you
pay me'"—and then reiterates that "no such word was used by us savages at that time; and the persons I am speaking of are living yet; they
could speak for us if they choose to do so" (10). Winnemucca here adds a
fourth voice to the mix, the hostile and "savage" voice in which her tribe
has never spoken but with which they have nonetheless been defined,

and implies that it is white silence which has allowed for the creation of this false Native American voice.

Winnemucca's conditional shift to the present tense in that moment ("if they choose to do so") indicates a continued hope that the second white voice, that of her at least potentially sympathetic readership, will speak up on behalf of Native Americans. But as she knows, such sympathetic speech must be prompted, and it is her text's avowed purpose to provide such prompting. Furthermore, she recognizes that doing so requires her to talk less about herself and more about, as the text's impersonal title indicates, the wrongs and claims of her tribe as a whole (her individual wrongs and claims may be no less worthy of attention, but could be more easily dismissed as unique or atypical).[59] "I will now stop writing about myself" (58) she vows at the start of chapter three, and later she spells out that narrative shift's implications: "Dear reader, I must tell a little more about my poor people, and what we suffer at the hands of our white brothers. ... Oh, my dear good Christian people, how long are you going to stand by and see us suffer at your hands?" (89). Winnemucca narrates the tribal history, then, as an explicit appeal to her readers' sympathy, requiring of them a sense not only of complicity ("at your hands") but also of connection to the Indians ("our white brothers"). And if Winnemucca has a smaller role as subject in this narrative, she still has a central role as creator of it, as bridge between the tribe and the reader. "Oh, it is a fearful thing to tell," she admits of one especially horrific episode, "but it must be told. Yes, it must be told by me" (77). In explicitly considering her role as interpreter, mediator between the two cultures (a role on which many critics focus), Winnemucca recognizes her voice's power and purpose.[60]

Yet the work of an interpreter goes both directions (back to one's people as well as out from them, that is), and thus the role's inherent influence is double-edged: the ability to speak truth to power is inextricably intertwined with a tendency to relay power's lies back to the powerless. In other words, Winnemucca's mediating role is another hybrid, one in which she serves as spokeswoman for both her tribe and the government. To her credit, she fully confronts the situation's complex realities, and includes her tribe's criticisms of her on these grounds. "Sister, I don't think it right that you should always tell everything to our people," her cousin Jarry argues after she has passed on an Indian agent's unpleasant directive, and Winnemucca can only reply, "Dear brother, I have not told anything but what I was told to tell them" (128). The similar structures of address in this sentence and Winnemucca's remarks to her "Dear reader," as well as her reference to her fellow Piutes as "them," indicate that, in her role as interpreter, she occupies a synonymous position toward both Native Americans and whites. Yet of course her words' potential negative impact on her tribespeople is immeasurably greater than on whites, and whenever she interprets she risks being complicit in the wrongs committed against her people. "You have a right to say I have sold you," she admits to them, because "it looks so. . . . I know I have told you more lies than I have hair on my head. I tell you, my dear children, I have never told you my own words; they were the words of the white people, not mine" (236).[61]

For one so convinced that her voice's power is the best means to help her people, it must be tremendously painful to admit that her words have often been co-opted for the exploitative policies of the whites and their government. And at times Winnemucca does become discouraged by that aspect of interpreting; this attitude is best illustrated in the moment when her brother Egan asks if she believes their family will lose their home to whites, and Winnemucca can only respond that "I have nothing to say. I am only here to talk for you all" (126).[62] Yet in each such instance she resists her despair, and does so, crucially, through the exercise of that same double-sided organ, her voice. "I am going to see my people dealt rightly by, and to stand by them, and I am going to talk for them just as long as I live" (129), she asserts, and the linkage of those three clauses exemplifies the continued strength and purpose which Winnemucca derives from her voice. Just as meaningful in that sentence is her use of "my people"—despite the distance created by her interpreter's role, Winnemucca is one of the Piutes, and her voice remains both personal and tribal in its origins and goals. When an army officer tries to lessen bad news by telling her, "It is nothing about you; it is about your people" (203), he separates the two identities in a way that Winnemucca cannot and would not want to if she could.

Life ends, as *Ploughed* does, in a moment that is very much physically as well as chronologically present. "After my marriage to Mr. Hopkins I visited my people once more at Pyramid Lake Reservation," Winnemucca reports in her final sentence, "and they urged me again to come

to the East and talk for them, and so I have come" (246). Here the resonances of Winnemucca's history as a lecturer are very strong—the feeling of her presence at this moment is tangible and impressive. Also here
are the continued connections between personal and tribal history; a
sentence which begins with Winnemucca's marriage moves immediately to her people and their situation on the reservation, and thus to
her role as tribal spokeswoman. But the sentence's most significant aspect is its sense of continuity between past, present, and future: as the
shift in verb tense indicates, Winnemucca has talked for her people before, will do so again (she is, her people know, "always ready to talk for
them" [140]), and is even doing so through this text. History, voice, narrative, and political purpose are inseparable in this moment, and this
final image of hybridity exemplifies both the inevitably complex reality
and the potential promise of Native American identity, voice, and history in this decade.

Among the documents and letters of support with which Winnemucca's text concludes is an "unsolicited" letter from one Roger Sherman
Day, a Nevada miner. Day writes to praise the Paiute people, to plead
with the government not to remove them to a reservation, and, most of
all, to recommend Winnemucca as a uniquely appropriate spokeswoman
for the tribe. "Miss Sarah can tell better than any one else why her kin-
dred should be let alone," he argues, and "she deserves the attention of
our best ears at Washington" (262). Unfortunately, Winnemucca's voice,
like those of Low Dorman, Carrie, Ramona and Alessandro, and Wolf
Killer, did not receive in this decade the attention—or, more accurately
and crucially, the response—which it deserved. Newspaper accounts
of the Ponca trials (to cite a prominent example) may have been well
read in their particular moment, but Indian wars continued through
Geronimo's 1886 surrender, and the reservation system has continued for
much, much longer. Even avowedly reformist measures like the Dawes
Act only contributed to the period's ongoing silencing, forgetting, and
erasure of Native American voices and histories.

Yet those sobering historical facts cancel out neither the existence
nor the value of those texts that did attempt to put forward alternative
narratives of silenced voices and forgotten histories. Harte's and Miller's cannot quite, despite their revisionist moments, escape the myths

of the Vanishing American; Jackson's depicts the relationship between one Native American struggling to reclaim her voice and history and another going mad due to the gradual destruction of both; and the most revisionist, Harsha's and Winnemucca's, are narrated by strong Native American voices that tell their own histories despite that task's inherent difficulties. But all of these texts indicate the depth and import of the Indian Question, and all make meaningful strides toward giving voice to Native American responses to that question. They still deserve the attention of our best ears.

3

"That's the Worst of Being a Woman. What You Go Through Can't Be Told"

Private Histories, Public Voices, and the Woman Question

Speaking before the Congressional Committee on Privileges and Elections in January 1876, the Unitarian reverend Olympia Brown emphasized her role as a representative female voice. Responding to male attempts to marginalize the suffragists, to the fact "that men are continually saying to us that we do not want the ballot; that it is only a handful of women that have ever asked for it," Brown countered that she spoke for "a general demand from the women in all the different States of the Union." Brown constructed herself not as these women's leader, nor even as their spokeswoman, but rather as simply a vessel for their voices, "bear[ing] testimony from the State of Connecticut" for "the women from the rank and file." And belying her own role as minister and public advocate, she further unified herself and those rank-and-file women by portraying their voices and goals as thoroughly private: they came "here with stammering tongues," as "the rank and file of the women of our country unaccustomed to such proceedings as these"; and they desired only "the province of voters . . . to stay at home and quietly read the proceedings of members of congress."[1] Such portrayals, like the claims of broad representation, were partly rhetorical strategies designed to sway Brown's unquestionably doubting and conservative audience, but they nonetheless provided particular and interconnected constructions of women's monologic voices, private experiences, and unified stance on suffrage.[2]

One might expect to find similarly unified depictions of women's

voices and histories in the weekly newspaper *The Woman's Journal,*
described on its masthead as "devoted to the interests of woman, to
her educational, industrial, legal and political equality, and especially
to her right of suffrage." Certainly the paper, and particularly the editorials of founders such as Lucy Stone and William Lloyd Garrison, did
often provide unified positions on those women's issues. But the *Journal's* literary contributions were more dialogic and multivalent, as exemplified by O. A. Cheney's short dramatic work "The Female Debating Society" (1876). In that text, four women and one man debate the
question "Is it just to withhold the ballot from women?" Unsurpris-
ingly, the man, Mr. Barker, embodies conservative chauvinism, while
two of the four women (Mrs. Barker and Miss Susan Snap) illustrate
impassioned suffragism. But as their names suggest, the Barkers and
Miss Snap are all similarly aggressive and quick to pass judgment; the
more sympathetic and rational voices belong to the two principal de-
baters, Miss Alice Winthrop on the affirmative and Mrs. Mary Lowell
on the negative. In an explicit critique of unproductive forms of debate, Mrs. Barker's and Miss Snap's interruptions meet with the disapproval of the Society's even-handed president, Mrs. Snow; Winthrop
and Lowell, however, maintain their respective positions but do so only
after fully and generously engaging with the other side's. "I have been
interested in listening to the arguments on the question," Mrs. Lowell
notes, and through that mutual interest, and the conversation which
it allows, Cheney's play includes and models productive women's dialogues in a setting quite removed from the privacy of the home (146).

In an attempt to make their voices heard at the national level, many
suffragists and women's rights activists constructed themselves as did
Brown: as spokeswomen for a unified, monolithic female constituency.
Their monologic emphasis is, as a political strategy through which to
change long-standing social realities and counter-entrenched opposition,
perfectly understandable. The period's public women had no shortage
of social issues on which to focus; suffrage was the top priority, but activists likewise emphasized marriage laws and customs, property rights,
workplace opportunities and difficulties, religious roles, and many other
issues.[3] But whatever the political motivations behind their univocal
narratives, they could not capture the variety of voices and viewpoints
included in debates over the woman question; a limitation that links the

reformers' narratives to the period's equally monologic progressive narrative. Such multivocal debates took place not only between women and men or conservatives and radicals but also within the suffrage movement (over issues such as race and temperance) and between reformers and women who articulated alternative visions of women's histories and goals (as evidenced by the Centennial Exposition's split between the Women's Pavilion organizers and the suffragist protesters).[4] Women who preferred to be more private likewise debated the woman question in their own minds and with each other, as both Cheney's play and the growing body of scholarship on the era's clubs and reading groups nicely demonstrate.[5]

Literary texts, whether written by radical women, conservative men, or any combination of gender and ideology in between, reduce even less easily to simple male-female or political binaries; such reductions elide the complex interplay of voices which constitute those texts. For example, reconsiderations of regionalist writing as an alternative, more female-friendly mode, while understandable in light of a century of belittling readings of the genre, nonetheless often construct regionalism in terms as monologic as those of its critics.[6] Nevertheless, more dialogic scholarship on nineteenth-century literature by women and on the woman question has often focused on voice's many formal and thematic meanings.[7] Voice itself can of course be forced into an overly dichotomized and politicized critical paradigm; discussions of "female voice" as if it were an easily identifiable, thoroughly distinct, and unequivocally positive category fall into this trap.[8] But close attention to individual texts' constructions of voice, alongside their similarly multifaceted constructions of history and the public/private duality, allows for an appropriately dialogic analysis of those texts and their visions of the woman question.

In Elizabeth Stuart Phelps's *The Story of Avis* the sympathetic narrative voice establishes, through both its heroine's struggles to find her artistic voice and its inclusions of other women's voices, the decade's principal dialogues: between women's private histories and public and professional aspirations; silence and voice; individualism and community; the relationships between women and men. Regionalist short stories such as Rose Terry Cooke's "Mrs. Flint's Married Experience" and Mary E. Wilkins Freeman's "On the Walpole Road," while not as cir-

cumscribed as has been argued, do focus on thoroughly private women's experiences, voices, and relationships, as observed by their distanced
narrators. However, Sarah Orne Jewett, the most enduring regionalist,
creates in *A Country Doctor* a woman whose public goals and powerful
voice, developed in the context of two competing visions of setting and
tradition, allow her to stretch her region's possibilities. Both Constance
Fenimore Woolson's "Miss Grief" and Henry James's *The Bostonians*
focus on women attempting, less successfully than Jewett's heroine, to
move into the world of public speech: Woolson's traditional male narrator cannot comprehend her tragic author-protagonist's history and voice;
while James's ambivalent narrator depicts a fierce discursive battle over
its central female's history, voice, and future. Finally, Frances Ellen Watkins Harper's and Sarah Piatt's poems provide unique formal encapsulations of the decade's dialogic debates over private histories, public
voices, and the woman question.

Phelps's *The Story of Avis* (1877), with its tragic narrative of the gifted
female artist Avis Dobell's unhappy and self-destructive marriage, has
long been read as one of the nineteenth century's most overtly feminist
novels. In one of the text's first reviews, the *New York Times* noted that
"indirectly the story is a partisan defense of women's rights," and prominent suffragist Lucy Stone argued in the *Woman's Journal* shortly thereafter that in fact the novel directly "raises the question more and more
asked by women, whether marriage, in the case of a woman, is compatible with the pursuit of other strong ruling tastes." Reviewers of distinct political persuasions naturally differed on this marital thesis' potential social effects, with the conservative *Philadelphia Inquirer* calling
it "a dangerous lesson to preach, and no less dangerous than untrue,"
and the more liberal *Woman's Journal* praising the novel's ability to "lead
a great many women for the first time to consider seriously their duties
and responsibilities." But however they depicted the text's social effects,
many reviewers shared a sense that its political emphasis had resulted
in literary shortcomings: the *Times* argued that, while the novel's radicalism might not result in social harm, "as a literary work—if any one
should regard it in that light—the harm would be undoubted" (2); *Times*
reviews of subsequent and in their opinion more aesthetically effective
Phelps works recalled with disdain "the phase represented by *The Story*

of Avis" and its "exaggerated vein"; and even the *Woman's Journal* admitted that *Avis* "is not likely to outlive a single generation."[9]

Twentieth-century scholars, many approaching the novel from an explicitly feminist perspective, have reiterated the focus on its radical gender politics and depiction of marriage. Susan Harris's description of the novel as "protest literature," as one of the most exemplary "portraits of power relationships from the point of view of the subordinate member" (*American* 207), emblematizes much *Avis* scholarship (both positive and negative).[10] And if critics have been less dismissive of the novel's literary merits than its contemporary reviewers, they have in one important way likewise minimized those merits in comparison with its politics: the glut of readings within a "protofeminist tradition," to use Lisa Long's term ("Heaven" 805), has led Long and other Phelps scholars to focus on other texts, in part because those works seem better able to support multifaceted, literary analyses.[11] Susan Donaldson rereads the novel's literary form and value impressively, but interestingly does so by connecting those elements to gender politics; Donaldson argues that *Avis* exemplifies the "deeply contested and heterogeneous nature of American literary realism and the close association of realistic discourse with hard-hitting critiques of conventions and abstract types in general and romance in particular, but also with the remaking of representations of masculinity and femininity—and by implication gender roles themselves"(107–8). This argument certainly reverses the tendency to move away from *Avis* in search of literary complexity, but still locates gender politics at the heart of any interpretation of the text.

While Avis unquestionably, powerfully, and politically depicts both an independent female artist and the negative effects of her bad marriage, I argue that it is even more noteworthy for its greatest literary success: the breadth and depth of its portrayal of women's histories and voices, its narrator's ability to introduce and maintain multivocal, heterogeneous, and often deeply contested dialogues over its central issues without losing sympathy for its titular heroine. Indeed, the implicit and explicit debates between its many female characters (and, occasionally, its male ones) over women's private and communal histories, silences and voices, and marital relationships reflect the developing and multivalent internal dialogue within Avis's own consciousness. The text's dialogues thus crucially shape its portrayals of both Avis specifi-

cally and women's issues generally, and, far from resolving into the binary political positions (or reversals of established such positions, as in
Donaldson) that prior criticism might imply, those dialogues remain
very much alive and ongoing at the novel's end.

Two distinct yet intertwined conceptions of women's dialogues are
presented in two particularly significant scenes. In one, the conversation between Avis and Susan Jessup (Wanamaker), her husband Philip's
former fiancée, such dialogue seems to be an ideal but impossible
goal. Susan, confronted with one of the period's most blatant gender
distinctions—her husband wants to move to Texas, and "the law compels
[her] to go with him, as if [she] were a horse or a cow"—visits Avis in
an effort to create female solidarity by admitting her prior relationship
with Philip. And despite the scene's centrality to the marriage plot—it
marks Avis's first strong reason to doubt her husband's character—it illustrates even more importantly these female voices' failures to articulate successfully either private history or communal identity. Susan's extended personal narrative notwithstanding, the novel focuses on Avis's
inability to articulate her responses: "her words went clumsily"; "She
tried to speak; but words looked distant and small, too small to be gath-
ered up"; "Some expression of sympathy hung confusedly upon Mrs. Os-
trander's lips; but she was not sure if she uttered it." Just as Avis remains
mostly unable to voice that sympathy, Susan's private memories deafen
her to what Avis can say: she simply "disregard[s] Avis' words, as if the
force of her own reflection [has] deadened her power of hearing." And
because of this complete lack of communication, Susan's voice, her reflection on her private history, likewise remains as silenced as it has always been: she begins by noting that she "never told it before," and despite her narrative concludes with the lament, "That's the worst of being
a woman. What you go through can't be told" (161–64).[12] A woman's private history, the scene suggests, is forever unfit for public airing, and
without such an airing no individual woman can share herself or her
voice with any larger female community. Moreover, just as Susan's new
husband causes her physical relocation, her old lover (Avis's new husband) contributes to this displacement between history and voice: Susan
has come to speak of Philip's place in her past, but his implicit presence
prevents her from truly communicating. And Philip, upon learning of
the conversation, demands even more thorough silence, complaining,

"in a deep, displeased voice," that Avis "discussed such a matter with a strange woman" (165).[13]

The scene's divisions between private and communal, history and voice, women and men, are prominent in all of the novel's dialogues; they are not, however, always depicted as so permanently separated. In fact, the second significant (and the text's most famous) scene, Avis's dream-vision of her artistic purpose, constructs an alternative account of these dialogic concerns in which they can be unified through and transcended by a new kind of aesthetic female voice. Suffering from "paralyzed inspiration" because of the Civil War's ongoing horrors—"Who could make a picture till the war was over?" she wonders—Avis retreats to her bedroom, "the dumb artist court[ing] the miracle of speech." While such a retreat might seem an evasion of the war and the outside world, the narrator constructs it instead as a unique and revelatory experience: "neither Raphael nor Titian could have taught her what she learned in one such self-articulate hour as this." The references to artists emblematic of a largely masculine tradition are pointed, since what Avis learns comprises a particularly feminine vision of history and artistic purpose. Seeing a room "full of women," historical personages from "Cleopatra . . . and Godiva" to "Jeanne d'Arc, and the Magdalene," Avis at first cannot imagine how to convert this female tradition into aesthetics: "these figures passed on, and vanished in an expanse of imperfectly-defined color like a cloud, which for some moments she found without form and void to her." Yet in her vision's climax she finds a form, a way to unify art and tradition, aesthetics and voice: "In the foreground the sphinx, the great sphinx, restored. The mutilated face patiently took on the forms and the hues of life; the wide eyes met her own; the dumb lips parted; the solemn brow unbent. The riddle of ages whispered to her. The mystery of womanhood stood before her, and said, 'Speak for me.' . . . she had seen her picture. To-morrow she could work." In this vision of her artistic work, Avis perceives a way to cross the gaps over which Susan laments. What women go through can be told; the silent, solitary, private histories can be made public and communal, given voice in her art (78–83).[14]

Shortly after the dream's completion, however, Avis has another, briefer "vision of battles" (83); and indeed rhetorical battles, debates between Susan's private, isolated, silent perspective, the dream's public, communal, voiced one, and many in between, dominate the novel's constructions of both its heroine's evolving consciousness and the woman question. The two aforementioned perspectives differ most obviously in their gender emphases—male abandonment and power cause Susan's private miseries, while female-only community produces Avis's public purpose—and it is easy to view the ongoing debates as thoroughly gendered. After all, the clearest antagonism to Avis's artistic goals and voice comes from Philip, a man consistently associated, from his initial appearance reading a literary passage in a "singularly musical voice" (5), with his powerful voice. His courtship of Avis constitutes a series of combative conversations, in which she voices liberated views of marriage ("I will never yield, like other women!" [67]) and her future ("I have different plans: at least I have different hopes" [59]), only to be overcome by "his penetrative undertone" (57). "He usually got what he sought in that reverberating tone," the narrator notes (109), and indeed he wins from Avis admissions of private, unvoiced, more traditionally feminine emotions: "I never said this before," she admits, "with the rapid, incisive utterance of one who is expressing what is so long familiar, and so long suppressed" (106). Having achieved this rhetorical victory, Philip marries Avis, an event explicitly opposed to her artistic goals: on their wedding day, Philip asks her, "what would you do if you had to choose now between us—the sphinx and me?" (127). Although Avis promises the Sphinx that she will "be true" to it and her artistic calling (117), throughout their largely unhappy marriage she time and again neglects her work for Philip and their children; particularly demanding of her attention is their son Van, who consistently functions as an extension of his father's masculine voice and will: "The child's voice and his father's chimed together oddly. . . . these two intensely wrought male personalities" (175).

Given all this, it is no surprise that so many critics analyze the novel as a proto-feminist tract on the dangers for women, particularly those with artistic talent and ambitions, of a male-dominated marriage system. However, to read its debates over the woman question through only that lens requires the elision, or at least confining to the role of unhappy wife, of a significant set of voices: *Avis*'s other women. Like Susan Jessup, each of these women, however brief her appearance in the novel, represents a distinct perspective that adds another layer to the dialogue and to Avis's own views. If Susan, one alternative wife for Philip, illustrates, in her tragic acceptance of privacy, isolation, and silence, one type of opposition to Avis's vision, then Barbara Allen, a second alternative spouse, exemplifies another contrasting position. At each moment in which she tempts Philip, Barbara is defined through her purposeful use of silence: unlike Philip's conversational courtship of Avis, his flirtation with Barbara consists largely of gazes, of which Barbara thinks "why spoil an innocent pleasure by talking?" (94); when discovered by Avis in a compromising position with Philip, Barbara remains silent, rejecting any possibility of dialogue (185–86); and after Philip and Barbara suffer a nautical misadventure, the narrator explicitly differentiates Barbara's desires for silence and privacy from Avis's public goals, noting that "Barbara could think of nothing worse than to be talked about" (196). Barbara pursues the same privacy, isolation, and silence of which Susan despairs, and the narrator generally treats Barbara's traditional desires, antagonistic as they are to her heroine's priorities and marriage, with understanding if not sympathy.[15] And the gap between Barbara's departing perspective (she "thought that she should marry a minister" [196]) and her fate (Coy wryly reports that she "had not married a minister, but only a New-York businessman; it was a trial for a Harmouth girl, but Barbara bore it well" [248]) highlights another story of women's marital and life experiences, one not quite included in *Avis* yet part of its multivocal canvas nonetheless.

In between the extremes provided by Susan, Barbara, and Avis, the novel identifies many other female voices and viewpoints. A rather cliché figure, common to the period's regionalist literature, which *Avis* both exploits and subverts is the New England widow. Avis briefly encounters one such widow in Philip's mother, symbolically named Waitstill and described by Avis as the "poor, plain, old mother," waiting for her son in her "poor, narrow, solitary home" (144). Those phrases define Waitstill entirely through the cliché, but underneath her plain, narrow façade and life, the narrator hints, exist both a meaningful history into which "her mind seem[s] to slip and wander" and a unique voice that she can find with "some effort of speech" (145). Yet her history and voice remain inaccessible by dialogue, as the final, sympathetic but silent exchange between Avis and Waitstill illustrates: "like spirits," the two meet "each other's eyes, and neither [speaks]" (146).[16] Similarly multifaceted but more vocalized is the novel's paramount version of this cliché, Avis's

Aunt Chloe. The narrator introduces Chloe as "a homeless widow, of excellent Vermont intentions, and high ideals in cupcake," a woman who
"in the course of a severe and simple life ... had known one passion,
and one only—the refined passion for flowers" (26). The description's
humor illustrates Chloe's principal role, as her domestic priorities and
traditional views consistently conflict with Avis.' Yet this humorous caricature does not thoroughly circumscribe Chloe's voice; in a brief but
telling moment, the newly engaged Avis asks Chloe if there is "nothing
that [she] ever wanted to be," and while Chloe's prize geraniums seem
to reply "we will never tell," Chloe herself admits, "in a subdued voice,"
that if she could "begin life over, and choose for [her] own selfish pleasure," she would have liked to be "a florist ... or a botanist." She "utter[s]
these words under her breath, as she might have some beautiful heresy"
(114–15), and returns to her private flowers and silence, but the moment
complicates any image of Chloe as simply Avis's traditional, humorous
foil. As with Waitstill, there clearly exists a complex history here, but one
that cannot quite be given shared, public voice, and these widows thus
provide counterpoints to Avis's artistic desire to speak for all women.
Both women could be read simply as further exemplifying marriage's
damaging effects, but that would conflate into a political type women
whose voices and histories, while linked to Avis's through their encounters with her, are unique to each.

Likewise unique, and placing Avis in a different familial context,
is the legacy of her mother's history and voice. At age nineteen, her
mother, also named Avis, left New York and a promising dramatic career to marry a thirty-five-year-old college professor. This marriage, the
narrator stresses, in no way foreshadowed Avis's and Philip's unhappiness; indeed, Avis's parents shared "a great love," one that made an
"Eden" of their "old-fashioned house" (23). But idyllic or no, the Do-
bells' house was old-fashioned, and her mother devoted her time to husband, daughter, and home, at the explicit expense of her "histrionic gift"
(25). Having abandoned a public career and voice for this traditional
role, Avis's mother adopted a silence of her own, one that the narrator describes quite differently from the doomed, desired, or domestic silences of Susan, Barbara, and Chloe. There was something "bird-like"
about the "certain reserve that was very marked in her," a "concealment"
which, like the robin's seemingly "exuberant frankness," is "the most im-

penetrable disguise in the world." As to what this silence concealed, "you may find out if you can" (23). Her mother, then, became a voluntary embodiment of the Sphinx, the mystery of woman, apparently happy in her choice of a private history but concealing in silence the depths of her true identity and voice. When her mother died before Avis's tenth birthday, the answer to her riddle died with her, and in this light Avis's artistic ambition becomes not only an aesthetic goal and communal female vision but also an attempt to "speak for" her namesake and the mysteries her silence had concealed.

The silence and mystery that result from Mrs. Dobell's death also open a space in the novel's dialogues and its heroine's consciousness for one of its few well-developed male voices: Mr. Dobell's. Avis acknowledges that voice's value when she asks her father to speak for her absent mother, wondering if, "in all those years, shut up in this quiet house, she ever knew a restless longing." In answer her father can only fall back, accurately but narrowly, on the traditions of marriage, replying, "Your mother was my wife . . . and my wife loved me" (25). His early responses to Avis's artistic desires seem similarly traditional and averse to dialogue; he calls her goals "nonsense," argues that he "can't have [her] filling [her] head with any of these womanish apings of a man's affairs," and orders her to "fret no more about 'being' this or that," since her "business at present is to 'be' a studious and womanly girl" (33–34). Yet Mr. Dobell is more multifaceted than these statements indicate; he has, the narrator notes, "a vein of broad tolerance in [his] sturdy nature" (28), and his decision to send Avis to Italy for further aesthetic education illustrates how their dialogues allow him to mine that vein, to shift his perspective in response to hers. Moreover, in articulating that decision he links both Avis and himself to her bird-like mother: "It is the custom, in the training of carrier-doves, to let them all loose from their places of confinement into the upper air . . . I let you go, my dear daughter, not without misgivings; but omnipotent Nature is wiser than I. I should be duller than the dullest bird among them all, if I could not trust you at her hands" (35). So this male perspective, which directly caused and still defends Mrs. Dobell's confinement, also helps the young Avis find her own wings. And his traditional but tolerant voice—one distinct from Philip's in its openness to female voices, which explains Mr. Dobell's wish that his wife, "a woman of rare penetration into human character," had lived to meet and articulate her perspective on Philip (115)—adds another multivocal layer to both Avis's mindset and the novel's dialogues. Taken together, Avis's parents illustrate that the voices of a woman's personal history are at once past and present, constant and changeable; and their joint influence on her development defies any simple separation into male-female or conservative-radical dichotomies.

Perhaps the novel's most complex perspective, and one that also combines tradition and subversion, is expressed by the female voice with which the text opens: Avis's childhood friend Coy Bishop. In many ways Coy is Avis without the public ambitions or voice; they marry and have children at around the same times, but Coy lives an apparently happy life in the same roles that stifle Avis's artistic impulses. Yet the opening pages, in which Coy observes Avis at a literary reading and contemplates the question, "What was it about her?" indicate that their relationship is more intricate than such plot details might suggest. Numerous statements in these pages highlight the women's differences in temperament and intelligence: Coy does not "wonder . . . very often," "being a blonde, with a small mouth and happy eyes"; "she [leaves] ideas to Avis"; she has "never been conscious of any depressing aspirations toward the college diploma"; and she calls Avis's typical mood "morbidness," with "the glibness of most unaccentuated natures in the use of this convenient word." Yet complicating such statements is the fact that the narrator has ceded this scene's point of view to Coy, lending the descriptions of her a degree of, frankly, coy self-consciousness. Moreover, given the depth and intelligence of the characterization of Avis provided by Coy's perspective here, it seems that Coy's mind and voice differ from Avis's not in their quality, but rather in their public articulation. The narrator prefaces one such characterization by calling it what "Coy would have said if she could," but clearly she could and in fact does say it, just not aloud (3–8). The difference between Coy and Avis, then, relates more to the dialogic of private and public, to the arena in which each woman feels most comfortable articulating her perspective, than to any fundamental distinctions in their natures.[17]

It is the question of women's natures, experiences, and voices on which the final encounter between Coy and Avis focuses. Avis, having lost her son, husband, and, apparently, ability or willingness to paint ("my style is gone . . . the stiffness runs deeper than the fingers" [244]), visits Coy, whose stability and happiness once again directly contrast Avis's experiences. But their dialogue, focused explicitly on their respective fates and implicitly on what these fates reveal about themselves and all women, exemplifies the complexity of both women's voices, and of the narrator's voice in its depiction of them:

> "You seem to keep pretty well," said Avis, after a silence . . . The words sounded superficial enough. Coy felt that Avis would rather be taken on her own level, and answered carelessly—
>
> "Pretty well, Avis. . . . I'll tell you—I never told it before . . . there is one thing I must admit: I do *not* like to ask John for money. There! But that is all, Avis."
>
> Was it all, indeed! It was a peaceful, pleasant story. . . . A spark sprang into Coy's incurious, gentle face.
>
> "It is nature!" she cried. "Explain it how you will."
>
> "But I," said Avis in a low voice, after an expressive pause, "*I* am nature too. Explain me, Coy."
>
> Coy did not answer. It was to be expected that Avis should be more or less unintelligible. (249)

Within these few lines, the narrator's voice and point of view mingle almost imperceptibly with the women's, producing an exchange as mysterious as it is multivocal. Where do the narrator's remarks end and the characters' free indirect speeches begin?[18] Who believes that Avis's words sound superficial? Who designates Coy's story pleasant and her face incurious? What do any of those adjectives connote? What does Avis's pause express, and are it and her low voice more or less unintelligible? To answer these questions would entail parsing out the three distinct perspectives, breaking the dialogue into identifiable monologues in a manner counterproductive to the scene's intentional intermingling. That is, I believe the scene's formal elements and effects make the answers, like the ostensible subject of women's natures, less important than the questions' continued presence, even here in the text's concluding pages, as dialogic aspects of women's histories and voices that can neither be silenced nor reduced to a single unifying perspective and that constitute crucial factors in each development of consciousness.

As the novel's final exchange illustrates, each consciousness can likewise influence future women's voices and perspectives. That exchange takes place between Avis and her daughter, Waitstill, whose name indicates not only her link to the future but also the continuing presence of the past; Wait connects to her namesake, Philip's silent mother, as Avis does her own mother and her quite different silence. The exchange in fact begins with a silence, with Avis and Wait "at home . . . more silently, perhaps, than usual." But Wait articulates, in her "distinct, impressive" voice, a vision of female community that can only be achieved through dialogue: " 'Mamma, I cannot read this story till I am old enough; but it is a pretty story, and I want to hear it. . . . read me—read me—read me till there is no more to read' " (249). Critics have made much of the Arthurian legend which Avis reads, noting the Grail quest's symbolic equivalents for both Avis and her daughter.[19] But just as significant in this final exchange, as with that between Coy and Avis, is the continued emphasis on women talking to one another, sharing, in both present and future (for there will always be "more to read"), their voices and the distinct perspectives and histories that lie behind them. It is in these multivocal dialogues about privacy and publicity, isolation and community, silence and voice, women and men, all moderated by the broadly sympathetic narrator's voice and all influencing the heroine's voice and perspective, that *The Story of Avis* best anticipates the decade's complex literary debates over the woman question.[20]

At *Avis*'s end, its heroine has invested in her daughter her hopes for women's future artistic success; that success might be slow in coming, as Waitstill's name implies, but it will also be significantly public and prominent.[21] Yet the literary genre in which female (as well as many male) writers achieved the next decade's greatest successes, regionalism (known then as local color), emphasized ordinary women's private histories and voices, not feminist artists' public ambitions. This emphasis, along with each writer's narrow geographic focus, led scholars for many years to dismiss regionalists such as Rose Terry Cooke and Mary E. Wilkins Freeman as similarly limited in theme and achievement, as, in Ann Douglas Wood's famous critique, sounding only a "note of attenuation, even impoverishment" (16). Some recent advocates of regionalism have swung the pendulum to the other extreme, arguing that regionalist writers constituted a subversive and vital alternative literary mode, what Josephine Donovan designates the "counter-tradition" of "woman-identified realism" (*New England* 2–3). But as these critical poles suggest, women's regionalist writing is best described as participating in the period's dialogues over the woman question, if from a particularly focused position. Short stories such as Cooke's "Mrs. Flint's Married Experience" (1880) and Freeman's "On the Walpole Road" (1886) are confined to depictions, in a somewhat detached narrative voice, of private, nearly silenced female histories; but they also hint at the possibilities for shared (and thus public) communication and the opportunities for change that can arise from such dialogues.

"Mrs. Flint's Married Experience" begins with the title character, currently known as "the Widow Gold," attempting to tell her daughter, Mindwell Pratt, about one of her life's most important events: the experience of losing a husband.[22] "Attempting" is the key word, however, for both the Widow and the narrator emphasize communication's limits: the Widow notes the contingencies of private history, admitting to Mindwell that "You can't never tell what it is to lose a companion till you exper'ence it"; while the narrator describes Mindwell as unable to respond adequately to her mother's narration, possessing "a reticence that forbade her to express sympathy, even with her mother's sorrow" (93). This shared lack of communicative female voice, moreover, is crucial to the story's plot and themes: both Deacon Flint's successful courtship of the Widow and her subsequent, deeply unhappy married experience (concisely foreshadowed in her name change, from Gold to Flint) depend upon the women's inability to articulate effectively any aspect of their experiences and views, particularly when contrasted with the Deacon's thorough dependence upon and mastery of words.

The Deacon's vocal power over the Widow is established throughout the courtship, and exemplified by his drawing up of a one-sided, abusive marriage contract. Quoting Scripture to defend his manipulations, the Deacon leaves the Widow "bewildered with the plausible phrases ballasted by a text" (104). The distinction between the two characters, the narrator argues in a detached voice that explicitly favors neither, is one of temperament as well as literacy: the Deacon is all talk, a "professor of religion" in whose spirituality Mindwell's husband "b'lieve[s] . . . jest so far forth as [he] hear[s] him talk, an' not an inch farther" (108); while the Widow, "like many another weak woman, . . . hate[s] words, particularly hard words" (104). Yet if the Widow is literally unable to voice either a reply to the Deacon or her prenuptial reservations, and thus forced into "concealing from her children the contract she [is] about to make" (105), Mindwell's silence on the matter is more a matter of choice. Although Mindwell tells her mother that she "don't skerce known how to speak about it," the narrator portrays her "habitual silence" as a conscious decision, and one with drastic negative effects; it "actually help[s], rather than hinder[s], this unpropitious marriage," whereas "a little more simple honesty of speech would have prevented it" (100–102). As the narrator's use of "unpropitious" here indicates, her detachment should not be equated with a lack of judgment on characters and events; rather it could be described as equanimity, since, in depicting the women's lack of communication, she judges them just as harshly as she does the Deacon's manipulative words.

Unfortunately for the Widow, this lack of communication, dictated by temperament on one side and choice on the other, continues to her wedding day and beyond. The narrator speculates at length on the Widow's bridal mindset, dispassionately but accurately highlighting the marriage's disproportionate benefits for the Deacon, but concludes by tersely noting that "The Widow Gold [the last time that name applies] did not tell" (106). Mindwell likewise does not allow any objections to be voiced: her husband, Sam, upon reading the marriage contract, begins to protest, but "Mindwell's touch on his arm arrest[s] the sentence," and he departs, "the half-finished sentence on his lips" (107). And when the Widow's granddaughters pay the newlyweds a visit and return with an extremely disturbing report on the Deacon's behavior toward his new wife, producing "tears in [Mindwell's] voice," she nonetheless quells those tears and remarks that "it isn't best to talk about a good many things that are true" (113–14). This emphasis on enforced silence, even on truths which cry out for comment, seems unnecessary and even cruel, but again, the narrator suggests that there is simply something in the private, isolated, traditional nature of a woman like the Widow (something apparently passed down to her otherwise modern daughter) that produces this preference for silence.[23]

Even the Widow's silence has its limits, however, and when she falls ill and the Deacon continues to mistreat her, she finally speaks out, claiming that she "b'lieve[s] [he'd] a sight rather [she] die than live" and then "pour[ing] out the long list of her sorrows into" the "faithful ear" of a female neighbor (118). Having found a way to voice her painful private experiences, the Widow is able to leave the Deacon, and for once it is he whose words fail: "for very shame's sake, [he] did not speak of her—for what could he say?" (119). Yet after taking this first step toward finding her voice, the Widow is confronted by the dominant public discourse of the story's Puritan-era setting: the discourse of the church. Within that language, the Deacon's voice possesses great power and authenticity, and the Widow and her supporters (particularly Mabel Eldridge, a "spirited" girl who has worked as a servant for the Flints and is far more willing than Mindwell to speak out [115]) are not very successful in their efforts to oppose him. The Widow is allowed to make a confession before the church elders, achieving a public but particularly limited voice: she admits that she "said and did things which under other Circumstances [she] should not have said or done" and expresses her willingness to "return to [her] Husband" (129). Fortunately, she does not get the chance to do so, although her escape is provided by the unfortunate and permanently silencing fact that she dies shortly after her confession.

For the most part, then, "Mrs. Flint's Married Experience" depicts a society in which its traditional heroine's private history, unvoiced and incommunicable, comprises her submissions to and destruction by the public and powerful voices of men like the Deacon. While younger, more liberated women like Mindwell and Mabel, along with more sympathetic men like Sam, seem unlikely to perpetuate such negative histories, they are likewise silenced, whether by choice (Mindwell) or powerlessness (Mabel). And even the narrator, while clearly aware of her story's silences and injustices, portrays them as both inevitable and historically distant, circumscribing any possibility of an alternative vision. However, there is an additional voice which occasionally surfaces in the text, a public voice that offers an unregulated, potentially subversive alternative to the church discourse. This voice, a sort of communal chorus, consists of Israel ("the village fool" and "the most independent man in Bassett, being regardless of public opinion" [97]) and Aunt Polly, the impoverished neighbor to whom the Widow finally articulates her painful history. While this earthy chorus, captured in a nearly impenetrable dialect, might be read as simply providing humorous glosses upon the story's action, it is without question the text's freest voice: Israel is described as being "free with the freedom of independent poverty to express pungently what he felt poignantly" (110), and in expressing their sympathetic, uncontrolled viewpoint, Israel and Polly illustrate that silent suffering and powerful pontificating are not the only options available in the story's society.[24]

While this alternative chorus appears only a few times in Cooke's text, a similar communal voice becomes the controlling viewpoint of Freeman's "On the Walpole Road." In fact, that text's communal, storytelling voice, shared between the elderly Miss Green and her young companion Almira, is at least as meaningful as the story which it tells, the tale of a forced, unhappy marriage and a deeply private woman slowly coming to articulate a partial voice. If that brief synopsis suggests a resemblance between Freeman's story within a story and Cooke's text, I believe the similarities are deliberate: Freeman's story about storytelling can be read as a response to Cooke's tale and others like it, and thus as something of a dialogic metatext about the limitations and possibilities of precisely the regionalist literary mode in which both Cooke and Freeman worked throughout their respective, lengthy careers.

"Walpole" begins by introducing, through dialogue, the theme of point of view, of the specificity and value of each individual perspective and voice. Judith Fetterley and Marjorie Pryse emphasize the opening descriptions of the two women, and particularly of Miss Green's "bristling chin," arguing that this conventionally unattractive detail locates these women outside societal conventions of beauty and marriage (155–57).[25] Yet while both women may well be single in the story's present (Miss Green, despite her title, is a widow; no reference is made to Almira's state), to link so explicitly the opening descriptions, the women's marital status, and the story's alternative vision is to impose a particular set of values upon a text that, at this early stage, seems decidedly neutral. This neutrality is best evidenced by the narrative voice, which describes the women and the Walpole Road in the same precise, observational tone. I would argue instead that the text first asserts its formal and thematic values when the women's dialogue begins, and particularly when Green advances an unorthodox position on "Gabriel's trumpet," about which she feels free to speak "as long as [Almira has] spoke of it." Almira responds "stoutly" to this freely expressed heresy by noting "That ain't accordin' to Scripture," to which Green replies,

> "It's accordin' to my Scripture. I tell you what 'tis, Almiry, I've found out one thing a-livin' so long, an' that is, thar ain't so much difference in things on this airth as thar is in the folks that see 'em. . . ."
>
> "You ought to ha' ben a minister, Mis' Green."
>
> "Wa'al, so I would ha' ben ef I had been a man." (28–29)

Despite her gender, Green indeed ministers to Almira at this moment, preaching her particular vision not just of Scripture, but also, and more importantly, of the centrality of vision itself. One's particular point of view, in Green's interpretation, defines both one's relationship to the world and one's identity, and as this passage (with its reliance on dialect to capture the sound of Green's and Almira's voices) exemplifies, one's point of view is always expressed in one's unique voice and in conversations with others who respond in their own voices and from their own points of view.[26]

Having established this construction of identity and community, point of view and voice, Green narrates the text's internal story. Because that story is told in a nonchronological fashion, it disrupts and reorients its audience's point of view: what seems to be a straightforward tale of a fortunate misunderstanding becomes instead a parable about the perils of silence. At first, Green's story centers on the time when she heard that her treasured Aunt Rebecca had died; heartbroken, she journeyed to Rebecca's home for the funeral, only to discover that Rebecca was alive and well and that her husband, Enos, had passed away. Only gradually, as Green reveals the forced nature of Rebecca's marriage to Enos (based on her mother's stubborn insistence) and preference for another local boy, Abner Lyons, does the symbolic resonance of Rebecca's reported death become apparent. And that resonance strengthens when Green recounts the one moment in which Rebecca articulated her own point of view on her future: at her wedding, when the minister asked if there were any obstacles, Rebecca "did speak up," saying that "thar' is an obstacle, an' I will speak, an' then I will forever hold my peace. I don't love this man I'm standin' beside of, an' I love another man" (36). Unfortunately, this voicing of her point of view dissuades neither her mother nor Enos from completing the wedding, and Rebecca is indeed forced to hold her peace, silenced—her voice, her point of view, and thus her identity, if not her physical body, killed—by an unwanted, unhappy marriage.

Of course silence does not necessarily entail death's permanence, and Green's story ends with a twist—once Enos dies, Rebecca is free to pursue her own vision of the future, marrying and spending her last few years with Abner. Green is careful not to depict this second marriage as an idealized antidote to Rebecca's first, noting that "sometimes [she] used to think [Rebecca and Abner] wa'n't so happy after all" and connecting this realization to another distinction between one's point of view and the dialogic realities of human relationships: "Aunt Rebecca didn't find anything just as she thought it was goin' to be" (39). But ideal ending or no, Rebecca has escaped both her reported death and her first marriage's forced silence, and Freeman's story concludes by suggesting this story of escape's potential value for both teller and hearer. At the outset of her tale, Green asked Almira if she had told her Rebecca's story before, and Almira replied that she "don't think [she] ever did" (30); but when the storytelling has concluded, Almira admits that, while she "liked to hear" Green, "it's kind of come to [her], as [she's] been listening, that [she] *had* heard it before . . . the last time [she] took [Green] to Walpole" (40). The juxtaposition of Almira's enjoyment of the tale with her acknowledgment of its repetition is crucial; there is something powerful enough in this story, and more exactly in the communal sharing of it, that makes it a sort of ritual, one that can and should be repeated. If the inefficacy of Rebecca's voice contributed directly to both her silencing and her symbolic brush with death, the strength of Green's storytelling voice, and the benefits of her communal mingling of her point of view with Almira's, make these women, by contrast, more deeply alive.[27]

If Cooke's story depicts the painful limitations of women's private histories and silenced voices, two of regionalism's principal subjects, Freeman's text indicates that the same world offers the potential for productive public—or at least communal—dialogue. Yet none of these fictional women, even the most liberated and outspoken (like Mabel or Green), resemble Phelps's Avis; none, that is, have aspirations to enter a larger world of truly public and professional voices. But those aspirations and that world—both central to the period's debates over the woman question—were not thoroughly foreign to the regionalist sensibility, as an early novel by the most enduring female regionalist, Sarah Orne Jewett, illustrates. Most Jewett scholarship focuses on her emblematically regionalist works, texts like *Deephaven* (1877), "A White Heron" (1886), and *The Country of the Pointed Firs* (1896); whether these critics seek to trace Jewett's limitations (as do Richard Brodhead and Michael Davitt Bell), advocate her strengths (Fetterley and Pryse and Josephine Donovan), or simply reread her work closely, they generally link her directly to scholarly debates over regionalism.[28] Through that lens, *A Country Doctor* (1884) becomes a relatively uninteresting anomaly, merely an excuse for "lectures from the author on the role of women in the professions" (Auchincloss 8–9).[29] But while *Doctor* is unquestionably Jewett's most overtly feminist work, particularly in its often didactic narrative commentary, she situates its portrayal of a strong, public female voice within a complex, dialogic setting where private history and communal tradition are both limiting and empowering.[30]

The atmospheric opening chapter, while tending toward melodrama, concisely establishes the limiting aspects of setting and tradition with which our heroine Nan Prince will have to contend. Nan's mother, carrying her infant daughter (a burden "too heavy for so slight a woman to carry"), wanders through "the dampness and increasing chill" of a dark November evening which foreshadows "the doom of winter." Both the burden of her young child and the gloom of the oncoming season explicitly point to a future too difficult for the woman to bear; but, as the remainder of the short chapter makes clear, it is really the past which both infuses the dark landscape and so oppresses her. She wanders first to a "brook, swollen by the autumn rains," which seems to be "crying out against a wrong or some sad memory"; she then finds herself near "an old burial place, a primitive spot enough," in which she senses a "legion of ghosts . . . chasing her and flocking around her and oppressing her from every side." And the connections between these natural or primitive settings and their ghostly legacies of a threatening past are highlighted when the woman "remember[s], one after another, the fearful stories she had known of that ancient neighborhood." The dark aspects of the woman's past, her history's sad memories, have become embodied in her setting's darkness, and this combination of tradition and environment is enough to silence the woman's voice, obliterate her identity, and sever her only connection to the future: in the chapter's final image, she collapses on her mother's doorstep, gives "one great sigh," and "[lies] still" while "the child [falls] from her grasp" (147–49).

With such an origin for both the novel and its heroine, it would stand to reason that Nan's relationship to her setting and history would be similarly negative, even destructive. And there are certainly indications in the descriptions of her early childhood—spent with her grandmother in the rural village of Oldfields, the place from which her mother attempted to escape and to which she reluctantly returned in that opening scene—that Nan has inherited these oppressive aspects of her mother's identity. An elderly neighbor complains that Nan "belongs with wild creatur's," as she has "just the same nature" (186), linking her with the primitive natural forces that threatened and eventually overwhelmed her mother. If she is indeed connected to those forces, it follows that Oldfields might hold the same destructive power over Nan that it apparently did over her mother. And Nan herself seems to recognize this rural setting's potential dangers: she dreams of an escape to the distant city where her aunt (her father's only known surviving relative) resides, "her imagination . . . apt to busy itself in inventing tales of her unknown aunt" (189).

Yet, as Bert Bender and Richard Adams argue, the novel's construction of inheritance is much more complex than such straightforward mother-daughter connections might indicate. If the young Nan bears these potential resemblances to her troubled and doomed mother, she exhibits more positive links with her father. Dr. Leslie, the kindly village physician who promises Nan's mother that he will look after the girl and takes her in after her grandmother's death, remarks upon Nan's interest in and propensity for medical work, noting that "her father studied medicine" and adding, "It is the most amazing thing how people inherit—" (187). Dr. Leslie does not finish the thought, but Jewett's narrator completes this vision of inheritance, noting of Nan, in one of the text's first didactic narrative passages, that "It seemed . . . as if she could do whatever she undertook, and as if she had a power which made her able to use and unite the best traits of her ancestors. . . . It might be said that the materials for a fine specimen of humanity accumulate through several generations, until a child appears who is the heir of all the family wit and attractiveness and common sense, just as one person may inherit the worldly wealth of his ancestry" (190). Adams connects this notion of concentrated inheritance to the late-nineteenth-century concept of the "epitome," "a method of forming an experience of historic transitions that binds the future to the past" (77); Bender links the novel to the recent theories of Darwinism, arguing that it is Nan's social fitness that produces her eventual success (97–103). While both are plausible historicist contexts for Jewett's construction of inheritance, most significant is her portrayal of the past as essentially dialogic, both "danger" and "promise" (Adams 69). Both the potential for silence and oppression exemplified by her mother and the opportunity for voice and profession provided by her father are inescapable parts of Nan's history, and the novel will explicitly situate her growth and development—its sole subject—within that dialogic framework.[31]

Even that description of her dialogic history, with mother on one side and father on the other, fails to capture the novel's complex construction of the past, and particularly the narrator's interweaving of multifaceted reflections on setting and gender into that construction. Despite the opening chapter's association of Oldfields with Nan's mother and her oppressive history, the village ultimately symbolizes the most productive kinds of traditions, those which contribute to Nan's strength of character, growth, and eventual professional success. In another didactic passage, the narrator reflects upon the nature of "an old-fashioned town like Oldfields," where "the old traditions survive in our instincts" (223). As the first-person pronoun suggests, there is a close relationship between the narrative voice and this setting's traditions, one mirrored in Nan's continuing ties to the village: even as she grows up, the townspeople note that "the young girl has clung with touching affection to the memory and association of her childhood," and that "the inherited attachment of generations seems to have been centered in her faithful heart" (247). And while Oldfields' positive traditions are, I will argue, finally brought back to Nan's maternal connections, they are also linked to the novel's most sympathetic male character, Dr. Leslie. Leslie has foregone opportunities for fame and fortune in the medical profession (symbolized by his friend Dr. Ferris) in favor of the titular role's limitations and comforts, serving in and of himself as an important tradition for Nan to connect with and emulate.

In opposition to Oldfields' productive traditions, Jewett sets the coastal city of Dunport, home once to Nan's father and still to her mysterious aunt, Anna Prince. Once again, setting and gender complicate the initial depiction of Nan's history; while it is apparently from her father that she inherits her initial inclination toward medicine, Dunport on the whole comes to represent a more limiting and oppressing kind of tradition. That representation is exemplified by Anna, described upon her first extended introduction as "a proud and stately woman of the old New England type: more colonial than American perhaps, and quite provincial in her traditions and prejudices" (273). As that description indicates, Anna is intimately connected to the past; she dwells in a house that "present[s] . . . nearly the same appearance" as it did in her grandmother's time (275) and within which one passer-by admits he "should be afraid of ghosts" (290). And the reference to ghosts, echoing the opening chapter's dark and oppressive past, indicates the particular kind of tradition to which Anna and Dunport are tied, one quite distinct from Oldfields'; while Dr. Leslie's traditionalism is a matter of choice, and one which limits neither his sympathy for Nan's progressiveness nor her ability to vocalize her ambitions, Anna is thoroughly defined and circumscribed by her traditions, and wishes the same for her niece.

Anna's tradition's limiting effects explicitly connect to voice, as exemplified by an extended discussion of Nan's professional ambitions and future. By this time the narrator has well established Anna's preference for privacy and silence, particularly on those aspects of her history which she cannot reconcile with her self-image: "she forbade, years before, any mention of her family troubles, and had lived on before the world as if they could be annihilated, and not only were not observable, but never had been" (298). She likewise prefers (in direct contrast to the talkative Dr. Leslie) to exert her influence on Nan silently, telling her only, "There are a great many things I hope you can understand, even if I have left them unsaid" (345). But Nan is not so easily swayed, and when she articulates her public, professional goals, Anna can no longer keep silent. She is supported in her opposition to women doctors by the even more traditional Mrs. Fraley, and together the two women argue strenuously for the value of tradition and privacy in women's lives, and the concurrent meaninglessness of the "plaudits of an ignorant public" (328).[32] Also taking that position is the novel's other principal male character and Nan's Dunport suitor, George Gerry, who both adds "his voice" to "the weaker ones in the parlor" and exemplifies, in his deeply traditional views and courtship of Nan, "the most powerful argument for their side of the debate" (330). While the didactic narrator easily counters this traditional position, contrasting for example Mrs. Fraley's domestic daughter's "life of bondage" with Nan's "freedom" (341),[33] Nan is not as willing to voice her opinions; the people of Dunport note that "the girl herself [is] disposed to talk very little about this singular fancy" (321), and Nan escapes the group discussion without engaging George on the topic.

If Dunport, with its emphases on tradition, privacy, and silence, does not provide a hospitable environment for Nan's progressiveness, public goals, and strong voice, the equally historical but more supportive Oldfields fully compensates. More exactly, and once again in complex contrast to the opening chapter, Nan's two most significant moments of voice, ambition, and growth directly link to her mother's death and legacy. The first such moment occurs the summer after her secondary school graduation, when she finds herself adrift, unsure of her future or her own mind. Wandering through the woods near a brook, Nan is "unconscious that she [has] been following her mother's footsteps, or that fate [has] again brought her here for a great decision" (252). While Anna desires only to forget the past's negative aspects, Nan has unknowingly duplicated her history's most painful element; and while Anna's amnesia, coupled with her narrow traditionalism, limit her voice and reinforce her private life, Nan's return to history allows her finally to articulate her public ambition: "Why should it not be a reality that she studied medicine?" (253). Having voiced this progressive desire, Nan has "the feeling of a reformer, a radical, and even of a political agitator," but the narrator adds that Nan has never been more traditional (in the positive, Oldfields, Dr. Leslie sense) than at this moment: "She seem[s] very old to herself, older than she ever [will] seem again" (258).[34]

This first moment of strong voice and ambition, however, does not fully decide Nan's future, for at this point she has not yet faced the perils and temptations of Dunport, Anna, and George. Once she has done so, and found herself unable (or, more precisely, unwilling) to articulate her public ambitions to George as forcefully as she had in Oldfields, the matter reaches a climax; as Dr. Leslie recognizes, this is "a critical time in the young girl's history," one that "either mean[s] a new direction of her life or an increased activity in the old one" (357). Although Nan does feel the pull of Dunport, George, and tradition, the narrator diffuses the tension by noting, in the text's most didactic (and least successful) passage, that "it counted nothing whether God had put this soul into a man's body or a woman's. He had known best, and He meant it to be the teller of new truth" (359). That truth, as the narrator constructs it, is that "the preservation of the race is no longer the only important question; the welfare of the individual will be considered more and more" (360–61). But as is the case throughout, Nan's own voice and experiences are more nuanced and effective tellers of the text's truths than the narrator, and in the final scene she returns once more to the site of her mother's weakness and her strength, revealing a final truth.[35]

This second and final repetition of the opening chapter is particularly symbolic since, the narrator stresses, it also takes place in November; now, however, that month is not the harbinger of winter's doom, but rather "an epitome of all the months of the year." Just as the temporal setting parallels but reverses the opening, so too has history's role shifted; no longer a dark, threatening presence which haunts one's life, it is now a rejuvenative force, as Nan discovers that "the old ties of affection and association [grow] stronger instead of weaker each year." Both shifts rely upon careful corrections of one's point of view: perceiving November for its own merits, rather than its relation to the dark months to come; envisioning one's connection to the past as a bond through which strength can flow, rather than as a chain that drags one down. Nan fully recognizes these transformations of setting and history, and "it seem[s] to her that she [has] brought all the success of the past and her hopes for the future to the dear old place that afternoon. Her early life [is] spreading itself out like a picture, and as she [thinks] it over and look[s] back from year to year, she [is] more than ever before surprised to see the connection of one thing with another." Having fully embraced the productive possibilities provided by Oldfields' setting and history, Nan again finds her strong, public voice and goals, saying, in the closing line, "O God . . . I thank thee for my future" (365–70).[36]

One criticism of Jewett's novel has been that it constructs its heroine as too unusual, too unique, to serve the socially productive role of spokeswoman for the period's ever-growing numbers of women with public, professional aspirations.[37] "She has a strange history, and is in a strange position," one of Nan's Oldfields friends remarks (233), but in fact her history and position were not nearly as strange in 1884 as they would have been even twenty years earlier. Neither were they atypical for the period's literature; not only were at least two other "woman doctor" novels published in the three years before Jewett's, but public and professional women of all kinds were increasingly common characters in the decade's literary works. However, such characters are not always as successful as Nan Prince, and as Constance Fenimore Woolson's "Miss Grief" (1880) and Henry James's *The Bostonians* (1886) illustrate, the failures—or at least the limitations—of such fictional professional women often intricately connect to dialogic debates over private and public, history and voice.

For much of the twentieth century, critical responses to Woolson focused on her famous relationship with James; from Leon Edel's dismissals of Woolson in his biography of James to Sharon Dean's and Cheryl Torsney's revisionist interpretations, the two writers' interactions and respective influences on each other's works dominated the first major treatments of Woolson.[38] This emphasis was only strengthened by the focus on the short story "Miss Grief," widely considered Woolson's masterpiece; that text's portrayal of a famous male writer's relationship with an older female writer has proven almost impossible to separate from Woolson's biography.[39] Thus, when recent critics reread Woolson, they usually do so, at least in part, by turning to other texts, reinforcing the circumscribed, biographical readings of "Grief."[40] But whatever the story's potential biographical resonances—Woolson wrote and published "Grief" before meeting James—it is more productively and revealingly analyzed on its own terms; for it provides, through Woolson's use of a male voice to narrate the tale of a female writer struggling to channel her powerful private voice into public, professional success, a unique depiction of the woman question's dialogic nature.[41]

The narrator's opening, highly self-conscious introduction illustrates his awareness of the interplay of private and public histories and identities intrinsic to the kind of public voice that comes with being a professional writer. "I find myself very well entertained in life," he notes, since, "I have all I wish in the way of society, and a deep, though of course carefully concealed, satisfaction in my own little fame; which fame I foster by a gentle system of noninterference. I know that I am spoken of as 'that quiet young fellow who writes those delightful little studies of society, you know'; and I live up to that definition" (248). This description of a writer's point of view and experiences comprises a series of complex mediations: concealing private satisfaction about public fame; fostering that fame through purposeful non-interference with the world's vision of one's self; and understanding how one is "spoken of" and carefully fitting one's actual (or performed?) identity to that public articulation. At each point, private, individual voice is and must be subsumed into the public voices which construct, maintain, and define a famous identity, an arrangement with which the narrator is in full and satisfied accord.

One reason for his happiness with this system of public definition is that, having established himself within it, the narrator can now participate as one of its defining voices. When he is continually visited by an unknown woman named (he believes) Miss Grief, the narrator falls comfortably into the role of public auditor and definer of this (to this point) private person: "My visitor should have a hearing," he decides, "but not much more: she had sacrificed her womanly claims by her persistent attacks upon my door" (250). The auditor here completely controls the possibility, terms, and length of any particular voice's performance; moreover, such dialogues are influenced not only by questions of private and public but also, and apparently most importantly, by gender. The latter issue requires an even more complex balancing act: this woman would not have received a hearing, and thus would not have been able to make her voice known, were it not for her aggressiveness, but in that aggressiveness she has apparently sacrificed femininity's more private aspects and caused the narrator to redefine her as a woman not worth much of a hearing. And that redefinition apparently extends to two of her most unique attributes, her voice and name: even after she tells the narrator that her name is Crief, he continues to refer to her as "Miss Grief," noting parenthetically that he "prefer[s] to call her so" (251).

When Miss Grief begins to speak at length, however, it becomes obvious that her voice is not one to be so easily defined and silenced. At first the narrator, while recognizing that voice's quality, continues to define and limit it: "Her voice," he admits, "was clear, low, and very sweet. . . . I was attracted by it, but repelled by her words" (252). Without quite saying so, the narrator attributes her voice's power to rather feminine qualities—its sweetness, its ability to attract—and concurrently dissociates those qualities from the content of her speech. But when that content becomes literary, giving the narrator no reason to be repelled by what Miss Grief says, he can focus more fully on the remarkable power with which she says it. It does not hurt that she is speaking words written by the narrator, but attributing his growing fascination with her voice only to writerly or male ego would oversimplify this moment's interactions of voice and text: "She began to repeat something of mine word for word, just as I had written it. On she went, and I—listened. I intended interrupting her after a moment, but I did not, because she was reciting so well, and also because I felt a desire gaining upon me to see what she would make of a certain conversation which I knew was coming. . . . So she went on, and presently reached the conversation: my two people began to talk. . . . Her very voice changed, and took, though always sweetly, the different tones required. . . . For she had understood me—understood me almost better than I had understood myself" (252). The narrator may be fond of the sound of his written voice, as it were, but he is willing to admit that he is equally—perhaps even more—fond of this woman's voice reading those words. And at least some of that fondness is due to her ability to move beyond the public definition and identity with which the narrator has become content; in reading his text, as he constructs this moment, she is also reading him, and her voice discovers a more private identity than even the narrator has perceived.

Yet such vocal mastery and insight, however effective and affecting they may be for her audience, do not constitute Miss Grief's identity and goals; she wishes instead to voice her own, equally powerful words. She is, the narrator learns to his initial "dismay," "an authoress," hopeful that the narrator's opinions and advocacy will help her make the long-sought move into the professional world of publication (253–54). And her hopes are justified, for the narrator's dismay does not survive his first reading of her manuscript, a drama which "thrill[s] [him] through and through more than once [with] its earnestness, passion, and power." While her speaking voice's aesthetic qualities most impressed the narrator, her written work, interestingly enough, strikes him as less successful in "the 'how'" than in "the 'what'"; its content contains "scattered rays of splendor" but its execution is full of "numerous and disfiguring . . . dark spots" (256). By the narrator's aesthetic standards, her written voice falls short of her speaking one; and Miss Grief might agree, for although she claims not to be "aware that there [are] any" faults in her work, she states that she "will not read it, but recite it." But if for Miss Grief the oral can supplement and strengthen the written, the narrator by contrast views the former as an impediment toward proper understanding of the latter, arguing that she will "recite it so well that we shall see only the good points, and what we have to concern ourselves with now is the bad ones" (258).

Unfortunately, this disagreement over the proper modes of literary performance foreshadows the broader receptions which Miss Grief's works receive. The narrator fulfills his promise to pass her works along to editor friends, but the responses are always the same: the texts' deficiencies "render [them] unavailable for publication," and "in fact, would 'bury [them] in ridicule' if brought before the public" (264). For these editors, as for the narrator himself, there is something in Miss Grief's aesthetics, something in her literary voice, not suitable for public display; perhaps they would feel differently if they heard her perform the works, but of course such individual, intimate vocalizing is not and cannot be part of the public dialogue into which literary texts enter upon mass publication. And once again, the narrator here implicitly connects voice and publicity to gender; he argues that Miss Grief's poems are not "evil," but "simply unrestrained, large, vast, like the skies or the wind," while his love interest, Isabel, who cannot "comprehend" the poems, is "bounded on all sides, like a violet in a garden bed. And [he] like[s] her so" (265). By opposing Miss Grief to Isabel—contrasting the objects of his literary and romantics affections—the narrator indicates that Miss Grief's voice and ambitions transcend limitation and yet, ironically, are unappealing to the broader, authoritative public world, and thus unfit for entrance into the professional venue of publication. And he also indicates that, ultimately, he too prefers the circumscribed woman.

The narrator may be, like Isabel, unable to comprehend the true power of Miss Grief's artistic voice, but he is unquestionably sensitive to her hopes and ambitions; that sensitivity drives not only his unsuccessful attempts to find a publisher, but also two important (if troubling) efforts he makes to link his voice with hers. First, his desire that her texts be "received" leads him to attempt secret revisions, believing that "the sieve of [his] own good taste . . . would serve for two." But again his literary taste clashes with Miss Grief's aesthetics, and he readily acknowledges that this effort "utterly fail[s]," that he cannot "succeed in completing anything that satisfie[s] [him], or that approache[s], in truth, Miss Grief's own work just as it" stands (264). The ease with which his publicly authorized voice identified and defined Miss Grief has faded in dialogue with her own strong, if more private, voice, but his resulting respect and appreciation for her cannot change the apparently impassable gap between her voice and the public world within which she wants it to succeed. All he can do for her, it turns out, is lie to ease the pain caused by that gap, which he does beside her deathbed in the story's climactic scene. In this second, more successful yet also more transient use of his voice for her purposes, the narrator, to support his lie that her drama ("Armor") "will appear," tells her "a romance invented for the occasion." The moment brings him to new artistic heights—he "venture[s] to say that none of [his] published sketches could compare with it"—but of course has no practical effects on Miss Grief's public silence (266–67).

Neither can the narrator's romantic lie alter Miss Grief's keen final awareness of her voice's distance from the desired public reception. Pointing out two "copybooks" full of additional writings, Miss Grief instructs him not to "look at them—[her] poor dead children," and to "let them depart with me—unread, as I have been" (268). She then consigns her literary ambitions to the realm of history, an aspect of her identity which she has kept thoroughly private: "It is all in the past now," she says, and the narrator admits that he "never knew more of her history than is written here. If there was more that [he] might have learned, it remained unlearned, for [he] did not ask" (268–69). Unable to bridge the gaps between his voice and hers, his public and her private history, the narrator has in some way, despite his efforts on her behalf, contributed to Miss Grief's failure to make her voice public. And that contribution is reflected in the narrator's final decision about her writings, one which he connects once more to gender:

> And the drama? I keep it here in this locked case. I could have had it published at my own expense; but I think that now she knows its faults herself, perhaps, and would not like it. . . .
> When I die 'Armor' is to be destroyed unread: not even Isabel is to see it. For women will misunderstand each other; and, dear and precious to me as my sweet wife is, I could not bear that she or anyone should cast so much as a thought of scorn upon the memory of the writer, upon my poor dead, "unavailable," unaccepted "Miss Grief" (269).

The narrator apparently shields Miss Grief from public reception and definition out of sympathy; however, as the story's opening paragraph highlights, such definitions are an inevitable part of contributing one's voice to the larger public world, and thus the narrator's sympathy provides just another unbridgeable gap separating Miss Grief from that world. Moreover, even here the narrator defines and limits Miss Grief—not only by using (and, quotation marks notwithstanding, validating) the editor's term "unavailable," but also by continuing to use the wrong name (affectionate or no, it is his own coinage and no part of her voice or identity) and by designating her both a woman and yet not fit to be shared with another woman. At the story's close, then, the narrator comes full circle, representing once again the public, authoritative voice with which he both begins the text and judges Miss Grief in their first encounters; a voice that she hopes to join but which seems to have no place for her powerful, unique, but ultimately private and silenced artistic voice.[42]

The conflicts between women's and men's voices, private history and public speech, and art and femininity are likewise central to *The Bostonians,* Henry James's ambivalent attempt to write what he famously called "an American story" about "the most salient and peculiar point in our social life, . . . the situation of women" (*Notebooks* 19).[43] The resulting novel's difficulty, even within the notoriously dense James ouevre, has perhaps become its most salient point, and has led many readers, including the author himself, to avoid extended considerations of it: James did not include the novel in the revised New York edition of his works, and some scholars to whose subjects (gender, history, silence) the text relates have likewise evaded it.[44] When critics have analyzed *Bostonians,* a primary goal has often been cutting through the ambivalence and pinning the novel down, determining on which side of the text's central, gendered conflict the narrator's (and usually the author's) sympathies truly lie.[45] After all, as that conflict's male figure, Basil Ransom, remarks to his female adversary, Olive Chancellor, "if . . . there is to be a discussion, there will be different sides, and of course one can't sympathize with both" (16). But while there are certainly victories and defeats in the text's conflicts over voice, history, and gender, its defining element is precisely debate: the ambivalent narrator's dialogic portrayal of such discussions, of the complex interactions of voice and silence, public and private, history and future, powerfully represents the era's debates over the woman question.[46]

The book's opening chapter effectively introduces those interactions. It begins with one woman, Luna Chancellor, speaking for another, her sister Olive; Luna tells a visitor that "Olive will come down in about ten minutes; she told me to tell you that. About ten; that is exactly like Olive. . . . She didn't tell me to say she was glad to see you, because she doesn't know whether she is or not, and she wouldn't for the world expose herself to telling a fib" (1). As Luna demonstrates, speaking for someone is a complex act, one in which the speaker can complete her duties precisely (repeating exactly what the absent voice has said; not telling what it has not) and yet at the same time subvert them by revealing things which the original speaker would not want the auditor to hear or know. Nonetheless, what follows, the first extended passage in the narrator's voice, indicates that there are likewise difficulties if one chooses not to speak for someone else: the narrator describes the Chancellors' visitor, their cousin Basil Ransom, noting that he comes "from Mississippi, and [speaks] very perceptibly with the accent of that country," but adding that "it is not in my power to reproduce by any combination of characters this charming dialect. . . . And yet the reader who likes a complete image, who desires to read with the senses as well as with the reason, is entreated not to forget that he prolong[s] his consonants and swallow[s] his vowels" (2). If speaking for someone has, in Luna's performance, constituted an undermining of that person's voice and identity, then not speaking for someone, the narrator's refusal to transcribe Basil's words in his own accented voice, also entails a slippage between that person's individual voice and identity and what is passed along to the audience.[47]

Given those perils of having one's voice mediated, either explicitly by a spokesperson or implicitly by the lack of one, it would seem that the most effective method of articulation is to speak directly for one's self. And indeed, both Basil's and Olive's own voices are described in this chapter as possessing some power, if of a specific, somewhat limited nature. Basil's power lies in two areas: his conversational skill with women, which the narrator describes as "the way in which a Southern gentleman spoke to ladies," including the use of "an elegant phrase" (4); and his use of silence to circumvent topics with which he is uncomfortable, as when Luna tells him about Olive's "radical" activities and he responds by saying "nothing for some time" (3). Olive's power, as the narrator describes it when she enters the room at the chapter's end, lies in her combination of honesty ("she never [goes] through any forms") and taste (she has "a cultivated voice"), producing a voice that is "low and agreeable" (5). And in introducing this pair of powerful voices, the narrator also introduces three other elements with which they connect and over which they have some control: gender, as illustrated by Basil's uses of voice with ladies and silence for radical feminism; and identity and history, as Luna illustrates by noting, on leaving Basil and Olive, that "in her absence Olive might give him any version of her she chose" (6).

Having introduced his two principal protagonists, the narrator in fact spends the remainder of the novel's exposition—which I believe ends the moment Verena Tarrant appears—giving his versions of the two characters. And those versions closely link to voice—not only because of Basil's and Olive's powerful voices and equally strong opinions on the subject of voice, but also due to the narrator's multidimensional point of view, his movement (through both dialogue and free indirect narration) into and out of many characters' viewpoints. In many ways, the visions of Basil and Olive that evolve over these pages are purposefully and thoroughly opposed to one another. Basil dislikes strong female voices, preferring "private and passive" Southern women to those who pursue "publicity" (7–8), whom he explicitly condemns as "a herd of vociferating women" (41)[48]; while Olive dislikes authoritative male voices and the rigid categories into which they classify women—she "hate[s]" the "epithet ... unwomanly overtures ... almost as much as she hate[s] its opposite" (10)—and is consumed with a desire to speak for women, as "the voice of their silent suffering [is] always in her ears" (30–31). Basil is strongly identified with and defined by his Southern past, is described as "very provincial" due to "the narrow range, as yet, of his experience" (7–8), and is quite pessimistic about the future—"he like[s] his pedigree, he revere[s] his forefathers, and he rather pitie[s] those who might come after him" (164); while Olive's focus on reform identifies her thoroughly with the future, puts her in the same category as a fellow reformer who to her "will never be old, [is] the youngest spirit I know" (16), and makes her much more optimistic.[49] And these contrasts are driven home in two early exchanges over reform and women's rights: in the first, Olive identifies herself as someone who is "interested in new ideas," who "care[s] for human progress," and who wishes to "plead the cause of the new truths," while Basil notes that he "never saw any" progress and has "never yet encountered in the world any but old truths" (15–16); and in the second, Olive speaks passionately about "the position of women" and her reformist goals regarding it, while Basil disagrees but does not fully articulate his opposition, choosing, when she asks him directly if he is "against [women's] emancipation," once again to redirect the conversation through silence (19–20).

If Basil and Olive are constructed from the outset as diametrical opposites, however, they share a central weakness and a corresponding goal. Both have a great deal of difficulty in and hesitancy about articulating public versions of their strong private voices, yet such articulation is the deep-seated ambition of both. Again, the narrator stresses that neither has any problem speaking in private: Olive is "quite a speaker [herself]," when she "let[s] [herself] go" (118) and "pour[s] forth these views" on the woman question (158); while Basil deploys his effective combination of voice and silence, depending on his conversational comfort level—"he like[s] to talk as well as any one; but he [can] hold his tongue, if that [is] more expressive, and he usually [does] so when his perplexities [are] greatest" (164). Both yearn to extend that expressive mastery into the public arena but find that transition difficult: Olive exclaims that she "want[s] to do something—oh, [she] should like so to speak," but recognizes that she has "none of that sort of talent ... no eloquence" (29), that in public settings she becomes "awkward and embarrassed and dry" (118); while Basil writes unpublished articles, hoping to "succeed some day in giving them adequate expression" (288), but finds himself partly repulsed by the idea of "prating in the market-place" (41) and mostly aware that he cannot prate effectively, that "perhaps they [don't] like the way he [speaks]. If they [can] show him a better way, he [is] willing to adopt it" (162). While there is a distinction between Olive's oral ambitions and Basil's written ones, foreshadowing Basil's later rhetorical single-mindedness and -voicedness in his conversations with Verena (as opposed to Olive's dialogic willingness to allow Verena to speak), both characters desire to extend their strong private voices and views into the public world, and the novel provides them with a medium through which they can do just that: Verena Tarrant.[50]

It may seem unusual to describe a character as a medium for vocalization, but Verena, as many critics have noted (and often complained), plays precisely such a role for much of the novel.[51] From her introduction she is characterized as a voice—not a character with a strong voice, but rather, in many ways, the instrument itself. In that first scene she gives a speech at a women's rights gathering, and her oration's content is nothing less than "the past history, the present condition, and the future prospects of [her] sex." Moreover, she believes that her gendered themes determine her audience and reception, that she "speak[s] only to women . . . for [she doesn't] expect [men] to like what [she] say[s]." But the positive responses to her speech, whether offered by other characters (female and male) or the narrator himself, ignore that content and focus exclusively on her voice: "She speaks so beautifully," in "a new style, quite original"; "the effect [is] not in what she" says, but in "the charming notes of her voice. . . . How prettily, indeed, she [makes] some of it sound"; "they may call it what they please, it's a pleasure to listen to it"; "It [is] generally admitted that the style [is] peculiar, but Miss Tarrant's peculiarity [is] the explanation of her success." Such descriptions separate not only Verena's content from her style, but also, and even more important, her voice from her will—as her father puts it, "The voice that [speaks] from her lips seem[s] to want to take that form," and her eloquence flows only after she "listen[s] for the voice." And Verena herself repeats in her oration this separation of voice from self, constructing women's ideal role as precisely such depersonalized vocal conduits: "the sound of our lips would become the voice of universal peace" (42-54).

What the sound of Verena's lips becomes for Basil and Olive, how-ever, is the representation of a much more specific desire: their respec-tive public ambitions. As the narrator describes Olive's feelings, Verena is what she has "been looking for so long" (67), and both seek explic-itly to "take possession of her" (66) and achieve their goals through her. Their attraction to Verena stems from their thoroughly aesthetic, formal views of her: Olive admits that she "should like to be able to say that [Verena is] my form—my envelope" (135); while Basil, in listening to an-other of Verena's speeches, notes that "her meaning [has] faded again into the agreeable vague, and he simply [feels] her presence, taste[s] her voice" (234). And they likewise share a desire to separate Verena from the past and recreate her as they see fit: Olive wants to remove her from her parents and her personal history, since "what she would [like] to impose on the girl [is] an effectual rupture with her past" (94); while Basil hopes to revise her understanding of American and women's his-tory, believing he "should be able to interpret history for [her] by a new light" (77-78).[52] But despite these nearly identical constructions of and ambitions toward Verena, Olive's and Basil's public goals are different in both form (Olive wants to speak, Basil to write) and content (Olive wants to publicize her optimistic, reformist visions of women's condi-tion and struggles; Basil his pessimistic views of women and the world), and their respective relationships with and ultimate plans for Verena are likewise distinct.

Those distinctions, moreover, are intimately connected to Olive's and Basil's widely disparate views of public, private, and the woman ques-tion. For Olive, that issue can only be publicly addressed by a woman— "it [is] a woman question; what they want [is] for women, and it should be by women" (125)—and so it is crucial that a woman with a "gift" like Verena's enter the public debate and "move the world with" her voice (70). Basil, however, detests Verena's role as "a public character" (75), be-lieving that the public arena should be reserved for men, that a voice like Verena's should be heard "privately, personally, . . . in the realm of family life and the domestic affections" (297), and that there her "facility . . . will simply make [her], in conversation, the most charming woman in

America" (341). And these contrasts shape one of their only exchanges on their respective plans for Verena:

> He asked her whether she supposed the girl would come out in public....
>
> "Come out in public!" Olive repeated, "in public? Why, you don't imagine that pure voice is to be hushed?"
>
> "Oh, hushed, no! it's too sweet for that. But not raised to a scream.... She oughtn't to become like the others. She ought to remain apart."
>
> "Apart—*apart?*" said Miss Chancellor; "when we shall all be looking to her, gathering about her.... she shall be an immense power for good." (81)

As this passage reiterates, both characters recognize and respect Verena's vocal power, but they construct it and its potential effects in radically different terms. Basil's emphases on the voice's sweetness and on keeping Verena apart reinforce his linked visions of femininity and privacy, while Olive locates Verena within a communal public space ("gathering about her") and describes her with the more masculine "immense."[53] And while Olive's construction is no less self-interested and controlling than Basil's, there is an element of violence in his goals which is absent from hers: he believes that "if he should become her husband he should know a way to strike her dumb" (280).[54]

Ironically, however, to achieve that violent silencing of Verena's public voice, Basil must engage her in a series of conversations. While the conversations are ostensibly private, they play out like public debates on the woman question and Verena's role within it; Verena recognizes the dialogues' close resemblance to her public performances, admitting that, "they tell me I speak as I talk, so I suppose I talk as I speak" (197). Moreover, both Verena and Basil describe the conversations' goals in explicitly rhetorical and argumentative terms, although with an important difference: Verena wants both to convert Basil ("I wanted him to hear ... because he is so awfully opposed!" [251]) and to understand his position ("I confess I am curious ... to hear the other side" [257]), while Basil desires only to convince his opponent that "the whole idea of women's being equal to men" is "balderdash" (276).[55] Basil's single-mindedness and monologia, which create further ambivalence in Verena—"a strange feeling came over her, a perfect willingness not to keep insisting on her own side" (287)—are two reasons for his greater conversational effectiveness. But there is another, more complex reason, combining Basil's unquestionable vocal skills, his status as a Southerner, and Verena's willingness to be silent and submissive: "His deep, sweet, distinct voice, expressing monstrous opinions with exotic cadences. . . . there was a spell upon her as she listened; it was in her nature to be easily submissive, to like being overborne. She could be silent when people insisted, and silent without acrimony" (287). The Southern element in Basil's voice and victory relates to a distinct, Reconstruction-era theme that parallels the novel's exploration of the woman question, and to which I return in chapter 4. But with or without that aspect, it is clear that Basil's effective voice is the key to achieving his objectives on two levels—convincing Verena of his position's merits but also, and more important, silencing her strong public voice in favor of private submission to his.[56] Verena recognizes this latter, much more personal goal of Basil's, but while she knows she should oppose it—asking of Olive, "how can I love him when he tells me he wants me . . . never to give another address, to open my lips in public?" (325)—she cannot help but remark upon "how wonderfully he can talk" (329). And thus, gradually but thoroughly, his "most effective and penetrating words" take hold, and for Verena "the truth change[s] sides" (335).

On the other side, of course, is Olive, who despite her own strong voice remains largely absent (not only literally, but also as an influence on Verena) from this series of crucial conversations. Critics have read this disparity between Basil's and Olive's voices as illustrating either the novel's unevenness or its favoritism toward Basil; while a case can be made for either position, it is worth noting that the narrator explicitly acknowledges Olive's unusual degree of silence. He notes that Olive does "not, during these dreadful days, talk continuously; she [has] long periods of pale, intensely anxious, watchful silence, interrupted by outbreaks of passionate argument, entreaty, invocation. It [is] Verena who talk[s] incessantly" (331). This description of Olive can be read as part of the overall construction of her as somehow diseased (perhaps connected to her pseudo-lesbian status),[57] but it also relates to the distinctions between Basil's and Olive's ambitions for themselves and for Verena-as-medium: Basil wants to develop his own public voice while silencing Verena's; Olive wants to find her public voice through encouraging Verena's. In Basil's monologic plan, if the vocal medium speaks back, he can simply overpower its voice with his own; in Olive's more dialogic vision, however, such a vocal discrepancy is harder to overcome. And the results of these two strategies are clear: Basil wins Verena and achieves his public voice, publishing his first article[58]; Olive loses Verena and is left in the famous final scene to find her own public voice (if she can).

Much has been written about that scene, and particularly about the narrator's perspective on two deeply ambiguous images: Verena's private emotional confluence of "glad"-ness and "tears," the latter of which are "not the last she [is] destined to shed" in her "union, so far from brilliant," with Basil; and Olive's unplanned first public oration, where the narrator leaves "whatever she should say to them" unspoken at the text's close (394).[59] Whatever one's position on the narrator's position here, however—and I have more to say about this scene in chapter 4, as I believe the final images of Basil and Verena relate most strongly to the novel's Southern themes—it is perhaps paramount that both narrator and text conclude with the same ambivalence toward Basil's and Olive's voices and ambitions that they have demonstrated from the opening chapters. It seems clear that all three characters' debates over public and private, voice and silence, men and women, and the woman question— debates which also include a wide variety of other voices on which I have not commented, including Miss Birdseye, Mrs. Farrinder, Mr. Pardon, and Doctor Prance (an echo of Jewett's Nan Prince)[60]—must be followed by many equally dialogic conversations before they can be in any way resolved.

As I have argued throughout this chapter, such conversations are the hallmark of the decade's literary engagements with the woman question. Moreover, two of the era's most significant writers worked within a literary form that embodies and exemplifies such a conversational approach: the dialogic poetry of Frances Ellen Watkins Harper and Sarah Piatt. Harper often connected the woman question to another social issue in which she had a lifelong stake, race; while Piatt linked the woman question to more conventional and seemingly sentimental subjects such as childhood and courtship. But both women wrote poems that in their content and form depict multivocal dialogues over the issues—history and future, private and public, women and men—so central to the decade's debates over the woman question.[61]

While Harper is best remembered for her fiction, and particularly for *Iola Leroy* (1892), her historical novel of Reconstruction, she was in her era, as Frances Foster notes, "the best known and best loved African-American poet prior to Paul Laurence Dunbar" (Harper, *Brighter* 4).[62] Much of that poetry, like the exceptional Aunt Chloe series from *Sketches of Southern Life* (1872), portrayed, in a complex mixture of dialect and poetic voice, the experiences and perspectives of slaves and ex-slaves before, during, and after the Civil War. Yet Harper did also turn her poetic voices to other contemporary subjects, and in "John and Jacob—A Dialogue on Woman's Rights" (1885) she deploys two such voices in an evolving debate over the woman question.[63] On a basic level, the poem seems to construct the type of rigid binary suggested by its title and its form, an alternating series of typographically separated statements from the two titular voices. Within that binary, Jacob stands for the past and women's private roles, arguing that he "don't believe a single bit / In those new-fangled ways / Of women running to the polls," preferring "the good old-fashioned times / When women used to spin, / And when you came from work you knew / Your wife was always in"; while John represents the future and women's public possibilities, contending that women should be "invite[d] . . . in to help / Us men to make [the polls] clean."[64]

Yet Harper subverts that binary structure in two significant ways. First, she narrows the gap between the two voices by allowing Jacob to participate fully in and learn from the dialogue. For example, when Jacob claims that "what [he] want[s] to know" is who will "stay at home to nurse, / To cook, to wash, and sew" if women get the vote, John replies that working women are already absent for much longer than voting women would be, and Jacob takes the point, replying: "Well I declare, that is the truth! / To vote, it don't take long." Although Jacob's conservative views are not disspelled by one such dialogic exchange, by the poem's end he can say that he "almost think[s] that [he] will go / And vote with Betsy Ann," a meaningful shift from his adamant opening stance.

And it is Harper's second subversion of the binary, her inclusion of the two voices' shared racial history, that best explains such a shift. In response to Jacob's claim that "women's voting's wrong," John cites that history and appeals to Jacob's perspective as an ex-slave:

> The masters thought before the war
> > That slavery was right:
> But we who felt the heavy yoke
> > Didn't see it in that light.
> Some thought that it would never do
> > For us in Southern lands,
> To change the fetters on our wrists
> > For the ballot in our hands.
> Now if you don't believe 'twas right
> > To crowd us from the track,
> How can you push your wife aside
> > And try to hold her back?

In these masterful lines, Harper connects conservatism on the woman question to the racial conservatism of both antebellum slaveholders and postbellum racists, and so uses history in two crucial ways: linking the period's conservative ideologies to the earlier era's, and thus exposing their continuing repressive effects; and appealing to the historical experiences of those who have suffered such repression to continue their work against it (in all forms) in the present. Her poem, then, puts not only pro-and anti-suffrage voices, but also past and present and the race and woman questions, in complex, evolving dialogue.[65]

While Harper constructs that dialogue through a pair of voices and perspectives, Piatt develops a new literary form in which to exemplify such heteroglossia: the dialogic lyric poem. Piatt has long been underappreciated; at best she merits a page or two in most studies of nineteenth-century poetry, including revisionist reconsiderations of women's poetry by Cheryl Walker, Emily Watts, and Elizabeth Petrino. Moreover, much of Piatt's work fits rather easily into such categories as courtship or children's poetry, and even the revisionists, when they reference Piatt at all, often discuss her through those categorizations.[66] What distinguishes Piatt from the many other writers (female and male) who worked in such genres, however, is her usage of a unique, difficult, dialogic style that adds depth and multivocality to almost all her poems. As her best critic, Paula Bennett, describes Piatt's "mature poetic," it consists of "a stripped-down kind of writing in which multiple speakers and direct and indirect dialogue give her thinking [a] hard, if typically subtle, edge" (*Poets* 144). And Piatt brings that dialogic style to bear on a profoundly individualistic poetic form, the lyric; her almost exclusively first-person poems still relay the speaker's "experiences, thoughts, and feelings" (as Abrams defines the lyric's content [6–7]), but do so within the complex contexts of other voices and perspectives as well as societal conversations and conventions.

Because Piatt's lyrical voices engage with such outside forces, it is easy to read her poetry in explicitly political terms, to view her as deploying a revisionist ideology toward her society's dominant voices and conventions. Bennett herself often takes that position, first (in an early article) constructing Piatt as a voice of "dissent" ("Descent") and later reading her lyrical mode, as opposed to lyric's generally "self-enclosed, intrasubjective nature," as "public speech" with an "expressive and mimetic power [that] is organized explicitly or implicitly for argumentative ends" (*Poets* 3–5). Some of Piatt's best poems do use their dialogic lyric voice for such argumentative and ideological purposes: in "A Woman's Counsel" (1876) the narrator responds to her male suitor's self-centered and self-aggrandizing voice with her own cynical version of him and his love (67–68); while in "After the Quarrel" (1878) a mother advises her jilted daughter that there are other voices besides men's (such as that of "a bird") and that even if "no one should love" her she can be satisfied with loving artistic figures such as Shakespeare and Raphael (86–87). Yet such lyrical voices' revisionist power should not overshadow Piatt's more truly dialogic works, those in which the lyric voice engages an evolving series of other voices and perspectives without coming to a particular position by the poem's conclusion. These include "The Palace-Burner" (1872), "From North and South" (1878), and my chapter's concluding text, "A Pique at Parting" (1879).

Since "Pique" is relatively short, and far too complex to paraphrase effectively, I will include it in full:

Why, sir, as to that—I did not know it was time for the moon to rise,
    (So, the longest day of them all can end, if we will have
        patience with it.)
One woman can hardly care, I think, to remember another one's
    eyes,
        And—the bats are beginning to flit.
        . . . We hate one another? It may be true.
        What else do you teach us to do?
        Yea, verily, to love you.

My lords—and gentlemen—are you sure that after we love quite all
    There is in your noble selves to be loved, no time on our
        hands will remain?
Why, an hour a day were enough for this. We may watch the wild
    leaves fall
        On the graves you forget. . . . .It is plain
        That you were not pleased when she said—Just so;
        Still, what do we want, after all, you know,
        But room for a rose to grow?

You leave us the baby to kiss, perhaps; the bird in the cage to sing;
    The flower on the window, the fire on the hearth (and the fires
        in the heart) to tend.
When the wandering hand that would reach somewhere has become
    the Slave of the Ring,
        You give us—an image to mend;
        Then shut with a careless smile, the door—
        (There's dew or frost on the path before;)
        We are safe inside. What more?

If the baby should moan, or the bird sit hushed, or the flower fade
    out—what then?
        Ah? the old, old feud of mistress and maid would be left
        though the sun went out?
You can number the stars and call them by names, and, as men, you
    can wring from men
        The world—for they own it, no doubt.

We, not being eagles, are doves? Why, yes,
We must hide in the leaves, I guess,
And coo down our loneliness.

God meant us for saints? Yes—in Heaven. Well, I, for one, am
    content
        To trust Him through darkness and space to the end—if an
            end there shall be;
But, as to His meanings, I fancy I never knew quite what He meant.
        And—why, what were you saying to me
        Of the saints—or *that* saint? It is late;
        The lilies look weird by the gate.
        . . . Ah, sir, as to that—we will wait. (91–92)

As the title suggests, "Pique" ostensibly fits within the category of court-ship poems, although, like "A Woman's Counsel," it undermines more than upholds the conventions of literary courtship. It begins, for ex-ample, by subverting one of courtship poetry's most stock images, the moon; the speaker barely notices that celestial body, and when she does acknowledge its ascent it is not in any romantic or metaphorical context, but rather the pragmatic recognition that it signals day's end. Yet while "Counsel" focuses on the discrepancies between the conventions and re-alities of literary courtship, "Pique" moves quickly beyond that theme and, as illustrated by its shift in structure of address from an individual "sir" to the collective "lords—and gentlemen," into the broader, public world of voices and perspectives on the woman question.

A number of distinctive formal elements contribute to the poem's dialogic lyric voice and perspective. The nonstandard punctuation, and particularly her use of dashes, ellipses, semicolons, and parentheses, dis-rupts any monologic sense of a continuous or consistent speaker's voice, indicating the multiple and often-conflicting voices and perspectives that can be contained within a single subjectivity. The many phrases suggesting hesitancy or ambivalence, including "I think," "perhaps," and "I guess," likewise illustrate the lack of certainty or stability in the speaker's voice and positions, or, more exactly, in her articulation of those positions to her audience. Similarly, her use of interjections, words and phrases such as "after all, you know," "ah," and "why, yes" that do not directly contribute to a line's grammar or meaning, creates the poem's sense of ongoing conversation; phrases that only have meaning in relation to another's remarks (such as "as to that," with which the poem begins and ends) heighten that conversational atmosphere. In both its shifting speaker and evolving conversations, "Pique" is quite different from "Counsel," where the speaker confidently and consistently responds to her suitor's previous comments and actions, and he is given no chance to reply; here it is as if both the speaker's voice and the debate itself are refined and redefined with each stanza.

Moreover, the poem's most overarching formal element, its stanzaic structure, illustrates how voice, position, and conversation can likewise evolve within a single poetic unit. Each stanza is divided by both rhyme scheme and line placement into two distinct sections, but those respective divisions overlap: the rhyme scheme, ababccc, groups lines 1–4 and lines 5–7 together, while the line placement, with lines 1 and 3 beginning at the extreme left and lines 4–7 indented, groups the lines in that way. Those overlapping structures highlight line 4 as a link between the sections, and thus a midpoint and turning point of each stanza; and the fourth line consistently does indicate a shift in the speaker's subject and voice, as illustrated by the punctuation utilized in each instance (four dashes and an ellipsis). While there are also vocal and positional shifts within each stanza's first and last three lines—as indicated by the presence of such punctuation marks there—the turns provided by the fourth lines are at once more unexpected (the first stanza's "And—the bats are beginning to flit" being the most surprising) and more crucial, as they consistently shift both the stanza's entire perspective (whether from private situation to public conventions, as in stanza 1; or abstract philosophy to concrete conversation, as in stanza 5) and the poem's thematic engagements with gender.

Each stanza, in fact, engages with a different gender-related theme: (1) women's community and interrelationships; (2) women's roles within and without romantic relationships; (3) the limitations of marriage and domesticity; (4) men's and women's respective authoritative and artistic opportunities; (5) religion and women's destinies. Yet as the multifaceted formal elements illustrate, those themes are considered not in a static or monologic manner, but rather with the constant sense of conversation, development, hesitancy, and nuance that comprises a genuinely dialogic approach. In stanza 5, for example, the speaker begins by responding to a statement provided by a (most likely) male conversant, that "God meant [women] for saints"; she agrees but immediately complicates that agreement with a dash followed by the modifying phrase "in Heaven." She then articulates what is, she stresses, a personal position on religion: that she, "for one," is content to trust God until the end, again with the hesitant, slightly heretical modification (after a dash) "if an end there shall be." She begins, in the always pivotal line 4, to elaborate, but is seemingly interrupted and once again responds to the other voice; her response, however, now involves questioning her conversant's statement, position, and, possibly, seriousness (if the emphasized phrase "that saint" indicates that her male conversant has referred to stanza 1's other woman with such religious terminology). In the fifth and sixth lines she seems to abandon these complex, dialogic philosophical discussions for concrete reflections on the hour and setting, although that domestic setting's beauty ("the lilies") is undercut by the "weird"-ness that suggests the continued presence of dissonant ideas. And finally, after another shifting (and somewhat evasive) ellipsis, she responds once more to her now definitely male conversant (she calls him "sir") with the phrase "as to that," a normally concrete reply here made abstract by the absence of a specific referent; she furthers the abstraction, but nonetheless indicates its communal importance, with the simple concluding phrase "we will wait." Precisely what it is that they (women) will wait for is unclear but clearly crucial and will, like all of the poem's thematic content, be constructed and reconstructed through the shifting voices, evolving positions, and dialogic exchanges which constitute its lyric voice.

In Piatt's final line and lyric voice can be found respectively the potential weakness and the great strength of the decade's literary debates over the woman question. The weakness arises when one examines a line like "we will wait"—or a character like Basil Ransom, or a theme like Avis's failed marriage—in a monologic vacuum, analyzing its gendered meanings as if they can be simplified to the binary oppositions and political conflicts that drive ideology from either end of the spectrum and that allowed for the construction of the progressive national narrative. But the strength is evident when one reads such a line—a character, a theme—in light of the texts' and period's complex, multivocal, dialogic discussions of private and public, speech and silence, history and future, men and women. Within such an analysis, it becomes clear that what women (and men) go through can be told, if in a wide variety of forms and voices; and, just as important, those narratives can be effectively and productively read and responded to as well.

4

"Quite the Southern Version"

The Lure of Alternative Voices and
Histories of the South Question

The Centennial Exposition's May 10, 1876, opening featured a Southern author in a prominent and reconciliatory role. Foremost among the opening ceremony's artistic works was the Centennial Cantata, a short poem set to music; the Centennial Commission had specifically desired a Southern poet to write the Cantata's words and musical cues, and had settled upon Sidney Lanier, nationally known for his poem "Corn" (1874). Lanier was a Confederate veteran who had begun his literary career in Reconstruction's early days with a novel (*Tiger Lilies* [1867]) and poems (such as "Laughter in the Senate" [1868]) that celebrated the South's "heart" in explicit contrast to the North's "brain." But Lanier had increasingly seen reconciliation as the best hope for his region's and nation's future, and his Cantata reflected that belief. Most noteworthy is the poem's one reference to the Civil War, an explicit call for Americans to "Toil when wild brother-wars new-dark the Light, / Toil, and forgive, and kiss o'er, and replight." From its definition of the Civil War past as a darkening of the American light (rather than a glorious if lost cause) to its future-focused emphasis on mutual forgetfulness and silence as the surest paths to regaining that light and kindling a romance of reunion ("plight" meaning "to pledge one's self in betrothal"), Lanier's poem exemplifies the reconciliatory position's principal attitudes ("Centennial" 260).[1]

Yet a speech given later that month illustrates that reconciliation did not define all prominent Southerners' historical constructions and future goals. Invited to give the annual Decoration Day (later Memorial Day) Address at New York's Brooklyn Academy of Music, the Southern veteran and politician Roger A. Pryor articulated an alternative perspective on the region's and nation's past and future. Decoration Day was intrinsically more historically focused than the forward-looking, progressive Centennial Exposition, and Pryor reiterated yet critiqued that focus's specifics. While thanking the occasion's planners for their "overture of reconciliation," Pryor's speech constituted a thorough and passionate argument that the dominant national view of the Civil War and regional history was profoundly inaccurate. He emphasized Reconstruction, a "dismal period" the terrible history of which, Pryor implied, had yet to be told in full. But neither did Pryor accept the period's visions of slavery, either as "the cause of secession" or as ended by Northern hands; instead, he waited for the day when "impartial history" could narrate a more accurate version of the Southern past. And despite Pryor's hardly impartial—in fact vehemently unreconstructed—attitudes, his presence at the New York ceremony indicated that these pro-Southern positions were explicitly intended for Northern ears and productive purpose. That is, Pryor's emphasized less the Lost Cause and more one he considered still quite salvageable: converting the North, through his powerful voice, to his views on history, region, and future.[2]

In the decade after Reconstruction's end, Southern voices and narratives of history came to dominate the literary dialogue over their region and its role in the American future. During the Reconstruction era, that dialogue had been predominantly composed of romances of reunion, narratives in which both sides's divisive history and extreme voices were forgotten or ignored in favor of national reconciliation—and which reached their apotheosis in Lanier's Centennial Cantata. While such romances continued to appear in the post-Reconstruction decade (as illustrated by S. Weir Mitchell's *In War Time*), they were largely supplanted in popularity and significance by conversion narratives, works in which Southern voices such as Pryor's articulated their alternative history and perspective and convinced the nation of their validity and value. Despite the efforts of diverse Southern authors like Richard Taylor, John Esten Cooke, and Frances Butler Leigh, the most powerful conversion narratives were produced by two Northern novelists, Henry Adams and

Henry James. Yet if Adams and James seemed to give in to the lure of the Southern voice and past, there were other writers from both regions, including Constance Fenimore Woolson and Mary N. Murfree, who constructed more complex, balanced, and multivocal histories of and dialogues about the South question. And providing the decade's most effective reply to the Southern version of voice and history was Albion W. Tourgée, whose *A Fool's Errand* not only responded to the conversion narratives and reinserted race back into the national discussion of the South question, but also represented a dialogic innovation in the form of the historical novel.[3]

As Nina Silber has thoroughly documented, there arose in the postbellum years a "conciliatory culture," one dominated by "the idea of reunion as it was imagined, and occasionally acted upon, mostly by northerners" (2–4). This culture's literary manifestation was the "romance of reunion," a novel in which (typically) a Northern man and Southern woman forget the divisive history of slavery, sectionalism, and Civil War, set aside their divergent and extreme views, and find love and a shared national future. While the title of the most famous such novel, John W. DeForest's *Miss Ravenal's Conversion from Secession to Loyalty* (1867), suggests that the plot required a greater change by the Southern character, Silber's comprehensive survey of the genre indicates that most often "forgetfulness" and conversion were central aspects of both sides' evolutions toward reconciliation and reunion.[4] And a brief analysis of a romance of reunion from our decade, Mitchell's *In War Time* (1884), reinforces this shared conversion's prominence and characteristics.

Mitchell's novel, set among the Philadelphia medical community during the war's later years, overtly criticizes regional extremes. The protagonist, Dr. Wendell, is a classic New Englander, descended from "generations of Yankees whose acuteness had been directed chiefly into the thorny tracks of biblical exegesis" (19); and he has transplanted that heritage to his new Philadelphia home, bringing "the old furniture from a home on Cape Cod, in which some generations of Puritan divines had lived" (22). Yet this illustrious history's heir is a coward, a thief, and a liar: Wendell, it is revealed, deserted his regiment and abandoned his medical duties, and in the course of the novel he lies about this history, steals a child's inheritance to cover his own debts and lies about that, and eventually deserts again, fleeing to the West a broken man.[5] While no Southerner comes off as badly as this son of New England, the novel's most Southern character, the symbolically named "Carolina gentleman" Henry Gray, is similarly extreme in his regional heritage and prejudices; he can refer to Northerners only as "damned Yankees" and is destined to dwell on his "ruined home," the "desolated South" (344–46, 350–51). Neither Wendell nor Gray seems able to move America into the postbellum future; that role is left to those characters who occupy more of a middle ground, both literally (being from Philadelphia) and figuratively. And the two exemplary such characters, and hero and heroine of the romance of reunion, are dashing young Philadelphian Arthur Morton and Hester Gray, an orphaned Southerner who has been raised in the city.[6]

Despite their middle-ness of heritage, however, Arthur and Hester do possess more extreme views that they must compromise before uniting in marriage. Arthur, upon meeting the "perfectly rabid rebel" Henry Gray, must leave "the room in five minutes, as red as a peony" (173); while Hester, as the war progresses and her native region falters, admits that, even among Philadelphia's Union sympathizers, she "must have [her] own feelings about the South" (239). Yet both are willing to moderate and even silence their views to support the other, even in the most emotionally charged circumstances: when Hester is bothered by Arthur's strong reaction to Lincoln's assassination, Arthur recognizes that "it has troubled her as a Southern woman" and promises that he "shall never so speak again" (281–83); and when Hester's cousin Henry confronts her about her engagement to Arthur, accusing her of having "so far forgotten [her] home, and [her] blood, and [her] dead father [a Confederate soldier]," she replies that "no obligation can make it right for [her] to hear such words about the man" she loves (350). Such silence of moderation and compromise is contagious—when Arthur meets Henry again, both men "carefully avoid the topics which [are] still very bitter in men's mouths" (354)—and, Mitchell clearly believes, was the most effective method for reconciling and reuniting North and South in the immediate postbellum era of his conclusion, a moment when divisive history and extreme positions still dominated the national dialogue.[7]

More than a decade after that historical moment, the participation in the national Centennial Exposition of Sidney Lanier, one of the most

prominent Southern authors, indicated that these emphases on reconciliation were now central to the nation's literary dialogue over the South
question. And Lanier's Cantata, especially the depiction of the Civil War
and its appropriate national response, illustrated the South's concur-
rence with the reconciliationist attitudes. That is, while Lanier's poem
no more represents all Southerners' views than the romances of reunion
do all Northerners', both exemplify a predominant element of their regions' attitudes by 1876.[8] Even after ten years of controversial and often
divisive Reconstruction, mutual reconciliation seemed to be the foremost wish of most white Americans. Yet Pryor's Decoration Day speech
highlighted a vocal minority of white Southerners with quite distinct
positions on the regional and national pasts and futures, and in the subsequent decade his group became an increasingly dominant voice in the
national conversation.

That shift was already culturally underway by the Centennial month,
as evidenced by the Tom Show advertisements' transformation with
which my book begins. But at the level of national identity it truly began
with the controversial 1876 presidential election, which ended Federal
Reconstruction and drastically altered the nation's regional balance; the
so-called Compromise of 1877 ceded significant priority to Southern attitudes and goals in exchange for a Rutherford B. Hayes presidency. Illustrating that concession is an April 1877 *Nation* editorial which voiced
a decidedly Southern sentiment on the Compromise's racial effects: "the
negro will disappear from the field of national politics" (Blight, *Reunion*
138). If slavery and race had been tacitly ignored in the reconciliationist
texts, they were more actively repressed and controlled in pro-Southern
narratives like the *Nation*'s.[9] And the decade that followed witnessed the
development of three interrelated Southern ideas that significantly influenced Northern perceptions of the region and nation. The first was the
New South, a conception of Southern progress and promise that arose
over the course of the decade and was codified in Henry Grady's famous
1886 address.[10] Despite the New South imagery's forward-looking nature, it brought with it an increased emphasis on two mythical conceptions of the Southern past: the plantation legend of the Old South and
the Lost Cause.[11] Since the historical situations encompassed by those
ideas were, by definition, irrevocably lost to present and future Southerners, the focus lay instead on remembering and voicing those histo-

ries, both within the region and to a national (and especially Northern) audience. Scholars have long debated the precise relationship between the New South advocates and the proponents of these mythic historical ideals, and the related question of whether continuity or change predominates in Southern history and thought[12]; but whatever the answers, all three concepts functioned together in this post-Reconstruction era, through forms as diverse as *Scribner's* magazine, travel writing, and the deification of Robert E. Lee, to convert the North to the value of Southern voices, views, and history.[13]

Throughout the decade, Southern writers such as Taylor, Cooke, and Leigh argued for and articulated that Southern version of history, identity, and region; but the most effective depictions of Northern conversion were constructed by two eminently Northern authors: Adams in *Democracy* and James in *The Bostonians*. Such conversion narratives' popularity and predominance, paired with the plantation tales of Joel Chandler Harris and Thomas Nelson Page, led Tourgée to voice his famous 1888 complaint that the nation's literature had "become not only Southern in type, but distinctly Confederate in sympathy" ("South" 412). Yet there were dissenting authors on both sides of the Mason-Dixon line, writers who had not been fully converted to the Southern perspective and who portrayed (in texts such as Woolson's "Rodman the Keeper" and Murfree's *Where the Battle Was Fought*) the history of and dialogue over the South question as much more complex, balanced, and multivocal.[14] And it was Tourgée himself who developed a new form for the historical novel, one which could embody as well as contain the South question's dialogic nature by including a variety of voices and versions of history—including those of African Americans—without ceding ultimate authority or sympathy to any one of them.

In the years following Reconstruction, a wide variety of Southerners made the case that their unique voices and histories had not been adequately articulated and understood in the previous era. Richard Taylor, a reconciliatory former Confederate soldier who had been educated in the North and was close friends with Henry Adams and his Bostonian circle, wrote *Destruction and Reconstruction: Personal Experiences of the Late War* (1877) because he believed, as the book's opening sentence claims, that "the history of the United States" was in large measure "as yet unwritten" (9), and he hoped that, by "making [his] small voice heard," he could help rectify that gap (268).[15] John Esten Cooke, one of the predominant Southern novelists since the 1850s, set *The Virginia Bohemians* (1880) in a deeply traditional "Dream-land" (9) where "the old regime [is] gone, but the old ways linger" (49), where life at an unreconstructed Confederate general's home is "not precisely like its old self under the past regime, but [is] as near an approach to it ... as the last half of the inexorable nineteenth century will tolerate" (52), and where even freed slaves make a "supreme protest against the new order of things" (157).[16] And Frances Butler Leigh, whose mother, British actress Frances Anne Kemble, had published the controversial anti-slavery *Journal of a Residence on a Georgian Plantation in 1838–1839*, chimed in with her own *Ten Years on a Georgia Plantation Since the War, 1866–1876* (1883).[17]

Leigh's text particularly illuminates these Southern conversion narratives' goals and methods. Leigh argues that the history that her text encompasses has never been depicted, that "the truth [of] the condition our part of the South was in ... never has been known" (33), but adds her conviction that "some day justice will be done, and the Truth shall be heard above the political din of slander and lies, and the Northern people shall see things as they are, and not through the dark veil of envy, hatred, and malice" (23). As indicated by the "political din," Leigh believes that during Reconstruction it was impossible for the Southern voice to be heard, that in fact her "words were powerless" at that time (52). But while her historical voice was severely limited, her authorial voice can and must use its power to recount that history while it still has relevance to the present: Leigh notes at the outset that she "was often asked at the time ... to write some account of [her] own personal experience," since "soon everything will be so changed" (2), and the entire work answers that oft-repeated request. Moreover, one of Leigh's two primary formal choices is to include as much evidence of her historical situation and voice as possible, by "copying" letters "written at the time" (6). Such evidence, she believes, will speak for itself, and this authentic voice and history's power to alter outsiders' perspectives of the South is illustrated by Leigh's second formal device: the inclusion of letters from her Northern brother-in-law and British husband. Leigh's husband is her ideal auditor, possessing as he does "the fresh and unbiased mind of a foreigner who [has] no traditions, no old associations, and no prejudices ... to influence him" (106); but her brother-in-law represents a Reconstruction-era Northerner, so it is the text's clearest victory when he recognizes that "the people at the North [have] no idea of the real state of things at the South" and lends his voice to the Southern cause, testifying that his sister-in-law should remain the plantation's owner (41–42).[18]

Despite the passion and formal sophistication of such Southern arguments for their own perspective and history, the decade's most eloquent and effective Southern voices—and most elaborate depictions of Northern conversion by those voices—can be found in the male protagonists of two Northern novels: John Carrington in Henry Adams's *Democracy* (1880) and Basil Ransom in Henry James's *The Bostonians* (1886). According to C. Vann Woodward, one of the first and best scholars of this character type (including Ungar from Herman Melville's epic poem *Clarel* [1876] as well), in the 1880s "Southern spokesmen of the old critique of Yankee 'progress'" were "champions of the Lost Cause" and thus "discredited from the outset," so "it remained for Northern writers . . . to acknowledge the relevance of the Southern tradition and bring to bear that point of view in their critique of American society. . . . The Southerner serves as the mouthpiece of the severest strictures upon American society. . . . the views he does express and the tradition he represents are assured a sympathetic reception" (*Burden* 109–10). While the era's popular literature's gradual domination by the Southern (and often Lost Cause) perspective—Tourgée's rise in "Confederate sympathy"— complicates Woodward's point about "discredited" Southern voices, his overall argument about the use of this Southern history and perspective in these Northern works remains convincing, and serves as a touchpoint for many subsequent readings.[19]

Yet if Woodward accurately identifies this common character type in these three quite different works, he less convincingly dismisses these characters' relevance to the South question. After referencing the authors' biographical "ambivalence" in their "attitudes toward the South," Woodward portrays the South question as relatively minor in these works. "The South or the Southern hero, past or present," he continues, "was a useful foil," one to whom these authors "turned . . . in search of the values and traditions they [and America] had lost" (136–39). While the three texts (and all their authors' works, for that matter) certainly share a consistent ambivalence, they also differ notably in their construction and deployment of the Southern voice and past. And I believe that only Melville's Ungar functions, like all of that allegorical poem's secondary characters, as an abstract, theoretical type; that is, Ungar's Southern heritage and Confederate experiences, like his partial Native American and Catholic ancestries, do seem chosen by Melville simply to maximize the character's "estranged" and "refugee" status, the "personal pain" which is the legacy of his "memories," and his pessimistic, passionate, but ultimately powerless critique of Gilded Age America.[20] While those aspects likewise relate to Adams's and James's Southern characters, their Southern identities and histories connect more fully to their voices, perspectives, and prominence in their respective texts.

Many analyses of Adams's novel focus on the two most common readings since its controversial anonymous publication: as a heavily autobiographical roman à clef and a bitingly pessimistic depiction of the Gilded Age political scene. In the former, John Carrington is usually linked to one of Adams's Southern friends (James Lowndes, Lucius Lamar, or Richard Taylor, among others); in the latter, Carrington becomes a mouthpiece for Adams's own historical and moral critique of modern politics.[21] The novel is without question deeply autobiographical and profoundly political, and Carrington relates to both characteristics; but neither reading of him, nor those which counter that Adams constructs Carrington as part of what is wrong with the political scene rather than a critic of it, focus closely enough on how Carrington's Southern experiences and voice connect him to the novel's heroine and contribute directly to his ultimate position of vocal, historical, and moral authority.[22]

While Carrington comes to occupy that prominent position, however, the novel's principal perspective belongs to its heroine, Madeleine Lee. Virtually all readings of the novel address Madeleine, and many conclude that her specifically female point of view on American politics and life is the text's defining element (foreshadowing Adams's second novel *Esther* [1884], where gender is even more central).[23] Yet to my knowledge none have pointed out that the opening chapter connects Madeleine's two most distinctive characteristics, her voice and sense of history, to her Southern ties. The first sentence introduces Madeleine as "Mrs. Lightfoot Lee," a name which resonates with both distant (Revolutionary) and recent (Civil War) Southern history, and throughout the chapter she is either Mrs. Lightfoot Lee or Mrs. Lee; the narrator does not disclose her first name until the second chapter (3–8). Those surnames describe both Madeleine and her late husband, "a descendant of one branch of the Virginia Lees" (4); and while the opening chapter focuses on Madeleine's mental and social state after her husband's death, this constant usage of his Virginia names connects her not just to him, but also to his region and ancestry. Moreover, the narrator describes Madeleine as "bitter against New York and Philadelphia, Baltimore and Boston" (4), a geographical dismissal that conspicuously stops just North of her husband's Virginia (and of Washington, where she will spend the remainder of the novel).[24] Having introduced Madeleine as concurrently affiliated with the South and opposed to the North, the narrator describes two traits that distinguish Madeleine from many female peers: she has a strong and aggressive voice ("What does she expect to get from her sharp tongue?" [6]) and a sense of history ("She was perhaps, the only woman in New York who knew something of American history" [7]). And as Carrington illustrates, both traits intimately connect to the South.

The close relationship between Carrington's Southern identity, history, and voice is established within a few lines of his initial appearance. Like most postbellum Southerners, he is linked to recent history, of the war (he "carried his musket modestly through a campaign or two") and of Reconstruction (he has left his family's "worn-out plantation" to practice law in Washington). But Carrington's historical ties go back further: to the Old South, as Madeleine thinks that he has "something of the dignity—others call it stiffness—of the old Virginia school"; and, most importantly, to the Revolutionary era, since Madeleine describes him as "a type . . . [her] idea of George Washington at thirty." Carrington's role in recent historical events is common to his generation and thus largely unrelated to his particular identity or character, while the more distant historical connections are unique, individual, and telling—a distinction driven home by the fact that the latter connections are made explicitly by Madeleine (they are her "idea" of him). And Carrington's voice reiterates his closer ties to the earlier history: while he generally talks "rather slowly and almost with effort," he is most talkative on the history of American democracy and its origins in the Revolution (12–13).[25]

In fact, Carrington serves for much of the text as a spokesman for democracy's ideals, particularly as embodied by men like Washington.

That role, moreover, is an explicitly alternative one, a philosophical counterpoint to the novel's other dominant male, political voice: Senator Ratcliffe. Ratcliffe represents the nation's other two regions, the North and West: his ancestry is Northern ("the family is a New England one"); his personal history Western ("he went West very soon after leaving college" and is now a senator from Illinois); and his voice retains elements of both regions (at a dinner party he tells "stories in Yankee and Western dialect") (14, 31).[26] And Carrington and Ratcliffe's regional contrast foreshadows their many antagonistic dialogues, conducted "in a hostile spirit" (31) and culminating in the novel's most famous scene, the visit to Mount Vernon. There Carrington, Ratcliffe, and Madeleine carry on an extended conversation about George Washington, with Ratcliffe calling Washington largely "an abstract virtue" whose "old clothes" no longer fit the political climate, and Carrington defending him as a rare "honest public man" whose type is sorely missed in the contemporary climate (68–71).[27]

In this scene and other similar dialogues, Carrington does seem to be Woodward's authorial spokesman, and as Woodward notes, the South question is not particularly important to such scenes. Carrington's Southern identity may provide him with the experiences and views necessary to express an alternative theory of American democracy and politics (one that Adams would second), but it is the theory, not the region, that matters at these moments. Yet there is another, more complex historical excursion and dialogue later in the novel, one that echoes but also inverts the Mount Vernon visit, focusing on specifics of regional history and voice rather than abstractions of national myth and political theory. Carrington and Sybil, Madeleine's sister, ride across the Virginia border into Arlington, site of both one of the largest Union cemeteries and Robert E. Lee's former house. The cemetery's presence makes Carrington "moody and abstracted, . . . troubled with memories of civil war and of associations still earlier, belonging to an age already vanishing or vanished." These negative historical reflections are naturally difficult to voice, leading Carrington to "groan in the silence of his thoughts," but Sybil begins to bring out Carrington's voice, asking him "what all these graves" mean. Once he tells her, her perspective begins to change; at first she is upset that he fought against Northern soldiers, but gradually her "sympathy" for him, coupled with a tour through Lee's abandoned house, opens her to the possibility of hearing and even sharing a Southern point of view on the place and the war (108–10).

Such a receptive auditor is precisely what Carrington has been seeking: "He want[s] some one to share his feelings," and having found her he quickly breaks his silence on the past. Moreover, he does so by connecting the recent and distant pasts, bridging the gap which has been in place since his first appearance. "We thought he was to be our Washington," he admits of Lee, and, in light of the Mount Vernon scene and the text's use of the first president, this simple statement reframes Carrington's recent and regional histories as potential continuations of the democratic ideals with which he has been associated. And this reframing allows for the subsequent conversation's two linked conversions. First, Sybil is converted to the Southern narrative of the war: she has "everything to learn," and with her "attention . . . so closely fixed on his story," she is soon "in imagination rushing with him down the valley of Virginia, . . . or gloomily toiling back to the Potomac after the bloody days at Gettysburg, or watching the last grand debacle on the road from Richmond to Appomattox." As the use of "gloomily" and "debacle" indicates, Sybil's perspective merges with Carrington's, leading directly to the second conversion, a shared epiphany about Madeleine's current situation and prospects of marriage with Ratcliffe. "I dislike Mr. Ratcliffe as much as you do;—more perhaps," Carrington reveals, and with Sybil's reply that Carrington is their "only hope. She will listen to you," they transfer their conversational, historical synergy into a forward-looking "alliance" which seeks to use his voice to change the course of contemporary history (110–14).[28]

The text's final third becomes a more pointed conflict between Ratcliffe's and Carrington's voices, one which emphasizes the difficulties faced by the Southern voice but also the strength provided by its unique history and perspective. The first time Carrington attempts to explain his feelings to Madeleine, he is unable to do so; Ratcliffe has made him a seemingly generous job offer in the current administration, and Carrington "dare[s] not trust his voice" to explain to Madeleine why he will refuse (116–18). Here Ratcliffe's insider status and power trump Carrington's outsider perspective and voice. But Carrington returns to Sybil and narrates more of his personal and regional history, telling "her all his private circumstances" in the postbellum South and giving her "for the first time a clear view" of him (125), and having done so he gains the ability to articulate his views to Madeleine.[29] He does, to great effect: his "tone and words pierce through all Mrs. Lee's armour," and, even more significantly, they remind her of other words "which had never been uttered to her before except by lips now dead and gone," her late husband's (130–31). Carrington reminds Madeleine of not only her personal history but also her attraction to the Southern voice, and for both reasons she "will never think of [him] again as [she] would have done if [he] had not spoken" (134). While Ratcliffe's own strength and power are sufficiently tempting to hold Madeleine's attraction even after this scene, the seeds of Carrington's ultimate victory have been sown. And they come to fruition in a letter from Carrington that thoroughly destroys Ratcliffe's chances, partly by indicating the depths of the senator's corruption, but also by reminding Madeleine of her "loyalty to her husband's memory," which "she had forgotten" (162–65). So reminded, Madeleine rejects Ratcliffe's final marriage proposal, making clear that it is primarily the senator's voice that has comprised his power and that Carrington has defeated: "Never speak to me or recognize me again!" (181).

Critics have made a great deal of the novel's conclusion, in which Madeleine seemingly abandons America and democracy, traveling abroad, expressing a wish to "live in the Great Pyramid and look out for ever at the polar star," and noting in a letter to Carrington (in the text's final sentence) that "the bitterest part of all this horrid story is that nine out of ten of our countrymen would say I had made a mistake" (182–84). Certainly these final pages are dominated by cynicism and despair, echoing Adams's own developing thoughts about his homeland and foreshadowing his increasing identification with Europe. Yet there is at least one American who would support Madeleine, the Southerner Carrington, and Sybil's final words to him—"If I were in your place I would try again after she comes home" (184)—suggest that Carrington's voice might yet complete the conversion process begun by reminding Madeleine of her affinity with the Southern perspective. That is, just as Madeleine's decision to reject Ratcliffe derives directly from her understanding of and reinforced attraction to the Southern voice, *Democracy*'s epilogue suggests that an optimistic American future might just be found by pursuing that attraction.[30]

If Adams's novel leaves its conversion narrative's completion to an underdetermined and uncertain future, Henry James's *The Bostonians* ends with the ultimate conversion: the young, divided heroine chooses the Southern hero over her family, her career, and, most relevantly, his Northern opponent. *Bostonians'* construction of the American future is thus much clearer, although the narrator's position on that future remains ambivalent. As I argue in chapter 3, however, the novel's central topic is indisputably the woman question, and the presence of complex gender as well as regional themes creates the disunity and confusion upon which many critics have remarked. Aaron Shaheen impressively unifies the novel's gendered and regional emphases, arguing that Basil Ransom "reifies the Arcadian image of the South in the form of Verena Tarrant," thus "forming Verena into the ultimate embodiment of the Southern landscape" (180–92); while Shaheen's work is innovative and convincing, I believe it does not engage fully enough with Basil's goals for his own and the American futures, many of which he shares with Olive (although there are important distinctions), nor with voice's centrality for all three protagonists. In chapter 3 I analyze those elements as they relate to gender; here I read the novel's triangle, conflicts, and conclusion in regional terms.

Critics interested in exploring the novel's gendered themes have a variety of possible focal points—Verena's speeches on women's issues; her relationships with Olive and Basil; Olive herself and her personality, relationships, and views; Luna Chancellor; Mrs. Farrinder and Miss Birdseye; Doctor Prance—but for those whose subject is the South question, James constructs a single, dominant image of the region in his male protagonist, Basil Ransom. Accordingly, critical attention has centered on that construction, and more exactly on discerning the narrator's (and thus, implicitly or explicitly, James's) attitudes toward his character. The most common interpretation of those attitudes comprises an acknowledgment of the narrator's ambivalence followed by an argument that the Southerner is nonetheless the novel's hero; Charles Anderson, for example, notes that Basil "reveals a certain ambivalence [in James] that raises some interesting problems in technique" but concludes that he "becomes properly speaking the hero" and that the text comprises "the triumph of a Mississippian in more than just plot" (309–31). Basil does emerge victorious in his battle with Olive for Verena's loyalty and future, but it is only partly true that "the importance of the struggle lies in the fact that the victor is the southerner" (Anne Rowe 129–36); James's emphases on voice and history in both that struggle and his Southern protagonist are just as key to the text's regional themes.[31]

On the novel's opening page, Luna asks her cousin Basil the question that will dominate the text's depiction of the South's role in Gilded Age America: "What's the good of being a Southerner?" (1). Basil does not answer here, and in fact the defining aspect of Southern identity over the text's first hundred pages seems to be its incommunicability. The narrator establishes this theme in his initial description of Basil, when he admits that although Basil speaks "very perceptibly with the accent of that country [Mississippi]," "it is not in [the narrator's] power to reproduce by any combination of characters this charming dialect." Basil's accent is thus a characteristic which the reader "is entreated not to forget" and yet an aspect that will remain invisible, uncommunicated, throughout the text (2). And while the narrator's refusal to communicate that accent can be partly attributed to James's disdain for local color fiction (with its wide variety of authentically rendered accents), it also reflects Basil's own unwillingness, at this point in the novel, to communicate his Southern identity and experiences to a national (and especially a Northern) audience. That unwillingness is illustrated by Basil's inner response when Mrs. Farrinder asks him to speak to a women's rights meeting about the "social and political condition of the South": "To talk to those people about the South—if they could have guessed how little he cared to do it! . . . To be quiet about the Southern land, not to touch her with vulgar hands, to leave her alone with her wounds and her memories, not prating in the market-place either of her troubles or her hopes, but waiting as a man should wait, for the slow process, the sensible beneficence of time—this was the desire of Ransom's heart" (41). As this complex passage indicates, Basil's silence is not due to any desire to shed his own Southern identity, despite his decision to emigrate to the North; he simply does not believe that it is the right time to discuss that identity and all that it represents, particularly in any manner that could be constructed as an attempt to "sell" his native region. Yet the passage also suggests that such a time will arrive, and that since Basil is "waiting" for it, he will be willing to speak about the South when it does.[32]

In fact, Basil is not merely waiting for the moment when it will be possible and productive to speak about the South; he is seeking out such an opportunity, or more exactly a medium through which he can develop his voice. He is in this way, as Susan Mizruchi argues (to complicate images of Basil as nostalgic or caught in the past), "decidedly ambitious" (152). And in that ambition, Basil is not only Olive's antagonist (although he is clearly that, as exemplified by the distinction between Mississippi and Boston, the Deep South and the heart of New England) but also her double: both have strong views which they believe are crucially important to the American future; both are not quite willing or able to express those views themselves; and both are immediately and powerfully attracted to Verena, a character defined by (and even as) her voice and who thus can help them articulate their views and shape the future. However, there is an important difference: Olive wants Verena to speak for her, while Basil hopes to use Verena as an ideal dialogic audience against whom he can develop his arguments and whose voice he can then subsume into his own. And the narrator foreshadows Basil's success through his experiences with Newton, Luna's son: "He had been very nice to Newton, told him all about the war (quite the Southern version, of course . . .), and Newton did nothing but talk about him, calling him 'Rannie,' and imitating his pronunciation of certain words" (137). As this brief but crucial passage suggests, once Basil can articulate his Southern version of history, he will be able to convert his audience, not only to that narrative's validity, but also to the attractiveness of his previously incommunicable Southern accent and identity.

Before reaching that conversion narrative's apex, however, the novel provides, in the famous Memorial Hall scene, a red herring of sorts. In that scene, and particularly in Basil's reaction to the memorials to the Northern Civil War casualties, the narrator suggests that Verena and Basil's relationship is a classic romance of reunion, and reconciliation (with its emphasis on mutual forgetfulness and forgiveness) the novel's ultimate regional theme. As Basil "read[s] with tenderness each name and place—names often without other history, and forgotten Southern battles," he does indeed forget, "now, the whole question of sides and parties" (210). Michael Kreyling uses this moment to argue that Basil does not believe in the Lost Cause, and that in fact he is willing, in both his relationship with Verena and his Northern interactions more generally, to "put the past behind him" ("Nationalizing" 394). Yet describing the text's regional themes in such reconciliationist terms elides two critical points: Olive, not Verena, is the novel's most representative Northerner and Basil's bitter opponent at every turn, while Verena is as undefined in her regional heritage as she is in most other ways; and Basil's primary goal is to find a medium through which he can articulate his historical views and alternative perspective. That is, he might well be willing to reconcile with fellow veterans, but they are not the Northerners with whom he is struggling throughout the novel, nor those to whom he must make the case for his unique point of view. In light of those points, the Memorial Hall scene is largely an aberration, a brief detour from the conversion narrative which largely comprises the regional aspect of Basil and Verena's developing relationship.[33]

That conversion narrative reaches its turning point in Basil and Verena's New York conversations, particularly the final one in Central Park. In chapter 3 I discuss the two conversants' different goals and tactics in these dialogues, how Basil's single-minded determination to convince Verena overpowers her desire for a free and fair exchange of ideas. But Basil's Southern voice likewise contributes to Verena's conversion to his "intensely conservative" perspective (285–86), as illustrated by one of the text's most unusual and significant passages: "A strange feeling came over her, a perfect willingness not to keep insisting on her own side, and a desire not to part from him with a mere accentuation of their differences. Strange I call the nature of her reflections, for they softly battled with each other as she listened, in the warm, still air, . . . to his deep, sweet, distinct voice, expressing monstrous opinions with exotic cadences" (287). Although the narrator goes on to attribute this "spell . . . upon her as she listen[s]" to Verena's "easily submissive . . . nature," a significant part of Basil's vocal power here derives (as it apparently did in his instruction of young Newton) from his voice's distinctiveness, his Southern accent's exotic cadences. In fact, that accent is far more important in the conversion process than any particular arguments of Basil's; while Carrington converts Madeleine to his perspective through a combination of sound reasoning and reminders of her Southern affiliations, in Basil's case the reasoning is subsumed into the spell cast by his voice, so distinct from the Northern voices to which Verena is accustomed. Or, more precisely, reason follows voice in this case, for Verena comes to discover (despite Olive's immediate removal of her from Basil's pres-

ence) that Basil's "words, the most effective and penetrating he had uttered, had sunk into her soul and worked and fermented there," and
"she had come at last to believe them, and that was the alteration, the
transformation. . . . It was simply that the truth had changed sides" (335).
Even monstrous opinions, it seems, when uttered in a voice as effective
as it is distinctive, can be converted into truth, and Verena has under-
gone just such a conversion process.

Yet the opinions were described as monstrous, highlighting another
aspect of the text's construction of both Basil and Verena's conversion:
the narrator's ambivalence toward them. The complexity and insta-
bility of James's use of point of view in *Bostonians,* particularly when
compared to his use of a single narrative consciousness in almost every
other work of published fiction, has been well documented, and emphasizes the distance between the narrator and all his characters, including
Basil—a distance that contrasts with the clearer proximity between Adams's and his Southern character's ideas.[34] For that reason, Basil's conversion of Verena is best read, in regional terms, less as James's position
on what the post-Reconstruction future should be than as a depiction
of what it will be. Such a reading, moreover, allows for an analysis of the
novel's complex conclusion that does not depend on unraveling James's
attitudes toward it. At least two things about that ending are clear: Basil
emerges victorious in his battle with Olive, removing Verena (by a combination of "muscular force" and her own volition) from the Boston
auditorium which was to host her greatest speaking engagement; and
Olive is left behind to fill in as best she can. Entirely uncertain, however, are both how Olive will perform in that role—we have only Basil's
speculations that "whatever she should say to them (and he thought
she might indeed be rather embarrassed), it [is] not apparent that they
[are] likely to hurl the benches at her"—and what Basil and Verena's future will hold; Verena says "I am glad" but at the same time sheds tears
that, "with the union, so far from brilliant, into which she [is] about to
enter, . . . [are] not the last she [is] destined to shed" (393–94).[35]

Without determining the narrator's or James's position on these developments, and keeping in mind the novel's constructions of regional
voice and identity, an analysis of that conclusion could read like this:
The Southern voice has converted the larger national audience to its
perspective and version of history and the two are poised to enter once

again into a union, although not without misgivings on the nation's part; despite its attraction to the South, it remembers that region's monstrous opinions and the damage to the union which they caused.[36] The stronger and more resilient Northern voices have resisted this conversion (it was, after all, never particularly directed at them in the first place) and can, if they choose, articulate their own visions of past and future, although for now it seems likely that they will not meet with the same success as the South. The novel foreshadows that lack of success in the fate of Miss Birdseye, whose formerly influential Northern, abolitionist voice speaks to increasingly small and insignificant postbellum audiences, as exemplified by Basil's recognition that "the only persons . . . to whom her death made a real difference were three young women in a small 'frame-house' on Cape Cod" (350).[37] Finally, while James neither explicitly endorses the Southern perspective nor portrays the Northern one as corrupt and dangerous (both of which Adams does), he nonetheless constructs this Southern victory as the seemingly inevitable end toward which postbellum dialogues over the South question are tending, given the power, attractiveness, and effectiveness of the Southern voice. For both Adams and James, then, as for Southern authors such as Taylor, Cooke, and Leigh (notwithstanding the various writers' notably different degrees of personal investment and enthusiasm), the future holds not simply reconciliation between the regions, but conversion of the nation by the Southern voice and version of history.

Southern partisans and Northern converts were not the only writers to consider the South question in the post-Reconstruction decade, but their formidable joint influence on the era's literary production has tended to shape critical readings of even those authors who constructed different Southern images. For example, Constance Fenimore Woolson's Southern stories have been collectively described as her attempt to "extol every southern virtue available and to capitalize on each unique aspect of a passing way of life" (Anne Rowe 62); similarly, one of the few references to Mary Noailles Murfree's novel *Where the Battle Was Fought* (1885) dismisses it as "represent[ing] the type of work which enlisted Northern sympathy for the devastation wrought by Northern invasions" (Buck 213–14).[38] Certainly some of Woolson's stories fit into the era's dominant literary discourses about the South, from a romance of reunion to a nostalgic depiction of race to a bitter conversion narrative; and Murfree's well-known collection *In the Tennessee Mountains* (1884) depicts as deeply attractive the Southern preference for tradition and conservatism over progress and change. But in the authors' best works on the South, they are able, both by constructing settings that embody the past's presence and by developing powerful, interregional dialogues, to portray the complex interplay of history and voice that truly constitutes the South question.

Woolson has been described as a germinal figure, both chronologically and generically, in the Northern construction of the postbellum South: Fred Pattee claims that "her pen was the first to picture for Northern readers the war-desolated South" ("Constance" 130); and Paul Buck calls her "the only Northern author who made a positive contribution to the development of the Southern genre" (203). While later recoveries and redefinitions have challenged both positions, the fact remains that Woolson was distinctively focused on the South in the 1870s, living in St. Augustine, Florida, from 1873 to 1879 and writing about the entire region in travelogues, in editorials, and in the stories collected in *Rodman the Keeper: Southern Sketches* (1880). And there exists in many of those writings—and, just as importantly, in Henry James's famous assessment of *Rodman*'s value "when regarded in the light of the voicelessness of the conquered and Reconstructed South"—a common thread of attraction to and sympathy for the South that has led to the image of Woolson as one of the earliest and most fervent Northern literary converts.[39]

For critics seeking to confirm such perceptions, *Rodman* contains ample evidence. There is for example "Old Gardiston," a note-perfect romance of reunion in which the strong but threatened Southern belle and the sympathetic Northern soldier gradually abandon their grudges, forgive and forget, and unite in marriage, while the one character interested in the past, the belle's antiquarian cousin Copeland, is a naïve fool; for good measure, "Gardiston" also contains a thoroughly Southern account of Reconstruction, highlighted by the assertion that "the unhappy State had fallen into the hands of double-faced, conscienceless whites, who used the newly enfranchised blacks as tools for their evil purposes" (116). Even more obvious in its sympathies and objectionable in its version of history is "King David," a bitingly satirical account of a Northern reformer's total failure as a schoolteacher for freedmen, in which a traditional Southern planter offers the most rational perspective, the freed slaves turn quickly and thoroughly to drink and mischief of all kinds, and the reformer returns to the North, having not found "the blacks what he expected" (275).[40]

Perhaps the most troubling, and certainly unique, of Woolson's pro-South stories is her version of a conversion narrative, "In the Cotton Country." In this tale, a first-person narrator who is clearly Woolson herself relates her own conversion to the Southern perspective, through a series of encounters with a forlorn, ruined farmwoman and her symbolically mute grandson. More exactly, Woolson lets that woman convert the narrator and reader directly, ceding narrative voice over to the Southerner for the story's final two-thirds. And the narrator makes clear her intent in so ceding the storytelling voice: "In time I succeeded in building up a sort of friendship with this solitary woman of the waste, and in time she told me her story. Let me tell it to you. I have written stories of imagination, but this is a story of fact, and I want you to believe it. It is true, every word of it, save the names given, and, when you read it, you whose eyes are now upon these lines, stop and reflect that it is only one of many life-stories like unto it" (184). It is this story that likely prompted James's comment about Woolson's speaking for the voiceless South, and "Cotton" certainly allows a particular Southerner to articulate a story that resonates with a larger set of postbellum Southern experiences and views. Yet that story is one in which Southerners are constantly and entirely victimized, whether by Northern aggression during the war or black-dominated Reconstruction government after it, and the woman comes to a nostalgic, hopeless, pained conclusion (one with which Woolson concludes her story, with no framing comments of her own) that exemplifies the Old South and Lost Cause constructions of Southern history:

Let him [her grandson] grow up under the new regime; I have told him nothing of the old. . . . It seems we were wrong, all wrong; then we must be very right now, for the blacks are our judges, councilors, postmasters, representatives, and law-makers. That is as it should be, isn't it? What! not so? But how can it be otherwise? . . . I do not know anything certainly any more, for my world

has been torn asunder, and I am uprooted and lost. . . . Let us alone;
we will watch the old life out with [the old country], and when her
new dawning comes we shall have joined our dead, and all of us,
our errors, our sins, and our sufferings will be forgotten. (195–96)

This speech's underhanded political and racial commentary is bad
enough, but far worse is the assertion that this Southern voice and version of history have not been heard (and thus, implicitly, that they need
the aid of a Northern voice like Woolson's); in fact, they were already at
this moment beginning to dominate the literary and cultural dialogues
about the South question, thanks in no small measure to stories like
"Cotton."[41]

All this evidence notwithstanding, however, Woolson could construct
narratives which portrayed the complex realities of postbellum Southern
history and voice, as exemplified by the collection's titular, first, and best
story, "Rodman the Keeper." In this story of a Northern veteran living
in the South and serving as "keeper of the dead" at a Union cemetery
built on a Confederate prison's former site, and particularly in her inter-
woven constructions of the cemetery as metaphor for the past's influential presence and of interregional dialogues that privilege no one voice
or version of history, Woolson fully undermines the overly simplistic regional images developed in her aforementioned stories and in so many
of the period's narratives of the South question.[42] For example, instead
of the racial clichés of "David" and "Cotton," the story includes a brief
but moving description of freed slaves placing flowers on the Union
graves in celebration of Memorial Day (32–33). Similarly, the story sets
up a potential (if May–December) romance of reunion between John
Rodman and Bettina Ward, the daughter of a Confederate veteran, but
concludes with a highly charged conversation, rather than an engagement, between the two.

Memorial Day and charged conversation, past and dialogue, are in
fact the story's principal, interconnected subjects, and they are developed in a unique and effective (if somewhat melodramatic) manner.
The opening descriptions of both the nearby Southern town and Rodman's role at the cemetery construct the past as a fixed entity, if one
broad enough to embody simultaneously loss and nostalgia, ruin and
escape from the present. The town is, Rodman notes, in a "second es-

tate" that bears close if degraded resemblance to its antebellum "first estate"—he observes "the pleasant, rambling old mansions, each with its rose-garden and neglected outlying fields, the empty negro quarters falling into ruin, and everything just as it stood when on that April morning the first gun was fired on Sumter." This state of ruined similitude is due partly to necessity (the war's losses, in population and otherwise) and partly to nostalgia, to "sorrow for the lost cause" and a desire to replicate the Old South where "everywhere magnificence went hand in hand with neglect." Rodman seems to critique the nostalgia while understanding the necessity, but regardless his work obligations separate him from this temporal standstill's future implications and relationship to the South question: "It is part of a great problem now working itself out," but that has no connection to him, as he is "not here to tend the living, but the dead" (10–11). The town and Rodman, then, are similarly fixated on and fixed in the past by both desire and necessity, and concurrently isolated from the larger world because of it.

Yet no sooner has this isolation been established than it is challenged, by an unlikely but appropriate source: the voice of the past. In response to Rodman's articulation of his duties, "a voice seem[s] to rise from the still ranks below . . . the [cemetery's] long mounds," arguing, "'While ye have time, do good to men. . . . Behold, we are beyond your care'" (11). Apparently no one, not even a solitary gravekeeper, can entirely escape from the world and its dialogues, for the past contained in those graves has its own voice. Even if the world prefers not to acknowledge it—as the narrator notes, for most visitors to such a cemetery the graves "seem already a part of the past, that near past which in our hurrying American life is even now so far away" (12)—that voice will make itself heard, intruding into present considerations and circumstances. And as its response to Rodman indicates, the past's voice does not fit any preexisting images, but brings its own perspective to the conversation, establishing dialogue where there has been only monologue.

Despite the past's challenge to his preferences for it and isolation, Rodman welcomes such dialogue, and furthers it by developing imaginary but meaningful conversations with some of the deceased veterans under his care. On one level his responses indicate a continued and rather morbid (if humorous) attraction to the past, as when he instructs one John Andrew, "Now then, don't fancy I am sorrowing for you; no doubt you are better off than I am at this very moment" (13). But the dialogues also suggest another factor in Rodman's choice of profession: he hopes to rediscover and validate his own experiences and identity through his work at the cemetery. He imagines that he and one of the fallen soldiers are "friends even now although separated for a time," and together they "wander" in memory "over the whole seven days" battle, in which both men had fought (15). Even more significantly, he fixates on the grave of one "—Rodman," whom he names "Blank Rodman" and of whom he notes, "It might easily have been John. And then, where should *I* be?" (15). This fallen Rodman reifies the living one's connections to the past yet illustrates the distinction made by the past's voice: Rodman is still alive, carrying his history and identity with him into the present, and thus not a blank like his buried namesake.

Significantly, it is shortly after this moment that Rodman makes his first Southern acquaintance, a disabled Confederate veteran living out his final days in a small house near the cemetery, with whom Rodman takes the next steps toward genuine dialogue. There is a sense in which this shell of a man is physically no different from the deceased veterans with whom Rodman converses; indeed, when Rodman discovers the veteran and says, "Excuse me. I thought nobody lived here," the Southerner's bitter but accurate reply is, "Nobody does. . . . I am not much of a body, am I?" (17). Yet while the deceased soldiers' histories are buried with them, this veteran, Ward De Rosset, retains his war memories—they are, in fact, all that is left him—and those memories form the core of his relationship with Rodman from its initiation. After exchanging a few pleasantries, the two men "remain silent, busy with their own thoughts; for each had recognized the ex-soldier, Northern and Southern, in portions of the old uniforms, and in the accent" (18). Distinct as those histories and voices are, they also symbolize the men's connections in experience and identity, which provoke Rodman to overcome his desire for isolation, move De Rosset into his more comfortable home, and help care for him as the destruction begun by his war wounds is completed.

In taking this step, Rodman quite literally transfers his care from the dead to the living (or at least to some in-between state), just as the voice of the past had instructed, and so it is entirely appropriate that he discusses the step with that voice. Moreover, this conversation is the first in which Rodman does not simply state his own responses to the dead, but also imagines at length their reply, as articulated by his doppelganger Blank Rodman. And despite his own Northern birth and Union war service, Rodman now imagines himself as occupying a middle ground between North and South, telling the soldiers that "the war is over, and you Northerners have gained every point for which you fought." Blank Rodman takes a similarly generous position, replying that he is "glad the poor Confederate [is] up in the cottage, and he [does] not think any less of the keeper for bringing him there." Or at least, Rodman notes, "That is what he would have said" (23–24); and in this meta-reflection on his imaginary conversations, Rodman indicates not only his awareness of their artificiality but also, and more importantly, that they represent an earnest attempt to come to terms with the history represented by the Northern veterans and to place that history in dialogue with this Southerner's past and identity.

Having constructed such a dialogue, Rodman can take the next step, sharing his own personal history with De Rosset. Although the narrator has made a point of withholding any details of Rodman's war experiences or reason for coming South after the war, mirroring Rodman's reticence on those topics, the keeper now admits, in response to De Rosset's queries, "I don't know that I have any objection to telling the story. I am not sure but that it will do me good to hear it all over myself in plain language again" (35). And tell it he does, narrating in the text's longest section of continuous dialogue a story in which war experiences disrupt and alter his life in every imaginable way, much as they did for so many Southerners: his mother dies while he is away, his fiancée "turn[s] false," he sells the family farm and loses the money, and his "health fail[s]," prompting him to move South in search of that region's "healing climate" (36). While this tale of woe is almost as melodramatic as the farm woman's narration in "Cotton," there is a key difference: Rodman tells this story not to elicit sympathy for questionable political views, nor to offer an ideological alternative to a larger national narrative, but rather and simply to connect with another person, and particularly one as superficially different as De Rosset, through shared history and identity.

If the story ended with this exchange or offered it as the only model of interregional dialogue, it would be in two ways too simplistic in its construction of history and voice. For one thing, De Rosset is as fully fixed in history as Rodman, in both his emphasis on his war experiences and his proximity to his own cemetery mound, and thus does not suggest history's connections to the present or the future. For another, the similarities in the men's experiences, and the corresponding ease with which they can connect and transcend their regional distinctions, could be read as a homosocial romance of reunion, albeit one in which shared remembering (rather than forgetting) is the basis for reconciliation. Yet De Rosset is not the story's only Southern voice, and the other, his young cousin Bettina Ward, complicates both the historical emphasis and the reconciliationist nature of Rodman and De Rosset's relationship. For despite Bettina's initial description as a classic Southern belle, "young and dimpled and dewy; one of the creamy roses of the South" (25), she is more closely affiliated with the future, with the South's uncertain relationship to its past (her dying cousin), and with a bitterness toward the North that Bettina exemplifies by noting of Northern women who put flowers on Southern soldiers' graves that "They must be angels. We have no angels here" (34).

The story does not offer answers to the questions Bettina represents; nor does it unite her in marriage with a Northern soldier like Rodman, as might be expected of the postbellum belle. It does, however, provide at its conclusion a balanced, unresolved dialogue between Bettina and Rodman that concisely expresses those questions' significance. De Rosset has died, but Bettina returns to the cemetery a final time, "mov[ing] to and fro among the mounds, pausing often." When Rodman asks why she has come, she offers only a partial reply: "Because Ward was here—and because—because—never mind. It is enough that I wished to walk once among those mounds." It seems that the connection between her family's history and that represented by the Union cemetery has changed Bettina somewhat, but she also notes that she is attempting to leave the past behind, moving to Tennessee to "begin a new existence." Rodman will not let her abandon the past so quickly, arguing that she has "scarcely begun the old [existence]" and asking her to "write [her] name in . . . the visitors' register," to prove that she "can think gently of the men who lie there under the grass." But despite her time among the mounds, Bettina does not write, offering instead a final articulation of the past's painful hold on her: "Shall I, Bettina Ward, set my name in black and white as a visitor to this cemetery, where lie fourteen thousand of the soldiers who killed my father, my three brothers, my cousins; who

brought desolation upon all our house, and ruin upon all our neighborhood, all our State, and all our country?—for the South is our country,
and not your North. Shall I forget these things? Never!" To inscribe her
name in this national register, Bettina argues, would be to turn her back
on the Southern version of the war, and that philosophical abandonment of her history and identity is clearly less possible than her upcom-
ing geographical relocation. And Rodman understands her voice and
position, responding: "Nothing can change you. . . . I know it, I have
known it all along; you are part of your country, part of the time, part of
the bitter hour through which she is passing. Nothing can change you; if
it could, you would not be what you are, and I should not—But you can
not change. . . . Follow your path out into the world. Yet do not think,
dear, that I have not seen—have not understood" (37–40). Rodman recognizes the ways in which Bettina is fixed in and by the past, bringing
the story full circle. Yet its constructions of history and dialogue have
not been static—Rodman has been changed by his conversations with
the dead soldiers, the nearly dead De Rosset, and the painfully living
Bettina; and, despite Rodman's assertion that Bettina can not change,
her brief visit to the cemetery, caused by her cousin's presence and connections there, indicates that in the South new perspectives on and dialogues about history and identity are likewise possible.[43]

Just as the stereotypical Southern narratives in Woolson's *Rodman the
Keeper* have overshadowed the more original and dialogic title story, the
continued scholarly attention to Murfree's *In the Tennessee Mountains*
(published, as were all her early works, under the pseudonym Charles
Egbert Craddock) has obscured what I would argue is a more significant text, her novel *Where the Battle Was Fought*. The focus on *Mountains* is certainly understandable, as the collection is an exemplary local color text, and thus of interest not only for its stories' humor, pathos,
and formal skill, but also as an autobiographical, geographical, linguistic, and sociohistorical document.[44] Yet *Mountains*' stories are linked just
as strongly by an emphasis on and preference for a deeply traditional
Southern viewpoint; Murfree's Old South and Lost Cause do not explicitly connect to slavery or race, and so seem less objectionable than
Virginia's or the Deep South's, but they nonetheless oppose and triumph over a modern, cultured, forward-looking voice closely tied to the
North. And so it is easy to group Murfree with other postbellum writ-

ers who romanticized the South, and concurrently to dismiss *Battle* as "the type of work which enlisted Northern sympathy for the devastation wrought by Northern invasions" (Buck 213–14).[45]

The few critics who analyze *Battle* at any length, however, agree—despite distinct viewpoints on the novel's quality and modern relevance—that it is anything but a typical postbellum Southern text. Edd Parks, who emphasizes the novel's autobiographical elements, notes that Murfree "has no sectional purpose to serve," which was "far from the usual Southern point of view, fifteen years after the war" (102–3, 116); while Sarah Gardner, in the context of women's Civil War narratives, explicitly contrasts Murfree with those Southern "authors of the immediate post-war era" who "shared the belief that Southern majesty and grandeur rested with Confederacy," arguing that Murfree "never identified with the Confederacy" (104–5).[46] And while *Battle* does contain elements typical of the period's Civil War literature—a romance between a Union soldier and the daughter of a Confederate general with a deep allegiance to the Old South; plot developments and secret revelations that serve to reunite the regions—it constructs them, and the histories and regions they symbolize, in original and complex ways. More specifically, Murfree's novel (like "Rodman") both constructs a setting in which history has a living presence and voice and develops dialogues between its principal characters that reflect and alter each one's perspective on regional history and identity.

Before discussing those effective aspects of Murfree's text, I should note that even her most melodramatic and convoluted plot strand represents an original construction of postbellum Southern history and voice. In this plotline, a corrupt Southern gentleman attempts to swindle a noble widow out of her family estate, and the tool he uses is "a curious twist in the law, the interregnum or period of legal grace allowed to those Confederates who had been 'beyond the seas' during or after the Civil War" (Parks 78–79). In order to capitalize on the Northern generosity toward Southern veterans with this specific history, the villain resuscitates the widow's deceased relative, employing an actor to portray the Confederate. The result is mostly a series of sinister, secret conversations between the two men and desperate, teary times for the widow, interspersed with an occasional digression into the finer details of inheritance law; nevertheless, this plot device nicely undermines two key aspects of postbellum history. First, it unearths a little known aspect of Northern amnesty toward the Confederate South, and exposes it as an opportunity for self-interested and destructive revisions of the historical record that separate upstanding Southerners from their family, past, and home. Second, it demonstrates that Civil War memories and regional identity can themselves be manipulated, and are thus not necessarily the hallowed ground that Lost Cause proponents would portray. And as I will argue, this plotline's conclusion connects it effectively to the novel's broader images of regional history, identity, and voice.

The first, and unique, such image is suggested by the title: the Civil War battlefield on which most of the text's action occurs. The book's first two paragraphs introduce that setting in two distinct but inter-connected ways:

It is said that a certain old battlefield in Tennessee is haunted in these peaceful times. Often there comes out of the dark silence the sudden wild blare of the bugle chilling the blood of distant fire-side groups. Then the earth throbs with the roll of drums and the measured tread of martial hosts. A mysterious clangor, as of the clash of arms, fills the air. A flash—it is the glinting of bayonets above the grim earthworks which still loom up against the vague horizon.

And yet there are those who can hear, in the military music and the tumultuous voices of victory and defeat, only the rush of the wind across the vast historic plain; who can see, in the gleaming phantoms that hold the works, only the mist and the moon; who can feel, in the tremor of the earth beneath a charging column, only the near approach of the railway train thundering through the cavernous limestone country. (1)

Most apparent in this dichotomous depiction of the battlefield's ef-fects (besides the prose's overly florid nature, characteristic of Murfree's style throughout) is the distinction between those residents who are "haunted" by the past and those who are not, but the passage includes two other key elements. For one thing, the haunted version of the battle-field is specifically introduced as a narrative: "It is said" that the past still lingers in this way. Yet at the same time, this self-conscious narrative of haunted history is formally constructed as the truth, as evidenced by the use of direct phrases ("it is the glinting of bayonets"); while the second paragraph's rational, sensory perceptions are constructed, through the repetition of and primacy given to the haunted version ("who can hear, in the military music . . . , only the rush of the wind"), as a delusion from which "those" few (contrasted with the unnamed, and thus implicitly larger, group that "says" the haunted version) suffer. In other words, the voice of history symbolized by the haunted battlefield is explicitly introduced as a narrative produced by the Southern voices that inhabit it, but one no less—and perhaps more—real and influential because of it.

Having established that strong connection between the battlefield's history and the town's Southern voice, Murfree goes one step further by literally situating her text's most localized characters, the ferryman Tom Toole and his fugitive brother-in-law Graffy, within the battlefield itself. Graffy explicitly connects to the battlefield's historical presence: he has killed a man in self-defense and takes refuge in the field's "empty powder magazine," where he is continually frightened by yet also mirrors the ghostly "harnts," with his "vague presence" suggesting "hallucination" more than man (83–86). And Toole, who alone knows Graffy's secret location, closely links to Southern and historical voices: the former because his speech is represented with the text's most elaborate use of dialect; the latter since he uses his powerful singing voice to communicate unobtrusively with both Graffy and the battlefield's spirits while performing his daily duties: "Sometimes there were war songs; sometimes quaint antiquated ditties which his grandfather had brought here . . . ; often he sang a certain old hymn, and its dominant iteration—'Peace—peace—be still!'—resounded in its strong constraining intensity far and wide over the battlefield— . . . thrilling through the haunted thickets, and breaking the silence with a noble pathos where the shadowy pickets lurked and listened" (85). In his singing of these old songs, which speak to personal, regional, and Confederate histories yet explicitly ease all three pasts' painful associations, Toole indicates the complexity and power of Murfree's depiction of the living, connected presence of history and voice on the battlefield.

Also living on the battlefield and tied to its history is one of the novel's two most significant characters, the one-armed Confederate veteran General Vayne. Vayne lives with his daughter Marcia, his young son, and a few remaining servants in a half-ruined house that almost too obviously mirrors that history: it is "dismantled and desolate, ris[ing] starkly above the dismantled desolation of the plain" (2). And upon the general's initial appearance, Murfree links his perspective just as closely to the past: the narrator names him "the unreconstructed" (5), and the general admits that he is "conservative in [his] views," since "conservatism . . . is the moral centripetal force that curbs the flighty world" (6). The dichotomy between the general's affiliation with a glorious past and his present realities (exemplified by his house's condition) could be read as satirical, as the narrator hints by noting that, "with his young family growing up around him and only privation in the present and this mortgaged ruin to leave them as an estate, he [is] a marvelously apt illustration of the ignoble fact, failure—a fact of which he [is] most profoundly, most pathetically, unconscious" (14). Yet as she does so often, Murfree later complicates this image: Vayne recognizes that he has grown "dulled in suffering for the past" of the "Lost Cause" (107–8), but also notes, in a significant exchange with Marcia (who generally symbolizes the future), that it is only their proud past to which they can turn for continued hope (112–13).[47]

If the general is thus tied to, obsessed with, and limited by his regional past and identity, the novel's second protagonist, John Estwicke, symbolizes the possibilities and dangers of severing such ties. Estwicke is what the general calls one of "these home-made Yankees, these Southern Yankees," a Tennessee resident (from the same area) who chose to join the Union army (15, 7–8). While Estwicke is perfectly willing to defend that choice—indeed, it constitutes a primary cause of his "inordinate personal pride" (7)—it has apparently produced a deep aversion to the Southern Civil War past; as Marcia notes in their first meeting, Estwicke "has a morbid horror of that battlefield. And a reason for it" (9). Perhaps in response to that historical aversion, Estwicke has developed a guiding philosophy that renders the past immediately useless and meaningless: upon witnessing a sunset, for example, he states that "it's gone forever. There's no resurrection for a dead day. It's a type of the irrevocable. And what is done—is done" (123). But just as the general's historical and regional emphases do not go unchallenged, neither will circumstances allow Estwicke to maintain these rigid dichotomies between past and present, South and himself. Those dichotomies are partly, symbolically undermined from the novel's outset, when Tom Toole mistakes Estwicke for a dead Confederate of whom he is "the livin' image" (20–21); although this resemblance remains a mystery until the conclusion, it immediately indicates that Estwicke is closer to history and region than he would admit. And instrumental in those connections' gradual unfolding are Estwicke and Marcia's dialogues.

The most overt such exchange illustrates both Marcia's symbolic connection to the future and that connection's roots in her regional and historical identity. In response to Estwicke's philosophy about dead days, Marcia replies, "To-day has left its mark on the world—a vast deal of useful work has been done everywhere. And 'To-morrow' is already sailing on the high seas, and bright and early in the morning she will be here." It would be easy for this blithe optimism to seem powerless and even silly in the face of not just Estwicke's pessimism, but also the destruction and hopelessness that surround Marcia; but Murfree stresses that Marcia's statement actually derives from her specific experiences and identity, and thus strikes Estwicke as courageous and powerful. "Instead of bewailing the ruin of the war, she busie[s] herself in picking up the pieces. . . . He sigh[s]—he [is] only reminded of the faith and affection which [bind] together that little home-circle in perfect peace, here where the battle was fought" (123–24). Indeed, Marcia's declaration, like all their dialogues, occurs on the battlefield, and her perspective and influence blend with its historical power to change Estwicke. At first he claims that, while aware of the "solemn oration in the [field's] air" and "thrilled by the electric eloquence," he does not "hear it," largely because he refuses to connect with it; "I have never had a home," he maintains (146). But over the course of the novel and their conversations, "Marcia and nature together [do] much to soften the traces of that terrible event" (310), and with the field's history no longer so terrible to Estwicke, he can start to admit his own connections to past and place, promising Marcia that some day he must "tell [her] something more—the great trouble and haunting sorrow of my life." Having begun that process, they can likewise begin to make peace with the battlefield's pain: "The tread of martial feet shook the ground. And all unheeding—here where the battle was fought—youth, and love, and life rode bravely through the spectred twilight" (281–82).

Richard Cary argues, in the most extended analysis of *Battle*, that

Estwicke and Marcia's love signals a triumph of North and future over South and past, that "the discord between Vayne and Estwicke" symbolizes "the struggle between forces of the South and the North for ascendancy of the past over the present" and thus that "in the outcome Miss Marcia predicts the emergence of a new South, one born out of coalition with the strength and vision of the North (Estwicke) that triumphs over the old traditions (Vayne) and infuses the new generation (Marcia) with a germ of hope for the future" (117–19). But this schematic reading, besides eliding such complexities as Estwicke's regional and historical duality, Vayne's self-consciousness of his obsession with tradition, and Marcia's own regionally and historically influenced perspective on the future, also misses a crucial corollary of Estwicke's dialogic development: its influence on the general. Estwicke's renewed connections to region and past, exemplified by his rescue of Graffy (the battlefield's ghost) from an exploding keg of gunpowder (a symbolic echo of the war), lead the general to question his own dichotomy between glorious past and ruined present, heroic Confederates and invading Union soldiers. And that questioning both liberates him from the mythic past's hold and reminds him of those historical details worth remembering: "His own fine deeds of valiance stretched out in the darkness of the Lost Cause like the brilliant track of a falling star. He had thought them then only prosaic duty; now they had loosed all hold on his memory. But every enthusiastic pulse throbbed in accord with this fine deed that another man had done" (359). The Lost Cause may now be dark for the general, but his own past, and its connections to Estwicke, can affect him more deeply than such myths ever could, and with that emotional impact comes the possibility of a future: "I have not the slightest objection," he replies to Marcia's desire to marry Estwicke (359).

Before that union can be finalized, however, Estwicke must keep his promise and reveal his full history and identity to Marcia and her father, in the novel's lengthy concluding scene. His narrative and its connections to the novel's other main plotline are convoluted, but boil down to this: Estwicke's father was John Fortescue, the dead Confederate soldier who was related to the noble widow and whose identity the villain's actor friend assumed in order to cheat that widow out of her inheritance. This final revelation not only unifies the plot but also substantiates Murfree's complex, interconnected constructions of region and history. Est-

wicke is not only from the region, it is also in a very real sense his father, and his connection to it goes far beyond geography—he is, as Toole
noted, a "living image" of his father, and, just as importantly, speaks
"with his voice" (392–93). The novel's title thus assumes a new level
of meaning, for this battle pitted Estwicke against his father as well as
his region, and "the stern, savage old battlefield, indelibly marked with
its own irrevocable history" (417), is for him at once the site of an unquestionable break with the Southern past and a permanent, inescapable reminder of his ties to that past. Despite the pain occasioned by his
narrative—at first Estwicke claims that he "can't talk about this thing—
it kills" him (417)—it does allow him to recapture his own history and
identity, to wrest them back from two impostors (the villainous actor
and Estwicke's own self-denying role) and make them part of his continued movement into the future. And it is precisely Murfree's construction of the past's living presence in every aspect of her characters' identities and voices that turns the text's final exchange—in which Marcia
claims that Estwicke's father has witnessed his changes because "God is
so good," and the lovers "turn toward the east and the future" (423)—
from overly optimistic reconciliationist cliché into a hard-earned, open-
ended acknowledgment of the need to build an interregional future that
incorporates the regional past's painful but vital details.

⟜

In their best works from the decade, then, Woolson and Murfree engage with and complicate the era's dominant narratives of Southern history and voice: reconciliation and conversion. The most formally innovative such engagements, however, were developed by Albion W. Tourgée
in his two historical novels of Reconstruction, *A Fool's Errand* (1879) and
Bricks Without Straw (1880). As is well known, Tourgée was as deeply invested in Reconstruction's politics, promise, and process as he was in cri-
tiquing its failures and the subsequent rise of the Southern voice and
version of history, and so critical readings of his novels have been overwhelmingly biographical and political. Scholars have almost uniformly
dismissed the novels' formal aspects as either nonexistent, thoroughly
traditional and romantic, or, occasionally, a combination of both.[48] Biography and politics certainly constitute the Reconstruction historical
novels' starting points and ultimate purposes, but their most significant

feature is Tourgée's development of a new form for historical literature, one that can adequately contain, represent, and analyze the multivocal nature of the South question's histories and dialogues.

Before describing that new form's key elements, I believe it is important to reiterate (especially given my aversion, throughout this study, to overly biographical or political readings of literary texts) my agreement with the description of these novels as primarily and profoundly influenced by Tourgée's biography and politics. The biographical basis for *Fool's,* and in particular for its protagonist Comfort Servosse, has been thoroughly established; while *Bricks* strays further from Tourgée's specific experiences, it just as clearly relies on people, places, and events he knew and witnessed in the Reconstruction South.[49] And both novels' political themes and goals—with *Fool's* focused on Southern politics, *Bricks* more centrally concerned with race, and both attempting to counter the period's most aggressively pro-Southern voices and narratives— are equally paramount.[50] Yet when critics move directly from such biographical and political readings to reductive points about Tourgée's form—as in the common claim that both novels suffer from an overly didactic narrative voice—I believe they do an injustice to his formal innovations; those innovations in fact allow Tourgée to represent the complexities of biography and politics, the dialogic nature of his own experiences and of history and voice in the Reconstruction South.[51]

The brief "Letter to the Publishers" with which Tourgée begins *Fool's* both indicates that work's biographical basis and points toward its formal goal and first innovation. Tourgée suggests the text's biographical nature by explicitly comparing the book to his own person, arguing that he does not want to write a "Preface" since "it is like a man introducing himself." Instead, he uses the Letter to discuss his subject's historical precedents—famous fools and their errands—and then drives home that subject's close connections to the text's author by signing the Letter, as he did the first edition's title page, "One of the Fools." The Letter introduces not only this general tone of biographical identification and self-deprecation, but also, in its closing paragraph, a bold formal goal: "honest, uncompromising truthfulness of portraiture" (5–7). As noted above, when Tourgée's novels are credited with formal consistency at all, they are usually categorized as romantic; that categorization derives from both his philosophical opposition to realism, voiced in a number of essays and reviews, and many of the novels' plot devices: star-crossed lovers, moonlit chases, secret documents, mistaken identities, and so forth.[52] But Tourgée's reliance on such romantic devices should not obscure his primary, realistic formal goal, and it is precisely through his more unorthodox stylistic elements, such as the relationship between the voices of his foolish narrator and foolish protagonist, that he most fully achieves that goal.

That narrative relationship can best be described as a multifaceted bifurcating of the text's dominant point of view. On one level, that bifurcation occurs in the naming of the protagonist, as reflected in the novel's first sentence: "The Fool's patronymic was Servosse; his Christian name, Comfort" (9). As evidenced by this introduction, the protagonist is constructed from the outset in two distinct ways: his actual self, as defined by his name; and his perceived self, identified as the Fool. But of course, the title page and introductory Letter are signed "One of the Fools," and so this dichotomy between self and perception has already been complicated by a link to the text's narrative voice. Is the narrator the same Fool as his protagonist? And how exactly does either Fool relate to the fictional self known as Comfort Servosse? The usual critical response has been to connect all three identities to that of Albion Tourgée, actual historical self; to argue that Tourgée takes an ironic stance toward his own biography, calling himself the Fool and narrating his story through that lens. But this argument, while accurate as far as it goes, does not acknowledge the second level of narrative bifurcation produced by the text's divisions: that of voice. The novel's narrative voice is most exactly described as shared between Comfort Servosse's earnest voice and the narrator's ironic one, with the latter revealing the former's foolish undercurrents. A prominent example of this bifurcation of voice can be found when Servosse decides to move back to the postbellum South:

> "Oh," he replied, "there must be great changes, of course! Slavery has been broken up, and things must turn into new grooves; but I think the country will settle up rapidly, now that slavery is out of the way. Manufactures will spring up, immigration will pour in, and it will be just the pleasantest part of the country. I believe one-fifth of our soldiers—and that the very best part of them too—will find homes in the South in less than two years, just as soon as

they can clear out their old places, and find new ones there to their mind."

So he talked, forgetful of the fact that the social conditions of three hundred years are not to be overthrown in a moment, and that differences which have outlasted generations and finally ripened into war, are never healed by simple victory,—that the broken link can not be securely joined by mere juxtaposition of the fragments, but must be fused and hammered before its fibers will really unite. (24–25)

As this passage suggests, the division of narrative voice also represents a division in temporal situation and perspective: Servosse, located within his historical moment, generally looks forward, articulating a vision of the future; while the narrator, located within the moment of composition, looks backward, not simply at his protagonist (with all the virtues of hindsight) but also at the historical realities that complicate or undermine Servosse's vision of the future. And all the divisions comprised by this bifurcated narrative voice constitute important elements of Tourgée's realistic form of the historical novel, since they represent an attempt to capture an individual's perspective in both history and that history's subsequent narration.

Just as the bifurcated narrative voice allows Tourgée to construct his protagonist's evolving perspective in that multifaceted manner—and it does evolve, with Servosse's views gradually developing into a much closer approximation of the narrator's ironic, historically situated standpoint—so too does it create space for other voices and perspectives. That is, while a more traditional first-person narrative voice would typically serve as a novel's dominant perspective, this bifurcated voice, with its emphasis on the way in which any perspective is concurrently perceived by all those surrounding it, demands the inclusion of other voices. Once again, this multivocality occurs on at least two levels: the voices of other significant characters, including the Southern partisan Squire Hyman and the radical freedman Uncle Jerry, who express distinct perspectives on both Servosse and Southern history and politics; and more abstract voices that represent particular regional and historical viewpoints. While the former voices illustrate the breadth of Tourgée's realistic depiction of the postbellum South, the latter are more

indicative of his innovations in the historical novel's form. These abstract voices are concisely introduced in an early passage on varying perceptions of Union soldiers, who

> received different names in different localities. In some they were
> called "Boys in Blue," "The Country's Hope," and "Our Brave
> Soldier-Boys;" while in others they were termed "Lincoln's Hire-
> lings," "Abolition Hordes," and "Yankee Vandals." It may be ob-
> served, too, that the former methods of distinguishing them pre-
> vailed generally in the States lying to the north, and the latter in
> those lying to the south, of what used to be called "Mason and
> Dixon's line." Both meant the same thing. The difference was only
> in the form of expression peculiar to the respective regions. All
> those names, when properly translated, signified *Fools.* (20)

The narrator's belief that he can "properly translate" these various viewpoints and state most succinctly their overarching meaning exemplifies the voice so many critics have designated "didactic." Yet without dis-
missing that didactic narrator's existence, I believe it is important not to
elide the passage's connections of voice to geography ("the form of expression peculiar to the respective regions") and history ("what used to
be called"). Those connections, and the formal innovations with which
Tourgée represents such regional and historical voices, constitute significant aspects of his realistic historical novel.

Two extended passages exemplify Tourgée's multivocal, metanarra-
tive forms. The first is found in one of the text's narrative digressions,
chapters in which the narrator steps back from his protagonist to relate his version of historical details. In this chapter, "How the Wise Men
Builded," the narrator provides his account of Reconstruction's early
years, and his strong opinions about where Reconstruction's architects
miscalculated and failed would seem to validate descriptions of his didactic voice. But far from existing in a self-contained vacuum, the narrator's analysis is founded upon regional and historical voices; he separates
those voices into two distinct eras ("Ante Bellum" and "Post Bellum")
and quotes their opinions in a series of short sections entitled "The
Northern Idea of the Situation," "The Southern Idea of the Situation,"
"The Northern Idea of the Southern Idea," "The Southern Idea of the

Northern Idea," and so on (138–40). There is awkwardness in Tourgée's
structure here—a more experienced novelist might work these opposing positions into his narrative's dialogues—but this form also achieves
two meaningful effects. For one thing, it indicates how certain voices
and versions of history can become so closely associated with certain
regions at certain times that genuine dialogue becomes impossible; one
can imagine an infinite extension of this structure ("The Northern Idea
of the Southern Idea of the Northern Idea") in which each side continually redefines its perception of the other's voice. And this formal
choice likewise illustrates how any future historical analysis or narrative
of a moment like Reconstruction necessarily depends on such regional
voices, and thus, whatever its analytical distance from either side, runs
the risk of contributing to the process of dichotomous definition.

This sort of divided rather than dialogic interregional interaction was
not the era's only unproductive rhetorical and historical situation, however, nor its most significant. As Tourgée himself argued in his 1888 article about pro-Southern literary trends, the period also witnessed an increased presence of and national reliance upon a particular and highly
partisan Southern voice and version of history. And Tourgée, in constructing the Southern popular press's voice and dominance, also includes and complicates that trend in his innovative historical novel. The
thirtieth chapter, "A Thrice-Told Tale," nicely illustrates, through the
construction and dissemination of a particular version of a prominent
Northern reformer's murder, Tourgée's formal and thematic use of this
journalistic voice. The chapter is divided into three sections, each narrating the event in a different voice; the first comprises the voice of the
press, since, as the chapter's first sentence states, "the newspapers told it
first." Not only does the press thus articulate the initial account of the
murder, it also strongly influences later accounts. At the conclusion of
the newspapers' narratives, Tourgée notes that "so the act passed into
current history; and the great journals of the North recorded with much
minuteness" the details provided by their Southern counterparts. The
Southern version can even influence an antagonistic audience such as
Servosse, since "thus it first came to the Fool's ears." But the chapter's
remaining two sections bring new versions to those ears, articulated in
distinct voices—a more objective Southern perspective in section two; a
freedman's dialect voice in section three—which complicate and under-

mine the newspapers' straightforward narrative. Yet while these individual voices persuade Servosse to reexamine the history—and "upon further investigation, [he] learn[s] several facts strongly confirmatory of this strange story" as narrated by the freedman—they are of course much less heard and thus much less influential (in either the South or the nation) than the partisan and increasingly dominant voice exemplified by the pro-South press (205–23).

All these formal innovations, then, allow Tourgée to include, place in dialogue, and analyze a variety of voices within his realistic historical novel. A final characteristic which serves the same purpose is the inclusion of letters. While this particular device was by no means new to the American historical novel—one of the first, Catherine Maria Sedgwick's *Hope Leslie* (1826), includes a number of letters—Tourgée utilizes it in interestingly dialogic ways. Some of the letters provide additional instances of and commentaries on Servosse's voice, as he writes to various Northern advisors (collectively referred to by the narrator as "Wise Men"), details his experiences in and views of the South, and receives their replies and perspectives. The narrator is often openly critical of those responses, and concurrently of Servosse for relying on these geographically and philosophically distant advisors, and these letters could thus further illustrate the didactic narrative voice. Certainly they have that effect, although they also allow significant space for alternative perspectives (whether Servosse's or his conversants') to be presented in full and in their individual voices. But more clearly and thoroughly dialogic are those letters penned by Servosse's wife, Metta, who supports her husband's Southern efforts but does not hesitate, in these private missives to Northern friends, to articulate her own, quite distinct perspective on the South and their experiences there. And her letters are explicitly presented as alternatives to Servosse's voice and vision: the first letter is introduced, after a reference to Servosse's initial happiness with his new Southern home, with the question "Why attempt to paint the delights of that first winter at Warrington?"; and the letter itself, which "show[s] the feelings of the young wife," certainly does not paint such delights, depicting the family's new environment in a realistic voice that fully acknowledges the region's history ("It did seem terribly lonely and desolate when we first arrived. . . . The poor Confederacy must have been on its last legs when it gave up") and nicely counters Servosse's forward-looking optimism (45–46). Indeed, throughout the text Metta's letters complicate further Servosse's voice and perspective, indicating that not only detached Northerners or partisan Southerners, but even sympathetic soul mates, can take a quite distinct view of the experiences and environment described in Tourgée's realistic historical novel.

As a number of critics note, *Fool's* gradually becomes a romance of reunion, with Servosse's daughter Lily and a former Southern slave-holder's son playing the roles of the conflicted but ultimately united interregional lovers. Moreover, *Bricks Without Straw*, despite some of the era's only overtly critical literary depictions of the Ku Klux Klan and anti-black violence, as well as continued reliance on multiple voices, letters, and other formal innovations, focuses even more fully on such a romance: its reformist Northern schoolteacher heroine learns that she is connected by family history to a Southern plantation, the heir to which she comes to love; and that conservative Southern hero gains a different perspective and becomes the text's most explicit spokesman for Tourgée's own views of the South, Reconstruction, and the importance of education.[53] Yet despite their resonances with this earlier, more simplistic literary representation of the South question, both of Tourgée's Reconstruction novels, and especially the groundbreaking *A Fool's Errand*, emphasize in their subjects and exemplify in their formal innovations a complex, dialogic construction of voice, history, and region that engages with, but does not succumb to the lure of, the Southern version of those narratives.

That Southern version had by my decade's end become a dominant voice in not only cultural, but also, as Adams's and James's novels illustrate (if with differing degrees of enthusiasm), literary dialogues over the South question. But as Woolson's, Murfree's, and Tourgée's texts indicate, the period's most balanced literary engagements with the South question were those which acknowledged and modeled the dialogic nature of Southern (as well as Northern and national) voices, histories, and identities. Such texts are not necessarily able to refrain entirely from endorsing a particular version—certainly Tourgée's novels, with their overt connections to his biography and politics, are not consistently objective—but they likewise complicate that endorsement, both philosophically and formally, in ways that the conversion narratives generally do not. Similarly, while Woolson, Murfree, and Tourgée unquestionably engage with literary forms such as the romance of reunion or the conversion narrative, they make those forms part of, rather than the primary medium for, their dialogic depictions of voice, history, and the South question in the post-Reconstruction era.

Tourgée's novels are significant for another reason as well: they explicitly connect the South question to race in ways that many of the decade's other works on the subject do not. James's inclusion of a former abolitionist such as Miss Birdseye only highlights the ways in which conversion narratives must silence such racially focused voices in order to allow the South to make its case; Woolson's "Rodman" does include African American characters, particularly in the complex Memorial Day scene, but focuses, as does Murfree's novel, on the dialogues and reconciliations between white Union and Confederate soldiers and their families. While the absence of race as a central theme does not circumscribe the ability of these texts to engage the South question in complex and dialogic ways, its presence in Tourgée's novels further illustrates his texts' thematic breadth and formal complexity. And the connections between the South and race questions take center stage in what I would argue is the decade's most formally and thematically rich work of historical literature: George Washington Cable's *The Grandissimes*.

5

"The Way They Talked in New Orleans in Those Days"

Voice and History in and on *The Grandissimes*

The short opening chapter of George Washington Cable's novella "Madame Delphine," published in 1881 and included in subsequent editions of the collection *Old Creole Days,* makes explicit the geographical, historical, and linguistic project with which Cable's early fictional works were constantly engaged. The four-page chapter, entitled "An Old House," utilizes a striking second-person narrative voice found nowhere else in the novella (or the collection as a whole, for that matter). At first the chapter's "you" seems to be simply a more elegant stand-in for "one," as in the opening phrases: "A few steps from the St. Charles Hotel, in New Orleans, brings you to and across Canal Street, the central avenue of the city." But it quickly becomes clear that the chapter is tracing not a generalized tour of New Orleans taken by a universalized figure, but rather a specific path followed by a particular "you": the first paragraph concludes by noting that "the crowd . . . will follow Canal Street," and the second opens with, "But you turn, instead, into the quiet, narrow way."

Cable's use of "instead" here is crucial, for the path on which he leads his audience in this chapter is constructed as an explicit alternative to the dominant New Orleans narratives. That path represents first and foremost a historical alternative, one pursued by "a lover of Creole antiquity, in fondness for a romantic past." The past to which it leads is "ancient and foreign-seeming," distant both chronologically and culturally from that to which the reader is accustomed; and it is concurrently in danger of disappearing, both in reality ("every thing has settled down [into] a long sabbath of decay") and memory ("names in that region elude one like ghosts"). But it is kept alive through the alternative languages, the multivocal history, it contains: the narrow way on which narrator and reader walk is still called "the Rue Royale" by the aforementioned antiquarian; while its residents note in their distinct dialect, referring to the chapter's titular, seemingly abandoned house, that "Yass, de 'ouse is in'abit; 'tis live in."

That house, with its "quadroon" inhabitants descended from the beautiful and tragic Madame Delphine, who lived there "sixty years ago and more" (4), is the chapter and story's destination (1–4). And the historical tale which the house and Delphine comprise, one connected to the race, woman, and South questions, exemplifies themes central to Cable's early literary texts. Yet just as important as that destination is the journey itself, the alternative walking tour through a New Orleans whose histories and languages represent richly multivalent and -vocal alternatives to the dominant narratives but were in danger of disappearing by the late nineteenth century (a danger that has recently and powerfully reemerged). Guiding his readers to and through that city, constructing and revealing for them those histories and voices, were at the heart of Cable's unique yet exemplary literary mission.

Voice and history intertwine both formally and thematically through much of the American historical literature published in the post-Centennial decade. And in no single text are those two interconnected elements more central, or the decade's social themes more resonant, than Cable's *The Grandissimes,* which was serialized in *Scribner's* in 1879–1880 and published in book form in 1880. Cable's sprawling novel of New Orleans in the years following the Louisiana Purchase deals with each of my four structuring questions: primarily the race question, but also the South, woman, and (to a lesser degree) Indian questions. And its form, a complex mixture of local color, romance, and realism that has continually defied critical attempts at definition, centers on the interrelationships of language, identity, communication, the construction of narratives, and the past's power and presence. Moreover, the novel's infamous editorial process, while containing elements of the conservative pressures that so many scholars describe, itself constitutes an ad-

ditional level of dialogue, one in which the *Scribner's* readers and Cable
exchange their own views on voice and history and out of which arise
important changes in and meanings of the text itself. Both in and on its
pages, then, *The Grandissimes* exemplifies the intricate interactions of
voice and history which constitute the great significance and power of
the decade's historical literature.

    While I read Cable's novel's form and content, its style and politics,
as inextricably interconnected, some recent scholars have argued that
Grandissimes criticism has been too formalist, has paid too little attention to political concerns. Etienne de Cussac begins his analysis of the
novel's "gothic strategy" by arguing for the need not to "overlook" the
text's "political implications" (137), while Thomas Fick and Eva Gold,
discussing the novel's mulattoes, contend that "the political nature of
Cable's novel may have been responsible for the relative paucity of criticism" on the text (68). But such assessments, while possibly accurate for
these critics' particular subjects, do not gibe with the overall trends in
Cable scholarship; from the first extensive analyses by Edmund Wilson,
Philip Butcher, Arlin Turner, and Louis Rubin to recent reappraisals by
Barbara Ladd, Gavin Jones, and Stephanie Foote, *Grandissimes* readings
consistently emphasize political themes such as race, class, gender, and
nationalism, and concurrently connect Cable's historical novel to the
historicist conditions of its post-Reconstruction publication.[1]
    Critics have had three excellent reasons for so focusing their atten-
tion. For one thing, there is the aforementioned generic confusion: the
novel is a "blend of romance and realism" (Butcher 46) in which, most
critics agree, the romantic elements (particularly the ubiquitous love triangles and voodoo curses) are generally the weaker ones.[2] While I argue
that those romantic elements connect to the novel's use of language
and storytelling, thus constituting vital aspects of its constructions of
voice and history, they do tend toward what Newton Arvin terms "a dis-
tasteful streak of sentimentality" (vi); critical readings therefore often
focus on the realistic aspects, which are much more easily linked to
Cable's reformist impulses. Those impulses, and more broadly Cable's
well-known and overtly political biography (which includes criticism of
both the Old and New Souths, essays in favor of race equality and inte-
gration, and his 1885 masterwork of Southern dissent, *The Silent South*),

provide a second rationale for political readings of the novel.[3] Thirdly, Cable himself wrote, in the essay "My Politics" (1888–89), that he "meant to make *The Grandissimes* as truly a political work as it has ever been called" (Rubin, *George* 78–79), adding in his diary that the novel "contained as plain a protest against the times in which it was written as against the earlier times in which its scenes were set" (Ekstrom 56); even critics who would generally avoid the intentional fallacy find it difficult to ignore such explicit authorizations for their political readings.

Whatever one's position on authorial intentions, Cable's statements, like many other aspects of the text, make clear that it is in an intensely political work. Yet it is first and foremost a novel, not a polemic like *Silent* or a didactic essay such as "The Freedmen's Case for Equity," and overtly political scholarship risks conflating such disparate genres. That is, political readings can reduce this vast, complex work of fiction to a set of ideological statements on subjects such as race, region, and gender, and can concurrently envision the critic's primary task as formulating an evaluation of and reply to those statements. For example, Kersten Piep's provocative recent reading, which analyzes *Grandissimes* and Lydia Maria Child's *A Romance of the Republic* as idealistic but flawed "liberal versions of Reconstruction," focuses on Cable's critiques and reifications of "prejudices" and comes to the evaluative conclusion that "blacks in *The Grandissimes* neither effect nor contribute to historical progress" (185). That conclusion shortchanges the role of African American voices in the novel's vision of history; but more importantly, Piep's overall analysis, like all those which move too fully into the political realm, elides the text's formal complexities and significance: Cable's constructions of language, identity, communication, narration, and the past, his central images of voice and history, lead directly to the novel's thematic engagements with the race, South, woman, and Indian questions.[4]

The novel's opening scene encapsulates its interconnected constructions of voice and history. Its first sentence seems to establish a clear division between past and present, introducing the setting as "the city we now call New Orleans, in the month of September, and in the year 1803." But the setting is a masked ball, an occasion where the citizens disguise themselves as various characters, including their distant ancestors, and thus a moment when the boundaries between past and present are more porous. One group of citizens in particular, on whom the chapter focuses, are dressed as "a group of first colonists," including a French soldier who reminds an observer of "great-great-grandfather Fusilier's portrait" and an "Indian Queen" who is the "ideal" image of "his wife, Lufki-Humma." This historical representation entails language as well as costume: the man disguised as Lufki-Humma speaks with the "saucy . . . familiarity of . . . the slave dialect" when he rebukes the venerable Agricola Fusilier, "Don't you know your ancestors, my little son!"; Agricola both replies and expresses his disapproval of the recently completed Louisiana Purchase in "the rumbling pomp of his natural voice" and in "unprovincial French"; and the crowd comments on the scene in "Louisiana French." The narrator gradually moves away from these broad issues of history and language and toward the specific interrelationships and budding romances between the four primary characters, noting that "all this is an outside view; let us draw nearer and see what chance may discover to us behind those four masks" (1–3). But the historical and linguistic masks that comprise each individual's identity within and relationship to a multicultural and -lingual society such as 1803 New Orleans can never be entirely discarded; in other words, as is so often the case in the novel, the romance is founded on this carefully constructed framework of linguistic and historical complexity, and so can be properly analyzed only with an eye toward the outside view.

Perhaps that outside view's primary element, and certainly the historical setting's most noteworthy aspect, is the use of languages. *Grandissimes* is heteroglossic in the term's fullest sense—the first one hundred pages alone depict or refer to no less than nine distinct languages or dialects: Louisiana French, Parisian French, standard English, German, slave dialect, Creole or Plantation French, English with an extreme French accent, and Choctaw (a local Indian language). In part this heteroglossia indicates the text's realistic goals: the narrator wants to represent "the way they talked in New Orleans in those days" (26); and William Evans, having studied the novel's phonology at length, concludes that Cable's dialect representations are "reasonably accurate" and "a significant part of Cable's attempt to preserve something of a unique and valuable, but declining, culture" ("French" 220).[5] That type of cultural preservation, however, is inherently a political act, the expression of a particular version of the past and its value, and Cable's linguistic variety can also be read as a subtle, subversive revision of English-dominated histories of America and a concurrent argument for including multilingual versions of the past in the national discourse.[6] As Gavin Jones argues, "Cable's depiction of dialect . . . gets to the heart of the cultural hybridity that, for him, characterized New Orleans society," and his work thus "demonstrates what a powerful tool of counter-hegemonic subversion dialect could be" (124, 133).[7] And Cable's choice of 1803—the year of the Louisiana Purchase, and so of the transition from French to American rule of New Orleans—as his setting and of Joseph Frowenfeld, a recent German immigrant, as his organizing narrative consciousness and moral point of view exemplify this multilingual historical revisionism.

Despite these connections to Cable's realism and revisionism, however, the novel's use of languages most directly relates to its themes of identity, communication, and narration. The narrator is concerned throughout with defining and describing characters' regional and racial identities, and he consistently does so through their use of and attitudes toward language. The proud and conservative Agricola, for example, perfectly expresses his identity with the exclamation, spoken in his typical "manner that might be construed either as address or soliloquy" (85), that "English is not a language, sir; it is a jargon!" and the concurrent admission that "you must not expect an old Creole to like anything in comparison with *la belle langue*" (48–49). Honoré Grandissime, however, occupies a position between the old Creoles and the city's new inhabitants, as encapsulated in his use of English: "his pronunciation was exact, yet evidently an acquired one. While he spoke his salutation in English, he was thinking French" (35). And other main characters are likewise identified through their unique languages: the white heroines, Aurore De Grapion Nancanou and her daughter Clotilde, inhabit a private space outside of public New Orleans society, and are described at a critical point as having "come to themselves now, . . . speaking in their peculiar French" (66); and Clemence, a highly articulate and opinionated former slave whose identity and goals remain mysterious for much of the text, is intimately connected to "the often audacious, epigrammatic philosophy of her tongue" (249).

While language and identity are thus closely linked in the narrator's construction of individual characters, they are made most meaningful in those moments when they are communicated to others. The novel's most obvious questions of communication, as in any text that uses dialect extensively, relate to the narrator-reader relationship; Cable's narrator acknowledges that relationship on many occasions, including the aforementioned reference to "the way they talked," which he follows by instructing his readers to "note the tone" if they "care to understand" Louisiana's history and present situation (26). But unique to Cable's novel, and more central to its themes of voice and history, is the issue of communication between characters, particularly those who speak different languages or dialects. Virtually every dialogic exchange in the novel is as much about understanding and intelligibility as about the particular information to be relayed, and those aspects are explored in their full range of complexity: from a story told in a "patois difficult, but not impossible, [for the auditor] to understand" (10); to an "audible answer" in French that an English speaker "could not understand" (12); to a listener who "may not have understood English, but [who] comprehended, nevertheless" (135). In other words, despite the accuracy and breadth of Cable's linguistic representations, he emphasizes the moments when those languages intersect, the social conditions under which languages coexist and through which speakers attempt to make their voices and stories heard and understood.

Almost every voice in the novel, in fact, has a unique and important story to tell, and these issues of communication and understanding are especially paramount because of that constant presence of storytelling, of narrative production.[8] Some are narratives of self, as when the two male protagonists, Frowenfeld and Honoré, tell each other their personal stories to convey their respective pasts and identities "in full detail" (36). Some are narratives of region, as when Dr. Charlie Keene and Raoul Innerarity provide Frowenfeld with, respectively, an external and internal perspective on New Orleans history and life. And some are narratives of defining historical events; in that category falls the story of Bras-Coupé, African monarch turned slave turned rebel, whose tragic history forms a backdrop for many of the text's exchanges and events. Bras-Coupé's story occupies center stage in the novel, both figuratively and literally: it is alluded to but not narrated (at least not to Frowenfeld and so not to the reader) on four occasions in the first half, each time with the same emphasis as Honoré's claim that "that negro's death changed the whole channel of my convictions" (38); and finally, in two long chapters at the novel's exact midpoint, the narrator conflates three virtually simultaneous tellings (by Raoul, Honoré, and his mixed-race half-brother of the same name) into one triangulated version that does "not exactly follow the words of any one of these" (169). No one voice can do justice to this story's contents and complexity, this triangulation suggests; it requires an amalgamation of voices and perspectives to tell it fully and accurately.

Indeed, the Bras-Coupé legend, a slightly revised version of Cable's twice-rejected story "Bibi," is a narrative of unquestionable power and a deeply felt critique of slavery and Southern race relations, and one that has received the attention of virtually all Cable critics[9]; I would simply highlight the story's connections to the novel's depictions of voice and history. For one thing, before Raoul can tell his version of the story to a gathering of young Creoles, he must sing a number of traditional songs, which Cable represents with both their French lyrics and (in one case) musical notes; Raoul sings these songs in part because of an explicit connection to Bras-Coupé, whom he "heard . . . sing" one of them, but also due to an implicit link between the Creole identity conveyed by the songs and the regional and racial history comprised by the story. When his auditors ask Raoul, "that master of narrative and melody," for "Une chanson Creole! Une chanson des negres!" they make clear the ties between song and story, people and history (166–68). And the narrator's decision to tell a collective version of the story, one that begins "Bras-Coupé, they said" (169), formally and clearly indicates that the Bras-Coupé narrative speaks both of and for the Creole community.

Within that narrative, voice and history occupy prominent and interconnected positions. One of the challenges Bras-Coupé poses to his Creole slave master is his voice, and more exactly his language, a tribal tongue known as Jaloff that is apparently rare among the plantation slaves. In order to develop a working relationship with the slave, the master must "get an interpreter . . . and come to an understanding," and that interpreter is found in Palmyre, a beautiful fellow slave who "has picked up as many negro dialects as [Agricola] know[s] European languages" and with whom Bras-Coupé, after hearing her speak "in the dear accents of his native tongue," falls in irrevocable, tragic love (172–74). Later, when Bras-Coupé's understanding with his master has come to a violent end, he stands over the Creole, "making strange signs and passes and rolling out in wrathful words of his mother tongue what it needed no interpreter to tell his swarming enemies was a voudou malediction" (181). A curse is first and foremost a vocal attempt to keep the past alive and powerful in the future, and Bras-Coupé's curse, significantly, is articulated in Creole—a mixture of his own voice and his new region's language—and translated by Cable's narrator into New Orleans's newest language: "*Mo cé voudrai que la maison ci là et tout ça qui pas femme' ici s'raient encore maudits!* (May this house and all in it who are not women be accursed)" (187). And when Bras-Coupé's rebellion fails and he lies on his deathbed, his final words, voiced with great difficulty, indicate both a spiritual return to the past and a move into the linguistic future: "'To—' the voice failed a moment; the departing hero essayed again; again it failed; he tried once more, lifted his hand, and with an ecstatic, upward smile, whispered, 'To—Africa'—and was gone" (193). While Bras-Coupé's dying wish, like his attraction to the linguistically familiar Palmyre, illustrates his continued connections with his African past, his uses of Creole (in the curse) and English (on his deathbed) indicate the inescapable relationships with the present and future into which he and his history have been brought. Those relationships continue to resonate long after Bras-Coupé's demise, as Honoré admits when he concludes his version of the story by telling Joseph, "You may ponder the philosophy of Bras-Coupé in your study, but *I* have got to get rid of his results" (198). And indeed every character in the novel, even a recent arrival such as Frowenfeld, lives, speaks, and acts under (in the text's most famous phrase) the "shadow of the Ethiopian" (156).

The Bras-Coupé story is broadly historical in a number of ways, from its sweeping geographical scope (it covers Africa, the middle passage, the Grandissime plantations, and the swamps of Louisiana) to its encapsulation of a wide variety of the slave system's key aspects (arrival, language, working conditions, slave-master relations, religion, slave marriages, rebellions, punishment). But it just as meaningfully conveys history's intimacy and power within individual lives, families, and relationships. Revealing crucial aspects of the experiences, identities, loves, hatreds, and motivations of most of the novel's central characters, from Agricola and the two Honorés to the slave women Palmyre and Clemence, the story exemplifies the novel's continuous depictions of history's living presence and force within both a society like New Orleans and its individual inhabitants. That presence and force are concisely symbolized by Bras-Coupé's curse, a prime example of a romantic device with a realistic and thematic purpose; the curse suggests how historical actions and figures resonate into the present, exerting an influence (often through language) that far outlasts their specific existence. It is that influence, more than any concrete effects of Bras-Coupé's life, rebellion, or death, that Honoré calls his "results"; and Cable's constructions of history, in the Bras-Coupé story and elsewhere, indicate that "getting rid" of those results is both nearly impossible and counterproductive.

While the Bras-Coupé story is the text's central image of history's power and presence, as well as its most significant engagement with the race question, there are other, equally effective such images that connect to the decade's other social questions and to voice and narration. In the novel's first extended act of storytelling, Dr. Keene tells Frowenfeld an early episode in the histories of the De Grapion and Grandissime families, while concurrently providing Cable with an apt (if self-deprecating) symbol for his text. Keene, the narrator notes, "was a poor story-teller. To Frowenfeld—as it would have been to any one, except a Creole or the most thoroughly Creolized Americain—his narrative, when it was done, was little more than a thick mist of strange names, places, and events; yet there shone a light of romance upon it that filled it with color and populated it with phantoms. Frowenfeld's interest rose—was allured into this mist—and there was left befogged" (15). In this short passage, the narrator not only introduces the omnipresent issues of language, identity, communication, and narrative, but also suggests how a story built upon those issues, and illuminated with the romance of local color and historical content, can attract its readers' attention. Yet in this construction of storytelling such attention is not rewarded with any resolution, and indeed Keene's story—which describes the romanticized circumstances under which the Grandissimes became connected to Lufki-Humma and her Tchoupitoulas tribe, providing the novel's only outright engagement with the Indian question—raises rather than answers questions about its historical subject, illuminating the distant origins of the ongoing feud between the Grandissimes and De Grapions but providing no details on their evolving relationships or present descendants. But the tale's unsatisfying conclusion—Frowenfeld is left "weary-eyed," admitting that "there are so many Grandissimes, [he] cannot distinguish between" them (29)—serves two key points. Formally, it requires additional investigation from Frowenfeld in order to yield a completed history, an investigation that produces the text's ever-present dialogues and narratives. And thematically, it indicates that the early histories represented by both the Creole "Family Trees" (the chapter's name) and Native Americans cannot be isolated or treated as concluded narratives, but must instead be kept open, subject to further investigation, if meaning is to be made of them.

If Keene's story concerns the most public kind of history, a region's communal past, then the Nancanou women's voices and identities represent a circumscribed, private form of history particular to their gender. The reference to their "peculiar French" distinguishes the two women from their fellow Creoles, and in fact Aurore and Clotilde's lives are almost entirely isolated from New Orleans society, restricted to their small home. The outside world's only view of them is that which infiltrates their residence: "you could see from the street or the opposite windows that [Aurore] was a wise householder" (63). Yet such isolation is not their only option, as Aurore reveals by remembering that her late husband was "teaching [her] to speak English" (66). The narrator likewise connects her to that new language by abruptly changing her name to Aurora, claiming that "it sounds so much pleasanter to anglicize her name" (70).[10] And as the novel progresses it is English that moves Aurora out of her restricted sphere: first when the outside world and history force themselves upon her, in the form of a letter (in English) from Honoré requesting their unpaid rent; and later when she articulates to Frowenfeld her own perspective on that society and past. That narrative, comprising the chapter "Aurora as a Historian," begins with a comment on Aurora's unique voice: "Alas! the phonograph was invented three-quarters of a century too late. If type could entrap one-half the pretty oddities of Aurora's speech—the arch, the pathetic, the grave, the earnest, the matter-of-fact, the ecstatic tones of her voice— . . . ah! but type—even the phonograph—is such an inadequate thing" (145). Even as she leaves her isolation and begins to participate in the outside, English-speaking world's communication and narration, Aurora's voice and perspective remain distinctive, even inimitable. But despite this apparent shortcoming of narrator-reader communication, the character-

ization of Aurora's voice is an argument for her communication with
Frowenfeld and the new society he represents; the narrator cannot speak
for her, and so it is up to Aurora to articulate her history of herself, her
friend Palmyre, and the limitations and dangers which constitute the
woman question in that place and time. And while her narration's historical vision is largely negative, she ends with a more positive image:
the strong resemblance between Clotilde and a painting of her most re-
vered ancestor, her grandmother. "Clotilde is my gran'-mamma" (148),
she concludes, and the connection between the strong historical and
the present woman, as well as Aurora's link to both—there is "a certain
family resemblance between [Aurora's] voice and that of [Clotilde]"
(45)—establish the presence and promise of women's histories.[11]

The novel's construction of historic houses provides yet another intricate image of history's presence and force, as well as its potential disappearance. As the narrator describes these houses, they are at once important, "rising above the general surroundings," and isolated, reminding
the viewer of a man "searching for a friend who is not there and will
never come back." Moreover, they symbolize a history both enduring
("displaying architectural features which identity them with an irrevocable past") and in danger of erasure ("if, indeed, they were not pulled
down yesterday"). As such, they provide a multifaceted historical symbol for the South question—unique to the region and cut off from the
rest of the nation, impossible to escape but easy to forget or ignore.[12]
Exemplifying that complex history is the novel's central house, "the
great mother-mansion of the Grandissimes" (a Southern echo of Hawthorne's House of the Seven Gables). "Do not look for it now," the narrator instructs the reader, for "it is quite gone" (157–58), but the house's
intimate and irrevocable interconnections with the Grandissimes' destiny illustrate that a physical disappearance cannot end this historic
home's influence. And as with all the novel's images of the past, the
house represents both the negative force of traditions, "the sentiments
and prejudices" of the fathers, and the constructive potential of a revisionist historical understanding, the righting of "our dead father's mistakes" (219) through an "unbroken and harmonious Grandissime family
gathering, . . . without reproach before all persons, classes, and races,"
toward which Honoré constantly works (159).[13]

Finally, if the historic houses symbolize a certain section of New Orleans society and thus a certain perspective on the South question, Cable provides a more comprehensive geographic, historical construction in the crowd's public voice. With the Louisiana Purchase that crowd's language has changed, both officially and informally: "Nouvelle Orleans had become New Orleans, and Louisiane was Louisiana" (45); and "the odd English of the New Orleans street-urchin was at that day just beginning to be heard" (203). But the older language and voice will not disappear without a fight, as is evident in both the scene where passers-by mock the new governor Claiborne in "the French of the late province" (88) and the extended, multivocal conversation which makes clear that "Louisiana is going to state her wants" (235). Besides developing these public versions of the city's new and old voices, Cable also constructs in Frowenfeld an outsider who can observe and analyze those voices. Significantly, Frowenfeld describes his subject as a text, "this newly found book, the Community of New Orleans"; and although "much of it [is] in a strange tongue," he resolves to comprehend it nonetheless, paying particular attention to its historic aspects, those "leaves" covered by "much dust" (103). And by the novel's end, thanks to the varied communications and narrations I have described, Frowenfeld does come to speak the city's language and understand its history, as evidenced by his successful visit to that most historic Creole house, the Grandissime mansion; a visit during which Frowenfeld's linguistic inquisitiveness is returned in kind, with every member of the family "contriv[ing] to understand Frowenfeld's English" and thus to comprehend their city's future (304).

As these many, interconnected examples indicate, history is the driving motivation for each of the novel's characters and plots, including those not analyzed here: Raoul's paintings of key events from Louisiana history; Agricola's conservative nostalgia and opposition to Americanization; the mulatto, free man of color Honoré's attempts to share in his family's heritage; the ex-slaves Clemence and Palmyre's deep-seated hatreds of the conservative Grandissimes. Even the love triangles which drive the text's sentimental plots (and which have driven so many critics to distraction) are, like their romantic counterparts the voodoo curses, themselves driven by history, by the pain and promise of the past's living presence.[14] History is, in short, ever-present in the novel, the most powerful force at society's broadest and most intimate levels. But despite that presence—or perhaps precisely because history in *Grandissimes* is not limited to particular events, locations, or bodies of knowledge—the past is ultimately accessible only through stories, and thus through voices (with their accompanying questions of language, identity, communication, and narration). It might seem that such a historical vision, one so tied to stories and voices, constitutes a nineteenth-century precursor to the postmodern historical novel; that Cable portrays history and historical knowledge as meaningless or even nonexistent outside of the narratives which construct them. But I would argue instead that history is the most real and meaningful (as well as constant) element of Cable's novel, and that the text's depiction of history's force is only strengthened by its emphasis on voice. And the conclusion's most powerful element, Clemence's fate, reiterates the effectiveness of this conjunction of history and voice, this location of the past's presence and power in the perspectives, accents, and stories of a city's, culture's, and country's citizens.

Much of *Grandissimes'* conclusion more befits a romance of reunion (albeit a rather complex one, along the lines of Murfree's and Tourgée's) than a revisionist historical novel. Conservative old Agricola is dead, and his traditions and prejudices with him, although the history represented by Agricola and his dying words, "Louis—Louisian—a—for—ever," lives on in the inscription on his tomb (328). Nonetheless, the man and his era have passed, and two pairs of star-crossed young lovers have married, reconciling the differences that divided them: Frowenfeld and Clotilde have crossed their racial, cultural, and linguistic barriers; while Honoré and Aurora have mended their families' rifts and reunited the clan in the Grandissime mansion.[15] And the two characters who fit least easily into such reconciliations, Honoré the f.m.c. and Palmyre the former slave, have removed themselves as obstacles by moving to France; Honoré's suicide there does cast a pall over the text's final pages, but the action seems largely motivated by his unreconciled love for Palmyre, and thus by a history that is painful but not particularly relevant thematically.[16] While all these characters' complex voices, identities, and histories have by no means been erased, they are more difficult to perceive in the hazy glow of sentimental romance that has enveloped the text.

The one character who stands most completely outside that light throughout the novel, however, is Clemence. The ex-slave street peddler (marchande des calas) never hesitates to express, in her "audacious" voice, hard truths about her race, gender, and region; the best example is her extended dialogue with Keene in which she shatters a number of myths about slavery's idyllic nature and concludes by arguing that "white folks is werry kine. Dey wants us to b'lieb we happy—dey *wants to b'lieb* we is. W'y, you know, dey 'bleeged to b'lieb it—fo' dey own cyumfut" (249–51). Cable's phonological accuracy here is no longer the issue; noteworthy instead is the accuracy and pointedness of Clemence's voice and historical vision, expressed in that distinctively black, Southern dialect.[17] And it is Clemence's voice that is most profoundly altered in her final scene, when, caught in a steel trap while attempting to plant a voodoo curse on the Grandissime property, she begs for her captors to spare her life:

> "Oh, *Miché* Jean Baptiste, I di'n' mek dat ah! *Mo té pas féça!* I swea' befo' God! Oh, no, no, no! 'Tain' nutt'n' nohow but a lill play-toy, *Miché.* Oh, sweet *Miché Jean,* you not gwan to kill me? I di'n' mek it! It was—ef you lemme go, I tell you who mek it! Sho's I live I tell you, *Miché Jean*—ef you lemme go! Sho's God's good to me—ef you lemme go! Oh, God A'mighty, *Miché Jean,* sho's God's good to me."
>
> She was becoming incoherent. (314)

She is indeed becoming incoherent, and not simply in the literal sense: her voice, once so firmly and effectively under her control, is slipping back and forth between languages and levels of dialect; and her racial identity, once so strong, has splintered so far that she is willing to incriminate Palymre (her oldest and only friend) to save herself. Or perhaps both changes are simply performances, desperate attempts by a trapped and outnumbered woman to put over one last trick on her Creole former masters. Regardless, Clemence's voice, which had so effectively revised history's mythic narratives, is no match for history itself, whether the heritage represented by the Grandissime family or the horrors of slavery and lynching represented by this brutality: her captors win a confession of Palmyre as the curse's mastermind and then kill Clemence anyway, shooting her in the back as she runs away from the trap.[18]

While Clemence's death embodies the nadir of the novel's themes, a moment in which an incoherent voice encounters an inescapable history and meets an inhuman death, her character throughout the text illustrates those themes' potential power. When Clemence articulates her critiques, as when Aurora tells her story or Honoré and Frowenfeld engage in dialogue, the novel's depiction of history's presence is deepened and amplified by its vision of voice, its recognition that nowhere is the past more forcefully present than in the languages, identities, and stories which constitute all voices. And that recognition, in turn, highlights the importance of communication—of genuine dialogue—for the development of any complex, meaningful historical understanding. Early in the novel, Honoré admonishes Frowenfeld that "it is of no use to talk" (37), but the text's close and continued connection of dialogue and narration to historical revision and accuracy thoroughly belies such a statement.

Coincidentally but significantly, communication and dialogue were also central to the process of revising Cable's novel for its initial *Scribner's* serialization. Cable's usual editor, Richard Watson Gilder, was in Europe throughout the editing process, and he turned the task over to his understudy, Robert Underwood Johnson. Johnson, in turn, recruited two Southern readers, Irwin Russell (author of the famous dialect poem "Christmas Night in the Quarters") and Sophia Bledsoe Herrick (daughter of Southern partisan Albert Taylor Bledsoe and an editor of the *Southern Review*), to provide their own reactions to the manuscript. With all three readers making frequent remarks and corrections, almost every page of *The Grandissimes*' printer's copy has at least one editorial comment; moreover, Cable was unusually active in the editorial process and provided his own written responses (sometimes a single word, but often a lengthy reply) on a remarkable number of those pages.[19]

Ever since Edmund Wilson referred to "the constant carping and nagging to which [Cable] had to submit" during the novel's editing and placed much of the blame for Cable's artistic decline on such editorial harassment (580), the scholarly account of this process has been overwhelmingly negative. Arlin Turner greatly enlarges upon Wilson's account, including extended quotations from the manuscripts, rejected pages of text, and additional correspondence between Cable and Johnson (among other materials), but similarly depicts Cable as the process's embattled victim (95–99); Louis Rubin follows suit, while also blaming Cable for his own inability to self-edit and thus his tendency to submit to the *Scribner's* positions (*George* 77–78); and Barbara Ladd reiterates this narrative, arguing that Cable's politics were likewise compromised by the editors' conservatism (46–50). While there is certainly some truth to this account (as Turner's chosen quotations demonstrate), and while one of the manuscript's central lessons is unquestionably "how solidly [Cable's] writing was founded on history and sure observation" (Turner 99), a closer examination of the printer's copy reveals that the dominant mode of discussion among readers and author is dialogue. That is, Cable and his readers engage in an extensive, complex, and often quite productive series of conversations about his text, communications of their particular visions of voice and history that result (whether they leave the text unchanged or significantly altered) in another level of formal and thematic dialogue over the novel's central issues.[20]

Before analyzing a few such dialogic moments, I believe that it is important to acknowledge this section's relationship to reader-response theory. I have not practiced reader-response criticism elsewhere in this study; nor can I do justice here to its methodologies or goals. To put it succinctly, my reading of Cable's manuscripts relates to reader-response in my argument that the text's meaning is (in some cases) actively constructed through these interactions between author and readers, and concurrently that our scholarly understanding of the text is deepened and strengthened by examining those interactions. However, in this case the responses are not separate events, occurring after the text's publication and in discrete settings, but are rather part of a dialogue with the author, one occurring during the process of composition and revision. And thus my use of these reader responses does not eliminate or lessen the importance of the author and the meanings he hopes to impart to his text (as, I believe, some reader-response critics seek to accomplish through their work); instead, an analysis of these responses indicates how Cable both was involved in and utilized dialogues in constructing his novel's forms and themes.[21]

The author-reader dialogues that most clearly complicate the dominant narrative of the editorial process are those from which Cable and his novel benefit; and indeed, some of the text's most impressive formal elements received such aid. For example, of the introduction to Aurora's voice "as a Historian," one of the readers (most likely Johnson, although the comment is unsigned) points out that "Part of this can't be done even by the phonograph!" and Cable adds the distinction; the change highlights Aurora's voice's uniqueness and inimitability and strengthens the subsequent narration's power and significance.[22] Even more important is Johnson's suggestion, in regard to a particular thought of Palmyre's, that "This sounds a little stilted in her words. It had better be related than quoted"; Cable not only makes the change, adding his own comment that the result is "Much better," but consistently adds free indirect discourse, and thus an additional layer of complex narrative voice, throughout the text during the editorial process (m325; 178). And any doubt that Cable was aware of and appreciated such benefits is quelled by the author's response at any earlier moment, when Johnson has persuaded him to cut an overly long, redundant section of Frowenfeld's thoughts: "I hope to be able to some day tell you by word o' mouth how highly I value your criticisms," Cable replies, indicating both the dialogues' conversational nature and his gratitude for them, as well as his own willingness to use nonstandard idioms (m204; 113).

More complex and interesting than these straightforward changes, however, are those moments when Cable disagrees and does not take his readers' advice. While such moments could be read as Wilsonian carping and nagging, the readers' comments and Cable's replies form an additional level of dialogue about voice and history (among other topics) that can only deepen our understanding of the text itself. A minor, humorous example concerns Cable's description of the Grandissime plantation at the time of Bras-Coupé's arrival; Cable notes that "everybody wore clothes—children and lads alone excepted," and when a reader crosses out "and lads," Cable asks that it be left in, adding, "Please let me tell the naked truth." His senses of history and humor prevail, and the text is left unchanged (m311; 171). Much more important is the extended dialogue over Clemence's death speech. When one reader (likely Russell) indicates that her speech goes on for too long, Johnson at first sides with Cable, noting that "it would be unnatural for the old negress not to pour of a perfect flood of words." By the next manuscript page, however, all three readers are in apparent agreement about the speech's length, arguing that "half the quantity of her talk while in the trap would be twice as effective and so in inverse proportion down to half a

page of it. The scene is strong. Eds." Taking the comment for the carefully considered criticism that it certainly is, Cable attempts to shorten
the scene, admitting that he has "made a poor attempt to scratch out
some of it but think[s] [he is] only hurting it." Anxious to keep the editorial dialogue alive and productive, he adds that he "hope[s] it is unnecessary to say that [he] would accept the above suggestion if [he]
could see [his] way to doing so advantageously or without injury to the
story." The speech went into the final version, unchanged and unshort-
ened, and its length and gradual descent into incoherence are vital to its
meaning; and our sense of that meaning is only heightened by an awareness of this dialogue over the passage's length (m596–97; 313–14). Also
interesting are the truly multivocal editorial conversations, such as the
responses to the first interaction between Bras-Coupé and his master,
Don José: the two stare each other down and José, impressed, instructs
his underlings to "Get an interpreter and come to an understanding"
with the slave. Russell comments that "This whole scene is very improbable," but Johnson and Herrick, convinced by Cable's construction
of character and history, "Don't think so," and the scene remains (m314;
172–73).

Finally, it must be noted that *Grandissimes'* manuscript pages do occasionally prove that dialogues and conversations, despite my emphasis
on them throughout this study, are not perfectly balanced nor, necessarily, the most productive form of composition and construction. That
is, there are moments where the readers (whether through their oft-
remarked conservatism or simple artistic differences) convince Cable
to change his novel in ways that diminish his formal and thematic
achievements. The manuscript version, for example, includes an extended section of Bras-Coupé's thoughts, reflections on his goals, and
plans which begin his story's second chapter. The section is unique both
for its connections and distinctions between African American and Native American histories—Bras-Coupé thinks about joining "the hostile
Chickasaws" but recognizes that "the Indians were themselves slaveholders" and opts against it—and for its acknowledgment of the rebellious
slave's conflicting motivations: his rational desire for self-survival and
his emotional attachment, "true as truth," to Palmyre. In this case the
editorial process oversimplifies Cable's construction of his character:
Johnson comments on this moment that "it seems inartistic to have Bras

Coupé bestowing any thought upon anything—he acted so thoroughly
from impulse," and Cable concurs, eliminating the reflections entirely
and beginning that second chapter with the simple "Bras-Coupé let the
autumn pass, and wintered in his den" (m334; 183). Johnson's reasoning
makes sense, given the thoroughly physical and emotional construction
of Bras-Coupé which Cable has developed, and as the text stands it is
easier, without any clear indication of Bras-Coupé's thoughts, for him
to become the multifaceted historical legend that is his principal role in
the novel; yet it is difficult not to regret the loss of this unique passage,
and with it the chance for another layer of voice and history in the construction of the enslaved king.

Even more complex is an extended deleted passage on the future
family history of the novel's most fully realized black character, Clemence. Just after her historical debate with Keene, the narrator contrasts
Clemence's heritage and temperament with those of "us"; much of it remains in the novel, including the powerful historical image of Clemence
as "heiress" to the centuries of pain and violence to which her people
have been subject and which have "left her the cinders of human feelings." In the manuscript version, however, Cable brings this inheritance
metaphor up to his own era, writing of Clemence that

> Her grandchildren came through our late civil war. Everybody
> wondered at them. They were not like white people at all. They
> served their masters and mistresses with song and laugh, through
> good news and bad, seemingly unconscious of the great threatened
> overturning. It was a great puzzle; but it was very simple. Its cause
> was the long habit of neutrality. The tyrannous coward is parti-
> san, the servile coward is neutral. To the Southern slave events had
> never before born any import. Except in an isolated case here and
> there, hope could not penetrate the hard shell of that old habit
> of neutrality until "de Yankees" were right in the door yard; but
> the instant hope entered, fidelity to master was gone, and so was
> Cuffee. But we need not look into philosophy. All we care to state is
> that Clemence was a type; because in all matters of strife between
> whites and whites, she played the neutral.

Of this section Johnson argues, despite its stated avoidance of philosophy, that, "These philosophical 'asides' are as philosophy good, as

novel writing superfluous and in the way. [The prior page] gives all that is necessary about Clemence's antecedents." Cable is persuaded, cutting the paragraph and noting that he "believe[s] that as it stands now there isn't a better passage in the book" (m472; 251). The published passage is certainly still impressive, and on the cut section Johnson is right, to a point: this is not novel writing in any traditional sense. But it does exemplify Cable's innovative historical novel's connections between past and present, voice—while the slaves are only quoted with "de Yankees," their neutral performances are clearly public articulations of a particular viewpoint, distinct from their private voices and views—and history. And while there is in the cut passage, as in the published novel, cause for political objection ("servile coward" a prime example), there is also evidence of the originality and importance of Cable's formal and thematic developments. His complex constructions of voice and history do get "in the way" of a straightforward, simplistic sense of story or history, but that, as much as any effect of his masterpiece of a historical novel, is precisely the point.

To be faithful to Cable's point, however, requires a thorough and honest examination of the historical record, and in that light it is difficult to argue that *The Grandissimes'* complex visions of voice, history, and society had any discernible, practical influence on his readers or his era. The most noteworthy responses to the novel, in fact, were antagonistic: Creole "poet-priest" Adrien Rouquette anonymously published a pamphlet entitled *Critical Dialogue Between Aboo and Caboo on a New Book; or A Grandissime Ascension* (1880) which, while relevant in its appropriation of Cable's themes of voice, dialogue, and communication, was mostly a thorough savaging of Cable and his portrayals of Creole society, the South, and African Americans; and New Orleans's general response, while less vitriolic than Rouquette's, was negative enough to begin the process of alienation which ended in Cable moving his home and family to New England. While the national reception was much more favorable, including such interesting formal responses as William Dean Howells' remark to Cable that he and his wife were so enamored of the "Nancanou ladies" and "the charm of their English" that they had decided to "speak nothing else now but that dialect" (Turner 99), it is hard to argue that Cable's constructions of voice and history had any immediate or explicit influence on the larger national dialogues (too often, as I have argued, monologues) on the race, South, gender, or Indian questions, much less the progressive historical narrative.[23]

The same objection could, of course, be raised about each of my chapters and arguments, and thus about my study as a whole. As the decade and century progressed toward their ends, the race question moved inexorably toward the nadir of Jim Crow, segregation, and the lynching epidemic; the South question, concurrently, toward Northern indifference, Federal inaction, and the triumph of reactionary and repressive forces throughout the region and indeed the nation; and the Indian question, most thoroughly and destructively of all, toward the Dawes Act, the reservation system's full implementation, and the end for many decades of any pretense of Native American sovereignty or independence. Progress was made (if gradually and partially) only on the woman question, and those achievements are much easier to trace to the unifying, political voices of the suffrage movement and women's rights reformers—voices that in their monologic tendencies were to some degree assimilable into the national narrative, particularly with the suffragists' focus on white women at the expense of African Americans—than to literature's multivocal and -valent dialogues. All of these trends were exemplified at the 1893 Chicago Exposition, which both represented the national narrative's apotheosis and foreshadowed its extension onto the international stage. And all the trends reveal a larger question about my study's historical emphasis: given the future that we now know was in store, are not the majority of scholars right to analyze the Gilded Age in the explicit context of the transition to the twentieth century? In other words, what is the value of looking backward, or more exactly looking at those texts which look backward, in an era moving so quickly, for better or (more often) for worse, forward?

In answer, I would turn to the texts themselves, the complex works of fiction, nonfiction, and poetry on which I have focused. As those texts make clear, our understanding of the present and plans for the future are always built on visions of the past, and those visions—whether of slavery, Indian wars, women's lives, the Civil War, New Orleans society, or any of the other histories with which the texts are centrally concerned—are always most manageable when they are most simplistic and monologic. The progressive national narrative's rise over this decade reflects the dominance of just such a unifying, monologic vision. Yet as these texts consistently demonstrate in their content and model in their form, the past is deeply dialogic, and an accurate construction of history thus requires formal engagements with voice and narration, language and dialect, communication and silence. And while these literary texts are not first and foremost political works, nor didactic statements about their themes or social questions, they are formal constructions of voice and history that challenge simplistic portrayals of those issues and require both close readings and further investigations, and thus entrance into the dialogues of narrative and history, from their readers and critics. In contesting the past and reconstructing the nation, these texts formally and thematically exemplify the presence, power, and pertinence of history and dialogue for their society and future, and for ours.

Conclusion

Despite the dialogic complications provided by my chapters' literary texts, the period under consideration ended with the monologue clearly triumphant. If the 1876 Centennial Exposition represented a strong and distinctive recurrence of a progressive national historical narrative, and a series of 1886 events illustrated that narrative's firm entrenchment a decade later, then the 1893 World's Columbian Exposition served as the narrative's apotheosis. A *Chicago Tribune* editorial on the Exposition's opening ceremonies opined without hesitation that the festivities marked "the beginning of the world's millennium. That is to say," the editors added for those readers who had not yet internalized the progressive narrative's terms, "the booming of the cannon ushered in a new era in the world's history" (Litwicki 47). Notwithstanding the reiteration of "world's" in those formulations (and in the Exposition's name and ostensible purpose), it was a particular vision of America's history and future that the Chicago Fair most thoroughly embodied; a vision that had never been expressed more clearly and that would indeed shortly thereafter expand dramatically onto the world's stage.

The Exposition exemplified the consensus narrative's three central elements: its emphasis on the nation's material development and prowess; its construction of a nostalgic vision of past glories that augmented the present's power; and, most importantly, its progressive vision of a glorious, millennial future. While some Exposition historians see continuations of Gilded Age contrasts in the dichotomy between Midway and Court of Honor, I argue that the former's depiction of the foreign as exotic antecedent to American civilization was not only perfectly in keeping with the progressive narrative, but in fact foreshadowed that narrative's next stage: the imperialist extensions of the late 1890s. The social questions that offered spaces for dialogic complications of the narrative at and after the Centennial were in Chicago more clearly assimilated into or silenced by the monologue: Southern voices and histories now central to the national narrative, as illustrated by the choice of unreconstructed Southerner James Lynch for the Exposition's welcoming poet; women's voices and histories moving in that direction with a presence that reinforced the narrative's progressivism and hierarchies; and African American and Native American voices largely absent, their histories constructed from other perspectives. Yet the latter groups also offered two alternative narratives—the pamphlet *The Reason Why the Colored American Is Not in the World's Columbian Exposition* and Chief Simon Pokagon's speech "The Red Man's Greeting"— that kept their voices and histories alive in Chicago. And those texts, like the many complex historical literary texts published in and around the Exposition year, built upon earlier historical literature's dialogic models, envisioning a multivocal past and pointing toward more inclusive and democratic national futures.

Just as at the Centennial, much of what was displayed at the Columbian Exposition constituted representations of and tributes to America's material prowess; but where the progressive historical narrative underpinning the Centennial's materialism was often merely implied or expressed in specific texts such as Whittier's Hymn, in Chicago that narrative was present in full force throughout. As John Cawelti argues, "the image of a new, purer Renaissance bursting forth from the chrysalis of American material and moral progress pervaded every aspect of the fair" (339). Illustrating that pervading connection of material to national progress was the Exposition's use of electricity: the highlight of the opening ceremonies was when President Grover Cleveland "pressed a gilded button sending electricity pulsating through the fair site," with striking results both material ("machinery rumble[d] ... water gushed") and national ("a shroud fell from Daniel Chester French's

giant . . . gilded Statue of the Republic") [Schlereth 277].[1] The larger-
than-life depictions of America expressed in such imagery directly co-
rollated to the Gilded Age's nascent nationalism (the Pledge of Allegiance was drafted by Francis Bellamy in response to the Exposition's
glories)[2]; and both that nationalism and the Exposition's grand visions
likewise linked to the progressive historical narrative's idea of America.
The fair was indeed the most concrete and thorough "actualizing [of] a
progressive vision" that the nation had ever witnessed (Judith Adams,
"American" xix); the consensus historical narrative seemed everywhere
triumphant on the White City's spacious grounds.[3]

As the previous chapters have demonstrated, that progressive narrative required not an elision of American history, but rather the construction of a particular—nostalgic, selective, linear—vision of that
past. And such a historical perspective was likewise significantly present at the Columbian Exposition. J. T. Harris, Chairman of the Exposition's National Commission, expressed that perspective's main thrust
quite succinctly in his first speech, discussing the aftermath of Columbus's discovery: "It remained for the Saxon race to people this new land,
to redeem it from Barbarism, to dedicate its virgin soil to freedom, and
in less than four centuries to make of it the most powerful and pros-
perous country on which God's sunshine falls" (Greenhalgh 98). Much
more famous and influential in American historiography and thought,
but in many ways simply an extended version of Harris's claim, was
Frederick Jackson Turner's lecture "The Significance of the Frontier in
American History," delivered at the American Historical Association's
Chicago gathering. While Turner's thesis illustrated specifically a new
national perspective on the West, it more broadly represented the progressive narrative's three key rhetorical modes: the jeremiad, as Turner
exalted the Western past and wondered if the 1890 census's "closing of
the frontier" meant a permanent fall from it; the elision of alternative
histories, with Turner's negligible references to Native Americans in the
Western past or present; and the millennial vision, with his claim that
since Columbus's days "America has been another name for opportunity," and his prescient belief that "the American energy will continually
demand a wider field for its exercise" (59–60).[4] On those multiple but
interconnected levels, Turner provided historical visions to complement
the progressive narrative; his address "reaffirmed the very idea of His-

tory for a public well schooled in the characteristic designs of American progress" (Daehnke 2–5).[5]

However, the Gilded Age American public was schooled not only in progress, but also in the contrasts and conflicts that had concurrently helped constitute the past quarter century. Set alongside the White City's splendors, events such as the Panic of 1893, the four-year depression that followed, and most overtly the Pullman Strike that dominated Chicago life for much of 1894 clearly highlighted those contrasting realities' continued existence. Many recent Exposition historians have emphasized the unintentional but irrepressible presence of such contrasts within its grounds; for such scholars, Neil Harris notes, "where once the exposition symbolized consensus, unity, and agreed-upon values, we now spot smothered dispute" (44). Such scholars, including John Cawelti, John Kasson, and Lawrence Levine, focus on the divergence between the Midway's lowbrow entertainments and the Court of Honor's highbrow exhibits; Levine argues that there is "no better symbol of the growing [cultural] fragmentation" than the gap between those two areas.[6] But while the Midway's definition of culture might have been quite different from the Court's, I believe that both places played symbiotic roles in the Exposition's construction of an agreed-upon and essential element of consensus and unity: the progressive historical narrative. A millennial vision of past progress toward an ideal future, after all, needs an alternative against which that progress can be contrasted, and the Midway's international exhibits—or, more accurately and relevantly, the American perceptions of them—provided just such an alternate narrative. Frederick Law Olmstead suggested this relationship between Midway and Court in a letter to Daniel Burnham, the Exposition's chief of construction, noting that responses to the Court would improve if it were to hire "varieties of heathen" from the Midway (Kasson 22–23); that perspective not only made the Midway into "an early form of touristic consumption" (Hinsley, "World" 363), but also allowed its less "civilized" inhabitants to reinforce American views of their civilization's progress.[7]

The Exposition's connection of the progressive national narrative to the larger international community also provided a prophetic glimpse into the immediate American future. The progressive narrative had always constituted a broad vision of the future as much as the past, and its Exposition incarnation was no exception. Emblematic of that perspective on the future, and particularly of its optimism, were the seventy-four topical "Chapters of Forecasts" commissioned by the American Press Association in honor of the Exposition; the essays covered a range of subjects but largely shared the perspective expressed by New York minister Thomas De Witt Talmage in the series' debut piece, "World Improving All the Time." Despite Talmage's world-encompassing emphasis, the essayists mostly focused their attention on the national future, but as implied by Thomas Dixon Jr.'s statement in his piece that "democracy will reign triumphant to the farthest limits of civilization," Americans were at this moment beginning to link their own and the international future to an unprecedented degree (Walter, ed. 95). And in many ways the Exposition served as both index and impetus for this American "coming of age on the world scene" (Orvell 59–60).[8] Most importantly, the hierarchical view of America's progressive relationship to world civilization (or lack thereof) embodied in the Midway-Court dialectic provided a clear rationale for the move from a nationalist to an imperialist narrative; a transition defined by Robert Rydell as building from "idealized American past" and "faith in America's future" ("Racist" 254) to the "culture of imperial abundance" ("Imperial") that America would become by the early twentieth century.[9]

If the Exposition's version of the national narrative foreshadowed the world's incorporation, it just as clearly represented the assimilation of my study's four social questions. Gail Bederman's assertion that "the millennial perfection embodied in the Exposition was composed of equal parts of white supremacy and powerful manhood" (31) encapsulates the fair's relationship to the South, woman, race, and Indian questions.[10] That relationship was most complete in the Exposition's subtle but significant endorsement of the Southern conversion narrative. Where Sidney Lanier's Centennial Cantata had enshrined the reconciliationist vision of Southern and national history at the 1876 Exposition, in 1893 a central occasional text—James D. Lynch's "Columbia Saluting the Nations," chosen as the welcoming poem—reflected the conversion narrative's triumphant national role. "Columbia" seems simply to replicate, in lines such as "Catch the head-light of the ages, leave the darkening past behind" (7), the progressive historical narrative's broad strokes. But when read in the context of the works that established the Reconstruction lawyer Lynch's literary credentials—the historiographic conversion narrative *Kemper County Vindicated* (1879), with its attempt to speak for oppressed Southerners "whose voice of defense was forever hushed" (6); and the mini-epic *Redpath, or, the Ku Klux Tribunal* (1877), which depicts the conversion of a Republican reformer (and prominent abolitionist's namesake) into a thorough sympathizer with the Klan's perspective—Lynch's historical progressivism seems predicated on the erasure of the specific past (and present) details of slavery and racial violence. And the Exposition's unanimous selection of Lynch for this essential role indicates just how fully those Southern views had been incorporated into the national historical narrative by this time.[11]

In many ways women's presence at the Exposition seemed to represent an important revision of that narrative. In 1876 women had been forced to raise their own funds and go before Congress to argue for a Women's Pavilion, but the Columbian Commission appointed a 115-member Board of Lady Managers to participate in the Exposition planning from the outset; and while the 1876 Pavilion had almost entirely excluded political issues, leading to the July 4 suffragist protests, in 1893 the week-long World's Congress of Representative Women prominently included Susan B. Anthony, Elizabeth Cady Stanton, Lucy Stone, and other public and political women from America and Europe. It thus certainly seems reasonable to argue that "women's involvement in the fair greatly advanced the cause of women's suffrage and other issues" (Bolotin and Laing 156–58).[12] But if the Exposition at least potentially contributed to a more positive future for American women, it did so by explicitly constructing a progressive vision of their past. That vision was hierarchical, as evidenced by the Woman's Building's contrasting murals: Mary Mac-Monnies's "Primitive Woman," which featured what MacMonnies called "the simplest draped figures of women . . . in a landscape background that . . . is certainly not in America" (Weimann 206–7); and Mary Cassatt's forward-looking series, which included "Young Women Plucking the Fruits of Knowledge and Science" and "Young Girls Pursuing Fame."[13] And it was exclusive: African American women's voices and histories were largely silenced and elided in the Woman's Building.[14] In both these ways, the Exposition's image of new womanhood was linked to the progressive national narrative, situating, as Charles Bonney noted in the Women's Congress's opening address, "the magnificent

achievements of women in the upward and onward march of civilization" (*World's* 8–9). As T. J. Boisseau argues, the "female fair organizers"
did "their utmost to tailor a new standard of American womanhood to
complement and augment the fair's promotion of the United States as a
pre-eminent modern nation" (72).[15]

Silencing, elision, and hierarchical, stereotypical historical constructions in fact dominated the Exposition's inclusions of both African and
Native Americans. African Americans were far outnumbered on the
grounds by Africans themselves, and the average response to the latter
group was to characterize them as the people most opposite to American
civilization's advanced state; that characterization is evident not only in
a caption for an illustrated Exposition guide, which describes African
Americans as at least more civilized than "their barbarous countrymen"
(Rydell, "Racist" 264), but also and even more tellingly in the remark
of Frederick Douglass (usually no advocate for the progressive narrative) that "as if to shame the Negro, the Dahomians are here to exhibit
the Negro as a repulsive savage" (Trachtenberg, *Incorporation* 220–21).[16]
And the Exposition's most prominent individual African American likewise directly contributed to the progressive historical narrative: Nancy
Green, a former slave and longtime Chicago servant, won a prize for
her enormously popular performance as Aunt Jemima, a "plantation
mammy" telling "nostalgic tales of plantation life" (Rydell, "Contend"
xix).[17] With international and national images like these dominating the
Exposition's depictions of African Americans, it is no wonder that many
of them viewed the fair as "a moral regression" (Rudwick and Meier
361) or even "the definitive failure of the hopes of emancipation and reconstruction" (Carby 5).

Native Americans faced a similar combination of primitivist and
stereotypical classifications at the Exposition. The exhibits of cultural
artifacts—which, while assembled by early anthropologists not unsympathetic to the Indian cause, were presented in "a little mean-
looking building in the midst of . . . grand and imposing structures,"
to quote a Board of Indian Commissioners official (Muccigrasso 151)—
were treated as remnants of an earlier and less civilized culture that had
(in a narrative paralleling Turner's) appropriately and helpfully given
way before the next stage of progress. A few of those exhibits did depict
Natives as potential converts to that progressive narrative: Reid Badger

describes a father-son diorama which portrayed the adult as "savage" but "his child in the dress of civilization" (105). But the more popular Native American representations, the Indian performers in Buffalo Bill's Wild West Show (located just outside the Exposition grounds), were depicted as antagonists of progress: in the show's oft-repeated and virtually unchanging narratives, the "savage and ferocious" Natives were "dramatically repulsed" by Cody and his heroic counterparts (Muccigrasso 148–51). All in all, Native Americans' relationships to the fair's progressive narrative were the most absolute and oppositional of any group; as Paul Greenhalgh forcefully argues, the 1893 depiction of Native Americans had "deteriorated" from that at the 1876 Exposition, where they were already "cast . . . as immoral savage[s]" (100).[18]

Yet even in the face of such sweeping and limiting characterizations, African and Native Americans did articulate dialogic complications of the Exposition's progressive monologue, giving "fresh expression to the subversive voices of dissent" (Downey xix). African Americans did so in part by organizing "Jubilee" or "Colored People's Day," featuring a keynote speech by the aged but still eloquent Frederick Douglass; while he did refer to the savage Dahomians, he also cleverly turned the Exposition itself into an outdated artifact, calling it "a whited sepulcher."[19] And even more dialogic, historical, and impressive was the pamphlet *The Reason Why the Colored American Is Not in the Columbian Exposition,* a series of essays authored by Ida B. Wells, Douglass, Irvine Garland Penn, and Ferdinand L. Barnett and distributed to Exposition visitors. In "this presentation of their side of the question" (81), as Barnett describes it in his titular closing essay, the four authors both engage constructively with and offer an alternative to the progressive historical narrative. On the one hand, they utilize that narrative's terms to illustrate the Exposition's failure to commemorate their race's historic successes, arguing that "the exhibit of the progress made by a race in 25 years of freedom as against 250 years of slavery, would have been the greatest tribute to the greatness and progressiveness of American institutions which could have been shown the world" (3). And on the other hand, they acknowledge the historical vision of slavery at the progressive narrative's core—how it has "been asserted" in the postbellum era "that slavery was a divine institution"—and "avail [themselves] of the opportunity" they have constructed to offer a counternarrative (66–67). Some

African American leaders objected to the pamphlet, worrying that it would bring embarrassing or even damaging attention to their absence from the Exposition; but the text instead highlights the elisions present in the progressive narrative itself, and demonstrates what is lost through those erasures.[20]

A somewhat more elegiac but no less powerful and dialogic response to such historical elisions was presented by Potawatomi chief Simon Pokagon. Pokagon was asked by the Exposition organizers to ring a replica of the Liberty Bell during the opening ceremonies; the inclusion of a Native American at this moment, while certainly not as limiting or dismissive as the exhibits' or shows' characterizations, nonetheless clearly embodies the Exposition's emblematic transition from primitive to civilized American culture. The bell, that is, was tolling for Pokagon and all the noble but departing Natives for whom he stood. But Pokagon offers, in the speech "The Red Man's Greeting" with which he followed the symbolic act, a different vision of both the Exposition and American history. He begins by reconstructing the absent, alternative narrative over which the Exposition's historical vision has been built: he instructs his audience that while they "rejoice over the beauty and grandeur of this young republic," they should "not forget that this success has been at the sacrifice of our homes and a once happy race"; and notes that "where stands this 'Queen City of the West' once stood the red man's wigwams." He then narrates an extended Native American version of the significance of the frontier to their history, a tragic articulation of "those days that tried [their] fathers' souls." Pokagon acknowledges white voices' power to characterize Native Americans as (among other things) "treacherous, vindictive, and cruel"; and "in answer to the charge" he uses the perspectives of his audience's "own historians" to demonstrate such characterizations' falseness. And while Pokagon ends with what seems to be an elegiac reiteration of the Vanishing American trope, an image of "the incoming tide of the great ocean of civilization ris[ing] slowly but surely to overwhelm" Indians, his entire text—which he subsequently printed, circulated at the fair, and continued to sell until his death in 1899—represents a refusal to accept that future without a dialogic historical response (29–35).

Just as the Exposition's emphasis on the progressive historical narrative neither silenced nor elided the voices and histories contained in and constructed by *Reason* and "Greeting," the monologic narrative's cultural dominance by the century's final decade likewise continued to be challenged by dialogic historical literary texts connected to all four social questions. The years surrounding the Chicago fair included many such texts in a variety of genres: historical novels such as S. Alice Callahan's *Wynema* (1891; generally considered the first novel by a Native American woman) and Frances Harper's *Iola Leroy* (1892); nonfiction works such as Anna Julia Cooper's personal and feminist essays in *A Voice from the South* (1892) and Ida Wells's journalistic exposés on lynching (culminating in *A Red Record* [1895]); poetry such as Paul Laurence Dunbar's debut collection *Oak and Ivy* (1892) and new works by Sarah Piatt and Helen Hunt Jackson; and collections of short fiction and folktales by Grace King, Kate Chopin, and Joel Chandler Harris. The national historical narrative had certainly become more entrenched in the post-Centennial decades, incorporating or dominating many alternative voices and histories; but historical literature remained a particularly potent space in which such dialogic alternatives could be constructed for their own moment and modeled for future decades and literary texts.

Emblematic of those alternatives and their explicit connection to the American future are *Iola Leroy*'s final few pages. James Christmann argues that the novel's dual climaxes—chapter 20's rural church meeting and chapter 30's philosophical conversation between "Friends in Council"—represent "competing voice-paradigms" and alternative African American communities: the former Southern, emotional, and dialect driven; the latter Northern, rhetorical, and more vocally sophisticated. In Christmann's analysis, Harper wavers between the two modes throughout but (as the term "competing" suggests) ultimately cannot sustain both's power and possibility, choosing to emphasize the Northern mode. Central to the distinction between the two is the implied gap between the African American past and future; as Christmann notes, the Southern scene is necessarily linked to "slave and folk stereotype[s]," while the Northern one seems to embody "bourgeois progress" into "mainstream culture" (5–18). And in choosing to emphasize the latter, Harper would thus also be reifying the progressive historical narrative,

casting her lot fully with the future; that reading of *Iola* could argue that
such a fate for the past is foreshadowed in and inevitable from the novel's
subtitle, *Shadows Uplifted*.[21]

Certainly there is much in Harper's novel, and especially its dual climaxes, to support such a reading. Yet the Northern climax is not the
text's endpoint, and its final chapter, "Conclusion," complicates the
aforementioned distinctions. For one thing, Iola and her new husband,
Dr. Latimer, return to "their home in North Carolina," soon to be joined
by the rest of Iola's family; and this historical Southern home's connection to their planned future of racial uplift is articulated, in dialect
voice, by Aunt Linda, who claims that she "seed it in a vision dat some-
body fair war comin' to help us" (456). Those intersections between the
African American past and future are exemplified by the fate of the final
character discussed in the novel, Grandmother Johnson, who "was glad
to return South and spend the remnant of her days with the remaining
friends of her early life" but at the same time is "in full sympathy with
her children for the uplifting of the race" (460–61). And the narrow-
ing of the past-future distinction is even more strikingly represented
through a formal element: the closing paragraphs' sudden shift from
past to present tense, within the span of two sentences about Iola's work
in this new yet familiar community: "Together [Iola and the town's pas-
tor] planned meetings for the especial benefit of mothers and children.
When the dens of vice are spreading their snares for the feet of the
tempted and inexperienced [Iola's] doors are freely opened for the instruction of the children before their feet have wandered and gone far
astray" (459). Iola focuses on providing a positive direction for the future, in explicit contrast to the current direction. Yet in the chapter's
Southern, familiar, and familial context, Iola's forward-looking work is
powerfully rooted in her own and her racial past, and so her vision of
the future—like the shift in tense—is much more historical and dialogic
than the progressive narrative. The final two lines of Iola's closing poem
read "Yet the shadows bear the promise / Of a brighter coming day"
(463), and the concluding chapter illustrates the meaning of both that
ambiguous image and the text's subtitle: it is precisely the past's dialogic
shadows that offer the best chance for the future, and those shadows, far
from being swept away by the progressive narrative's millennial light,
must be illuminated by historical knowledge so they can be uplifted into

a genuinely progressive future.[1] As *Iola Leroy* forcefully demonstrates, at stake in the intersections between the consensus narrative and its literary contestations was not only how America would remember its past but also how it would imagine and construct its present identity and future course. Just as the national narrative's nostalgic and linear history meshed nicely with its progressive and millennial visions of the future, so too did historical literature's multivocal and -valent constructions of the past produce corollary images of the future. Like the literary texts themselves, those futures were complex, uncertain, and always potentially assimilated into the dominant monologue; but they were also, at their best, dialogic, inclusive, and democratic. No two such visions nor the forms through which they were imagined were ever entirely alike, and each demands close attention to its specifics: whether Twain's dialect-driven raft community or Chesnutt's shifting and competing narrative voices and stories; Harsha's imagined first-person Native American narrator or Winnemucca's efforts at cross-cultural and linguistic mediation; Phelps's multivocal world of women or Piatt's dialogic lyric poetic speaker; Woolson's romantic and haunted Southern ground or Tourgée's multigeneric innovations in the historical novel; Cable's polyphonic literary landscape or his manuscript's conversational textual terrain; Pokagon's final plea for broadened national memory and sympathy or Iola's work to achieve racial and regional uplift. But all these texts and the many others I have read shared a fundamental commitment to striving toward a more multivocal and democratic future by contesting the past and reconstructing the nation in Gilded Age America.

Notes

Preface

1. See "Advertising *Uncle Tom*."

2. Harris "hasten[s] to say" that Stowe had "attacked the possibilities of slavery with all the eloquence of genius," but nonetheless reiterates that "the same genius painted the portrait of the Southern slave-owner, and defended him" (39).

3. The autobiography as a whole both critiques and endorses unifying American myths, illustrating "the dynamic interplay between the marginal and dominant in cultural forms and power structures" (Scheckel, "Home" 223).

4. For models of such scholarship, see Levin; Henderson; Hughson; Mizruchi; Cowart; Wesseling; David Price; Rody.

5. For my terms, see Bakhtin; Todorov; Bal. For voice and American literature, see McKay; Nettels; Wald; Looby; Donaldson; Levander, *Voices;* Gavin Jones; Elliott; Holmes; Minnick.

Introduction

1. Ingram's description of the Indian exhibits, for example, is located between, and indistinguishable from, reports on "The Fishery Resources of This Country" and the "Patent Office" (147–52).

2. Quoting more nostalgic sections of Whittier's Hymn, Badger contends that the Exposition "turned its face from the new age and searched with Whittier for lost innocence in the American past" (27); but nostalgia for a glorious past was actually perfectly compatible with (and often a corollary to) such visions of a glorious future. Most assess-

ments of the Exposition depict it as forward-looking; see Cawelti 324–34; Greenhalgh
127–30; Schlereth 267–77.

3. Throughout this study, I use "progressive" to refer to this particular (and conservative) vision of America and its history. I know that the similarity to the later liberal reform movement might be confusing, although Progressivism has often been seen as related to this progressive historical perspective. Regardless, the centrality of progress to
the vision in question makes the term too apt to be discarded.

4. Conn argues that the vision's progressive element often overshadowed the religious ones, that in fact progress is "the American faith" (209–10); Saum similarly traces a
postbellum "Waning of Providence" and waxing of nationalist faith.

5. For the merging of "social criticism" with "the errand" (*Jeremiad* xi, xiv), see
also Bercovitch, *Rites* 63; Lears; Ernest 6–8. Hofstadter articulates this duality most succinctly: "The United States was the only country in the world that began with perfection and aspired to progress" (*Age* 35–36). For certain "cataclysmic" jeremiads as distinct
from the millennial view, see Jaher; Painter, *Standing*.

6. Bercovitch emphasizes this philosophical combination's enduring nature, arguing that rituals of consensus constitute "the forms and strategies of cultural continuity"
(*Rites* 30). See also the many editions of Davis, ed.; Samet. For a critique of consensus
scholarship, see Ellis.

7. For veterans' groups, see McConnell; Logue 82–130; Blight, *Reunion* 171–210;
Grant. For war memories as hindering consensus and needing to be "live[d] down" by
both sides, see Current.

8. Timothy Smith argues that memorials truly began to serve this unifying purpose
after the 1889 founding of the national Memorial Day holiday.

9. "The war was thus the source of a new American confidence to achieve" (Dawes
68). For the shift in understandings of historical time, see Conn 25–26; this progressive
vision was at once historical and historiographic, could "be both America's historical fate
and the way Americans would come to understand their history" (Conn 26). For changing notions of time in the period, see Stephen Kern.

10. For the Women's Committee and Pavilion, and "the cultural interplay between
womanhood and sisterhood" (114), see Cordato. See also Weimann 1–4; Greenhalgh 174–
97; Schlereth 275–76. For the July 4 protest, see Coté 115; for the text of the "Declaration,"
see Scott and Scott, eds. 90–95.

11. See Greenhalgh 100.

12. Rydell, like most Exposition historians, replicates its emphasis on material progress by focusing on national economics and America's place in world markets; his readings of the Native American exhibits are convincing but tied to those topics. Even more
exemplary of this tendency is Goodheart's argument that "many groups aspired to participate as producers in the Centennial . . . those who failed did so because they failed as
capitalists" (76).

13. Earlier figures such as Lydia Maria Child and Catherine Maria Sedgwick produced such alternative histories, but sectional crisis and Civil War eradicated the Indian

Question from the public consciousness. And while they did bring the issue back into the national dialogue, Helen Hunt Jackson (whose advocacy began a few years after the Centennial) and her contemporary reformers still represented a minority of the era's perspectives on Native Americans and their history. Even the early anthropologist Lewis Henry Morgan, who was unusually sympathetic to the Native Americans' cause, agreed with the progressive historical vision, arguing in 1881 that "in studying the condition of the Indian tribes . . . we may recover some portion of the lost history of our own voice" (Trachtenberg, *Incorporation* 35–36).

14. See Philip Foner.

15. One could fit abolition into such progressive accounts, by arguing that America's victory over slavery represented another trend toward national perfection. But the histories and voices of figures such as Douglass and Allen would wholly challenge such a perspective; for such African American historical alternatives from the era, see Savage 89–128; Kathleen Clark; Maffly-Kipp.

16. For voice and nationalism, see Lloyd; for late-nineteenth-century nationalism, see Hobsbawm; for a link of millennialism to nationalism, see Anthony Smith 109–12.

17. For patriotism, see Davies 28–345; Jonathan Hansen. For Social Darwinism, see Hofstadter, *Darwinism;* Hawkins; Ryan, ed. For the era's dominant ideas, see Commager 3–81; Saum.

18. On corporations and public policy, see Sklar; Zunz. On imperialism and expansionism, see LaFeber; Rosenberg; Blum.

19. On the memorials, see Kammen 101–31; Savage; Mills and Simpson, eds.; Timothy Smith. On history's institutionalization, see Sternsher; Noble, *End* 16–40; Fitzpatrick 13–50.

20. For the dime westerns, see Klein 65–130; for local color and nationalism, see King.

21. For Progressivism, see Hofstadter, *Age;* Wiebe; Chambers. For naturalism, see Howard; Michaels; Lawlor; Link. Michaels's link of naturalism to consensus—"in naturalism, . . . all fictions . . . are corporate fictions" (213)—goes much further than would I.

22. See Levine and Story 2–5.

23. See Bell and Abrams 11–23; Schneider 33–43.

24. Moreno and Levine and Story are the only scholars I have found that reference Laboulaye's stance on the Civil War, much less acknowledge its importance to the Statue. Warner exemplifies the progressive interpretation, claiming that the Statue "does not record the past. . . . It anticipates continuously a future that is always in the process of becoming" (3–15); see also Bishop 13–40. Kotler mentions Laboulaye's post-assassination tribute to Lincoln, but argues that "from its very beginnings, the Statue of Liberty was designed to be a beacon, a universal symbol, for the spread of freedom and self-government everywhere" (1–16).

25. Strong goes further with this vision, calling the end of the nineteenth century "second in importance" only to "the birth of Christ" (13).

26. For *Our World*'s chronology, see Berge 184. See also Muller; Robert Smith.

27. See Hartmann 95–119.

28. For Haymarket, see Avrich; Dabakis; Carl Smith 101–74.

29. For such debates, see Harris, ed.; Burt, ed. For the era's "adversary tradition," see John Thomas.

30. The other two essays diverge from Trachtenberg, arguing that incorporation and the consensus narrative more productively influenced the future; those essays not only continue the forward-looking scholarly emphasis, but could even be said to replicate the Gilded Age's own attitudes (Leverenz; Livingston, "*Incorporation*"). See also Haskell; Livingston, *Economy*.

31. Wiebe notes that one "ethical evasion" that bolstered contemporary corruption was to "idealize the past and the passing" (39); Trachtenberg defines Frederick Jackson Turner's goal as providing "a connected and unified account of the progress of civilization across the continent" (*Incorporation* 13). Lears's subjects were deeply interested in the past (if often a distant and European one)—"the most powerful critics of capitalism have often looked backward rather than forward" (xviii)—but he ultimately sees their historical interests as assimilated "to the mainstream" (xix–xx), complementary to the capitalist progressive vision. One clear exception is Orvell, who identifies an alternative American tradition (the "Whitmanesque patrimony" [156]) from which the era's dominant culture broke; yet he only discusses this past at length in his first chapter, and then only through one key figure (Whitman) whose principal role is as a model for Orvell's twentieth-century subjects.

32. For an extension of Michaels's work (by a student of his), see Kerkering's analysis of whether nineteenth-century texts were complicit with or resistant to racial discourse.

33. I make a related argument about *Gone with the Wind*'s full complicity with a political position similar to Page's—although only after an extended reading of that novel—in "'What Else.'"

34. See Santayana; Dawidoff.

35. Kaplan here opposes Richard Chase's "profoundly ahistorical thesis that . . . Americans do not write social fiction" (2), but Chase's *The American Novel and Its Tradition* (1957) comes from a profoundly different era; more recent scholars, including Kaplan, Pizer, Michael Davitt Bell, Brook Thomas, Barrish, and Wonham, emphasize realism's social contexts and functions as much as its formal characteristics. Even those critics, including Glazener and Warren, who most fully critique realism for its "affiliation with powerful groups" (Glazener 12) still focus on its relationship to the era's social undercurrents. For realism and audience, see Hochman; Goodman.

36. Foundational in that debate is Sinclair Lewis's 1930 Nobel Prize address; he accuses Howells of having "the code of a pious old maid whose greatest delight was to have tea at the vicarage" (Michael Davitt Bell 37). See also Michael Davitt Bell 17–37; Kaplan 15–64; Pizer 70–85.

A subcategory of realism that complicates this contrast is local color, which is often nostalgic and conservative in its historical vision yet realistic in its portrayal of regional distinctions and dialects. I am not overly concerned with labels such as genteel, realistic, or local color, but have more to say about region, dialect, and history in the following chapters.

37. Other recent dialect scholars likewise highlight this era; see Elliott 35–88; Holmes 28–31, 46–61; Minnick 1–27.

38. By "presentist" and "futurist," I simply mean that primary texts (and scholarship) engaged with those themes focus on the nation's present and future; since such texts are not centrally concerned with constructing a vision of the past, I do not read them as historical literature.

CHAPTER 1

1. Moses, *Golden* 70–72; Blight, *Reunion* 315–19. See also Blight, *Frederick.*

2. See Moses, *Afrotopia* 96–135; Fulop.

3. Frederickson 198–227; Moses, *Golden* 59–102; Moses, *Afrotopia* 96–135; Howard-Pitney.

4. For debates over Elkins's controversial work, see Lane, ed.

5. Although even reconciliation required particular versions of slavery and race; see Blight, *Reunion* 98–139.

6. John David Smith traces this scholarly shift (3–13), and thoroughly documents the period's "obsession" with slavery (15–99). Prescient as ever, DuBois in the 1930s identified the existence and historiographic significance of these ante- and postbellum connections ("Propaganda").

7. See De Nevi and Holmes, eds.

8. See Guion Griffis Johnson; Wynes. Even former abolitionists who continued to fight for African American rights were not immune to this condition; see McPherson.

9. See Lynn; Rosenwald 335–37; Minnick 1–27.

10. For a complex version of this argument that "racial formal effects were imagined to reinforce rather than resist the commitment to racial identity," see Kerkering.

11. See Simms, "Irwin"; Jean Wagner 51–59; MacKethan, "Plantation" 211–12.

12. For Russell, Harris, and other dialect writers (particularly Thomas Nelson Page), see Hubbell 788, 795–96.

13. Sundquist gives a good overview of dialect criticism (*Wake* 294–323); see also Minnick 28–41.

14. Minnick's question quoted from Rickford and Rickford. See also Holmes.

15. Wolfe includes Harris's stuttering and fear of reading aloud (81–82). For the dual personality quote, Mark Twain's divided authorial self, and African American double consciousness, see Wyatt-Brown 155–78. For a representative negative analysis of Harris, see Birnbaum.

16. Birnbaum portrays the relationship between standard and dialect language in *Uncle* differently, arguing that, in terms of "the politics behind the procedures for articulating this relation," "written dialect poses as a representation when often it has no constituency—it presents speech spoken by no one" (37, 41). Certainly Harris's use of

dialect can serve such political ends, as my discussion of the "Sayings" illustrates. But in the "Legends," the power of Remus's voice, coupled with the tales' content, far outweighs whatever abstract authoritative weight the narrator's standard English carries.

17. "The Wonderful Tar-Baby Story" has a long history, in both Harris's own writings (he revised it four times) and African American folklore. See Pedersen, "Rewriting"; Keenan.

18. For Harris's support of the New South and his friendship with Henry Grady, see Rubin, "Uncle." For Harris's nostalgic opposition to certain New South changes, see Mixon 73–84. For the revisions of "Story," see Montenyohl.

19. "A Story of the War" also couples Harris with the period's most prominent nostalgic Southern writer: Thomas Nelson Page. Page's "Marse Chan; A Tale of Old Virginia" likewise concerns a zealously loyal slave narrating his master's antebellum life (what the slave calls the "good ole times," "de bes' [he] ever see" [10]) and heroic war exploits; the master dies in the war but the slave remains on the plantation to care for ("wait on" [3]) the master's old dog. Page and Harris are often lumped together as equally regressive writers; see Diffley 176–90. That charge does disservice to the "Legends," but is more accurate to "Story" and the "Sayings" that follow.

20. For the conflict between Harris's historical vision and his dependence on an African American storytelling voice, see MacKethan, "Plantation" 214–16; Humphries. MacKethan connects Uncle Remus to both sides, arguing that Remus "provides a simplistic way back to the world of lost innocence" but that he also, as "master of his folktale narratives," is a "shrewd role player" (216).

21. I use "propaganda" as a purposeful echo of DuBois's *Black Reconstruction in America* (1935); its final chapter, "The Propaganda of History," deconstructs the nostalgic vision of Southern history that dominated academic and popular circles in the late nineteenth and early twentieth centuries.

22. Critics disagree on whether *Nights* marks a step forward or backward for Harris. Light sees the legends' multiple versions as an improvement in Harris's treatment of race (95–98); Cartwright calls *Nights* Harris's aesthetic "masterpiece" (115). Hedin, however, argues that Uncle Remus's oral and subversive powers, and with them Harris's thematic and aesthetic significance, decline with each book in the series (83–90).

23. See Light 95–98.

24. For satire, see Wieck 135–36. For serious, see Pedersen, "Negro"; Bolend 30–40; Carkeet. Sewell, the authority on Twain's languages, focuses on the note's concluding sentence and argues that Twain's point, masked by his humor, lies in the idea of "talking alike" and language conventions (108–9).

25. Messent makes a parallel case that in the Notice "the whole question of voice, its authority, weaponry at its command, trustworthiness, and relation to other voices, has been swiftly and incisively introduced" (206); see also Kleiman. Lynn connects Twain's use of language to his humor (198–245).

26. See McKay 148–50; Nichols.

27. For Huck and society's languages, see Sewell 107; Wonham, "Disembodied" 4; Blakemore 29; Stephen Railton 395.

28. As Berret notes, black characters in minstrel shows (a form of entertainment to

which Twain was professedly indebted) could provide both humor and social critique. Twain "adopts the chief strategy of the minstrel show, the use of a black character or black persona as a mouthpiece for humor, social criticism, and deep personal sentiment" (38). See also Lott.

29. J. Hillis Miller defines Huck's language at these moments as "good/ideal," one of three categories he identifies in the novel; the other two are "bad/false" and "solitude/ silence" (40–41). See also Kaul 292–99; Rosenwald 338–41.

30. For Messent, the time "restored" by these pastoral "idylls" is "folkloric," in contrast to the rest of the novel's historical time (227). Burns focuses instead on the book's overall "subtle but active past-tense structure" to claim that "the timelessness of the river is paradoxically end-stopped by time" (53). The pastoral sections are indeed interrupted and ended by time (or by history), but that does not diminish their ahistorical quality's effects on voice.

31. Schmidt describes these recurrences as "the disintegration of Huck's identity into warring factions" (46). For Brook Thomas, such elements' presence makes Huck's voice forever "derivative," and thus "Huck's real choice . . . between speech and silence" ("Languages" 7).

32. For Jim's voice, here and elsewhere, as intentionally subverting Huck's intentions, and thus Jim as a trickster or signifying figure, see Shafer; Godden and McCoy.

33. For Twain and Bakhtin, see Berthoff 27; Messent 204–42.

34. See Cox 400; Berret 47–49; Poirier 101; Lindberg 48.

35. For the ending and antebellum realities, see Cecil. For the postbellum era, see MacLeod. For both, that Twain began the novel due to the need for "a contemporary indictment of the antebellum South," see Egan 66–134. See also Mixon 85–97.

36. Leonard sees the "white inside" comment as one of the novel's "double-edged declarations," arguing that what truly makes Jim "white inside" is "his ability to control the rhetorical situation" (147–48); Bollinger centers her analysis on this moment, arguing that in it Huck and Jim jointly speak the "the language of care," as opposed to "the dominant voice of the society in which" they live, "the language of justice" (38, 46). Leonard's point relates nicely to Jim's earlier logical victories over Huck, and Bollinger's distinctions help define Huck and Jim's separation from the language systems around them, but I see evidence of neither double-ness nor alternative languages at the "white inside" moment.

37. Wyatt-Brown argues that even Huck's last act of "lighting out" is portrayed, due to his necessary separation from Jim, as tragic (177–78).

38. Gilbert's and Titus's degree of authorship in the *Narrative* is a point of critical contention; as I argue, they definitely affect the text's construction of voice. However, the book's primary purpose is to give Truth the opportunity to tell her life story, so it certainly qualifies as an autobiography.

39. Many critics provide definitions of the subgenre, including Starling, Bontemps, Davis and Gates, and Francis Smith Foster (Waters 43); these definitions emphasize different particulars but concur on voice and history's centrality to the narratives' purpose and composition.

40. "Black people had to represent themselves as 'speaking subjects' before they could

even begin to destroy their status as 'objects,'" and they "could become 'speaking' subjects only by inscribing their 'voices' in the written word" (Gates, "Gronniosaw" 10–11).

41. An analysis of the differences between *Life* and Douglass's other narratives is outside of this study's purview; see Ernest 140–79; Wald 73–105; Holmes 8–24.

42. Truth "purposefully anchored herself in slavery" throughout her public life (Painter, "Difference" 158). Most critics reiterate this emphasis, treating the later text as simply a revised and extended version. Douglass-Chin differentiates between the two, calling the 1878 version more of an autobiography (66), but he refers largely to the inclusion of Truth's own words (the 1878 text has more), which would not undermine its continued identity as slave narrative.

43. Van Leer argues that this distinction between Douglass's young and old perspectives exists throughout, and that "the contrast between the two voices confers full authority on neither" (129). However, this contrast does not prohibit Douglass from articulating a revisionist historical argument that is, if anything, too univocal.

44. Sekora identifies this function of the slave narratives, their connection of personal details to a broad historical system, as the "personal history of slavery" (157–70).

45. See Wilson Moses, "Freely" 76; Warren, "Frederick" 254. For the black oral tradition and Douglass's oratory, see Lampe.

46. Sundquist argues that in Douglass's second autobiography, *My Bondage and My Freedom,* he was already moving away from the *Narrative*'s historical (slave) self, "detaching himself . . . from the objectified selves of the past" (*Wake* 83–93).

47. This version of the Sandy encounter was new to *Life*: in the *Narrative* Douglass does not elaborate on the conversation's details, while in *Bondage* he does represent some of Sandy's comments in dialect form. See Goddu and Smith 839.

48. "Language is [Douglass'] tool, and in mastering language, he declares himself a free and sovereign subject" (Dupuy 32–33).

49. For the relationship of Douglass's voice to African American and slave voices as positive, see Sisco 212; Goddu and Smith 823–24; McBride 151–72. For it as more problematic, see Kibbey and Stepto 189; Rothenberg 52; Boudreau, *Sympathy* 88–89. For Douglass's "doubleness," see Valerie Smith 20–28.

50. "The voice most in evidence among [Douglass'] black constituents was a voice in discord with his own: that of the black preacher" (Warren, "Frederick" 258). Truth was one of the strongest such oppositional voices, as her famous "Frederick, is God dead?" rejoinder proves; "a woman needed boldness to speak out in such a 'deep, peculiar voice, heard all over the house' in disagreement with Douglass" (Bush 65). For Douglass on Truth's "ungainly dialect," see Moses, *Creative* 50.

51. The speech is transcribed in the "Book of Life" section, 133–35. This transcription, which Truth presumably saw (and at least distributed), complicates Painter's argument that the well-known version of "Ain't I a Woman" was largely created by Frances Gage twelve years after its delivery; certainly it is possible that Truth did not read or know of the "Book of Life" version, but it was literally in her hands during her lifetime.

52. Samra's is the most negative take: Gilbert "smothers Truth's voice with her own Anglicized morality and style," so we must "search for [Truth's] narrative" in her

"speeches and letters" (158–59, 167). See also Yellin 80–87; Merish 216–28. Humez argues instead that "Truth's own eloquent expressions of both feeling and moral principle influenced Gilbert's decision to avoid the distancing effect of dialect and create a highly dignified-sounding representation of her speech" (46).

53. For "Ain't," see *Life* 103–12, 259–62, 281.

54. It is unclear whether Truth's dialect voice was entirely natural or partly performative. Samra argues that "Truth had no other option, perhaps no desire, to speak a language other than black English vernacular" (162); Fitch and Mendziuk contend that Truth "seemed to enjoy using her quaint style to amuse her audiences and bring down her opponents" (38), and that "the power of [her] rhetoric came from her successful construction of an autobiographical character that coincided precisely with what audiences actually saw when she spoke before them" (83). Regardless, the *Narrative* fails to represent her voice in all its effectiveness and power. Again, Painter argues that the dialect voice was a creation of Truth's white biographers.

55. See Brodhead 177–210; Petrie. McWilliams gives a more literary reading of the journals, concluding as I do that Chesnutt's "attitude in the journals to black vernacular speech is . . . complex and conflicted" (23–42). See also Minnick 77–98.

56. "Chesnutt accomplishes the vernacular imperative by transforming local vernacular materials . . . into something that speaks well beyond the community which produced them" (Barbara Baker 30). Chesnutt's dissatisfactions with dialect writing are well known, including his remark that "there is no such thing as a Negro dialect," only "English pronounced as an ignorant old Southern Negro would be supposed to speak it" (Burnette 446). But that attitude did not prevent Chesnutt from using black dialect to great effect in the conjure tales, nor from representing it with "accuracy" there (Foster 1; Minnick 77–98). For a more negative reading of Chesnutt's remark and relation to dialect, see Holmes 52–61.

57. In these years Chesnutt also published local color stories such as "Tom's Warm Welcome" and nonracial character sketches such as "A Bad Night" and "Cartwright's Mistake" (all 1886). While all three use first-person narration interestingly, I focus on stories that deal explicitly with racial issues.

58. For "Uncle" and the conjure tales, see Gleason.

59. "The subordination of Gainey's voice and his perspective . . . find unexpected support from a dialect speaker at the story's conclusion" (McWilliams 69). For William Andrews, these early stories take a uniformly "detached" and "condescending" view of local blacks (*Literary* 18–19).

60. I analyze the 1887 version, in keeping with both my chronological focus and my attention to Chesnutt's early work. Chesnutt made a few significant revisions for the story's inclusion in *The Conjure Woman* (1899); see Burnette.

61. See Babb; Werner; Sundquist, *Wake* 323–59; Nowatzki; Matthew Martin.

62. On Chesnutt's mixed response to Page's "Marse Chan," see Price 257–76; Elliott 63–76.

63. Wonham reads *The Conjure Woman* as operating on three "historical registers": the antebellum era; post-Reconstruction; and the turn of the century ("Plenty" 131–32);

only the first two are significantly present in this earliest conjure tale. See also Mixon 101–18; Keely 642–48.

64. Chesnutt distinguishes Julius from Remus more strikingly in the 1899 version, inserting an additional descriptive paragraph delineating Julius's apparently mixed-race identity.

65. For Julius-centered arguments, see Melvin Dixon; Terry; Babb; Joyce Scott. For John, see Burnette 452–53; Nowatzki 24–25. For Annie, see Nowatzki 26; Duncan 92.

66. Wonham argues instead that while both voices are powerful, neither can hear the other; that there is a "permanent discontinuity between John's latinate, bourgeois idiom and Julius' earthy black dialect" ("Curious" 65).

67. For a different take on the conjure woman, see Bost 223–24 n56.

68. For such issues in these turn of the century works, see Gunning 48–76; Boeckmann 138–73.

CHAPTER 2

1. For biographical, largely pessimistic readings of the ending, see Benn; Graulich; Christine Smith 25. Darlis Miller likewise reads the story biographically, but admits that "the voice was not lost . . . an artist can find satisfaction in the West" (107–9). Richard's reading parallels mine: Foote "accesses her readers' memories to contrast shrinking eastern possibilities for home and female community with the alternative of western potential" (42).

2. "Akin to Frederick Jackson Turner and, indeed, to the temper of her times, Foote usually excluded Native Americans from her landscape" (Blend 98–99).

3. For Standing Bear and his lecture tour, see Mathes and Lewitt; Dando-Collins.

4. Smith and Slotkin (*Fatal*) trace these changes at length; see also Kolodny; Hyde; Truettner, ed.; Rosowski; Murdoch.

5. See Noble, *Historians;* Limerick 17–32; Nash.

6. See Wecter 341–63; Bold; Marcus Klein 65–130; Denning; Bridger.

7. For such historians, the "Indian was pictured as an obstacle to Western settlement and the coming of civilization" (Berkhofer 109); to fit Natives into that role, "narratives like Turner's deny [them] a history" (Brook Thomas, "Frederick" 275–92). See also Kerwin Klein; Lawlor 41–57.

8. As Murdoch notes of the Buffalo Bill-type hero, "his real job was removing Indians" (40). Trachtenberg attributes this violence to psychological factors: "an Indian presence persisted as the underside, the lasting bad conscience, within the prevailing conception of 'West,' calling for repeated ritualistic slaying in popular 'Westerns'" (*Incorporation* 28). Hall contends that the participation of some Native Americans (such as Sitting Bull) allowed the shows to serve, in a way, as "educational and cultural enrichment" (141), but his argument pales in the face of a show such as the one referenced.

9. See Weeks 176–233. Critics such as Slotkin (*Regeneration* 17), Cheryl Walker (*Indian*), and Bellin argue persuasively for a significant Native presence in nineteenth-century American myths and literature, but they focus on antebellum texts.

10. For governmental Indian policy, see Priest; Hagan; McDonnell. For the period's reformers, see Mardock 150–228; Prucha; Hinsley, *Savages;* Hoxie; Spack.

11. See Stedman; Hanson; Deloria; Scheckel, *Insistence;* Bergland; Sherry Smith; Huhndorf.

12. For poetic "cultural fusions" as blurring the divisions between Native and white authors and texts, see Lincoln.

13. For such Native voices from the period, see Hoxie, ed.

14. For the Cherokees, see McLaughlin; for Wounded Knee, see Gonzalez and Cook-Lynn.

15. For literary critical alternatives to sovereignty, see Krupat, *Red;* Pulitano.

16. I am indebted to two anonymous readers for *ESQ* for their thoughtful responses.

17. Ruppert's text is often cited as a starting point for cultural mediation's resurgence in Native American literary criticism; see also Szasz, ed. For extensions of the concept to particular texts, see Walker, *Nation* 139–63; Silkü.

18. I am certainly not the first to suggest that white authors can also perform acts of cultural mediation; see for example Sarah Wilson.

19. Waterhouse puts Harte's influence in different, if equally strong, terms: he was the "cause of fictional motifs" which produced later Western writers like Miller (61).

20. While the two recent biographies of Harte narrate this trajectory in fuller and more complex terms, the basic outline remains the same. See Nissen; Scharnhorst, *Opening.*

21. See Morrow, "Predicament" 181–88; Scharnhorst, "Whatever." Glover advocates a "reconsideration" of Harte's "later work" (any post-1878 text), but does not analyze particular texts at length.

22. As a footnote of Harte's indicates, "The first word of Pope's familiar apostrophe is humorously used in the far West as a distinguishing title for the Indian" (11). Low's self-adoption of this "distinguishing title" illustrates his attempts to define his own history and identity.

23. Walterhouse argues instead that the presence of a half-breed "tragic hero" helps reduce Harte's novella to the level of trite melodrama (58). See also Duckett, "Portrayal." For a recent analysis of this figure, see Henry Brown.

24. There may be an element of autobiography in this moment; Scharnhorst argues that Harte's "own mixed ethnicity prompted him to portray characters of mixed white and Indian blood sympathetically" (*Opening* 14).

25. For Harte and Diggers, see Duckett, "Indian."

26. "Miller, who often portrayed his personal past as heroically linked to Native American cultures, is borrowing some of the authorial light cast by John Rollin Ridge" (Lewis 81). For *Life,* see Lewis 87; Keiser 233–48.

27. See Marberry; Frost.

28. Walterhouse also notes "the Indian propaganda seemingly inherent" in *Shadows* (70–71).

29. The name Logan resonates with Native American history and literature. There

is Chief Logan, whose speech Jefferson includes in *Notes on the State of Virginia* as an example of Native Americans' "eminence in oratory" and whose fate, expressed in that speech's final sentences—"Who is there to mourn for Logan? Not one"—resembles that of Miller's hero (Jefferson 123–24). There is also the hero of John Neal's 1822 Native American novel *Logan: A Family History;* see Nelson, *National* 61–101.

30. Miller follows Logan's death with a brief, nonspecific account of Logan's father; it is "now whispered" that he was "the son of an officer made famous in the war annals of the world." This "brief sketch," he concludes, "is about all there is to tell of the young man who lay dead in chains" (172–74). This addendum serves the same purpose as Harte's coda, allowing Miller to satirize white society without changing his Native American hero's apparently inevitable disappearance.

31. See Lee Mitchell for nineteenth-century accounts of the vanishing American wilderness.

32. For the remainder of this section I refer to "the narrator" rather than "Miller"; Miller locates his narrative voice amid the text's voices, and my semantic move is meant to reinforce that positioning. I do not believe that the narrator differs in opinion from Miller, only that he is more closely tied to these characters and histories.

33. See Moylan, "Reading"; Stevens; Aleman 61.

34. For Jackson's political goals, see Phillips 251–52. For responses to the novel's popular success, see Moylan, "Materiality"; Padget; DeLyser.

35. See Nevins 284; Dorris xvii. Senier likewise argues for the importance of "stirring up the common association between Jackson and the Dawes Act," and models a more complex rereading of the novel, if one still focused on its relation to Indian reform (29–72). For Jackson's reform work, see Mathes.

36. See Nevins 269–85; Luis-Brown 821–23; Vickers 45–53.

37. For Jackson's researches, see May; Sandos. For nostalgia, see Starr 54–63; Goldman; Bryan Wagner. For Mexican-American readings, see Gutierrez-Jones 50–69; Jacobs; Rosenthal; Irwin.

38. For Alessandro's and Ramona's not-quite-Indian identities, see Moylan, "Reading" 163–64; Gutierrez-Jones 60–61; Stevens 161; Herndl 266–70; Aleman 63. Byers argues instead that in their lack of specificity "Alessandro and Ramona are made to represent not simply individuals or even tribes of Indians, but all Indians" (344–45). For Ramona as exemplary mixed-blood character, see Henry Brown 134–45.

39. Dorris sees this moment as more negative: in using the new name, Ramona "intentionally cuts herself off from her past" (xiv). That is accurate if her past is the *hacienda,* but I believe the renaming relates more to Alessandro and Ramona's Indian identity than to the Morenos and her Mexican upbringing.

40. For Wardrop, the canyon exemplifies the novel's visions of a "mother-centered world" and connects to Ramona's quest to discover her birth mother's identity (27–38).

41. Gutierrez-Jones calls the dialect "rather unfortunate" (62). Bryan Wagner contends that it is "deployed both as an instrument of political critique and as an exotic commodity" (14); while Phillips claims that by having only white Americans speak in dialect, Jackson "expresses solidarity with oppressed groups by inverting the ordinary

regionalist method of transcribing local vernaculars" and thus "distinguish[ing the minorities] as the societal 'norm'" (39).

42. As Moylan argues, Aunt Ri's "conversion" represents a rejoinder to critics who focus on particular reader responses more than Jackson's own text; that conversion is clearly "intended for the readers as well" ("Reading" 155–57). For a contrasting take on Aunt Ri, see Gonzalez.

43. It is left to Aunt Ri and her family to "advance the novel's critique of U.S. imperialism," while Ramona and Alessandro "are crushed, literally rendered speechless" (Bryan Wagner 13). Gutierrez-Jones is harsher on this silence, arguing that in it "Jackson has again premised disengagement on incapacity rather than volition," part of her portrayal of "an essentially invisible Native American population" (64, 66).

44. For critiques of the ending, see Scheick 45; Nevins 280; Goldman 68; Rosenthal 135–36; Aleman 63; Phillips 259–61. For Luis-Brown it instead symbolizes "the mixed-race American future that Ramona embodies," with "the mantle of Americanness passe[d] from the United States to Mexico" (823, 829).

45. Gutierrez-Jones claims instead that the daughter Ramona exemplifies the conclusion's "assimilationist assumptions," its "denial of an entire historical period representing *mestizaje* (the mixing of racial heritages) itself" (63, 68).

46. See Lee Mitchell on *Ramona* as "a telling critique of American values from what [Jackson] assumed was an indigenous point of view" (262); Herndl on "mestiza discourse" and the possibility of "authentic voice" in nineteenth-century literature (262–64); Padget's "critique [which] frames the novel as a site of interpretation in which the possibilities of Indian reform and the position of Native Americans within U.S. society were debated" (836); and Senier on "polyvocality," *Ramona*'s ability to fit into the "incorporation of America" narrative while at the same time "flirting with the possibility of alternative norms" (51–53).

47. Jackson's review appeared in the February 26, 1881, issue of *The Critic*. See May 67; Phillips 252.

48. This narrative device likewise distinguishes *Ploughed* from Harsha's other, equally political but less interesting fictions, such as *A Timid Brave* (1886).

49. It was one of their lectures that first led Jackson to sympathize with Native Americans. For La Flesche, see Marion Brown; "Bright Eyes." She later married journalist Thomas H. Tibbles, who penned his own reform novel, *Hidden Power* (1881).

50. The plough metaphor also contrasts Euro-and Native American land use, with the Euro-American reliance on the plough more efficient but more damaging than Natives' use of the hoe.

51. Other sites similarly augment the novel's Native American credibility by naming Bright Eyes its editor; the editor was the aforementioned (and white) J. B. Gilder.

52. The conflation of text, composition, and reader is not astonishing; such conflations have a long history in the novel ("Reader, I married him"). It is, however, a striking counter-narrative to the Vanishing American stereotype, particularly given otherwise revisionist novels such as *Ramona*'s concluding deference to that all-powerful image.

53. Winnemucca's Indian name was "Thocmetony," and her 1881 marriage to Lewis

H. Hopkins makes her authorial credit Sarah Winnemucca Hopkins; however, since I focus on her construction (in English) of her identity and history as Native American spokeswoman, and since most critics refer to her as Sarah Winnemucca, I will use that name. Similarly, I follow critical and anthropological consensus in using "Paiutes"; in my textual discussions I use Winnemucca's spelling. See Canfield; Zanjani.

54. "Much criticism of this book [is] preoccupied with separating its different voices and techniques" (Senier 94): "ethnohistory" (Fowler 40); "memoir style of male auto-biography" (Sands 275); "autoethnographic text" (Spack 10–11); "ethnoautobiography" (Tisinger 173).

55. See Brumble 63; Fowler 40; McClure 37; Zanjani 239; Tisinger 175. It is worth noting that, unlike in most written transcriptions of oral narratives, transcriber and narrator are here one and the same.

56. As with slave narratives edited by white activists, there is always "the possibility of outside manipulation" of the author's voice and text (Peyer 386), but I (and virtually all critics) believe that *Life* is "primarily [Winnemucca's] effort and not that of Mary Mann" (Fowler 40).

57. See Olney.

58. See Georgi-Findlay 224, 245; Cheryl Walker, *Indian* 139–63; Ruoff, "Early" 89; McClure 31; Lape 45; Senier 92; Carpenter 72; Tisinger 190. Sands argues that "the text is not a polyphony; only the single voice of Winnemucca actually narrates dramatic events and characters" (278).

59. For the text's title (in relation to Miller's *Life Amongst the Modocs*), see Carpenter 73.

60. Discussions of Winnemucca as mediator often relate to her dialogism; see Schweninger; Anderson 125–26.

61. Lape connects the tribe's criticisms to the "half-breed" stereotype, arguing that Winnemucca "is shaped by her people into the image of the half-breed interpreter, whose words cannot be trusted" (44).

62. Spack argues that "the book had become an example of one of its major themes: the futility of using the written word in English" (97); Senier agrees that "in some sense, to tell the story of Indians speaking to whites in the nineteenth century is necessarily to tell a story of failure, the failure of the audience," but also acknowledges the potentially radical power of Winnemucca's voice and text (104).

CHAPTER 3

1. For the speech, including Brown's assessment that "the men were not moved by her appeal," see Coté 113–15; see also Neu; Greene.

2. For the question of whether to emphasize rhetorical or historical contexts in suffrage scholarship, see Dow; Heilmann.

3. See Clinton; Kugler; Goldberg; Matthews.

4. For race and suffrage, see Gordon, ed.; Penn-Terborg. For temperance and suffrage, see Giele.

5. See Karen Blair; Theodora Martin; Anne Scott 79–184; Gere. For the clubs and the next generation, see Tarbox. For the period's many perspectives, see also Herman; Morilley; Howard and Torrent, eds.; Des Jardins.

6. For the exemplary belittling, see Wood; see also Sundquist, "Realism"; Michael Bell 167–204; Brodhead 107–41. For reconsiderations, see Donovan, *New England;* Donna Campbell; Inness and Royer, eds.; McCullough; Fetterley and Pryse. For other approaches, see Jordan, ed.; Hönnighausen; Renza.

7. See Dobson; Bardes and Gossett; Cutter, *Unruly;* Tracey; Cognard-Black.

8. See the provocative essays in Bauer and McKinsty, eds. Gilbert and Gubar's germinal book likewise simplifies voice; one of its defining questions is "If the Queen's looking glass speaks with the King's voice, how do its perpetual kingly admonitions affect the Queen's own voice?" (46).

9. The later *Times* quotes are from December 10, 1882: August 6 and 22, 1881: 3. For all other reviews, see Phelps 273–78.

10. For positive feminist readings, see Stansell 246–51; Donovan, *New England* 95–97; Kelly; [Kessler] Phelps xiii–xxxii; Shapiro 39; Coultrap-McQuin. For a more negative response, see Mary Bennett 80–84.

11. See Gail Smith; Watson; Dicker.

12. Dobson uses this quote to argue that "the awareness of what 'can't be told' haunts women's literature in nineteenth-century America, . . . is the primary expressive dilemma" (99).

13. Huf sees Susan here as pleading for Avis to pass along her history: "if just one woman will confide her story to another," Huf paraphrases Susan, "then all women would one day know how to avoid the once unavoidable—woman's fate" (56). While Avis's artistic work can be read as a response to Susan's vision of isolation and silence, it is difficult to attribute such hope to Susan herself. For a more ambivalent take on this scene, see Thomson 578.

14. For links of this artistic vision to Phelps's, see Williams 153; Privett 181; Cognard-Black 118. For contrasting arguments about the Sphinx imagery, see Jack Wilson; Barker.

15. Certainly sympathy seems absent from the boating scene, which ends with a series of humiliations for Barbara: she is "hauled in, hand over hand, like a mackerel-net"; an eel "jump[s] into [her] lap"; and Philip notices "how it alter[s] Barbara's appearance to have her curls washed straight." Yet Philip is equally humiliated; more exactly, these humiliations are his perception of "this grotesque, satiric ending to a highly-wrought experience" (191–92). While the scene might thus be read as a failure of Barbara's strategy of silence—she has no voice to counter Philip's perceptions—I believe the narrator's unsympathetic judgments are directed mostly at Philip.

16. Cognard-Black argues that, in response to this scene, "Avis takes up the mother's unspoken sorrow, turning the expected silent suffering of conventional womanhood into a forceful and vocal rejection of men's wrongs" (136–37). Avis's voice is more public and articulate than Waitstill's, but it is critical that Waitstill as yet does not voice a distinct history and viewpoint; turning Waitstill's silence into grist for Avis's mill undermines the text's multivocality.

17. Cognard-Black calls Coy Phelps's "ideal reader, which is why she begins and ends the narrative" (140).

18. For narrator's and free indirect speech, see Bal.

19. See Huf 48; [Kessler] Phelps xxxv–xxxvi; Jack Wilson 72; Susan Harris, "Dilemma" 30.

20. For the narrator as more "conflicted" in her depiction of Avis, see Tracey.

21. "Avis is not the New Woman" but "hopes that her daughter will be that woman" (Huf 48).

22. While Cooke's work is gaining attention, only a few critics specifically discuss "Flint's." See Newlyn 52–54; Donovan, *New England* 73–75, 81; Holly 65–80; Rohrbach 62–65.

23. For Cooke's constructions of women, see Toth; Kleitz; Donovan, "Breaking."

24. Fetterley and Pryse connect Cooke's dialect to narrative voice, arguing that the latter "serves primarily to authenticate and reinforce the dialect voice of her characters" (184–86). Stone perceives instead "a persistent dissonance between narrative commentary and narrative acts" (96–97).

25. Fetterley and Pryse do analyze how Freeman's opening paragraphs often "imply a change in the perspective from which things are seen" (179–84), but their discussion of "Walpole" focuses on their anachronistically feminist reading of the chin. For all we know, married, highly conventional elderly women in late-nineteenth-century rural New England might likewise have had bristling chins. For Freeman's connections of gender to nature, which relate to these descriptions, see Terrell Dixon.

26. Much of the best Freeman scholarship focuses on language and voice, although only Fetterley and Pryse, Johnsen, and Palumbo-DeSimone (37–42) reference "Walpole." See also Maik; Cutter, "Frontiers"; Orr. For point of view, see Bader.

27. Art is "a gift freely shared and gladly received" in "Walpole," producing a "satisfying relationship between artist and audience" (Johnsen 44, 54). For art and gender in Freeman, see Harris, "Dilemma" 27–38.

28. See Brodhead 142–76; Michael Davitt Bell 167–204; Fetterley and Pryse 222–26; Donovan, *New England* 99–118.

29. See Levy 31–63; Jennifer Campbell. Jewett herself contributed to this view, writing in a 1904 letter, "Indeed, I understand that 'The Country Doctor' [*sic*] is of no value as a novel, but it has many excellent ideas" (Fetterley and Pryse 392n3).

Similarly, many critics connect *Doctor* to the era's other "woman doctor novels," particularly Howell's *Dr. Breen's Practice* (1881), Phelps's *Dr. Zay* (1882), and Dr. Prance in James's *The Bostonians* (1886). See Masteller; Bender; Valerie Fulton. While often compelling, these readings are limited by their medical and (given Jewett's close relationship with her doctor father) biographical focuses.

30. For other multifaceted readings, see Shapiro 71–86; Richard Adams; Pryse.

31. Snow describes the construction of Nan's "gift" or "calling" as "both new and not new; its presentation of the themes of the gift and the calling is entirely traditional; its author's choice of central character is new" (138, 147).

32. Although Miss Prince and Mrs. Fraley are clearly in the wrong here, Johns accu-

rately notes that "Jewett's honesty as a writer is that she gives voice to" this alternative vision of women's roles and responsibilities (163); this inclusion of multiple voices, linked in complex ways to setting and gender, elevates the novel above the level of feminist polemic.

33. Never afraid of driving a point home through repetition, the narrator refers elsewhere to "Miss Fraley look[ing] at her young friend as a caged bird at a window might watch a lark's flight" (321).

34. Nan's access to her voice and goals through history here (and in the concluding scene) complicates Shapiro's argument that "at crucial points in the novel Nan is pictured literally following her mother's footsteps, but each time she turns away" (78). Nan does not emulate her mother's resignation and death, but her strength and voice at these moments derive from the past and her mother's legacy.

35. See Sherman 176–78, 188.

36. Richard Adams contends of this closing line that "Nan holds the lamentable, though reassuring, vision at book's end of a gradual falling away of the past" (79). However, Nan's belief in this productive future is connected throughout to the positive, Oldfieldsian past, and this final scene only cements that connection. See also Pryse 217–19, 228–30; Donovan, "Nan" 27; Michael Davitt Bell 185–88.

37. See Donovan, New England 105–6; Sherman 184; Levy 45–47. For Morgan, while such "concessions" do render Jewett's novel "weak," Nan represents a middle category between traditional womanhood and feminism (33–37). Roman describes Nan instead as "Jewett's paradigmatic girl-heroine" (32–35).

38. Edel vol. 2: 87, 203; Dean, "Constance"; Torsney, "Traditions."

39. For James-centered readings of "Grief," see Brehm; Boyd.

40. See Caccavari; Torsney, "Whenever." See also Koppelman.

41. For related readings see Torsney, Constance; Comment; Crumbley; Sofer 162–67.

42. Most critics focus on this side of the narrator's relationship with Miss Grief: see Grasso 110; Dean, Constance 187–89; Crumbley 86.

43. There is, of course, another central theme—the South and its role in postbellum America—with a corresponding body of scholarship; I address that theme in chapter 4.

44. See Walton; Yeazell, ed.; Sara Blair. Kasten posits another cause for such evasion, arguing that "with most feminist discussion of James focused on The Bostonians, [she] want[s] to consider the feminist dimension of other works" (16–17).

45. See Boudreau, "Narrative"; John Rowe, Other 41, 104–5; Daugherty. For scholars who note the ambivalence but define the sympathies, see Ender 99–133; Hugh Stevens 92–103; Person.

46. For related readings, see Page; Tanner, Scenes 148–75; Anthony Scott; Levander, "Bawdy"; Kearns; Joyce Rowe; Gooder.

47. For the accent, see Tanner, Scenes 158–59; Page 379–81.

48. The narrator hastens to add, parenthetically, that he is "but the reporter of [Basil's] angry formulae" (41). Critics have long debated the sincerity of such separations of narrator (and presumably author) from character; I prefer to focus on the construction of each character's voice, history, and identity.

49. For a class distinction, see McCormack 47–52.

50. For Basil and Olive's similarities and differences, see Salmon 25. For writing and orality, see Baren 84–85; Gooder 109.

51. For Verena as weak (both in her will and as a fictional character), see Appignanesi 46–48. For Verena as "medium," see Elizabeth Allen 83–116. Wilt, while acknowledging that "everywhere in the narrative Verena remains an object of interpretation," makes the rare argument that Verena has a "quest of her own" (298, 294); Hochman calls Verena a stand-in for James himself (81–83).

52. For history in the novel, see Hughson; Mizruchi; Greenwald 79–104; Salmon 18–19.

53. Auerbach (119–41) and Lovell argue that the novel undermines any possibility of female community and solidarity. See also Koistinen-Harris 35–62.

54. See Joyce Rowe. Fisher sees Basil's desire to remove Verena from the world of publicity and fame by any means necessary as largely in her best interests (174–79).

55. For rhetoric in the conversations, see Gabler; Ian Bell, "Language." Basil articulates a more extreme critique of the women's movement in his infamous rant about the "feminine, . . . nervous, hysterical, chattering, canting age" (292). While this passage, and the narrator's subsequent reference to Basil's "narrow notions" (292), have provided ample (if malleable) evidence for definitions of the narrator's sympathies, focusing on such statements' content elides the text's emphasis on formal elements such as voice and silence in these conversations.

56. For Basil's "spell" and supernatural imagery, see Howard Pearce; Wolstenholme; McClymer. See also Braude.

57. Early scholars of Olive's latent lesbianism tended to use it as evidence of her role as villainess; see Howe; Buitenhuis 146–47. Recent critics see Olive's sexuality as a more complex (if still, ultimately, tragic) aspect of her characterization; see Hugh Stevens 92–103; Jacob Jacobson 87–100.

58. Some critics argue that Basil's publication, appearing as it does in the potentially ironically named *Rational Review,* should not be read as a triumph. However, given the overarching emphasis on Basil and Olive's battle to control Verena's public voice and develop their own, I believe that the publication indicates Basil's decisive victory (if not necessarily a final one, as Olive's ambiguous public opportunity illustrates).

59. See Haslam 232–37; Fisher 178–79; Tanner, *Scenes* 166–74; Maxwell 18–33; Kahane 296–97; Chandler; Bertonneau; Person 120–23.

60. For Prance, see note 29; Ian Bell, "Curious"; Wegener. For Birdseye, see Heaton; Yellin 153–78; Hendler 147–52.

61. For nineteenth-century women's poetry as historical precisely in its multivocal complication of the public-private division, see Wolosky, "Claims"; Wolosky, "Poetry" 334–36.

62. See Foster, "Gender." For a representative overly brief assessment of Harper's poetry, see Watts 122–23. For extended readings, including the Aunt Chloe series, see Graham; Foster, *Written* 131–53; Melba Boyd 147–66; Bennison.

63. Even in the antebellum era Harper occasionally "redirect[ed]" her poetry away

from slavery, making her "less confined than any of her contemporaries" (Redding 38–39, 43). See Shirley Logan 44–69.

64. Harper makes a similar case for suffrage in her temperance novel *Sowing and Reaping* (1876–77), in which she depicts "women's suffrage as a necessary disciplinary tool to combat intemperance" (Peterson 49). Of course, African Americans faced much more immediate and violent threats at the Gilded Age ballot box than intemperance, providing another level of historical contextualization to complement those discussed here.

65. For dialogue in Harper's oratory, see Shirley Logan. Harper's conflation of race and women's rights here might also reflect the view (shared by Frederick Douglass) that African American voting rights was first a racial issue, and thus that black men should receive the vote before black women; see Thomas-Collier. See also Farah Griffin.

66. Walker does not discuss Piatt in *Nightingale;* she does include a page on Piatt in an essay that updates that book ("Nineteenth-Century"). Watts briefly references Piatt in *Poetry,* but only in the context of her children's poems. Petrino does not mention Piatt in *Emily* or "Nineteenth-Century."

CHAPTER 4

1. See Lanier, *Letters* 25–29, 136–42, 167–69; Gabin 89–120. For Lanier and the South (Old and New), see Rubin, *William* 107–44; MacKethan, *Dream* 18–35.

2. For Pryor's speech, see Blight, *Reunion* 89–93. See also Holzman; Waugh.

3. The South question might be seen as inextricably intertwined with the race question, dialect, and slavery (and thus with chapter 1). While I am not averse to such connections, and reference race in this chapter where appropriate (as I did with Southern themes in chapter 1), I do believe that this chapter's central themes—the Southern voice and past and their relationship to the North's and the nation's—were often treated in this period as a distinct question (partly for the historical and political reasons discussed in this chapter's introduction and to which Tourgée's novels respond) and merit a separate and extended treatment. I consider both questions in chapter 5.

4. See Buck; Appleby; Anne Rowe; Gaines Foster 63–75; Keely; Censer; Blight, *Reunion* 211–54.

5. Wendell is partly a negative version of Mitchell: "the hero of the novel is a study of just what Dr. Weir was *not*" (Burr 114–15); "there are hints that in this character Mitchell exorcised some of his personal devils" (Earnest 95–100). But despite these autobiographical elements, I agree that Wendell's "New England background [in contrast to Mitchell's lifelong Philadelphia identity] is a point that Mitchell emphasizes" (Levering 52–64).

6. Hester represents the height of evolution, an exemplar of "a masterful race" (Mitchell 350), and thus a promising sign for the country's future (as opposed to her older cousin Henry, who is debilitated by his fixation on the past); see Griffith 255–56. Arthur is similarly stronger and more future-oriented than his relatives. For Arthur and Hester as static and failed characters, see Gallman 11–17, 23–28.

7. For the novel and the war, see Kaledin; Long 33, 49–57.

8. Robert Penn Warren's critique of Lanier's choice to "advance his literary career by flattering the North" indicates one way in which Lanier did not speak for all Southerners of his or any era (De Bellis 21). See also Thomas Young on Lanier's "sacrifice," his willingness "to accept the cultural inferiority of his section and the dominant themes of the New South, even if in the process he had to abandon everything the Old South stood for" (110, 103).

9. Blight conflates the two attitudes, arguing that after the Compromise "a reconciliationist vision mixed with racism stood triumphant, ushering the emancipationist vision of the Civil War into an increasingly blurred past" (*Reunion* 138). While I agree on the period's historical blurriness, the reconciliationist vision was over the next decade increasingly subsumed under the pro-Southern (and often racist) conversion narratives. For the election and Reconstruction's end, see Buck; Woodward, *Reunion;* Polakoff; Gillette 300–362; Richardson 122–55.

10. See Woodward, *Origins;* Hubbell 693–836; Gaston; Mixon; Ayers.

11. For the plantation legend and Old South, see Gaines; William Taylor; MacKethan, "Plantation." For the Lost Cause, see Osterweis; Charles Wilson; Connelly and Bellows; Gray 75–121; Gallagher and Nolan, eds.; Blight, *Reunion* 255–99.

12. See Cash 101–85; Degler, *Place;* Kammen 101–31; Ashmere; Lynn Murray.

13. See Buck 220–35; Rayford Logan 165–275; Osterweis 30–65; Moore, "Paul"; Connelly; Connelly and Bellows 39–72; Gerster and Cords, eds. 43–58; Savage 129–61; Lynn Murray; Blum 87–119.

14. For Southern dissent, see Degler, *Other* 189–371; William Link; Dan Frost; Baggett.

15. See Edmund Wilson 299–307; Richard Weaver 174–76; Aaron 246–48; Riley.

16. The "village is intended to be typical" of postbellum Southern life (Beaty 148–49).

17. Plantation tradition texts can be seen as variations on the conversion narrative, enlisting an ex-slave's voice to convert the white auditor to the Southern perspective.

18. Leigh's book is "trying to 'teach' the postwar North . . . a more favorable view of Anglo-Southerners," partly through its formal awareness that all historical accounts are to some degree "contingent on lived experiences" (Nelson, *Principles* xxiv–xxv, xliii–xliv). See also Juncker 120–36.

19. See Tanner, "Henry"; Marcia Jacobson; Kreyling, "Nationalizing." For Adams, James, and history, see John Rowe, *Henry;* McCowen.

20. Melville 386, 400–404, 459–63. Ungar has an "improbable but symbolically rich triple minority status" (Buell 148). Karcher convincingly argues, in her analysis of race and slavery in Melville, that the poem's construction of Ungar locates it firmly in the tradition of "the de-ideologizing of the Civil War in the interests of reconciliation with the South" (281–91); but I agree with Aaron that "in *Clarel* the 'South' became a symbol for [Melville's] own moral landscape" (88–90), as did every element of the poem's world.

21. For Carrington's equivalents, see Stevenson 167–69; Samuels 80. For Carrington as mouthpiece, see Levenson 93–94; Lyon 26–27, 248–49n3.

22. For the counter-reading, see Schmitz; Kentleton. For Carrington's Southern status, see Kreyling, "Nationalizing"; Decker 146–56; Scheiber.

23. See Bardes and Gossett 164–66; Scheiber; Gilley.

24. For Adams's (and James's) "antipathy" for Boston, see McCowen 54.

25. Carrington otherwise "bear[s] in dignified silence his experience as a ruined and marginalized southerner" (Decker 148–49, 301n27), although it is the breaking of that silence that produces the novel's central plot developments and conversions.

26. Lyon focuses on the North-South contrast, calling Ratcliffe Daniel Webster to Carrington's George Washington (27).

27. See Lyon 29–30; Schmitz 159–60; Otten 272–73.

28. By the end of this scene "a dramatic shift of sympathy has taken place" (Otten 278–79). For the Arlington excursion and Carrington's role as a "nationalized Southerner, . . . ready to donate [his pastoral honor] to a Northern (national) character," see Kreyling, "Nationalizing" 388–89. See also Aaron 104–5.

29. "If [Carrington] is an inarticulate suitor in the present, he is able to find words for the past" (Levenson 94–95).

30. Dawidoff reiterates Madeleine's "choice of a principled past" but calls that past "beyond recall" and impossible to bring into the future (60–63). Schmitz argues that America is thoroughly "stripped of its gloried past and denied its splendid future" by the conclusion (167), while Samuels and Lyon contend that Madeleine may return and reunite with Carrington (Samuels 80; Lyon 34–36).

31. See Marcia Jacobson; Menikoff; Kreyling, "Nationalizing"; Quebe; Mizruchi 135–81; Limon 42–49.

32. Kreyling defines Basil as not a "nationalized Southerner," not one who seeks to "donate" his voice, history, and views to the cause of national union and future; he thus "preserves his heroism by resisting conversion into a national type" ("Nationalizing" 388, 401).

33. Aaron too uses this scene as evidence of Basil's status as "chivalrous Southerner" (159). For the novel and Civil War imagery, see Marcia Jacobson 268–74; Menikoff; Greenwald 93–99; Person 116–23.

34. For the narrator's ambivalence, see chapter 3, notes 42 and 43. For point of view and the South question, see Anderson 324–25; Mizruchi 160–69.

35. For the conclusion and the South question, see Marcia Jacobson 274–75; Menikoff 474; Anne Rowe 136; Mizruchi 177–81; Shaheen 185.

36. Removing any doubt about Basil's connections to that damage, James includes in this final section a subtle but disquieting comparison to John Wilkes Booth, noting that Basil feels "as he could imagine a young man to feel who, waiting in a public place, had made up his mind, for reasons of his own, to discharge a pistol at the king or the president" (375). Booth's reasons, of course, were far less his own and far more those of his region, its history, and its monstrous opinions.

37. For a connection of Miss Birdseye's "lost voice" to how "James's post–Civil War white feminists freely use the language of their antislavery feminist predecessors to signify their own oppression" yet "lack interest in the black men and women whose earlier enslavement had structured this discourse," see Yellin 153–78. See also chapter 3, note 58.

38. For women's Civil War writing, see Elizabeth Young.

39. For the James review and this argument, see Hubbell 733–37. See also Kern 46–96; Gross, "Negro" 8; Dean, *Constance* 33–35; Murray 107–11. For a contrasting reading, see Weekes.

40. For a different take on "King," see Wyatt-Brown 198–200.

41. For "In the Cotton Country" as "a failure because its language . . . traps Woolson in the Southern past and [its] romantic technique . . . tries unsuccessfully to recreate an imagined place," see Dean, *Constance* 36–37. For more positive readings, see Moore, *Constance* 56–57; Weekes 112; Wyatt-Brown 195–98.

42. Some critics do link "Rodman" to such overly simplistic images: Anne Rowe calls it just another Northern "vivid picture of the desolation of a once noble land," one that makes the pro-Southern case that "what is going on here is regrettable" (62–63); Weekes dismisses it as an example of "early-Reconstruction bias" against the South (106–7).

43. The story actually ends with a brief, ironic epilogue in which Rodman encounters the De Rosset home's new owner, an "energetic Maine [man]" who is "pulling down the old house" (41). But the conversation with Bettina more meaningfully concludes the themes of regional history, identity, and voice.

44. See Warfel; Enser; Fetterley and Pryse 186–88.

45. See Ridgely 91–93.

46. Parks describes *Battle* as slightly better than Murfree's later, more "typical historical novel[s]" (219); for a more negative take, as well as the only other extended reading I have found, see Cary 115–23.

47. Parks describes Vayne as "a type of the old Southern gentleman," "both fool and nobleman" (114), but it seems to me that his links to both roles, as well as his consciousness of the duality, distinguishes him from the type. Similarly, Gardner's point that "the inadequacy of the past—specifically, the Confederate past—to nurture the residents of Chattalla is most acutely felt by General Vayne" (105), while accurate, does not fully characterize Vayne's complex understanding of that past's role in his family's lives. See also Richard Weaver 307–8.

48. On the lack of form, see Cowie 521; Weissbuch 28n1; Limon 70. On Tourgée as romanticist, see Becker 70; Olsen 238–39; Aaron 149. For an exemplary combinatory argument, see Simms, "Albion" 168–69.

49. See Gross, *Albion* 58–86; Olsen 223–41; Magdol; Aaron 197–98.

50. See Robert Sommer; Short. For Tourgée as in some ways pro-South, see Buck 234–35; Edmund Wilson 529–48; Anne Rowe 32–53; Hardwig. See also Carter.

51. For the didacticism, see Cowie 524–26; Gross, *Albion* 61, 68–69; Short 243, 263–64.

52. For Tourgée on realism, see Simms, "Literary Realism."

53. For Tourgée and romances of reunion, see Gross, *Albion* 101–2; Anne Rowe 48–53.

Chapter 5

1. Wilson 548–87; Butcher 46–56; Turner 89–104; Rubin, *George* 77–96; Ladd 37–84; Jones 100–133; Foote 98–123.

2. See Cowie 556–67; Chase 167–76; Eaton; Bendixen.

3. Some scholars see Cable as less politically progressive than such publications might indicate, but still focus on his postbellum politics, rather than his historical novel. See Friedman 99–117; Takaki 205–11; Frederickson 222–27. For a related reading of the novel's politics, see Handley 61–73.

4. For formal analyses, see Clemon; Ringe; Tipping.

5. "Cable was intensely interested in language, and his re-creation of Creole speech was the product of close observation and considerable literary labor" (Rubin, "Division" 29). Cable's dialect can also be laborious for the reader, and for the second (1883) edition he eliminated some of the more unnecessary and extreme moments; see Rubin, *George* 282n6; Evans, "French."

6. Multi- and bilingualism have become important terms in recent literary scholarship, often with exactly such revisionist aims. See Sollors, ed.; Doris Sommer, ed.

7. For a contrasting argument, see Foote 106–10.

8. See Ringe; Tipping.

9. "Bibi" was rejected by *Scribner's Monthly* and the *Atlantic Monthly;* see Kreyling, Introduction. See also Michael Campbell; Joseph Egan; Stephens; Alexander.

10. See Evans, "Naming."

11. See Rubin, *George* 89–92; Swann; Elfenbein 25–73.

12. For Cable's attitudes toward the South, see Aaron 272–73, 278–82.

13. For Honoré's goal as ahistorical, and Cable's past as a "nightmare of the present" from which his characters need to "cut loose" in order to "make the ideal future," see Jay Martin 100–105.

14. For miscegenation as another symbol for "relationships between the past and the present," see William Clark.

15. See Rubin, *George* 93–95; Goodspeed; Piep 177–78.

16. One could read this doomed love as symbolizing the complex relationships between freed blacks and slaves, mulattos and full-bloods, and Creoles and African Americans, but there is not much evidence to support such an analysis. For the surviving black characters' exile, see Handley 73; Foote 123.

17. Ladd notes that most of the novel's black characters share "silence (a refusal to speak or difficulty in speaking)" (75), rendering Clemence's effective voice even more significant.

18. For Clemence and her "minstrel-style" final speech, see Michael Campbell 170–73.

19. This printer's copy is held, in two volumes, at Harvard University's Houghton Library. For the readers' identities (they use initials), see Turner.

20. See also Ekstrom 60–64.

21. For an overview of early reader-response criticism, including an annotated bibliography, see Tompkins, ed. For historicist reader-response work, see Machor, ed. For a

link of reader-response and formalist criticisms, and an updated bibliography, see Davis and Womack.

22. The comment is on the left side of manuscript page 262; the published version appears on the novel's page 145. Future citations will be parenthetical in this manner: (m262; 145).

23. See also Rubin, *George* 97–100.

CONCLUSION

1. See Judith Adams, "Promotion."

2. See Schlereth 285–88; O'Leary 150–71.

3. See Neil Harris, "Dream"; Downey xvii–xviii.

4. See Noble, *End* 16–40; Ellis and Munslow; Lawlor 41–57; Conn 220–26.

5. Cawelti 345; Kasson 23–28; Levine 206–10. See also Ginger 15–34; Schlereth 277–88. My argument parallels Rosenberg's: "this Dream City flaunted America's faiths and glossed over its contradictions" (3–7).

6. For "the vision of unity" between the Exposition's spaces, see Badger 125–28; Orvell 34–35; Findling 1–35. For the "civilization" question, see Bederman 31–41.

7. See Bolotin and Laing 8, 156–58.

8. See Bederman.

9. See Muccigrasso 132–53.

10. For Lynch's selection, see the May 27, 1893, letter to Lynch from James Dickinson, Secretary of the Columbian Commission; it is attached to the Library of Congress's copy of "Columbia."

11. For the Congress, see Jamieson; Weimann 523–49. For other largely positive readings of women's Exposition presence, see Snyder-Ott; Greenhalgh 178–82; Muccigrasso 132–41; Gullett.

12. For primitive and foreign women at the Exposition, see Grabenhorst-Randall; Trump 215–58. Bederman argues that the Building's separate existence defined women as outside of civilization (33–35).

13. See Stetson; Weimann 103–24; Rydell, " 'Contend' " xvi–xvii. A few African American women such as Frances Harper did speak during the Women's Congress.

14. For feminism's links to turn-of-the-century corporate culture, see Livingston, *Feminism;* for women writers and Gilded Age cultural nationalism, see Sofer.

15. For a different take on the Exposition's African presence, see Christopher Reed 143–91.

16. See Manring 72–78.

17. See Rydell, "Racist" 263–67; Bederman 37–38. For a more positive take on the exhibits, see Conn 108–14; for the shows as alternatives to the progressive narrative, see L. G. Moses 129–40.

18. For Douglass's text, see Christopher Reed 193–94. See also Rudwick and Meier 354–61; Muccigrasso 146–47; Paddon and Turner, "Douglass's"; Christopher Reed 134–35.

19. See Massa 337; Rydell " 'Contend' " xi–xlviii; Christopher Reed xi–xiv; James

Davis. For such counter-narratives as constituting African American participation in the Exposition, see Bederman 38–40; Paddon and Turner, "African."

20. See Marilyn Elkins; John Earnest; Bizzell; Jackson.

21. That poetic image's significance to Harper's overall literary vision is highlighted by Frances Foster in the title of her anthology, *A Brighter Coming Day*.

Works Cited

Aaron, Daniel. *The Unwritten War: American Writers and the Civil War*. Madison: U of Wisconsin P, 1987.

Abrams, M. H. "The Romantic Period: Introduction." *The Norton Anthology of English Literature*, 4th ed., vol. 2. New York: Norton, 1979. 1–20.

Adams, Henry. *Democracy: An American Novel*. 1880. *Novels, Mont Saint Michel, The Education*. New York: Library of America, 1983. 1–184.

Adams, Judith A. "The American Dream Actualized: The Glistening 'White City' and the Lurking Shadows of the World's Columbian Exposition." *The World's Columbian Exposition: A Centennial Bibliographic Guide*. Ed. David J. Bertuca. Westport, CT: Greenwood, 1996.

———. "The Promotion of New Technology through Fun and Spectacle: Electricity at the World's Columbian Exposition." *Journal of American Culture* 18 (1995): 45–56.

Adams, Richard. "Heir Apparent: Inheriting the Epitome in Sarah Orne Jewett's *A Country Doctor*." *Constance Fenimore Woolson's Nineteenth Century: Essays*. Ed. Victoria Brehm. Detroit: Wayne State UP, 2001. 67–81.

"Advertising *Uncle Tom*." *Uncle Tom's Cabin and American Culture*. Ed. Stephen Railton, U of Virginia, June 25, 2005 <http://www.iath.virginia.edu/utc/onstage/ads/tsads hp2.html>.

Aleman, Jesse. "Historical Amnesia and the Vanishing Mestiza: The Problem of Race in *The Squatter and the Don* and *Ramona*." *Aztlan* 27.1 (2002): 59–93.

Alexander, Robert Allen Jr. "The Irreducible African: Challenges to Racial Stereotypes in George W. Cable's *The Grandissimes*." *Songs of the Reconstructing South: Building Literary Louisiana, 1865–1945*. Ed. Suzanne Disheroon-Green and Lisa Abnoy. Westport, CT: Greenwood, 2002. 123–33.

Allen, Elizabeth. *A Woman's Place in the Novels of Henry James*. New York: Martin's, 1984.

Allen, Leslie. *Liberty: The Statue and the American Dream*. New York: Ellis Island Foundation, 1985.

Anderson, Benedict. *Imagined Communities: Reflections on the Origin and Spread of Nationalism*. London: Verso, 1983.

Anderson, Charles R. "James's Portrait of the Southerner." *American Literature* 27.3 (1955): 309–31.

Anderson, Eric Gary. *American Indian Literature and the Southwest: Contexts and Dispositions*. Austin: U of Texas P, 1999.

Andrews, William. *The Literary Career of Charles W. Chesnutt*. Baton Rouge: Louisiana State UP, 1980.

——. "The Novelization of Voice in Early African American Narrative." *PMLA* 105.1 (1990): 23–34.

Appignanesi, Lisa. *Femininity and the Creative Imagination: A Study of Henry James, Robert Musil, and Marcel Proust*. London: Vision, 1973.

Appleby, Joyce. "Reconciliation and the Northern Novelist." *Civil War History* 10.2 (1964): 117–29.

Arac, Jonathan. Huckleberry Finn *as Idol and Target: The Functions of Criticism in Our Time*. Madison: U of Wisconsin P, 1997.

Ashmere, Susan Youngblood. "Continuity and Change: George Brown Tindall and the Post-Reconstruction South." *Reading Southern History: Essays on Interpreters and Interpretations*. Ed. Glenn Feldman. Tuscaloosa: U of Alabama P, 2001. 212–32.

Auchincloss, Louis. *Pioneers and Caretakers: A Study of Nine American Women Novelists*. Minneapolis: U of Minnesota P, 1965.

Auerbach, Nina. *Communities of Women: An Idea in Fiction*. Cambridge: Harvard UP, 1978.

Avrich, Paul. *The Haymarket Tragedy*. Princeton: Princeton UP, 1984.

Ayers, Edward L. *The Promise of the New South: Life after Reconstruction*. New York: Oxford UP, 1992.

Babb, Valerie. "Subversion and Repatriation in *The Conjure Woman*." *Southern Quarterly* 25.2 (1987): 66–75.

Bader, Julia. "The Dissolving Vision: Realism in Jewett, Freeman, and Gilman." *American Realism: New Essays*. Ed. Eric Sundquist. Baltimore: Johns Hopkins UP, 1982. 176–98.

Badger, Reid. *The Great American Fair: The World's Columbian Exposition and American Culture*. Chicago: Nelson Hall, 1979.

Baggett, James Alex. *The Scalawags: Southern Dissenters in the Civil War and Reconstruction*. Baton Rouge: Louisiana State UP, 2003.

Baker, Barbara. *The Blues Aesthetic and the Making of American Identity in the Literature of the New South*. New York: Lang, 2003.

Bakhtin, Mikhail. *The Dialogic Imagination: Four Essays*. Ed. Michael Holquist. Austin: U of Texas P, 1981.

Bal, Mieke. *Narratology: Introduction to the Theory of Narrative.* 2nd ed. Toronto: U of Toronto P, 1997.

Banning, Evelyn I. *Helen Hunt Jackson.* New York: Vanguard, 1973.

Bardes, Barbara, and Suzanne Gossett. *Declarations of Independence: Women and Political Power in Nineteenth-Century American Fiction.* New Brunswick: Rutgers UP, 1990.

Baren, Lynda S. *Eurydice Reclaimed: Language, Gender, and Voice in Henry James.* Ann Arbor: Michigan Research P, 1989.

Barker, Deborah. *Aesthetics and Gender in American Literature: Portraits of the Woman Artist.* Lewisburg, PA: Bucknell UP/Cranbury, NJ: Associated Univ. Presses, 2000.

Barnett, Louise K. *The Ignoble Savage: American Literary Racism, 1790–1890.* Westport, CT: Greenwood, 1975.

Barrish, Philip. *American Literary Realism, Critical Theory, and Intellectual Prestige, 1880–1995.* Cambridge: Cambridge UP, 2001.

Bauer, Dale M., and Susan Jaret McKinsty, eds. *Feminism, Bakhtin, and the Dialogic.* Albany: SUNY P, 1991.

Beaty, John O. *John Esten Cooke, Virginian.* Port Washington, NY: Kennikat, 1965.

Becker, George J. "Albion W. Tourgée: Pioneer in Social Criticism." *American Literature* 19.1 (1947): 59–72.

Bederman, Gail. *Manliness and Civilization: A Cultural History of Gender and Race in the United States, 1880–1917.* Chicago: U of Chicago P, 1995.

Bell, Ian F. A. "The Curious Case of Dr. Prance." *Henry James Review* 10.1 (1989): 32–41.

———. "Language, Setting, and Self in *The Bostonians.*" *Modern Language Quarterly* 49.3 (1988): 211–38.

Bell, James B., and Richard I. Abrams. *In Search of Liberty: The Story of the Statue of Liberty and Ellis Island.* New York: Doubleday, 1984.

Bell, Michael Davitt. *The Problem of American Realism: Studies in the Cultural History of a Literary Idea.* Chicago: U of Chicago P, 1993.

Bellin, Joshua. *The Demon of the Continent: Indians and the Shaping of American Literature.* Philadelphia: U of Pennsylvania P, 2001.

Bender, Bert. "Darwin and 'The Natural History of Doctresses': The Sex War between Howells, Phelps, Jewett, and James." *Prospects* 18 (1993): 81–120.

Bendixen, Alfred. "Cable's *The Grandissimes:* A Literary Pioneer Confronts the Southern Tradition." *The Grandissimes: Centennial Essays.* Ed. Thomas J. Richardson. Jackson: UP of Mississippi, 1981. 23–33.

Benn, Mary Lou. "Mary Hallock Foote in Idaho." *University of Wyoming Publications* 20.1 (1956): 157–78.

Bennett, Mary Angela. *Elizabeth Stuart Phelps.* Philadelphia: U of Pennsylvania P, 1939.

Bennett, Paula Bernat. "'The Descent of the Angel': Interrogating Domestic Ideology in American Women's Poetry, 1858–1890." *American Literary History* 7.4 (1995): 591–610.

———. *Poets in the Public Sphere: The Emancipatory Project of American Women's Poetry, 1800–1900.* Princeton: Princeton UP, 2003.

Bennison, Sarah Elizabeth. "The Poetry and Activism of Frances Ellen Watkins Harper." *Journal x* 6.2 (2002): 203–23.

Bercovitch, Sacvan. *The American Jeremiad.* Madison: U of Wisconsin P, 1978.

———. *The Rites of Assent: Transformations in the Symbolic Construction of America.* New York: Routledge, 1993.

Berge, William Henry. "The Impulse for Expansion: John W. Burgess, Alfred Thayar Mahan, Theodore Roosevelt, Josiah Strong, and the Development of a Rationale." Diss Vanderbilt U, 1969.

Bergland, Renée L. *The National Uncanny: Indian Ghosts and American Subjects.* Hanover: UP of New England, 2000.

Berkhofer, Robert. *The White Man's Indian: Images of the American Indian from Columbus to the Present.* New York: Knopf, 1978.

Berner, Robert L. *Defining American Indian Literature: One Nation Divisible.* Lewiston, NY: Mellen, 1999.

Berret, Anthony. "*Huckleberry Finn* and the Minstrel Show." *American Studies* 27.3 (1986): 37–49.

Berthoff, Werner. *American Trajectories: Authors and Readings, 1790–1970.* University Park: Penn State UP, 1994.

Bertonneau, Thomas F. "Like Hypatia before the Mob: Desire, Resentment, and Sacrifice in *The Bostonians* (An Anthropoetics)." *Nineteenth-Century Literature* 53.1 (1998): 56–90.

Billington, Ray. *America's Frontier Heritage.* New York: Holt, 1966.

Birnbaum, Michele. "Dark Dialects: Scientific and Literary Realism in Joel Chandler Harris' *Uncle Remus* Series." *New Orleans Review* 18.1 (1991): 36–45.

Bishop, Gordon. *Gateway to America: The Statue of Liberty, Ellis Island, and Seven Other Historic Places.* Medford, NJ: Plexus, 2003.

Bizzell, Patricia. "'Stolen' Literacies in *Iola Leroy*." *Popular Literacy: Studies in Cultural Practices and Poetics.* Ed. John Trimbur. Pittsburgh: U of Pittsburgh P, 2001. 143–50.

Blair, Karen J. *The Clubwoman as Feminist: True Womanhood Redefined, 1868–1914.* New York: Holmes, 1980.

Blair, Sara. *Henry James and the Writing of Race and Nation.* Cambridge: Cambridge UP, 1996.

Blakemore, Steven. "Huckleberry Finn's Written World." *American Literary Realism* 20.2 (1988): 21–29.

Blend, Benoy. "A Victorian Gentlewoman in the Rocky Mountain West: Ambiguity in the Work of Mary Hallock Foote." *Reading under the Sign of Nature: New Essays in Ecocriticism.* Ed. John Tallmadge and Henry Harrington. Salt Lake City: U of Utah P, 2000. 85–100.

Blight, David W. *Frederick Douglass' Civil War: Keeping Faith in Jubilee.* Baton Rouge: Louisiana State UP, 1989.

———. *Race and Reunion: The Civil War and American Memory.* Cambridge: Harvard UP, 2001.

Blum, Edward J. *Reforging the White Republic: Race, Religion, and American Nationalism, 1865–1898*. Baton Rouge: Louisiana State UP, 2005.

Boeckmann, Cathy. *A Question of Character: Scientific Racism and the Genres of American Fiction, 1892–1912*. Tuscaloosa: U of Alabama P, 2000.

Boisseau, T. J. "White Queens and the Chicago World's Fair, 1893: New Womanhood in the Service of Class, Race, and Nation." *Gender and History* 12.1 (2000): 33–81.

Bold, Christine. *Selling the Wild West: Popular Western Fiction, 1860 to 1960*. Bloomington: U of Indiana P, 1987.

Bolend, Sally. "The Seven Dialects in *Huckleberry Finn*." *North Dakota Quarterly* 36.3 (1968): 30–40.

Bollinger, Laurel. "'Say It, Jim': The Morality of Connection in *Adventures of Huckleberry Finn*." *College Literature* 29.1 (2002): 32–52.

Bolotin, Norman, and Christine Laing. *The World's Columbian Exposition: The Chicago World's Fair of 1893*. Urbana: U of Illinois P, 1992.

Bontemps, Arna. "The Slave Narrative: An American Genre." *Great Slave Narratives*. Ed. Bontemps. Boston: Beacon, 1969.

Bost, Suzanne. *Mulattas and Mestizas: Representing Mixed Identities in the Americas, 1850–2000*. Athens: U of Georgia P, 2003.

Boudreau, Kristin. "Narrative Sympathy in *The Bostonians*." *Henry James Review* 14.1 (1993): 17–33.

———. *Sympathy in American Literature: American Sentiments from Jefferson to the Jameses*. Gainesville: U of Florida P, 2002.

Boyd, Anne E. "Anticipating James, Anticipating Grief: Constance Fenimore Woolson's 'Miss Grief.'" *Constance Fenimore Woolson's Nineteenth Century: Essays*. Ed. Victoria Brehm. Detroit: Wayne State UP, 2001. 191–206.

Boyd, Melba Joyce. *Discarded Legacy: Politics and Poetics in the Life of Frances E. W. Harper, 1825–1911*. Detroit: Wayne State UP, 1994.

Braude, Ann. *Radical Spirits: Spiritualism and Women's Rights in Nineteenth-Century America*. Bloomington: Indiana UP, 2001.

Brehm, Victoria. Introduction. *Constance Fenimore Woolson's Nineteenth Century: Essays*. Ed. Brehm. Detroit: Wayne State UP, 2001. 7–17.

Bridger, Bobby. *Buffalo Bill and Sitting Bull: Inventing the Wild West*. Austin: U of Texas P, 2002.

Bridgman, Richard. *The Colloquial Style in America*. New York: Oxford UP, 1966.

"Bright Eyes." *Native American Women's Writing 1800–1924: An Anthology*. Ed. Karen Kilcup. Oxford: Blackwell, 2000.

Brodhead, Richard. *Cultures of Letters: Scenes of Reading and Writing in Nineteenth-Century America*. Chicago: U of Chicago P, 1993.

Brown, Dee. *The Year of the Century: 1876*. New York: Scribner's, 1966.

Brown, Henry J. *Injun Joe's Ghost: The Indian Mixed-Blood in American Writing*. Columbia: U of Missouri P, 2004.

Brown, Marion Marsh. *Susette La Flesche: Advocate for Native American Rights*. Chicago: Children's, 1992.

Brown, Olympia. "Speech of Rev. Olympia Brown to the Congressional Committee on Privileges and Elections, January 1877 [sic]." 1876. *Women and Social Movements in the United States, 1600–2000.* November 27, 2004, <www.alexanderstreet6.com/wasm/wasmrestricted/doctext/S10010 056-D0003.010.htm>.

Brumble, H. David III. *American Indian Autobiography.* Berkeley: U of California P, 1988.

Buck, Paul. *The Road to Reunion, 1865–1900.* Boston: Little, 1947.

Buell, Lawrence. "Melville the Poet." *The Cambridge Companion to Herman Melville.* Ed. Robert S. Levine. Cambridge: Cambridge UP, 1998. 135–56.

Buitenhuis, Peter. *The Grasping Imagination: The American Writings of Henry James.* Toronto: U of Toronto P, 1970.

Burnette, R. V. "Charles W. Chesnutt's *The Conjure Woman* Revisited." *CLA Journal* 30.4 (1987): 438–53.

Burns, Graham. "Time and Pastoral: the *Adventures of Huckleberry Finn.*" *Melbourne Critical Review* 15 (1972): 52–63.

Burr, Anna Robeson. *Weir Mitchell: His Life and Letters.* New York: Doubleday, 1929.

Burt, Elizabeth V., ed. *The Progressive Era: Primary Documents on Events from 1890 to 1914.* Westport, CT: Greenwood, 2004.

Bush, Harold. *American Declarations: Rebellion and Repentance in American Cultural History.* Urbana: U of Illinois P, 1998.

Butcher, Philip. *George W. Cable.* New York: Twayne, 1962.

Butterfield, Stephen. "The Use of Language in the Slave Narratives." *Negro American Literature Forum* 6.3 (1972): 72–78.

Byers, John. "The Indian Matter of Helen Hunt Jackson's *Ramona:* From Fact to Fiction." *American Indian Quarterly* 2.4 (1975–76): 331–46.

Cable, George Washington. *The Grandissimes: A Story of Creole Life.* 1880. New York: Penguin, 1988.

———. *The Grandissimes: A Story of Creole Life.* Scribner's manuscript. Houghton Lib., Harvard.

———. "Madame Delphine." 1881. *Old Creole Days.* New York: Scribner's, 1884. 1–81.

Caccavari, Peter. "Exile, Depatriation, and Constance Fenimore Woolson's Traveling Regionalism." *Women, America, and Movement: Narratives of Relocation.* Ed. Susan L. Robertson. Columbia: U of Missouri P, 1998. 19–37.

Calhoun, Charles W., ed. *The Gilded Age: Essays on the Origins of Modern America.* Wilmington: Scholarly Resources, 1996.

Campbell, Donna. *Resisting Regionalism: Gender and Naturalism in American Fiction, 1885–1915.* Athens: U of Ohio P, 1997.

Campbell, Jennifer. "'The Great Something Else': Women's Search for Meaningful Work in Sarah Orne Jewett's *A Country Doctor* and Francis E. Watson Harper's *Trial and Triumph.*" *Colby Library Quarterly* 34.2 (1998): 83–98.

Campbell, Michael L. "The Negro in Cable's *The Grandissimes.*" *Mississippi Quarterly* 27.2 (1974): 165–78.

Canfield, Gae Whitney. *Sarah Winnemucca of the Northern Paiutes.* Norman: U of Oklahoma P, 1983.

Carby, Hazel. *Reconstructing Womanhood: The Emergence of the Afro-American Woman Novelist.* New York: Oxford UP, 1987.

Carkeet, David. "The Dialects in *Huckleberry Finn.*" *American Literature.* 51.3 (1979): 315–32.

Carpenter, Cari. "Tiresias Speaks: Sarah Winnemucca's Hybrid Selves and Genres." *Legacy* 19.1 (2002): 71–80.

Carter, Everett. "Edmund Wilson Refights the Civil War: The Revision of Albion Tourgée's Novels." *American Literary Realism* 29.2 (1997): 68–75.

Cartwright, Keith. *Reading Africa into American Literature: Epics, Fables, and Gothic Tales.* Lexington: UP of Kentucky, 2002.

Cary, Richard. *Mary Noailles Murfree.* New York: Twayne, 1967.

Cash, W. J. *The Mind of the South.* 1941. New York: Vintage, 1991.

Cawelti, John G. "America on Display: The World's Fairs of 1876, 1893, 1933." *The Age of Industrialism in America: Essays in Social Structure and Cultural Values.* Ed. Frederic Cople Jaher. New York: Free Press, 1968. 317–63.

Cecil, L. Moffitt. "The Historical Ending of *Adventures of Huckleberry Finn.*" *American Literary Realism* 13.2 (1980): 280–83.

Censer, Jane Turner. "Reimagining the North-South Reunion: Southern Women Novelists and the Intersectional Romance, 1876–1900." *Southern Cultures* 5.2 (1999): 64–91.

Chambers, John Whiteclay. *The Tyranny of Change: America in the Progressive Era, 1890–1920.* New Brunswick: Rutgers UP, 2000.

Chandler, Katherine R. "Purchase of Power: The Conclusion of *The Bostonians.*" *English Language Notes* 32.3 (1995): 46–54.

Chase, Richard. *The American Novel and Its Tradition.* New York: Doubleday, 1957.

Cheney, O. A. "The Female Debating Society." *The Woman's Journal* 6 May 1876: 146.

Chesnutt, Charles W. "The Goophered Grapevine." 1887. *The Norton Anthology of American Literature, 1865–1914.* Ed. Nina Baym. New York: Norton, 2003. 782–89.

———. *The Journals of Charles W. Chesnutt.* Ed. Richard H. Brodhead. Durham: Duke UP, 1993.

———. *The Short Fiction of Charles W. Chesnutt.* Ed. Sylvia Lyons Render. Washington, DC: Howard UP, 1981.

Christmann, James. "Raising Voices, Lifting Shadows: Competing Voice-Paradigms in Frances E. W. Harper's *Iola Leroy.*" *African American Review* 34.1 (2000): 5–18.

Clark, Kathleen. "Celebrating Freedom: Emancipation Day Celebrations and African American Memory in the Early Reconstruction South." *Where These Memories Grow: History, Memory, and Southern Identity.* Ed. W. Fitzhugh Brundage. Chapel Hill: U of North Carolina P, 2000. 107–32.

Clark, William Bedford. "Cable and the Theme of Miscegenation in *Old Creole Days* and *The Grandissimes.*" *Mississippi Quarterly* 30.4 (1977): 597–610.

Clemon, John. "The Art of Local Color in George W. Cable's *The Grandissimes.*" *American Literature* 47.3 (1975): 396–410.

Clinton, Catherine. *The Other Civil War: American Women in the Nineteenth Century.* New York: Hill & Wong, 1984.

Cognard-Black, Jennifer. *Narrative in the Professional Age: Transatlantic Readings of Harriet Beecher Stowe, George Eliot, and Elizabeth Stuart Phelps.* New York: Routledge, 2004.

Commager, Henry Steele. *The American Mind: An Interpretation of American Thought and Character since the 1880s.* New Haven: Yale UP, 1950.

Comment, Kristin M. "The Lesbian 'Impossibilities' of Miss Grief's 'Armor.'" *Constance Fenimore Woolson's Nineteenth Century: Essays.* Ed. Victoria Brehm. Detroit: Wayne State UP, 2001. 207–23.

Conn, Steven. *History's Shadow: Native Americans and Historical Consciousness in the Nineteenth Century.* Chicago: U of Chicago P, 2004.

Connelly, Thomas L. *The Marble Man: Robert E. Lee and His Image in American Society.* New York: Knopf, 1977.

——, and Barbara L. Bellows. *God and General Longstreet: The Lost Cause and the Southern Mind.* Baton Rouge: Louisiana State UP, 1982.

Cooke, John Esten. *The Virginia Bohemians.* New York: Harper, 1880.

Cooke, Rose Terry. "Mrs. Flint's Married Experience." 1880. *"How Celia Changed Her Mind" and Selected Stories.* Ed. Elizabeth Ammons. New Brunswick: Rutgers UP, 1986. 93–130.

Cook-Lynn, Elizabeth. *Why I Can't Read Wallace Stegner and Other Essays: A Tribal Voice.* Madison: U of Wisconsin P, 1996.

Cordato, Mary Frances. "Toward a New Century: Women and the Philadelphia Centennial Exposition, 1876." *Pennsylvania Magazine of History and Biography* 107.1 (1983): 113–36.

Coté, Charlotte. *Olympia Brown: The Battle for Equality.* Racine, WI: Mother Courage, 1988.

Coulombe, Joseph. "Mark Twain's Native Americans and the Repeated Racial Pattern in *Adventures of Huckleberry Finn.*" *American Literary Realism* 33.3 (2001): 261–79.

Coultrap-McQuin, Susan. *Doing Literary Business: American Women Writers in the Nineteenth Century.* Chapel Hill: U of North Carolina P, 1990.

Cowan, Tynes. "Charles Waddell Chesnutt and Joel Chandler Harris: An Anxiety of Influence." *Resources for American Literary Study* 25.2 (1999): 232–53.

Cowart, David. *History and the Contemporary Novel.* Carbondale: Southern Illinois UP, 1989.

Cowie, Alexander. *The Rise of the American Novel.* New York: American, 1948.

Cox, James. "Remarks on the Sad Initiation of Huckleberry Finn." *Sewanee Review* 62 (1959): 389–405.

Craddock, Charles Egbert [Mary Noailles Murfree]. *Where the Battle Was Fought.* Boston: Osgood, 1885.

Crumbley, Paul. "Haunting the House of Print: The Circulation of Disembodied Texts in 'Collected by a Valetudinarian' and 'Miss Grief.'" *American Culture, Canons, and the Case of Elizabeth Stoddard.* Ed. Robert McClure Smith and Ellen Weinauer. Tuscaloosa: U of Alabama P, 2003. 83–104.

Current, Richard N. "From Civil War to World Power: Perceptions and Realities, 1865–

1914." *Legacy of Disunion: The Enduring Significance of the American Civil War.* Ed. Susan-Mary Grant and Peter J. Parish. Baton Rouge: Louisiana State UP, 2003. 207–21.

Curti, Merle. *Probing Our Past.* New York: Harper, 1955.

Cutter, Martha J. "Frontiers of Language: Engendering Discourse in 'The Revolt of Mother.'" *American Literature* 63.2 (1991): 279–91.

———. *Unruly Tongue: Identity and Voice in American Women's Writing, 1850–1930.* Jackson: UP of Mississippi, 1999.

Dabakis, Melissa. "Martyrs and Monuments of Chicago: The Haymarket Affair." *Prospects* 19 (1994): 99–133.

Daehnke, Joel. *In the Work of Their Hands Is Their Prayer: Cultural Narrative and Redemption on the American Frontiers, 1830–1930.* Athens: Ohio UP, 2003.

Dando-Collins, Stephen. *Standing Bear Is a Person: The True Story of a Native American's Quest for Justice.* Cambridge: Da Capo, 2004.

Daugherty, Sarah B. "James and the Representation of Women: Some Lessons of the Master(')s." *Questioning the Master: Gender and Sexuality in Henry James's Writings.* Ed. Peggy McCormack. Newark: U of Delaware P, 2000. 176–95.

Davies, Wallace Evan. *Patriotism on Parade: The Story of Veterans' and Hereditary Organizations in America, 1783–1900.* Cambridge: Harvard UP, 1955.

Davis, Allen F., ed. *Conflict and Consensus in American History.* Lexington, MA: Heath, 1968–1998.

Davis, James C. "'Stage Business' as Citizenship: Ida B. Wells at the World's Columbian Exposition." *Women's Experience of Modernity, 1875–1945.* Ed. Ann L. Ardis and Leslie W. Lewis. Baltimore: Johns Hopkins UP, 2003. 189–204.

Davis, Todd F., and Kenneth Womack. *Formalist Criticism and Reader-Response Theory.* London: Palgrave, 2002.

Dawes, James. "Counting on the Battlefield: Literature and Philosophy after the Civil War." *The Language of War: Literature and Culture in the U.S. from the Civil War through World War II.* Cambridge: Harvard UP, 2002. 24–68.

Dawidoff, Robert. *The Genteel Tradition and the Sacred Rage: High Culture versus Democracy in Adams, James, and Santayana.* Chapel Hill: U of North Carolina P, 1992.

Dean, Sharon. "Constance Fenimore Woolson and Henry James: The Literary Relationship." *Massachusetts Studies in English* 7.3 (1980): 1–9.

———. *Constance Fenimore Woolson: Homeward Bound.* Knoxville: U of Tennessee P, 1995.

De Bellis, Jack. *Sidney Lanier: Poet of the Marshes.* Atlanta: Georgia Humanities Council, 1988.

Decker, William Merrill. *The Literary Vocation of Henry Adams.* Chapel Hill: U of North Carolina P, 1990.

De Cussac, Etienne de Planchard. "The 'Gothic' Strategy of George W. Cable in *The Grandissimes.*" *Caliban* 33 (1996): 137–46.

Degler, Carl N. *The Other South: Southern Dissenters in the Nineteenth Century. 1974.* Gainesville: U of Florida P, 2000.

———. *Place over Time: The Continuity of Southern Distinctiveness*. Baton Rouge: Louisiana State UP, 1977.

Deloria, Philip J. *Playing Indian*. New Haven: Yale UP, 1998.

DeLyser, Dydia. *Ramona Memories: Tourism and the Shaping of Southern California*. Minneapolis: U of Minnesota P, 2005.

De Nevi, Donald P., and Doris A. Holmes, eds. *Racism at the Turn of the Century: Documentary Perspectives, 1870–1910*. San Rafael, CA: Leswing, 1973.

Denning, Michael. *Mechanic Accents: Dime Novels and Working-Class Culture in America*. London: Verso, 1998.

Des Jardins, Julie. *Women and the Historical Enterprise in America: Gender, Race, and the Politics of Memory, 1880–1945*. Chapel Hill: U of North Carolina P, 2003.

Dicker, Rory. "The Mirroring of Heaven and Earth: Female Spirituality in Elizabeth Prentiss's *Stepping Heavenward* and Elizabeth Stuart Phelps's *The Gates Ajar*." *Things of the Spirit: Women Writers Constructing Spirituality*. Ed. Kristina K. Groover. Notre Dame: U of Notre Dame P, 2004. 128–54.

Diffley, Kathleen. *Where My Heart Is Turning Ever: Civil War Stories and Constitutional Reform, 1861–1876*. Athens: U of Georgia P, 1992.

Dillard, J. L. *Black English: Its History and Usage in the United States*. New York: Random House, 1972.

Dippie, Brian. *The Vanishing American: White Attitudes and U.S. Indian Policy*. Middletown: Wesleyan UP, 1982.

Dixon, Melvin. "The Teller as Folk Trickster in Chesnutt's *The Conjure Woman*." *CLA Journal* 18.2 (1974): 186–97.

Dixon, Terrell F. "Nature, Gender, and Community: Mary Wilkins Freeman's Ecofiction." *Beyond Nature Writing: Expanding the Boundaries of Ecocriticism*. Ed. Karla Ambruster and Kathleen R. Wallace. Charlottesville: UP of Virginia, 2001. 162–76.

Dobson, Joanne. *Dickinson and the Strategies of Reticence: The Woman Writer in Nineteenth-Century America*. Bloomington: U of Indiana P, 1989.

Doenecke, Justus D. "Myths, Machines, and Markets: The Columbian Exposition of 1893." *Journal of Popular Culture* 6.3 (1973): 535–49.

Donaldson, Susan V. *Competing Voices: The American Novel, 1865–1914*. New York: Twayne, 1998.

Donovan, Josephine. "Breaking the Sentence: Local-Color Literature and Subjugated Knowledges." *The (Other) American Traditions: Nineteenth-Century Women Writers*. Ed. Joyce W. Warren. New Brunswick: Rutgers UP, 1993. 226–43.

———. "Nan Prince and the Golden Apples." *Colby Library Quarterly* 22.1 (1986): 17–27.

———. *New England Local Color Literature: A Women's Tradition*. New York: Ungar, 1983.

Dorris, Michael. Introduction. *Ramona: A Story*. New York: Penguin, 1988. iv–xx.

Douglass-Chin, Richard. *Preacher Woman Sings the Blues: The Autobiographies of Nineteenth-Century African American Evangelists*. Columbia: U of Missouri P, 2001.

Douglass, Frederick. *Life and Times of Frederick Douglass, Written by Himself*. 1881. New York: Collier, 1962.

Dow, Bonnie J. "Historical Narratives, Rhetorical Narratives, and Woman Suffrage Scholarship." *Rhetoric and Public Affairs* 2.2 (1999): 321–40.

Downey, Dennis B. *A Season of Renewal: The Columbian Exposition and Victorian America.* Westport, CT: Praeger, 2002.

Du Bois, W. E. B. *Black Reconstruction in America, 1860–1880.* 1935. New York: Russell, 1956.

Duckett, Margaret. "Bret Harte and the Indian of Northern California." *Huntington Library Quarterly* 18.1 (1954): 59–83.

———. "Bret Harte's Portrayal of Half-Breeds." *American Literature* 25.2 (1953): 193–212.

Duncan, Charles. *The Absent Man: The Narrative Craft of Charles W. Chesnutt.* Athens: U of Ohio P, 1998.

Dupuy, Edward. "Linguistic Mastery and the Garden of the Chattel in Frederick Douglass's *Narrative.*" *Mississippi Quarterly* 44.1 (1990–91): 23–33.

Earnest, Ernest. *S. Weir Mitchell: Novelist and Physician.* Philadelphia: U of Pennsylvania P, 1950.

Earnest, John. "From Mysteries to Histories: Cultural Pedagogy in Frances E. W. Harper's *Iola Leroy.*" *American Literature* 64.3 (1992): 497–518.

Eaton, Richard Bozman. "George Washington Cable and the Historical Romance." *Southern Literary Journal* 8.1 (1975): 82–94.

Edel, Leon. *The Life of Henry James,* 5 vols. Philadelphia: Lippincott, 1953–1972.

Egan, Joseph J. "Lions Rampant: Agricola Fusilier and Bras-Coupé as Antithetical Doubles in *The Grandissimes.*" The Grandissimes*: Centennial Essays.* Ed. Thomas J. Richardson. Jackson: UP of Mississippi, 1981. 74–80.

Egan, Michael. *Mark Twain's Huckleberry Finn: Race, Class, and Society.* London: Sussex UP, 1977.

Ekstrom, Kjell. *George W. Cable: A Study of His Early Life and Work.* Cambridge: Harvard UP, 1950.

Elfenbein, Anna Sharon. *Women on the Color Line: Evolving Stereotypes and the Writings of George Washington Cable, Grace King, Kate Chopin.* Charlottesville: UP of Virginia, 1989.

Elkins, Marilyn. "Reading beyond the Conventions: A Look at Frances E. W. Harper's *Iola Leroy, or Shadows Uplifted.*" *American Literary Realism* 22.2 (1990): 44–53.

Elkins, Stanley. *Slavery: A Problem in American Institutional and Intellectual Life.* 1959. Chicago: U of Chicago P, 1976.

Elliott, Michael A. *The Culture Concept: Writing and Difference in the Age of Realism.* Minneapolis: U of Minnesota P, 2002.

Ellis, Richard J., and Alan Munslow. "Narrative, Myth, and the Turner Thesis." *Journal of American Culture* 9.2 (1986): 9–16.

Ellis, William. *The Theory of the American Romance: An Ideology in American Intellectual History.* Ann Arbor: UMI Research P, 1989.

Ender, Evelyne. *Sexing the Mind: Nineteenth-Century Fictions of Hysteria.* Ithaca: Cornell UP, 1995.

Enser, Allison. "The Geography of Mary Noailles Murfree's *In the Tennessee Mountains.*" *Mississippi Quarterly* 31.2 (1978): 191–99.

Ernest, John. *Resistance and Reformation in Nineteenth-Century African-American Literature: Brown, Walker, Jacobs, Delany, Douglass, and Harper.* Jackson: UP of Mississippi, 1995.

Evans, William. "French-English Literary Dialect in *The Grandissimes.*" *American Speech* 46.3–4 (1971): 210–22.

———. "Naming Day in Old New Orleans: Charactonyms and Colloquialisms in George Washington Cable's *The Grandissimes.*" *Names* 30.3 (1982): 183–91.

Fetterley, Judith, and Marjorie Pryse. *Writing out of Place: Regionalism, Women, and American Literary Culture.* Urbana: U of Illinois P, 2003.

Fick, Thomas, and Eva Gold. "The Mulatto in *The Grandissimes:* Category Crisis and Crisis of Category." *Xavier Review* 21.1 (2001): 68–86.

Fielder, Leslie. *The Return of the Vanishing American.* New York: Stein & Day, 1968.

Findling, John E. *Chicago's Great World Fairs.* Manchester: Manchester UP, 1994.

The First Century of the Republic: A Review of American Progress. New York: Harper & Brothers, 1876.

Fisher, Philip. "Appearing and Disappearing in Public: Social Space in Late-Nineteenth-Century Literature and Culture." *Amerikastudien* 31.1 (1986): 81–100.

Fishkin, Shelley Fisher. *Was Huck Black: Mark Twain and African-American Voices.* New York: Oxford UP, 1993.

Fitch, Suzanne, and Roseann Mendziuk. *Sojourner Truth as Orator: Wit, Story, and Song.* Westport, CT: Greenwood, 1997.

Fitzpatrick, Ellen. *History's Memory: Writing America's Past, 1880–1980.* Cambridge: Harvard UP, 2002.

Foner, Eric. *Nothing but Freedom: Emancipation and Its Legacy.* Baton Rouge: Louisiana State UP, 1983.

———. *Reconstruction: America's Unfinished Revolution, 1863–1877.* New York: Harper & Row, 1988.

Foner, Philip S. "Black Participation in the Centennial of 1876." *Phylon* 39.4 (1978): 283–96.

Foote, Mary Hallock. "The Fate of a Voice." 1886. *Nineteenth-Century American Women Writers: An Anthology.* Ed. Karen L. Kilcup. Oxford: Blackwell, 1997. 341–59.

Foote, Stephanie. *Regional Fictions: Culture and Identity in Nineteenth-Century American Literature.* Madison: U of Wisconsin P, 2001.

Foster, Charles. "The Phonology of the Conjure Tales of Charles W. Chesnutt." *Publications of the American Dialect Society* 55 (1971).

Foster, Frances Smith. "Gender, Genre, and Vulgar Secularism: The Case of Frances Ellen Watkins Harper and the AME Press." *Recovered Writers/Recovered Texts: Race, Class, and Gender in Black Women's Literature.* Ed. Dolan Hubbard. Knoxville: U of Tennessee P, 1997. 46–59.

———. *Witnessing Slavery: The Development of Ante-bellum Slave Narratives.* Madison: U of Wisconsin P, 1979.

————. *Written by Herself: Literary Production by African American Women, 1746–1892.* Bloomington: U of Indiana P, 1993.

Foster, Gaines M. *Ghosts of the Confederacy: Defeat, the Lost Cause, and the Emergence of the New South, 1865 to 1913.* New York: Oxford UP, 1987.

Fowler, Catherine S. "Sarah Winnemucca, Northern Paiute, 1844–1891." *American Indian Intellectuals.* Ed. Margot Liberty. St. Paul, MN: West, 1976.

Franks, Kenny A. "Bright Eyes." *American National Biography Online.* February 2000. April 15, 2004, <www.anb.org/articles/20/20-00112.html>.

Frederickson, George. *The Black Image in the White Mind: The Debate on Afro-American Character and Destiny, 1817–1914.* Hanover, NH: Wesleyan UP, 1971.

Freeman, Mary E. Wilkins. "On the Walpole Road." 1886. *Selected Stories of Mary E. Wilkins Freeman.* Ed. Marjorie Pryse. New York: Norton, 1983. 27–40.

Friedman, Lawrence. *The White Savage: Racial Fantasies in the Postbellum South.* Englewood Cliffs, NJ: Prentice-Hall, 1970.

Frost, Dan R. *Thinking Confederates: Academia and the Idea of Progress in the New South.* Knoxville: U of Tennessee P, 2000.

Frost, O. W. *Joaquin Miller.* New York: Twayne, 1967.

Fulop, Timothy E. "'The Future Golden Day of the Race': Millennialism and Black Americans in the Nadir, 1877–1901." *Harvard Theological Review* 84.1 (1991): 75–99.

Fulton, Valerie. "Rewriting the Necessary Woman: Marriage and Professionalism in James, Jewett, and Phelps." *Henry James Review* 15.3 (1994): 242–56.

Gabin, Jane S. *A Living Minstrelsy: The Poetry and Music of Sidney Lanier.* Macon, GA: Mercer UP, 1985.

Gabler, Janet A. "The Narrator's Script: James's Complex Narration in *The Bostonians.*" *Journal of Narrative Technique* 14.2 (1984): 94–109.

Gaines, Francis Pendleton. *The Southern Plantation: A Study in the Development and the Accuracy of a Tradition.* Gloucester, MA: Peter Smith, 1962.

Gallagher, Gary, and Alan Nolan, eds. *The Myth of the Lost Cause and Civil War History.* Bloomington: U of Indiana P, 2000.

Gallman, J. Matthew. *"Touched with Fire?": Two Philadelphia Novelists Remember the Civil War.* Milwaukee: Marquette UP, 2002.

Gardner, Sarah E. *Blood and Irony: Southern White Women's Narratives of the Civil War, 1861–1937.* Chapel Hill: U of North Carolina P, 2004.

Gaston, Paul M. *The New South Creed: A Study in Southern Mythmaking.* New York: Knopf, 1970.

Gates, Henry Louis Jr. "Dis and Dat: Dialect and the Descent." *Afro-American Literature: The Reconstruction of Instruction.* Ed. Dexter Fisher and Robert Stepto. New York: MLA, 1979. 88–119.

————. "James Gronniosaw and the Trope of the Talking Book." *African American Autobiography: A Collection of Critical Essays.* Ed. William L. Andrews. Englewood Cliffs, NJ: Prentice-Hall, 1993. 8–25.

Georgi-Findlay, Brigitte. "The Frontiers of Native American Women's Writing: Sarah

Winnemucca's *Life Among the Piutes.*" *New Voices in Native American Literary Criticism.* Ed. Arnold Krupat. Washington, DC: Smithsonian Institution P, 1993. 222–52.

Gere, Anne Ruggles. *Intimate Practices: Literacy and Cultural Work in U.S. Women's Clubs, 1880–1920.* Urbana: U of Illinois P, 1997.

Gerster, Patrick, and Nicholas Cords, eds. *Myth and Southern History,* vol. 1. Urbana: U of Illinois P, 1989.

Giele, Janet Zollinger. *Two Paths to Women's Equality: Temperance, Suffrage, and the Origins of Modern Feminism.* New York: Twayne, 1995.

Gilbert, James. *Perfect Cities: Chicago's Utopias of 1893.* Chicago: U of Chicago P, 1991.

Gilbert, Sandra, and Susan Gubar. *The Madwoman in the Attic: The Woman Writer and the Nineteenth-Century Literary Imagination.* New Haven: Yale UP, 1979.

Gilder, Rodman. *Statue of Liberty Enlightening the World.* New York: NY Trust, 1943.

Gillette, William. *Retreat from Reconstruction, 1869–1879.* Baton Rouge: Louisiana State UP, 1979.

Gilley, B. H. "Power and Intuition: A Comparison of Women's Perception as Reflected in the Heroines of Henry Adams and John W. DeForest." *Midwest Quarterly* 39.3 (1998): 280–93.

Ginger, Ray. *Altgeld's America: The Lincoln Ideal versus Changing Realities.* New York: Funk & Wagnalis, 1958.

Glazener, Nancy. *Reading for Realism: The History of a U.S. Literary Institution, 1850–1910.* Durham: Duke UP, 1997.

Gleason, William. "Chesnutt's *Piazza Tales:* Architecture, Race, and Memory in the Conjure Stories." *American Quarterly* 51.1 (1999): 33–77.

Glover, Donald. "A Reconsideration of Bret Harte's Later Work." *Western American Literature* 8.3 (1973): 143–51.

Godden, Richard, and Mary A. McCoy. "Say It Again, Sam[bo]: Race and Speech in *Huckleberry Finn* and *Casablanca.*" *Mississippi Quarterly* 49.4 (1996): 657–82.

Goddu, Teresa A., and Craig V. Smith. "Scenes of Writing in Frederick Douglass's *Narrative:* Autobiography and the Creation of Self." *Southern Review* 25.4 (1989): 822–40.

Goldberg, Michael Lewis. *An Army of Women: Gender and Politics in Gilded Age Kansas.* Baltimore: Johns Hopkins UP, 1997.

Goldman, Anne E. "'I Think Our Romance Is Spoiled,' or, Crossing Genres: California History in Helen Hunt Jackson's *Ramona* and Maria Amparo Ruiz de Burton's *The Squatter and the Don.*" *Over the Edge: Remapping the American West.* Ed. Valerie J. Matsumato and Blake Allmendinger. Berkeley: U of California P, 1999. 65–84.

Gonzalez, John M. "The Warp of Whiteness: Domesticity and Empire in Helen Hunt Jackson's *Ramona.*" *American Literary History* 16.3 (2004): 437–65.

Gonzalez, Mario, and Elizabeth Cook-Lynn. *The Politics of Hallowed Ground: Wounded Knee and the Struggle for Indian Sovereignty.* Urbana: U of Illinois P, 1999.

Gooder, Jean. "Henry James's Bostonians: The Voices of Democracy." *Cambridge Quarterly* 30.2 (2001): 97–116.

Goodheart, Adam. "Last Summer of the Republic: The Centennial Exposition as Experiment and Experience." BA Thesis Harvard U, 1992.

Goodman, Susan. *Civil Wars: American Novelists and Manners, 1880–1940*. Baltimore: Johns Hopkins UP, 2003.

Goodspeed, Julie. "The Use of Endogamous Marriage in the Formation of Creole Identity in Cable's *The Grandissimes*, Chopin's 'Athenaise,' and King's 'La Grande Demoiselle.'" *Southern Studies* 9.4 (1998): 45–68.

Gordon, Ann D., ed. *African American Women and the Vote, 1837–1965*. Amherst: U of Massachusetts P, 1997.

Grabenhorst-Randall, Terree. "The Woman's Building." *Heresies* 1.4 (1978): 44–46.

Graham, Maryemma. Introduction. *The Complete Poems of Frances Ellen Watkins Harper*. New York: Oxford UP, 1987. xxxiii–lviii.

Grant, Susan-Mary. "'The Charter of Its Birthright': The Civil War and American Nationalism." *Legacy of Disunion: The Enduring Significance of the American Civil War*. Ed. Grant and Peter J. Parish. Baton Rouge: Louisiana State UP, 2003. 188–206.

Grasso, Linda. "'Thwarted Life, Mighty Hunger, Unfinished Work': The Legacy of Nineteenth-Century Women Writing in America." *American Transcendental Quarterly* 8.2 (1994): 97–118.

Graulich, Melody. "Profile: Mary Hallock Foote (1847–1938)." *Legacy* 3.2 (1986): 43–52.

Gray, Richard. *Writing the South: Ideas of an American Region*. Baton Rouge: Louisiana State UP, 1997.

Greene, Dana. Introduction. *Suffrage and Religious Principle: Speeches and Writings of Olympia Brown*. Metuchen, NJ: Scarecrow, 1985. 1–17.

Greenhalgh, Paul. *Ephemeral Vistas: The* Expositions Universelles, *Great Exhibitions and World's Fairs, 1851–1939*. Manchester: Manchester UP, 1988.

Grenwald, Elissa. *Realism and the Romance: Nathaniel Hawthorne, Henry James, and American Fiction*. Ann Arbor: UMI Research P, 1989.

Griffin, Farah J. "Frances Harper in the Reconstruction South." *Sage* 5.1 (1988): 45–47.

Griffith, Kelley. "Weir Mitchell and the Genteel Romance." *American Literature* 44.2 (1972): 247–61.

Gross, Theodore L. *Albion W. Tourgée*. New York: Twayne, 1963.

———. "The Negro in Literature of the Reconstruction." *Phylon* 22 (1961): 5–14.

Gullett, Gayle. "'Our Great Opportunity': Organized Women Advance Women's Work at the World's Columbian Exposition of 1893." *Illinois Historical Journal* 87.4 (1994): 259–76.

Gunning, Sandra. *Race, Rape, and Lynching: The Red Record of American Literature, 1890–1912*. New York: Oxford UP, 1996.

Gutierrez-Jones, Carl. *Rethinking the Borderlands: Between Chicano Culture and Legal Discourse*. Berkeley: U of California P, 1995.

Hadler, Jeffrey. "Remus Orthography: The History of the Representation of the African-American Voice." *Journal of Folklore Research* 35.2 (1998): 99–126.

Hagan, William T. *The Indian Rights Association: The Herbert Welsh Years, 1882–1904*. Tucson: U of Arizona P, 1985.

Hall, Roger A. *Performing the American Frontier, 1870–1906*. Cambridge: Cambridge UP, 2001.

Handley, George B. *Postslavery Literatures in the Americas: Family Portraits in Black and White*. Charlottesville: UP of Virginia, 2000.

Hansen, Jonathan M. *The Last Promise of Patriotism: Debating American Identity, 1890–1920*. Chicago: U of Chicago P, 2003.

Hanson, Elizabeth I. *The American Indian in American Literature: A Study in Metaphor*. Lewiston, NY: Mellen, 1988.

Hardwig, Bill. "Who Owns the Whip?: Chesnutt, Tourgée, and Reconstruction Justice." *African American Review* 36.1 (2002): 5–20.

Harper, Frances Ellen Watkins. *Iola Leroy, or Shadows Uplifted*. 1892. *Three Classic African-American Novels*. Ed. Henry Louis Gates, Jr. New York: Vintage Classics, 1990. 225–463.

———. "John and Jacob: A Dialogue on Women's Rights." 1885. *A Brighter Coming Day: A Frances Ellen Watkins Harper Reader*. Ed. Frances Smith Foster. New York: Feminist, 1990. 240–42.

Harris, Joel Chandler. *Nights with Uncle Remus: Myths and Legends of the Old Plantation*. Boston: Houghton Mifflin, 1883.

———. *Uncle Remus, His Songs and Sayings*. 1881. New York: Penguin, 1982.

Harris, Neil. "Dream Making." *Chicago History* 23.2 (1994): 44–57.

———, ed. *The Land of Contrasts, 1880–1901*. New York: Braziller, 1970.

Harris, Susan. "Mary E. Wilkins Freeman's 'A New England Nun' and the Dilemma of the Woman Artist." *Studies in American Humor* 3.9 (2002): 27–38.

———. *Nineteenth-Century American Women's Novels: Interpretative Strategies*. Chicago: U of Chicago P, 1992.

Harsha, William J. *Ploughed Under: The Story of an Indian Chief, Told by Himself*. New York: Fords, 1881.

Harte, Bret. "In the Carquinez Woods." 1882. *The Writings of Bret Harte*. Vol. 14. Boston: Houghton Mifflin, 1896. 1–125.

Hartmann, Thom. *Unequal Protection: The Rise of Corporate Dominance and the Theft of Human Rights*. New York: St. Martin's, 2002.

Haskell, Thomas L. "Capitalism and the Origins of the Humanitarian Sensibility." *American Historical Review* 90.2–3 (1985): 339–61, 551–66.

Haslam, Gerald. "Olive Chancellor's Painful Victory in *The Bostonians*." *Research Studies* 36.3 (1968): 232–37.

Hawkins, Mike. *Social Darwinism in European and American Thought, 1860–1945*. Cambridge: Cambridge UP, 1997.

Heaton, Daniel H. "The Altered Characterization of Miss Birdseye in Henry James's *The Bostonians*." *American Literature* 50.4 (1979): 588–603.

Hedin, Raymond. "Uncle Remus: Puttin' on Ole Massa's Son." *Southern Literary Journal* 15.1 (1982): 83–90.

Heilmann, Ann. "Introduction: Words as Deeds: Debates and Narratives on Women's Suffrage." *Women's History Review* 11.4 (2002): 565–76.

Henderson, Harry. *Versions of the Past: The Historical Imagination in American Fiction*. New York: Oxford UP, 1974.

Hendler, Glenn. *Public Sentiments: Structures of Feeling in Nineteenth-Century American Literature*. Chapel Hill: U of North Carolina P, 2001.

Herman, Sandra R. "Loving Courtship or the Marriage Market?: The Ideal and Its Critics, 1871–1911." *American Quarterly* 25.2 (1973): 235–54.

Herndl, Diane Price. "Miscegen(r)ation or Mestiza Discourse?: Feminist and Racial Politics in *Ramona* and *Iola Leroy.*" *Beyond the Binary: Reconstructing Cultural Identity in a Multicultural Context*. Ed. Timothy B. Powell. New Brunswick: Rutgers UP, 1999. 261–75.

Hinsley, Curtis M. *Savages and Scientists: The Smithsonian Institution and the Development of American Anthropology, 1846–1910*. Washington, DC: Smithsonian Institution P, 1981.

———. "The World as Marketplace: Commodification of the Exotic at the World's Columbian Exposition, Chicago, 1893." *Exhibiting Cultures: The Poetics and Politics of Museum Display*. Ed. Ivan Karp and Steven D. Levine. Washington, DC: Smithsonian Institution P, 1991. 344–65.

Hobsbawm, E. J. "The Transformation of Nationalism, 1870–1918." *Nations and Nationalism since 1780: Programme, Myth, Reality*. Cambridge: Cambridge UP, 1990. 101–30.

Hochman, Barbara. *Getting at the Author: Reimagining Books and Reading in the Age of American Realism*. Amherst: U of Massachusetts P, 2001.

Hofstadter, Richard. *The Age of Reform: From Bryan to F.D.R.* New York: Vintage, 1955.

———. *Social Darwinism in American Thought*. 1944. New York: Braziller, 1959.

Holly, Carol. "The Cruelty of Husbands, the Complicity of Wives, and the Cooperation of Communities in Rose Terry Cooke's 'Mrs. Flint's Married Experience.'" *American Literary Realism* 33.1 (2000): 65–80.

Holmes, David G. *Revisiting Racialized Voice: African American Ethos in Language and Literature*. Carbondale: Southern Illinois UP, 2004.

Holzman, Robert S. *Adapt or Perish: The Life of General Roger A. Pryor, C.S.A.* Hamden, CT: Archon, 1976.

Hönnighausen, Lother. "The Old and the New Regionalism." *"Writing" Nation and "Writing" Region in America*. Ed. Theo D'haen and Hans Bertens. Amsterdam: VU UP, 1996. 3–20.

Howard, Angela, and Sasha Torrent, eds. *Opposition to the Women's Movement in the United States, 1848–1929*. New York: Garland, 1997.

Howard, June. *Form and History in American Literary Naturalism*. Chapel Hill: U of North Carolina P, 1983.

Howard-Pitney, David. "The Enduring Black Jeremiad: The American Jeremiad and Black Protest Rhetoric, From Frederick Douglass to W. E. B. Du Bois, 1841–1919." *American Quarterly* 38.3 (1986): 481–92.

Howe, Irving. "Introduction to *The Bostonians* [1956]." *Critical Essays on Henry James: The Early Novels*. Ed. James W. Gorgeno. Boston: G. K. Hall, 1987. 165–66.

Hoxie, Frederick A. *A Final Promise: The Campaign to Assimilate the Indians, 1880–1920*. Lincoln: U of Nebraska P, 2001.

——, ed. *Talking Back to Civilization: Indian Voices from the Progressive Era.* Boston: Bedford, 2001.

Hubbell, Jay B. *The South in American Literature, 1607–1900.* Durham: Duke UP, 1954.

Huf, Linda. *A Portrait of the Artist as a Young Woman: The Writer as Heroine in American Literature.* New York: Ungar, 1983.

Hughson, Lois. *From Biography to History: The Historical Imagination and American Fiction, 1880–1940.* Charlottesville: UP of Virginia, 1988.

Huhndorf, Shari M. *Going Native: Indians in the American Cultural Imagination.* Ithaca: Cornell UP, 2001.

Humez, Jean. "Reading *The Narrative of Sojourner Truth* as a Collaborative Text." *Frontiers* 16.1 (1996): 29–52.

Humphries, Jefferson. "Remus Redux, or French Classicism on the Old Plantation: La Fontaine and Joel Chandler Harris." *Southern Literature and Literary Theory.* Ed. Humphries. Athens: U of Georgia P, 1990. 170–85.

Hyde, Anne Farrar. *An American Vision: Far Western Landscape and National Culture, 1820–1920.* New York: New York UP, 1990.

Hymes, Dell. "In vain I tried to tell you." *Essays in Native American Ethnopoetics.* Philadelphia: U of Pennsylvania P, 1981.

Ingram, J. S. *The Centennial Exposition Described and Illustrated.* 1876. New York: Arno, 1976.

Inness, Sherrie A., and Diana Royer, eds. *Breaking Boundaries: New Perspectives on Women's Regional Writing.* Iowa City: U of Iowa P, 1997.

Irwin, Robert McKee. "*Ramona* and Postnationalist American Studies: On 'Our America' and the Mexican Borderlands." *American Quarterly* 55.4 (2003): 539–68.

Ives, Sumner. "The Phonology of the Uncle Remus Stories." *Publications of the American Dialect Society* 22 (1954).

——. "A Theory of Literary Dialect (1950)." *A Various Language.* Ed. Juanita V. Williamson and Virginia M. Burke. New York: Free Press, 1971. 145–77.

Jackson, Cassandra. "'I Will Gladly Share with Them My Richer Heritage': Schoolteachers in Frances E. W. Harper's *Iola Leroy* and Charles Chesnutt's *Mandy Oxendine.*" *African American Review* 37.4 (2003): 553–68.

Jackson, Helen Hunt. *Ramona: A Story.* 1884. Boston: Little, Brown, 1914.

Jacobs, Margaret D. "Mixed-Bloods, Mestizas, and Pintos: Race, Gender, and Claims to Whiteness in Helen Hunt Jackson's *Ramona* and Maria Amparo Ruiz de Burton's *Who Would Have Thought It?*" *Western American Literature* 36.3 (2001): 212–32.

Jacobson, Jacob. *Queer Desire in Henry James: The Politics of Erotics in* The Bostonians *and* The Princess Casamassima. Frankfurt: Lang, 2000.

Jacobson, Marcia. "Popular Fiction and Henry James's Unpopular *Bostonians.*" *Modern Philology* 73.3 (1976): 264–75.

Jaher, Frederic Cople. *Doubters and Dissenters: Cataclysmic Thought in America, 1885–1918.* London: Collier, 1964.

James, Henry. *The Bostonians.* 1886. New York: Knopf, 1992.

———. *Notebooks*. Ed. F. O. Matthiessen and K. B. Murdock. New York: Oxford UP, 1961.

Jamieson, Duncan R. "Women's Rights at the World's Fair, 1893." *Illinois Quarterly* 37.2 (1974): 5–20.

Jefferson, Thomas. *Notes on the State of Virginia with Related Documents*. Ed. David Waldstreicher. New York: Palgrave, 2002.

Jewett, Sarah Orne. *A Country Doctor*. 1884. *Novels and Stories*. Ed. Michael Davitt Bell. New York: Library of America, 1994. 143–370.

Johns, Barbara. "'Mateless and Appealing': Growing into Spinsterhood in Sarah Orne Jewett." *Critical Essays on Sarah Orne Jewett*. Ed. Gwen L. Nagel. Boston: Hall, 1984. 147–65.

Johnsen, Norma. "Pieces: Artist and Audience in Three Mary Wilkins Freeman Stories." *Colby Library Quarterly* 29.1 (1993): 43–56.

Johnson, Charles S. "The New Frontage of American Life." *The New Negro*. Ed. Alain Locke. 1925. New York: Simon & Schuster, 1992. 278–98.

Johnson, Guion Griffis. "Southern Paternalism toward Negroes after Emancipation." *The Negro in the South since 1865: Selected Essays in American Negro History*. Ed. Charles E. Wynes. University: U of Alabama P, 1965. 103–34.

Jones, Gavin. *Strange Talk: The Politics of Dialect Literature in Gilded Age America*. Berkeley: U of California P, 1999.

Jones, Gayl. *Liberating Voices: Oral Tradition in African American Literature*. Cambridge: Harvard UP, 1991.

Jordan, David, ed. *Regionalism Reconsidered: New Approaches to the Field*. New York: Garland, 1994.

Juncker, Clara. *Through Random Doors We Wandered: Women Writing the South*. Odense: U of South Denmark P, 2002.

Kachun, Mitch. "Before the Eyes of All Nations: African-American Identity and Historical Memory at the Centennial Exposition of 1876." *Pennsylvania History* 65.3 (1998): 300–323.

Kahane, Claire. "Hysteria, Feminism, and the Case of *The Bostonians*." *Feminism and Psychoanalysis*. Ed. Richard Feldstein and Judith Roof. Ithaca: Cornell UP, 1989. 280–97.

Kaledin, Eugenia. "Dr. Manners: S. Weir Mitchell's Novelistic Prescription for an Upset Society." *Prospects* 11 (1987): 199–216.

Kammen, Michael. *Mystic Chords of Memory: The Transformation of Tradition in American Culture*. New York: Random House, 1991.

Kaplan, Amy. *The Social Construction of American Realism*. Chicago: U of Chicago P, 1988.

Karcher, Carolyn L. *Shadow over the Promised Land: Slavery, Race, and Violence in Melville's America*. Baton Rouge: Louisiana State UP, 1980.

Kasson, John. *Amusing the Million: Coney Island at the Turn of the Century*. New York: Hill & Wang, 1978.

Kasten, Carren. *Imagination and Desire in the Novels of Henry James*. New Brunswick: Rutgers UP, 1984.

Kaul, A. N. *The American Vision: Actual and Ideal Society in Nineteenth-Century Fiction.* 1963. Oxford: Oxford UP, 2002.

Kaup, Monica, and Debra Rosenthal, eds. *Mixing Race, Mixing Culture: Inter-American Literary Dialogues.* Austin: U of Texas P, 2002.

Kearns, Michael. "Narrative Discourse and the Imperative of Sympathy in *The Bostonians.*" *Henry James Review* 17.2 (1996): 162–81.

Keely, Karen A. "Marriage Plots and National Reunion: The Trope of Romantic Reconciliation in Postbellum Literature." *Mississippi Quarterly* 51.4 (1998): 621–48.

Keenan, Hugh T. "Twisted Tales: Propaganda in the Tar-Baby Stories." *Southern Quarterly* 22.2 (1984): 54–69.

Keiser, Albert. *The Indian in American Literature.* New York: Oxford UP, 1933.

Kelly, Lori Duin. *The Life and Works of Elizabeth Stuart Phelps, Victorian Feminist Writer.* Troy, NY: Whitston, 1983.

Kentleton, John. "Henry Adams and *Democracy:* Public Morality versus Private Integrity?" *Halcyon* 9 (1987): 21–34.

Kerkering, John D. *The Poetics of National and Racial Identity in Nineteenth-Century American Literature.* Cambridge: Cambridge UP, 2003.

Kern, John Dwight. *Constance Fenimore Woolson: Literary Pioneer.* Philadelphia: U of Pennsylvania P, 1934.

Kern, Stephen. *The Culture of Time and Space, 1880–1918.* Cambridge: Harvard UP, 1983.

Kersten, Holger. "The Creative Potential of Dialect Writing in Later-Nineteenth Century-America." *Nineteenth Century Literature* 55.1 (2000): 92–117.

Kibbey, Ann, and Michele Stepto. "The Antilanguage of Slavery: Frederick Douglass's 1845 *Narrative.*" *African American Autobiography: A Collection of Critical Essays.* Ed. William L. Andrews. Englewood Cliffs, NJ: Prentice-Hall, 1993. 166–91.

King, Kimball. "Local Color and the Rise of the American Magazine." *Essays Mostly on Periodical Publishing in America: A Collection in Honor of Clarence Gohdes.* Ed. James Woodress. Durham: Duke UP, 1973. 121–33.

Kleiman, Ed. "Mark Twain's 'Rhapsody': Printing and the Oral Tradition in *Huckleberry Finn.*" *University of Texas Quarterly* 59.4 (1990): 535–48.

Klein, Kerwin Lee. *Frontiers of Historical Imagination: Narrating the European Conquest of Native America, 1890–1990.* Berkeley: U of California P, 1997.

Klein, Marcus. *Easterns, Westerns, and Private Eyes: American Matters, 1870–1900.* Madison: U of Wisconsin P, 1994.

Kleitz, Katherine. "Essence of New England: The Portraits of Rose Terry Cooke." *American Transcendental Quarterly* 47–48 (1980): 127–40.

Koistinen-Harris, Janice H. *Social Reform, Taste, and the Construction of Virtue in American Literature, 1870–1910.* Lewiston: Mellen, 2002.

Kolodny, Annette. *The Lay of the Land: Metaphor as Experience and History in American Life and Letters.* Chapel Hill: U of North Carolina P, 1975.

Koppelman, Susan. "The Politics and Ethics of Literary Revival: A Test Case—Shall We,

Ought We, Can We Make of Constance Fenimore Woolson a Kate Chopin?" *Journal of American Culture* 22.3 (1999): 1–9.

Korten, David C. *The Post-Corporate World: Life after Capitalism*. San Francisco: Berrett-Koehler, 1999.

Kotler, Neil G. "The Statue of Liberty as Idea, Symbol, and Historical Presence." *The Statue of Liberty Revisited*. Ed. Wilton S. Dillon and Kotler. Washington, DC: Smithsonian Institution P, 1994. 1–16.

Kreyling, Michael. Introduction. *The Grandissimes*. New York: Penguin, 1988.

———. "Nationalizing the Southern Hero: Adams and James." *Mississippi Quarterly* 34.4 (1981): 383–402.

Krupat, Arnold. *For Those Who Came After: A Study of Native American Autobiography*. Berkeley: U of California P, 1985.

———. *Red Matters: Native American Studies*. Philadelphia: U of Pennsylvania P, 2002.

———. *The Voice in the Margin: Native American Literature and the Canon*. Berkeley: U of California P, 1989.

Kugler, Israel. *From Ladies to Women: The Organized Struggle for Women's Rights in the Reconstruction Era*. Westport, CT: Greenwood, 1987.

Ladd, Barbara. *Nationalism and the Color Line in George Washington Cable, Mark Twain, and William Faulkner*. Baton Rouge: Louisiana State UP, 1996.

LaFeber, Walter. *The New Empire: An Interpretation of American Expansion, 1860–1898*. Ithaca: Cornell UP, 1963.

Lampe, Gregory P. *Frederick Douglass: Freedom's Voice, 1818–1845*. East Lansing: Michigan State UP, 1998.

Lane, Ann J., ed. *The Debate over Slavery: Stanley Elkins and His Critics*. Urbana: U of Illinois P, 1971.

Lanier, Sidney. "Centennial Cantata." 1876. *Poems of Sidney Lanier*. Ed. Mary Day Lanier. 1884. Athens: U of Georgia P, 1981. 259–61.

———. *Letters of Sidney Lanier: Selections from His Correspondence, 1866–1881*. Ed. Mary Day Lanier. New York: Scribner's, 1899.

Lape, Noreen Groover. *West of the Border: The Multicultural Literature of the Western American Frontiers*. Athens: U of Ohio P, 2000.

Lasch, Christopher. *The Culture of Narcissim: American Life in an Age of Diminishing Expectations*. New York: Norton, 1978.

Lawlor, Mary. *Recalling the Wild: Naturalism and the Closing of the American West*. New Brunswick: Rutgers UP, 2000.

Lears, T. J. Jackson. *No Place of Grace: Antimodernism and the Transformation of American Culture, 1880–1920*. Chicago: U of Chicago P, 1994.

Leigh, Frances Butler. *Ten Years on a Georgia Plantation Since the War, 1866–1876*. 1883. Savannah: Library of Georgia, 1992.

Leonard, James S. "Huck, Jim, and the 'Black-and-White Fallacy.'" *Constructing Mark Twain: New Directions in Scholarship*. Ed. Laura E. Skandera Trombley and Michael J. Kiskis. Columbia: U of Missouri P, 2001. 139–50.

Levander, Caroline. "Bawdy Talk: The Politics of Women's Public Speech in *The Lecturess* and *The Bostonians*." *American Literature* 67.3 (1995): 467–85.

———. *Voices of the Nation: Women and Public Speech in Nineteenth-Century American Literature and Culture*. Cambridge: Cambridge UP, 1998.

Levenson, J. C. *The Mind and Art of Henry Adams*. Boston: Houghton Mifflin, 1957.

Leverenz, David. "Trachtenberg, Haskell, & Livingston, Inc." *American Literary History* 15.4 (2003): 738–47.

Levering, Joseph P. *S. Weir Mitchell*. New York: Twayne, 1971.

Levin, David. *In Defense of Historical Literature: Essays on American History, Autobiography, Drama, and Fiction*. New York: Hill, 1967.

Levine, Benjamin, and Isabella F. Story. *The Statue of Liberty: National Monument*. Washington, DC: National Park Service, 1957.

Levine, Lawrence. *Highbrow/Lowbrow: The Emergence of Cultural Hierarchy in America*. Cambridge: Harvard UP, 1990.

Levy, Helen Fiddyment. *Fiction of the Home Place: Jewett, Cather, Glasgow, Porter, Welty, and Naylor*. Jackson: UP of Mississippi, 1992.

Lewis, Nathaniel. *Unsettling the Literary West: Authenticity and Authorship*. Lincoln: U of Nebraska P, 2003.

Light, Kathleen. "Uncle Remus and the Folklorists." *Southern Literary Journal* 7.2 (1975): 88–104.

Limerick, Patricia Nelson. *The Legacy of Conquest: The Unbroken Past of the American West*. New York: Norton, 1987.

Limon, John. *Writing after War: American War Fiction from Realism to Postmodernism*. New York: Oxford UP, 1994.

Lincoln, Kenneth. *Sing with the Heart of a Bear: Fusions of Native and American Poetry, 1890–1999*. Berkeley: U of California P, 2000.

Lindberg, John. "The *Adventures of Huckleberry Finn* as Moral Monologue." *Proteus* 1.2 (1984): 41–49.

Link, Eric Carl. *The Vast and Terrible Drama: American Literary Naturalism in the Late Nineteenth Century*. Tuscaloosa: U of Alabama P, 2004.

Link, William A. *The Paradox of Southern Progressivism, 1880–1930*. Chapel Hill: U of North Carolina P, 1992.

Litwicki, Ellen M. "'The Inauguration of the People's Age': The Columbian Quadricentennial and American Culture." *Maryland Historian* 20 (1989): 47–58.

Livingston, James. "*Incorporation* and the Disciplines." *American Literary History* 15.4 (2003): 748–52.

———. *Pragmatism and the Political Economy of Cultural Revolution, 1850–1940*. Chapel Hill: U of North Carolina P, 1997.

———. *Pragmatism, Feminism, and Democracy: Rethinking the Politics of American History*. New York: Routledge, 2001.

Lloyd, David. "Adulteration and the Nation: Monologic Nationalism and the Colonial Hybrid." *An Other Tongue: Nation and Ethnicity in the Linguistic Borderlands*. Ed. Alfred Arteaga. Durham: Duke UP, 1994. 53–92.

Logan, Rayford. *The Betrayal of the Negro: From Rutherford B. Hayes to Woodrow Wilson.* 1954. New York: Da Capo, 1997.

Logan, Shirley Wilson. *"We Are Coming": The Persuasive Discourse of Nineteenth-Century Black Women.* Carbondale: Southern Illinois UP, 1999.

Logue, Larry M. *To Appomattox and Beyond: The Civil War Soldier in War and Peace.* Chicago: Dee, 1996.

Long, Lisa A. "'The Corporeity of Heaven': Rehabilitating the Civil War Body in *The Gates Ajar.*" *American Literature* 69.4 (1997): 781–812.

———. *Rehabilitating Bodies: Health, History, and the American Civil War.* Philadelphia: U of Pennsylvania P, 2004.

Looby, Christopher. *Voicing America: Language, Literary Form, and the Origins of the United States.* Chicago: U of Chicago P, 1996.

Lott, Eric. "Blackface Minstrels Influenced Many Aspects of *Huckleberry Finn.*" *Readings on* Adventures of Huckleberry Finn. San Diego: Greenhaven, 1998. 137–47.

Love, Nat. *The Life and Adventures of Nat Love.* 1907. Lincoln: U of Nebraska P, 1995.

Lovell, Linda. "The Separation of Women in Henry James's *The Bostonians.*" *Publications of the Arkansas Philological Association* 16.2 (1990): 51–62.

Luis-Brown, David. "'White Slaves' and the 'Arrogant Mestiza': Reconfiguring Whiteness in *The Squatter and the Don* and *Ramona.*" *American Literature* 69.4 (1997): 813–39.

Lynch, James D. "Columbia Saluting the Nations: A Poem." Chicago: Thayer and Jackson, 1893.

———. *Kemper County Vindicated, and a Peep at Radical Rule in Mississippi.* New York: Hale & Sons, 1879.

———. *Redpath, or, the Ku Klux Tribunal: A Poem.* Columbus, MS: Excelsior, 1877.

Lynn, Kenneth. *Mark Twain and Southwestern Humor.* Boston: Little, 1959.

Lyon, Melvin. *Symbol and Idea in Henry Adams.* Lincoln: U of Nebraska P, 1970.

Machor, James L., ed. *Readers in History: Nineteenth-Century American Literature and the Contexts of Response.* Baltimore: Johns Hopkins UP, 1993.

MacKethan, Lucinda. *The Dream of Arcady: Place and Time in Southern Literature.* Baton Rouge: Louisiana State UP, 1980.

———. "Plantation Fiction, 1865–1900." *The History of Southern Literature.* Ed. Louis D. Rubin, Jr. Baton Rouge: Louisiana State UP, 1985. 209–18.

MacLeod, Christine. "Telling the Truth in a Tight Place: *Huckleberry Finn* and the Reconstruction Era." *Southern Quarterly* 34.1 (1995): 5–16.

Maddox, Lucy. *Removals: Nineteenth-Century American Literature and the Politics of Indian Affairs.* New York: Oxford UP, 1991.

Maffly-Kipp, Laurie F. "Redeeming Southern Memory: The Negro Race History, 1874–1915." *Where These Memories Grow: History, Memory, and Southern Identity.* Ed. W. Fitzhugh Brundage. Chapel Hill: U of North Carolina P, 2000. 169–89.

Magdol, Edward. "A Note on Authenticity: Eliab Hill and Nimbus Ware in *Bricks Without Straw.*" *American Quarterly* 22.4 (1970): 907–11.

Maik, Thomas A. "Dissent and Affirmation: Conflicting Voices of Female Roles in

Selected Stories by Mary Wilkins Freeman." *Colby Library Quarterly* 26.1 (1990): 59–68.

Manring, Maurice M. *Slave in a Box: The Strange Career of Aunt Jemima.* Charlottesville: UP of Virginia, 1998.

Marberry, M. M. *Splendid Poseur: Joaquin Miller—American Poet.* New York: Crowell, 1953.

Mardock, Robert Winston. *The Reformers and the American Indian.* Columbia: U of Missouri P, 1971.

Margolis, Stacey. "*Huckleberry Finn;* or, Consequences." *PMLA* 116.2 (2001): 329–43.

Martin, Jay. *Harvests of Change: American Literature 1865–1914.* Englewood Cliffs, NJ: Prentice-Hall, 1967.

Martin, Matthew R. "The Two-Faced New South: The Plantation Tales of Thomas Nelson Page and Charles Waddell Chesnutt." *Southern Literary Journal* 30.2 (1998): 17–36.

Martin, Theodora Penny. *The Sound of Our Own Voices: Women's Study Clubs, 1860–1910.* Boston: Beacon, 1987.

Marx, Leo. "The Vernacular Tradition in American Literature." *Studies in American Culture: Dominant Ideas and Images.* Ed. Joseph J. Kwiat and Mary C. Turpie. Minneapolis: U of Minnesota P, 1960. 109–22.

Massa, Ann. "Black Women in the 'White City.'" *Journal of American Studies* 8.3 (1974): 319–37.

Masteller, Jean Carwile. "The Women Doctors of Howells, Phelps, and Jewett." *Critical Essays on Sarah Orne Jewett.* Ed. Gwen L. Nagel. Boston: Hall, 1984. 135–47.

Mathes, Valerie Sherer. *Helen Hunt Jackson and Her Indian Reform Legacy.* Austin: U of Texas P, 1990.

Mathes, Valerie Sherer, and Richard Lewitt. *The Standing Bear Controversy: Prelude to Indian Reform.* Urbana: U of Illinois P, 2003.

Matthews, Jean V. *The Rise of the New Woman: The Women's Movement in America, 1875–1930.* Chicago: Dee, 2003.

Maxwell, Joan. "Delighting in a Bite: James's Seduction of His Readers in *The Bostonians.*" *Journal of Narrative Technique* 18.1 (1988): 18–33.

May, Antionette. *The Annotated* Ramona. San Carlos, CA: Wide World, 1989.

McBride, Dwight. *Impossible Witnesses: Truth, Abolitionism, and Slave Testimony.* New York: New York UP, 2001.

McCabe, James. *The Illustrated History of the Centennial Exposition.* Philadelphia: National Publishing Co., 1876.

McClure, Andrew. "Sarah Winnemucca: [Post]Indian Princess and Voice of the Paiutes." *MELUS* 24.2 (1999): 29–52.

McClymer, John. "Who Is Mrs. Ada T. P. Foat? And Why Should Historians Care?: An Historical Reading of Henry James' *The Bostonians.*" *Journal of the Gilded Age and Progressive Era* 2.2 (2003): 191–217.

McConnell, Stuart C. *Glorious Contentment: The Grand Army of the Republic, 1865–1900.* Chapel Hill: U of North Carolina P, 1992.

McCormack, Peggy. *The Rule of Money: Gender, Class and Exchange Economics in the Fiction of Henry James.* Ann Arbor: UMI Research P, 1990.

McCowen, George S. Jr. "Historical Consciousness in Henry Adams and Henry James." *Willamette Journal of the Liberal Arts* 1.2 (1984): 49–78.

McCullough, Kate. *Regions of Identity: The Construction of America in Women's Fiction, 1885–1914.* Stanford: Stanford UP, 1999.

McDonnell, Janet A. *The Dispossession of the American Indian, 1887–1934.* Bloomington: Indiana UP, 1991.

McKay, Janet Holmgren. *Narration and Discourse in American Realistic Fiction.* Philadelphia: U of Pennsylvania P, 1982.

McLaughlin, William G. *After the Trail of Tears: The Cherokees' Struggle for Sovereignty, 1839–1880.* Chapel Hill: U of North Carolina P, 1993.

McPherson, James M. *The Abolitionist Legacy: From Reconstruction to the NAACP.* Princeton: Princeton UP, 1975.

McWilliams, Dean. *Charles W. Chesnutt and the Fictions of Race.* Athens: U of Georgia P, 2002.

Melville, Herman. *Clarel: A Poem and Pilgrimage in the Holy Land.* 1876. Evanston: Northwestern UP, 1991.

Menikoff, Barry. "A House Divided: A New Reading of *The Bostonians.*" *CLA Journal* 20.4 (1977): 459–74.

Merish, Lori. *Sentimental Materialism: Gender, Commodity Culture, and Nineteenth-Century American Literature.* Durham: Duke UP, 2000.

Messent, Peter. *New Readings of the American Novel: Narrative Theory and Its Application.* London: MacMillan, 1990.

Michaels, Walter Benn. *The Gold Standard and the Logic of Naturalism: American Literature at the Turn of the Century.* Berkeley: U of California P, 1987.

Miller, Darlis A. *Mary Hallock Foote: Author-Illustrator of the American West.* Norman: U of Oklahoma P, 2002.

Miller, J. Hillis. "Three Problems of Fictional Form: First-Person Narrative in *David Copperfield* and *Huckleberry Finn.*" *Experience in the Novel.* Ed. Roy Harvey Pearce. New York: Columbia UP, 1968. 21–48.

Miller, Joaquin. *Shadows of Shasta.* Chicago: Jansen, 1881.

Mills, Cynthia, and Pamela H. Simpson, eds. *Monuments to the Lost Cause: Women, Art, and the Landscapes of Southern Memory.* Knoxville: U of Tennessee P, 2003.

Minnick, Lisa Cohen. *Dialect and Dichotomy: Literary Representations of African American Speech.* Tuscaloosa: U of Alabama P, 2004.

Mitchell, Lee Clark. *Witnesses to a Vanishing America: The Nineteenth-Century Response.* Princeton: Princeton UP, 1991.

Mitchell, S. Weir. *In War Time.* 1884. New York: Century, 1909.

Mitchell, W. J. T. "Narrative, Memory, and Slavery." *Cultural Artifacts and the Production of Meaning: The Page, The Image, and the Body.* Ed. Margaret J. M. Ezell and Katherine O'Keeffe. Ann Arbor: U of Michigan P, 1994. 199–222.

Mixon, Wayne. *Southern Writers and the New South Movement, 1865–1913.* Chapel Hill: U of North Carolina P, 1980.

Mizruchi, Susan. *The Power of Historical Knowledge: Narrating the Past in Hawthorne, James and Dreiser.* Princeton: Princeton UP, 1988.

Montenyohl, Eric L. "Joel Chandler Harris' Revision of Uncle Remus: The First Version of 'A Story of the War.'" *American Literary Realism* 19.1 (1986): 65–72.

Moore, Rayburn S. *Constance Fenimore Woolson.* New York: Twayne, 1963.

———. "Paul Hamilton Hayne and Northern Magazines, 1866–1886." *Essays Mostly on Periodical Publishing in America: A Collection in Honor of Clarence Gohdes.* Ed. James Woodress. Durham: Duke UP, 1973. 134–47.

Moreno, Barry. *The Statue of Liberty Encyclopedia.* New York: Simon & Schuster, 2000.

Morgan, Ellen. "The Atypical Woman: Nan Prince in the Literary Transition to Feminism." *Kate Chopin Newsletter* 2.2 (1976): 33–37.

Morilley, Suzanne M. *Women Suffrage and the Origins of Liberal Feminism in the United States, 1820–1920.* Cambridge: Harvard UP, 1996.

Morrow, Patrick D. "Bret Harte, Popular Fiction, and the Local Color Movement." *Western American Literature* 8.3 (1973): 123–32.

———. "The Predicament of Bret Harte." *American Literary Realism* 5.3 (1972): 181–88.

Moses, L. G. *Wild West Shows and the Images of American Indians, 1883–1933.* Albuquerque: U of New Mexico P, 1996.

Moses, Wilson J. *Afrotopia: The Roots of African American Popular History.* Cambridge: Cambridge UP, 1998.

———. *Creative Conflict in African American Thought: Frederick Douglass, Alexander Crummell, Booker T. Washington, W. E. B. Du Bois, and Marcus Garvey.* Cambridge: Cambridge UP, 2004.

———. *The Golden Age of Black Nationalism, 1850–1925.* New York: Oxford UP, 1988.

———. "Writing Freely?: Frederick Douglass and the Constraints of Racialized Writing." *Frederick Douglass: New Literary and Historical Essays.* Ed. Eric J. Sundquist. Cambridge: Cambridge UP, 1990. 66–83.

Moylan, Michele. "Materiality as Performance: The Forming of Helen Hunt Jackson's *Ramona.*" *Reading Books: Essays on the Material Text and Literature in America.* Ed. Moylan and Lane Stiles. Amherst: U of Massachusetts P, 1996. 223–47.

———. "Reading the Indians: The *Ramona* Myth in American Culture." *Prospects* 18 (1993): 153–86.

Muccigrasso, Robert. *Celebrating the New World: Chicago's Columbian Exposition of 1893.* Chicago: Dee, 1993.

Muller, Dorothea R. "Josiah Strong and American Nationalism: A Reevaluation." *Journal of American History* 53.3 (1966): 487–503.

Murdoch, David H. *The American West: The Invention of a Myth.* Cardiff: Welsh Academic Press, 2001.

Murray, David. *Forked Tongues: Speech, Writing, and Representation in North American Indian Texts.* London: Pinter, 1991.

Murray, Lynn. "'A Newly Discovered Country': The Post-Bellum South and the Picturesque Ruin." *Nineteenth Century Prose* 29.2 (2002): 94–119.

Nash, Gerald D. *Creating the West: Historical Interpretations, 1890–1990.* Albuquerque: U of New Mexico P, 1991.

Nelson, Dana D. *National Manhood: Capitalist Citizenship and the Imagined Fraternity of White Men.* Durham: Duke UP, 1998.

———. *Principles and Privilege: Two Women's Lives on a Georgia Plantation, Frances A. Kemble and Frances A. Butler Leigh.* Ann Arbor: U of Michigan P, 1995.

Nettels, Elsa. *Language and Gender in American Fiction: Howells, James, Wharton, and Cather.* Basingstroke: Macmillan, 1997.

———. *Language, Race, and Social Class in Howells's America.* Lexington: UP of Kentucky, 1988.

Neu, Charles E. "Olympia Brown and the Woman's Suffrage Movement." *Wisconsin Magazine of History* 43.4 (1960): 277–87.

Nevins, Allan. "Helen Hunt Jackson: Sentimentalist vs. Realist." *American Scholar* 10.3 (1941): 269–85.

Newlyn, Evelyn. "Rose Terry Cooke and the Children of the Sphinx." *Regionalism and the Female Imagination* 4.3 (1979): 49–57.

Nichols, Mary P. "*Huckleberry Finn* and Twain's Democratic Art of Writing." *Seers and Judges: American Literature as Political Philosophy.* Ed. Christine Dunn Henderson. Lanham, MD: Lexington, 2002. 17–32.

Niemtzow, Annette. "The Problematic of Self in Autobiography: The Example of the Slave Narrative." *The Art of Slave Narrative: Original Essays in Criticism and Theory.* Ed. John Sekora and Darwin T. Turner. Illinois: Western Illinois UP, 1982. 96–109.

Nissen, Axel. *Bret Harte: Prince and Pauper.* Jackson: UP of Mississippi, 2000.

Noble, David. *The End of American History: Democracy, Capitalism, and the Metaphor of Two Worlds in Anglo-American Historical Writing, 1880–1980.* Minneapolis: U of Minnesota P, 1985.

———. *Historians against History: The Frontier Thesis and the National Covenant in American Historical Writing since 1830.* Minneapolis: U of Minnesota P, 1965.

North, Michael. *The Dialect of Modernism: Race, Language, and Twentieth-Century Literature.* New York: Oxford UP, 1994.

Nowatzki, Robert C. "'Passing' in a White Genre: Charles W. Chesnutt's Negotiations of the Plantation Tradition in *The Conjure Woman*." *American Literary Realism* 27.2 (1995): 20–36.

Nugent, Walter. "The American People and the Centennial of 1876." *Indiana Magazine of History* 75.1 (1979): 53–69.

Odell, Ruth. *Helen Hunt Jackson.* New York: Appleton, 1939.

O'Leary, Cecilia Elizabeth. *To Die For: The Paradox of American Patriotism.* Princeton: Princeton UP, 1999.

Olney, James. "'I Was Born': Slave Narratives, Their Status as Autobiography and as Literature." *The Slave's Narrative.* Ed. Charles T. Davis and Henry Louis Gates, Jr. Oxford: Oxford UP, 1985. 148–75.

Olsen, Otto H. *Carpetbagger's Crusade: The Life of Albion W. Tourgée.* Baltimore: Johns Hopkins UP, 1965.

Orr, Elaine. "Reading Negotiation and Negotiated Reading: A Practice within 'A White Heron' and 'The Revolt of Mother.'" *CEA Critic* 53.3 (1991): 49–65.

Orvell, Miles. *The Real Thing: Imitation and Authenticity in American Culture, 1880–1940.* Chapel Hill: U of North Carolina P, 1989.

Osterweis, Rollin G. *The Myth of the Lost Cause, 1865–1900.* Hamden, CT: Archon, 1973.

Otten, Kurt. "The End of Political Innocence in the United States: Henry Adams, *Democracy,* and the Novel of Manners." *Fiktion und Geschichte in der anglo-amerikanischen Literatur.* Ed. Rudiger Ahrens and Fritz-Wilhelm Neumann. Heidelberg, Germany: Winter, 1998. 255–84.

Paddon, Anne, and Sally Turner. "African Americans and the World's Columbian Exposition." *Illinois Historical Journal* 88.1 (1995): 19–36.

———. "Douglass's Triumphant Days at the World's Columbian Exposition." *Proteus* 12.1 (1995): 43–47.

Padget, Martin. "Travel Writing, Sentimental Romance, and Indian Rights Advocacy: The Politics of Helen Hunt Jackson's *Ramona.*" *Journal of the Southwest* 42.4 (2000): 833–76.

Page, Philip. "The Curious Narration of *The Bostonians.*" *American Literature* 46.3 (1974): 374–83.

Page, Thomas Nelson. *In Ole Virginia, or Marse Chan and Other Stories.* 1887. Chapel Hill: U of North Carolina P, 1969.

Painter, Nell Irvin. "Difference, Slavery, and Memory: Sojourner Truth in Feminist Abolitionism." *The Abolitionist Sisterhood: Women's Political Culture in Antebellum America.* Ed. Jean Fagan Yellin and John C. Van Horne. Ithaca: Cornell UP, 1994. 139–58.

———. *Sojourner Truth: A Life, A Symbol.* New York: Norton, 1996.

———. *Standing at Armageddon: The United States, 1877–1919.* New York: Norton: 1987.

Palumbo-DeSimone, Christine. *Sharing Secrets: Nineteenth-Century Women's Relations in the Short Story.* Cranbury, NJ: Associated Universities P, 2000.

Parker, Robert Dale. *The Invention of Native American Literature.* Ithaca: Cornell UP, 2003.

Parks, Edd Winfield. *Charles Egbert Craddock (Mary Noailles Murfree).* 1941. Port Washington, NY: Kennikat, 1972.

Pattee, Fred. "Constance Fenimore Woolson and the South." *South Atlantic Quarterly* 38.2 (1939): 130–41.

———. *A History of American Literature since 1870.* New York: Century, 1915.

Pearce, Howard D. "Witchcraft Imagery and Allusion in James's *Bostonians.*" *Studies in the Novel* 6.2 (1974): 236–247.

Pearce, Roy Harvery. *Savagism and Civilization: A Study of the Indian and the American Mind.* Baltimore: Hopkins UP, 1967.

Pedersen, Lee. "Negro Speech in the *Adventures of Huckleberry Finn.*" *Mark Twain Journal* 13.1 (1966): 1–4.

———. "Rewriting Dialect Literature: 'The Wonderful Tar-Baby Story.'" *Atlanta Historical Journal* 30.3–4 (1986–87): 57–70.

Penn-Terborg, Rosalyn. *African American Women in the Struggle for the Vote, 1850–1920.* Bloomington: U of Indiana P, 1998.

Person, Leland S. *Henry James and the Suspense of Masculinity.* Philadelphia: U of Pennsylvania P, 2003.

Peterson, Carla L. "Frances Harper, Charlotte Forten, and African American Literary Reconstruction." *Challenging Boundaries: Gender and Periodization.* Ed. Joyce W. Warren and Margaret Dickie. Athens: U of Georgia P, 2000. 39–61.

Petrie, Paul R. "Charles W. Chesnutt, *The Conjure Woman,* and the Racial Limits of Literary Mediation." *Studies in American Fiction* 27.2 (1999): 183–204.

Petrino, Elizabeth. *Emily Dickinson and Her Contemporaries: Women's Verse in America, 1820–1885.* Hanover, NH: New England UP, 1998.

———. "Nineteenth-Century American Women's Poetry." *The Cambridge Companion to Nineteenth-Century American Women's Writing.* Ed. Dale M. Bauer and Philip Gould. Cambridge: Cambridge UP, 2001. 122–42.

Peyer, Bernd C. "Autobiographical Works Written by Native Americans." *Amerikastudien* 26.3/4 (1981): 386–402.

Phelps, Elizabeth Stuart. *The Story of Avis.* 1877. New Brunswick: Rutgers UP, 1985.

Phillips, Kate. *Helen Hunt Jackson: A Literary Life.* Berkeley: U of California P, 2003.

Piatt, Sarah. "A Pique at Parting." 1879. *Palace-Burner: The Selected Poetry of Sarah Piatt.* Ed. Paula Bernat Bennett. Urbana: U of Illinois P, 2001. 91–92.

Piep, Kersten H. "Liberal Versions of Reconstruction: Lydia Maria Child's *A Romance of the Republic* and George Washington Cable's *The Grandissimes.*" *Studies in American Fiction* 31.2 (2003): 165–90.

Pizer, Donald. *Realism and Naturalism in Nineteenth-Century American Literature.* Carbondale: Southern Illinois UP, 1984.

Poirier, Richard. "Huckleberry Finn and the Metaphors of Society." *Twentieth-Century Interpretations of* Adventures of Huckleberry Finn. Ed. Claude M. Simpson. Englewood Cliffs, NJ: Prentice-Hall, Inc., 1968. 95–101.

Pokagon, Simon. "Simon Pokagon Offers 'The Red Man's Greeting.'" 1893. *Talking Back to Civilization: Indian Voices from the Progressive Era.* Ed. Frederick E. Hoxie. Boston: Bedford, 2001. 29–35.

Polakoff, Keith Ian. *The Politics of Inertia: The Election of 1876 and the End of Reconstruction.* Baton Rouge: Louisiana State UP, 1973.

Price, David. *History Made, History Imagined: Contemporary Literature, Poiesis, and the Past.* Urbana: U of Illinois P, 1999.

Price, Kenneth. "Charles Chesnutt, the *Atlantic Monthly,* and the Intersection of African-American Fiction and Elite Culture." *Periodical Literature in Nineteenth-Century America.* Ed. Price and Susan Belasco Smith. Charlottesville: UP of Virginia, 1993. 257–76.

Priest, Loring Benson. *Uncle Sam's Stepchildren: The Reformation of United States Indian Policy, 1865–1887.* New Brunswick: Rutgers UP, 1947.

Privett, Ronna Coffey. *A Comprehensive Study of American Writer Elizabeth Stuart Phelps, 1844–1911: Art for Truth's Sake.* Lewiston, NJ: Mellen, 2003.

Prucha, Francis Paul. *American Indian Policy in Crisis: Christian Reformers and the Indian, 1865–1900.* Norman: U of Oklahoma P, 1976.

Pryse, Marjorie. "'I was country when country wasn't cool': Regionalizing the Modern in Jewett's *A Country Doctor.*" *American Literary Realism* 34.3 (2002): 217–32.

Pulitano, Elvira. *Toward a Native American Critical Theory.* Lincoln: U of Nebraska P, 2003.

Quebe, Ruth Evelyn. "*The Bostonians:* Some Historical Sources and Their Implications." *Centennial Review* 25.1 (1981): 80–100.

Railton, Ben. "'What Else Could a Southern Gentleman Do?': Quentin Compson, Rhett Butler, and Miscegenation." *Southern Literary Journal* 35.2 (2003): 41–63.

Railton, Stephen. "Jim and Mark Twain: What Do Dey Stan' For?" *Virginia Quarterly Review* 63.3 (1987): 393–408.

Redding, J. Saunders. *To Make a Poet Black.* 1939. Ithaca: Cornell UP, 1988.

Reed, Christopher Robert. *"All the World Is Here": The Black Presence at the White City.* Bloomington: Indiana UP, 2000.

Reed, James E. "American Foreign Policy, The Politics of Missions and Josiah Strong, 1890–1900." *Church History* 41.2 (1972): 230–45.

Renza, Louis A. *"A White Heron" and the Question of Minor Literature.* Madison: U of Wisconsin P, 1984.

Richard, Thelma Shinn. "Reconstructing Memory in the American West." *Community in the American West.* Ed. Stephen Tchudi. Reno: U of Nevada P, 1999. 31–53.

Richardson, Heather Cox. *The Death of Reconstruction: Race, Labor, and Politics in the Post-Civil War North, 1865–1901.* Cambridge: Harvard UP, 2001.

Rickford, John Russell, and Russell John Rickford. *Spoken Soul: The Story of Black English.* New York: Wiley, 2000.

Ridgely, J. V. *Nineteenth-Century Southern Literature.* Lexington: UP of Kentucky, 1980.

Riley, Harris D. Jr. "General Richard Taylor, C.S.A.: Louisianan, Distinguished Military Commander and Author with Speculations on his Health." *Southern Studies* 1.1 (1990): 67–86.

Ringe, Donald A. "Narrative Voice in Cable's *The Grandissimes.*" The Grandissimes: *Centennial Essays.* Ed. Thomas J. Richardson. Jackson: UP of Mississippi, 1981. 13–22.

Rody, Caroline. *The Daughter's Return: African-American and Caribbean Women's Fictions of History.* New York: Oxford UP, 2001.

Rohrbach, Augusta. *Truth Stranger than Fiction: Race, Realism, and the U.S. Literary Marketplace.* London: Palgrave, 2002.

Roman, Margaret. *Sarah Orne Jewett: Reconstructing Gender.* Tuscaloosa: U of Alabama P, 1992.

Rose, Anne C. *Victorian America and the Civil War.* Cambridge: Cambridge UP, 1997.

Rosenberg, Emily S. *Spreading the American Dream: American Economic and Cultural Expansion, 1890–1945.* New York: Hill and Wang, 1982.

Rosenthal, Debra J. "Race Mixture and the Representation of Indians in the U.S. and the Andes: *Cumandá, Aves sin nido, The Last of the Mohicans,* and *Ramona.*" *Mixing Race, Mixing Culture: Inter-American Literary Dialogues.* Ed. Monica Kaup and Debra Rosenthal. Austin: U of Texas P, 2002. 122–39.

Rosenwald, Lawrence. "American Anglophone Literature and Multilingual America." *Multilingual America: Transnationalism, Ethnicity, and the Languages of American Literature.* Ed. Werner Sollors. New York: NYU P, 1998. 327–47.

Rosowski, Susan J. *Birthing a Nation: Gender, Creativity, and the West in American Literature.* Lincoln: U of Nebraska P, 1999.

Rothenberg, Kelly. "Frederick Douglass's *Narrative* and the Subtext of Folklore." *Griot* 14.1 (1995): 48–53.

Rouquette, Adrien. *Critical Dialogue between Aboo and Caboo on a New Book; or A Grandissime Ascension.* New Orleans: 1880.

Rowe, Anne. *The Enchanted Country: Northern Writers in the South, 1865–1910.* Baton Rouge: Louisiana State UP, 1978.

Rowe, John Carlos. *Henry Adams and Henry James: The Emergence of a Modern Consciousness.* Ithaca: Cornell UP, 1976.

———. *The Other Henry James.* Durham: Duke UP, 1998.

Rowe, Joyce A. "'Murder, what a lovely voice!': Sex, Speech, and the Public/Private Problem in *The Bostonians.*" *Texas Studies in Language and Literature* 40.2 (1998): 158–83.

Rubin, Louis D. Jr. "The Division of the Heart: Cable's *The Grandissimes.*" *Southern Literary Journal* 1.2 (1969): 27–47.

———. *George W. Cable: The Life and Times of a Southern Heretic.* New York: Pegasus, 1969.

———. "Uncle Remus and the Ubiquitous Rabbit." *Critical Essays on Joel Chandler Harris.* Ed. R. Bruce Bickley Jr. Boston: G. K. Hall, 1981. 158–73.

———. *William Elliott Shoots a Bear: Essays on the Southern Literary Imagination.* Baton Rouge: Louisiana State UP, 1975.

Ruckwick, Elliott, and August Meier. "Black Man in the 'White City': Negroes and the Centennial Exposition, 1893." *Phylon* 26.4 (1965): 354–61.

Ruoff, A. LaVonne Brown. *American Indian Literatures: An Introduction, Bibliographic Review, and Selected Bibliography.* New York: MLA, 1990.

———. "Early Native American Women Authors: Jane Johnston Schoolcraft, Sarah Winnemucca, S. Alice Callahan, E. Pauline Johnson, and Zitkala-Sa." *Nineteenth-Century American Women Writers: A Critical Reader.* Ed. Karen L. Kilcup. Oxford: Blackwell, 1998. 81–111.

Ruppert, James. *Mediation in Contemporary Native American Fiction.* Norman: U of Oklahoma P, 1995.

Russell, Irwin. *Christmas-Night in the Quarters and Other Poems.* 1888. New York: Century, 1917.

Ryan, Frank X., ed. *Darwin's Impact: Social Evolution in America, 1880–1920.* Bristol: Thoemmes, 2001.

Rydell, Robert W. *All the World's a Fair: Visions of Empire at American International Expositions, 1876–1916.* Chicago: U of Chicago P, 1984.

———. "The Culture of Imperial Abundance: World's Fairs in the Making of American Culture." *Consuming Visions: Accumulation and Display of Goods in America, 1880–1920.* Ed. Simon J. Bronner. New York: Norton, 1989. 191–216.

———. "Introduction: 'Contend, Contend!'" Ida B. Wells, et al. *The Reason Why the Colored American Is Not in the World's Columbian Exposition: The Afro-American's Contribution to Columbian Literature.* Urbana: U of Illinois P, 1999.

———. "The World's Columbian Exposition of 1893: Racist Underpinnings of a Utopian Artifact." *Journal of American Culture* 1.2 (1978): 253–75.

Salmon, Richard. *Henry James and the Culture of Publicity.* Cambridge: Cambridge UP, 1997.

Samet, Elizabeth D. *Willing Obedience: Citizens, Soldiers, and the Progress of Consent in America, 1776–1898.* Stanford: Stanford UP, 2004.

Samra, Matthew. "Shadow and Substance: The Two Narratives of Sojourner Truth." *Midwest Quarterly* 38.2 (1997): 158–71.

Samuels, Ernest. "Introduction to *Democracy* [1961]." *Critical Essays on Henry Adams.* Ed. Earl Herbert. Boston: Hall, 1981.

Sandos, James A. "Historic Preservation and Historical Facts: Helen Hunt Jackson, Rancho Camulas, and Ramonana." *California History* 77.3 (1998): 169–85.

Sands, Kathleen Mullen. "Indian Women's Personal Narrative: Voices Past and Present." *American Women's Autobiography: Fea(s)ts of Memory.* Ed. Margo Culley. Madison: U of Wisconsin P, 1992. 268–94.

Santayana, George. *The Genteel Tradition: Nine Essays.* Ed. Douglas Wilson. 1967. Lincoln: U of Nebraska P, 1998.

Saum, Lewis O. *The Popular Mood of America, 1860–1890.* Lincoln: U of Nebraska P, 1990.

Savage, Kirk. *Standing Soldiers, Kneeling Slaves: Race, War, and Monument in Nineteenth-Century America.* Princeton: Princeton UP, 1997.

Scharnhorst, Gary. *Bret Harte: Opening the American Literary West.* Norman: U of Oklahoma P, 2000.

———. "Whatever Happened to Bret Harte?" *American Realism and the Canon.* Ed. Tom Quirk and Scharnhorst. Newark: U of Delaware P, 1994. 201–11.

Scheckel, Susan. "Home on the Train: Race and Mobility in *The Life and Adventures of Nat Love*." *American Literature* 74.2 (2002): 219–50.

———. *The Insistence of the Indian: Race and Nationalism in Nineteenth-Century American Literature.* Princeton: Princeton UP, 1998.

Scheiber, Andrew J. "The Widow and the Dynamo: Gender and Power in Henry Adams' *Democracy*." *American Transcendental Quarterly* 4.4 (1990): 353–69.

Scheick, William J. *The Half-Blood: A Cultural Symbol in Nineteenth-Century American Fiction.* Lexington: UP of Kentucky, 1979.

Schlereth, Thomas J. "The Material Universe of American World Expositions, 1876–1915." *Cultural History and Material Culture: Everyday Life, Landscapes, Museums.* Ann Arbor: UMI Research P, 1990. 265–99.

Schmidt, Peter. "The 'Raftsmen's Passage,' Huck's Crisis of Whiteness, and *Huckleberry Finn* in U.S. Literary History." *Arizona Quarterly* 59.2 (2003): 35–58.

Schmitz, Neil. "The Difficult Art of American Political Fiction: Henry Adams' *Democracy* as Tragical Satire." *Western Humanities Review* 25 (1971): 147–62.

Schneider, Richard H. *Freedom's Holy Light*. Nashville: Thomas Nelson, 1985.

Schweninger, Lee. "'Only an Indian Woman': Sarah Winnemucca and the Heroic Protagonist." *Native American Women in Literature and Culture*. Ed. Susan Castillo and Victor M.P. DaRosa. Porto, Portugal: Fernando Pessoa UP, 1997. 157–61.

Scott, Anne Firor. *Natural Allies: Women's Associations in American History*. Urbana: U of Illinois P, 1991.

Scott, Anne Firor, and Andrew M. Scott, eds. *One Half the People: The Fight for Woman Suffrage*. Philadelphia: Lippincott, 1975.

Scott, Anthony. "Basil, Olive, and Verena: *The Bostonians* and the Problem of Politics." *Arizona Quarterly* 49.1 (1993): 49–72.

Scott, Joyce Hope. "Who 'Goophered' Whom: The Afro-American Fabulist and His Tale in Charles Chesnutt's *The Conjure Woman*." *Bestia* 2 (1990): 49–62.

Scott, Sir Walter. *Waverly; or, 'Tis Sixty Years Since*. 1814. London: Penguin, 1972.

Sekora, John. "Comprehending Slavery: Language and Personal History in Douglass's *Narrative* of 1845." *CLA Journal* 29.2 (1985): 157–70.

Senier, Siobhan. *Voices of American Indian Assimilation and Resistance: Helen Hunt Jackson, Sarah Winnemucca, and Victoria Howard*. Norman: U of Oklahoma P, 2001.

Sewell, David R. *Mark Twain's Languages: Discourse, Dialogue, and Linguistic Variety*. Berkeley: U of California P, 1987.

Shafer, Aileen Chris. "Jim's Discourses in *Huckleberry Finn*." *Southern Studies* 1.2 (1990): 149–163.

Shaheen, Aaron. "Henry James's Southern Mode of Imagination: Men, Women, and the Images of the South in *The Bostonians*." *Henry James Review* 24.2 (2003): 180–92.

Shapiro, Ann R. *Unlikely Heroines: Nineteenth-Century American Women Writers and the Woman Question*. New York: Greenwood, 1987.

Sherman, Sarah Way. *Sarah Orne Jewett; an American Persephone*. Hanover, NH: New England UP, 1989.

Short, Gretchen. "The Dilemmas of Reconstructing the Nation in Albion W. Tourgée's *A Fool's Errand* and Charles W. Chesnutt's *The Marrow of Tradition*." *REAL 14: Literature and the Nation* (1998): 241–67.

Shumway, David. "Incorporation and the Myths of American Culture." *American Literary History* 15.4 (2003): 753–58.

Silber, Nina. *The Romance of Reunion: Northerners and the South, 1865–1900*. Chapel Hill: U of North Carolina P, 1993.

Silkü, Atilla. "Challenging Narratives: Cultural Mediation and Multivocal Storytelling in Louise Erdrich's *Love Medicine*." *Interactions: Aegean Journal of English and American Studies* 13 (2003): 89–101.

Simms, L. Moody. "Albion W. Tourgée on Literary Realism." *Resources for American Literary Study* 8.2 (1978): 168–73.

———. "Irwin Russell and Negro Dialect Poetry: A Note on Chronological Priority and True Significance." *Notes on Mississippi Writers* 2.2 (1969): 67–73.

Sisco, Lisa. "'Writing in the Spaces Left': Literacy as a Process of Becoming in the Narratives of Frederick Douglass." *American Transcendental Quarterly* 9.3 (1995): 217–24.

Sklar, Martin J. *The Corporate Reconstruction of American Capitalism, 1890–1916: The Market, the Law, and Politics.* Cambridge: Cambridge UP, 1988.

Slotkin, Richard. *The Fatal Environment: The Myth of the Frontier in the Age of Industrialization, 1800–1890.* New York: Atheneum, 1985.

———. *Regeneration through Violence: The Myth of the American Frontier, 1600–1860.* Middletown: Wesleyan UP, 1973.

Smith, Anthony D. *Nationalism and Modernism: A Critical Survey of Recent Theories of Nations and Nationalism.* London: Routledge, 1998.

Smith, Carl S. *Urban Disorder and the Shape of Belief: The Great Chicago Fire, the Haymarket Bomb, and the Model Town of Pullman.* Chicago: U of Chicago P, 1995.

Smith, Christine Hill. *Reading* A Victorian Gentlewoman in the Far West: The Reminiscences of Mary Hallock Foote. Boise: Boise State UP, 2002.

Smith, Gail K. "From the Seminary to the Parlor: The Popularization of Hermeneutics in *The Gates Ajar.*" *Arizona Quarterly* 54.2 (1998): 99–134.

Smith, Henry Nash. *Virgin Land: The American West as Symbol and Myth.* Cambridge: Harvard UP, 1950.

Smith, John David. *An Old Creed for the New South: Proslavery Ideology and Historiography, 1865–1918.* Westport, CT: Greenwood, 1985.

Smith, Robert Freeman. "Protestant Millenarianism and United States Foreign Relations at the End of the Nineteenth Century." *Hayes Historical Journal* 9.4 (1990): 24–35.

Smith, Sherry L. *Reimagining Indians: Native Americans through Anglo Eyes, 1880–1940.* New York: Oxford UP, 2000.

Smith, Timothy B. *This Great Battlefield of Shiloh: History, Memory, and the Establishment of a Civil War National Military Park.* Knoxville: U of Tennessee P, 2004.

Smith, Valerie. *Self-Discovery and Authority in Afro-American Narrative.* Cambridge: Harvard UP, 1987.

Snow, Malinda. "'That One Talent': The Vocation as Theme in Sarah Orne Jewett's *A Country Doctor.*" *Colby Library Quarterly* 16.3 (1980): 138–47.

Snyder-Ott, Joelynn. "Women's Place in the Home (That She Built)." *Feminist Art Journal* 3.3 (1974): 7–8, 18.

Sofer, Naomi Z. *Making the "America of Art": Cultural Nationalism and Nineteenth-Century Women Writers.* Columbus: Ohio State UP, 2005.

Sollors, Werner. *Beyond Ethnicity: Consent and Descent in American Culture.* New York: Oxford UP, 1986.

———, ed. *Multilingual America: Transnationalism, Ethnicity, and the Languages of American Literature.* New York: NYU P, 1998.

Sommer, Doris, ed. *Bilingual Games: Some Literary Investigations.* London: Palgrave, 2003.

Sommer, Robert F. "The Fools Errant in Albion W. Tourgée's Reconstruction Novels." *Mid-Hudson Language Studies* 5 (1982): 71–80.

Spack, Ruth. *America's Second Tongue: American Indian Education and the Ownership of English, 1860–1900.* Lincoln: U of Nebraska P, 2002.

Standing Bear. "What I Am Going to Tell You Here Will Take Me Until Dark." 1881. *The Heath Anthology of American Literature, Concise Edition.* Ed. Paul Lauter. Boston: Houghton Mifflin, 2004. 1594–96.

Stansell, Christine. "Elizabeth Stuart Phelps: A Study in Female Rebellion." *Massachusetts Review* 13.1–2 (1972): 239–56.

Starling, Marion Wilson. *The Slave Narrative: Its Place in American History.* Washington, DC: Howard UP, 1988.

Starr, Kevin. *Inventing the Dream: California through the Progressive Era.* New York: Oxford UP, 1985.

Stedman, Raymond William. *Shadows of the Indian: Stereotypes in American Culture.* Norman: U of Oklahoma P, 1982.

Stephens, Robert O. "Cable's Bras-Coupé and Merimee's Tamango: The Case of the Missing Arm." *Mississippi Quarterly* 35.4 (1982): 387–406.

Stepto, Robert B. "Narration, Authentication, and Authorial Control in Frederick Douglass's *Narrative* of 1845." *Afro-American Literature: The Reconstruction of Instruction.* Ed. Dexter Fisher and Stepto. New York: MLA, 1979. 178–91.

Sternsher, Bernard. *Consensus, Conflict, and American Historians.* Bloomington: Indiana UP, 1975.

Stetson, Erlene. "A Note on the Woman's Building and Black Exclusion." *Heresies* 2.4 (1979): 45–47.

Stevens, Errol Wayne. "Helen Hunt Jackson's *Ramona:* Social Problem Novel as Tourist Guide." *California History* 77.3 (1998): 158–67.

Stevens, Hugh. *Henry James and Sexuality.* Cambridge: Cambridge UP, 1998.

Stevenson, Elizabeth. *Henry Adams: A Biography.* 1955. New Brunswick: Transaction, 1997.

Stone, Marjorie. "Bleeding Passports: The Ideology of Woman's Heart in the Fiction of Hawthorne, Freeman, and Cooke." *Atlantis* 15.1 (1989): 91–102.

Strong, Josiah. *Our Country: Its Possible Future and Its Present Crisis.* New York: The American Home Missionary Society, 1886.

Sundquist, Eric J. "Realism and Regionalism." *The Columbia Literary History of the United States.* Ed. Emory Elliot. New York: Columbia UP, 1988. 501–24.

———. *To Wake the Nations: Race in the Making of American Literature.* Cambridge: Harvard UP, 1993.

Swann, Charles. "The Price of Charm: The Heroines of *The Grandissimes.*" *Essays in Poetics* 13.1 (1988): 81–88.

Szasz, Margaret Connell, ed. *Between Indian and White Worlds: The Cultural Broker.* Norman: U of Oklahoma P, 1994.

Takaki, Ronald. *Iron Cages: Race and Culture in Nineteenth-Century America.* Seattle: U of Washington P, 1982.

Tanner, Tony. "Henry James and Henry Adams." *Tri Quarterly* 11 (1968): 91–108.

——. *Scenes of Nature, Signs of Men.* Cambridge: Cambridge UP, 1987.

Tarbox, Gwen Athene. *The Clubwomen's Daughters: Collectivist Impulses in Progressive-Era Girls' Fiction.* New York: Garland, 2000.

Taylor, Richard. *Destruction and Reconstruction: Personal Experiences of the Late War. 1877.* New York: Appleton, 1879.

Taylor, William. *Cavalier and Yankee: The Old South and American National Character. 1963.* Cambridge: Harvard UP, 1979.

Terry, Eugene. "The Shadow of Slavery in Charles Chesnutt's *The Conjure Woman.*" *Ethnic Groups* 4 (1982): 103–25.

Thomas, Brook. *American Literary Realism and the Failed Promise of Contract.* Berkeley: U of California P, 1997.

——. "Frederick Jackson Turner, Joaquin Miller, and Finding a Home on the Range." *Jose Marti's "Our America": From National to Hemispheric Cultural Studies.* Ed. Jeffrey Belnap and Raul Fernandez. Durham: Duke UP, 1998. 275–292.

——. "Languages and Identity in the *Adventures of Huckleberry Finn.*" *Mark Twain Journal* 21.2 (1983): 7–10.

Thomas, John L. *Alternative America: Henry George, Edward Bellamy, Henry Demarest Lloyd, and the Adversary Tradition.* Cambridge: Harvard UP, 1983.

Thomas-Collier, Bettye. "Frances Ellen Watkins Harper: Abolitionist and Feminist Reformer, 1825–1911." *African American Women and the Vote, 1837–1965.* Ed. Ann D. Gordon. Amherst: U of Massachusetts P, 1997. 41–65.

Thomson, Rosemarie Garland. "Benevolent Maternalism and Physically Disabled Figures: Dilemmas of Female Embodiment in Stowe, Davis, and Phelps." *American Literature* 68.3 (1996): 555–86.

Tipping, Scholin. "'The Sinking Plantation-House': Cable's Narrative Method in *The Grandissimes.*" *Essays in Poetics* 13.1 (1988): 63–80.

Tisinger, Danielle. "Textual Performance and the Western Frontier: Sarah Winnemucca Hopkins' *Life Among the Piutes: Their Wrongs and Claims.*" *Western American Literature* 37.2 (2002): 171–94.

Todorov, Tzvetan. *Mikhail Bakhtin: The Dialogical Principle.* Minneapolis: U of Minnesota P, 1984.

Tompkins, Jane P., ed. *Reader-Response Criticism: From Formalism to Post-Structuralism.* Baltimore: Johns Hopkins UP, 1980.

Tomsich, John. *A Genteel Endeavor: American Culture and Politics in the Gilded Age.* Stanford: Stanford UP, 1971.

Torsney, Cheryl B. *Constance Fenimore Woolson: The Grief of Artistry.* Athens: U of Georgia P, 1989.

——. "The Traditions of Gender: Constance Fenimore Woolson and Henry James." *Patrons and Protégées: Gender, Friendship, and Writing in Nineteenth-Century America.* Ed. Shirley Marchalonis. New Brunswick: Rutgers UP, 1988. 161–83.

——. "Whenever I open a book and see 'Hoot, man,' I always close it immediately:

Constance Fenimore Woolson's Humor." *Studies in American Humor* 3.9 (2002): 69–82.

Toth, Susan Allen. "Character Studies in Rose Terry Cooke: New Faces for the Short Story." *Kate Chopin Newsletter* 2.1 (1976): 19–26.

Tourgée, Albion W. *A Fool's Errand By One of the Fools.* 1879. Cambridge: Harvard UP, 1961.

——. "The South as a Field for Fiction," *Forum* 6 (1888): 405–12.

Tracey, Karen. *Plots and Proposals: American Women's Fiction, 1850–1890.* Urbana: U of Illinois P, 2000.

Trachtenberg, Alan. *The Incorporation of America: Culture and Society in the Gilded Age.* New York: Farrar, 1982.

——. "The Incorporation of America Today." *American Literary History* 15.4 (2003): 759–64.

——, ed. *Democratic Vistas 1860–1880.* New York: Braziller, 1970.

Trennert, Robert A. "Fairs, Expositions, and the Changing Image of Southwestern Indians, 1876–1904." *New Mexico Historical Review* 62.2 (1987): 127–50.

Truettner, William H., ed. *The West as America: Reinterpreting Images of the Frontier, 1820–1920.* Washington, DC: Smithsonian Institution P, 1991.

Trump, Erik. "Primitive Woman—Domestic(ated) Woman: The Image of the Primitive Woman at the 1893 World's Columbian Exposition." *Women's Studies* 27.3 (1998): 215–58.

Truth, Sojourner. *Narrative of Sojourner Truth; a Bondswoman of Olden Time.* 1878. Salem, NH: Ayer, 1992.

Turner, Arlin. *George W. Cable: A Biography.* Baton Rouge: Louisiana State UP, 1966.

Turner, Frederick Jackson. "The Significance of the Frontier in American History." 1893. *Rereading Frederick Jackson Turner: "The Significance of the Frontier in American History" and Other Essays.* Ed. John Mack Faragher. New Haven: Yale UP, 1999. 31–60.

Tuverson, Ernest Lee. *Redeemer Nation: The Idea of America's Millenial Role.* Chicago: U of Chicago P, 1968.

Twain, Mark. *Adventures of Huckleberry Finn.* 1884. New York: Penguin, 1985.

Van Leer, David. "Reading Slavery: The Anxiety of Ethnicity in Douglass's *Narrative.*" *Frederick Douglass: New Literary and Historical Essays.* Ed. Eric J. Sundquist. Cambridge: Cambridge UP, 1990. 118–40.

Vickers, Scott B. *Native American Identities: From Stereotype to Archetype in Art and Literature.* Albuquerque: U of New Mexico P, 1998.

Wagner, Bryan. "Helen Hunt Jackson's Errant Local Color." *Arizona Quarterly* 58.4 (2002): 1–24.

Wagner, Jean. *Black Poets of the United States: From Paul Laurence Dunbar to Langston Hughes.* Trans. Kenneth Douglas. Urbana: U of Illinois P, 1973.

Wald, Priscilla. *Constituting Americans: Cultural Anxiety and Narrative Form.* Durham: Duke UP, 1995.

Walker, Cheryl. *Indian Nation: Native American Literature and Nineteenth-Century Nationalisms.* Durham: Duke UP, 1997.

──. *The Nightingale's Burden: Women Poets and American Culture before 1900.* Bloomington: U of Indiana P, 1982.

──. "Nineteenth-Century American Women Poets Revisited." *Nineteenth-Century American Women Writers: A Critical Reader.* Ed. Karen L. Kilcup. Oxford: Blackwell, 1998. 231–44.

Walter, Dave, ed. *Today Then: America's Best Minds Look 100 Years into the Future on the Occasion of the 1893 World's Columbian Exposition.* Helena, MT: American & World Geographic Pub, 1992.

Walton, Priscilla L. *The Disruption of the Feminine in Henry James.* Toronto: U of Toronto P, 1992.

Wardrop, Daneen. "The *Jouissant* Politics of Helen Hunt Jackson's *Ramona:* The Ground That Is 'Mother's Lap.'" *Speaking the Other Self: American Women Writers.* Ed. Jeanne Campbell Reesman. Athens: U of Georgia P, 1997. 27–38.

Warfel, Harry R. "Local Color and Literary Artistry: Mary Noailles Murfree's *In the Tennessee Mountains.*" *Southern Literary Journal* 3.1 (1970): 154–63.

Warner, Marina. *Monuments and Maidens: The Allegory of the Female Form.* New York: Atheneum, 1985.

Warren, Kenneth. *Black and White Strangers: Race and American Literary Realism.* Chicago: U of Chicago P, 1993.

──. "Frederick Douglass's *Life and Times:* Progressive Rhetoric and the Problem of Constituency." *Frederick Douglass: New Literary and Historical Essays.* Ed. Eric J. Sundquist. Cambridge: Cambridge UP, 1990. 253–70.

Warrior, Robert Allen. *Tribal Secrets: Recovering American Indian Intellectual Traditions.* Minneapolis: U of Minnesota P, 1995.

Waterhouse, Roger R. *Bret Harte, Joaquin Miller, and the Western Local Color Story: A Study in the Origins of Popular Fiction.* Chicago: U of Chicago Libraries, 1939.

Waters, Carver. *Voice in the Slave Narratives of Olaudah Equiano, Frederick Douglass, and Solomon Northrup.* Lewiston, NY: Mellon, 2002.

Watson, William Lynn. "'The Facts Which Go to Form This Fiction': Elizabeth Stuart Phelps's *The Silent Partner* and the Massachusetts Bureau of Labor Statistics Reports." *College Literature* 29.4 (2002): 6–25.

Watts, Emily Stipes. *The Poetry of American Women from 1632 to 1945.* Austin: U of Texas P, 1997.

Waugh, John C. *Surviving the Confederacy: Rebellion, Ruin, and Recovery: Roger and Sara Pryor during the Civil War.* New York: Harcourt, 2002.

Weaver, Jace. *Other Words: American Indian Literature, Law, and Culture.* Norman: U of Oklahoma P, 2001.

Weaver, Richard M. *The Southern Tradition at Bay: A History of Postbellum Thought.* 1968. Washington, DC: Regnery, 1989.

Wecter, Dixon. *The Hero in America: A Chronicle of Hero Worship.* New York: Scribner's, 1972.

Weekes, Karen. "Northern Bias in Constance Fenimore Woolson's *Rodman the Keeper: Southern Sketches.*" *Southern Literary Journal* 32.2 (2000): 102–15.

Weeks, Philip. *Farewell, My Nation: The American Indian and the United States, 1820–1890*. Arlington Heights, IL: Harlan Davidson, 1990.

Wegener, Frederick. "'A Line of Her Own': Henry James's 'Sturdy Little Doctoress' and the Medical Woman as Literary Type in Gilded-Age America." *Texas Studies in Language and Literature* 39.2 (1997): 139–80.

Weimann, Jeanne Madeline. *The Fair Women*. Chicago: Academy, 1981.

Weissbuch, Ted N. "Albion W. Tourgée: Propagandist and Critic of Reconstruction." *Ohio Historical Quarterly* 70.1 (1961): 27–44.

Welker, Glenn. "Susette La Flesche Tibbles." *Omaha Literature*. April 15, 2004, <www.indigenouspeople.net/omaha.htm>.

Wells, Ida B., et al. *The Reason Why the Colored American Is Not in the World's Columbian Exposition: The Afro-American's Contribution to Columbian Literature*. 1893. Ed. Robert W. Rydell. Urbana: U of Illinois P, 1999.

Werner, Craig. "The Framing of Charles W. Chesnutt: Deconstruction in the Afro-American Tradition." *Southern Literature and Literary Theory*. Ed. Jefferson Humphries. Athens: U of Georgia P, 1990. 339–65.

Wesseling, Elizabeth. *Writing History as a Prophet: Postmodernist Innovations of the Historical Novel*. Amsterdam: Benjamins, 1991.

White, Bruce. "The Liberal Stances of Joaquin Miller." *Rendezvous* 19.1 (1983): 86–94.

Wiebe, Robert H. *The Search for Order, 1877–1920*. New York: Farrar, 1967.

Wieck, Carl F. *Refiguring* Huckleberry Finn. Athens: U of Georgia P, 2000.

Williams, Susan S. "Writing with an Ethical Purpose: The Case of Elizabeth Stuart Phelps." *Reciprocal Influences: Literary Production, Distribution, and Consumption in America*. Ed. Steven Fink and Williams. Columbus: Ohio State UP, 1999. 151–72.

Williamson, Joel. *The Crucible of Race: Black/White Relations in the American South since Emancipation*. New York: Oxford UP, 1984.

Wilson, Charles Reagan. *Baptized in Blood: The Religion of the Lost Cause, 1865–1920*. Athens: U of Georgia P, 1980.

Wilson, Edmund. *Patriotic Gore: Studies in the Literature of the American Civil War*. New York: Oxford UP, 1962.

Wilson, Jack H. "Competing Narratives in Elizabeth Stuart Phelps's *The Story of Avis*." *American Literary Realism* 26.1 (1993): 60–75.

Wilson, Sarah. "Material Objects as Sites of Cultural Mediation in *Death Comes for the Archbishop*." *Willa Cather and Material Culture: Real-World Writing, Writing the Real World*. Ed. Janis P. Stout. Tuscaloosa: U of Alabama P, 2004. 171–87.

Wilt, Judith. "Desperately Seeking Verena: A Resistant Reading of *The Bostonians*." *Feminist Studies* 13.2 (1987): 293–316.

Winnemucca Hopkins, Sarah. *Life among the Piutes: Their Wrongs and Claims*. 1883. Reno: U of Nevada P, 1994.

Wolfe, Bernard. "Uncle Remus and the Malevolent Rabbit: 'Takes a Limber-Toe Gemmun fer ter Jump Jim Crow.'" *Critical Essays on Joel Chandler Harris*. Ed. R. Bruce Bickley Jr. Boston: G. K. Hall, 1981.

Wolosky, Shira. "The Claims of Rhetoric: Toward a Historical Poetics (1820–1900)." *American Literature* 15.1 (2003): 14–21.

———. "Poetry and Public Discourse, 1820–1910." *The Cambridge History of American Literature*, vol. 4. Ed. Sacvan Bercovitch. Cambridge: Cambridge UP, 2004.

Wolstenholme, Susan. "Possession and Personality: Spiritualism in *The Bostonians*." *American Literature* 49 (1978): 580–91.

Womack, Craig. *Red on Red: Native American Literary Separatism*. Minneapolis: U of Minnesota P, 1999.

Wonham, Henry. "'The Curious Psychological Spectacle of a Mind Enslaved': Charles W. Chesnutt and Dialect Fiction." *Mississippi Quarterly* 51.1 (1997–8): 55–69.

———. "The Disembodied Yarnspinner and the Reader of *Adventures of Huckleberry Finn*." *American Literary Realism* 24.1 (1991): 2–22.

———. *Playing the Races: Ethnic Caricature and American Literary Realism*. New York: Oxford UP, 2004.

———. "Plenty of Room for Us All: Participation and Prejudice in Charles Chesnutt's Dialect Tales." *Studies in American Fiction* 26.2 (1998): 131–46.

Wood, Ann Douglas. "The Literature of Impoverishment: The Women Local Colorists in America, 1865–1914." *Women's Studies* 1.1 (1972): 3–45.

Woodward, C. Vann. *The Burden of Southern History*. 1960. Baton Rouge: Louisiana State UP, 1993.

———. *Origins of the New South, 1877–1913*. Baton Rouge: Louisiana State UP, 1971.

———. *Reunion and Reaction: The Compromise of 1877 and the End of Reconstruction*. New York: Oxford UP, 1966.

Woolson, Constance Fenimore. "Miss Grief." 1880. *Women Artists, Women Exiles: "Miss Grief" and Other Stories*. Ed. Joan Myers Weimer. New Brunswick: Rutgers UP, 1988. 248–69.

———. *Rodman the Keeper: Southern Sketches*. 1880. New York: Harper, 1899.

World's Congress of Representative Women. Chicago: McNally, 1894.

Wyatt-Brown, Bertram. *Hearts of Darkness: Wellsprings of a Southern Literary Tradition*. Baton Rouge: Louisiana State UP, 2003.

Wynes, Charles E. Introduction. *Forgotten Voices: Dissenting Southerners in an Age of Conformity*. Ed. Wynes. Baton Rouge: Louisiana State UP, 1967. 3–10.

Yeazell, Ruth Bernard, ed. *Henry James: A Collection of Critical Essays*. Englewood Cliffs, NJ: Prentice-Hall, 1994.

Yellin, Jean Fagan. *Women and Sisters: The Antislavery Feminists in American Culture*. New Haven: Yale UP, 1989.

Young, Elizabeth. *Disarming the Nation: Women's Writing and the American Civil War*. Chicago: U of Chicago P, 1999.

Young, Thomas Daniel. "How Time Has Served Two Southern Poets: Paul Hamilton Hayne and Sidney Lanier." *Southern Literary Journal* 6.1 (1973): 101–10.

Zanjani, Sally. *Sarah Winnemucca*. Lincoln: U of Nebraska P, 2001.

Zunz, Olivier. *Making America Corporate, 1870–1920*. Chicago: U of Chicago P, 1990.

Index